Mary of Guise in Scotland

To my parents and sisters

Mary of Guise in Scotland, 1548–1560

A Political Career

Pamela E. Ritchie

TUCKWELL PRESS

First published in Great Britain in 2002 by
Tuckwell Press Ltd
The Mill House
Phantassie
East Linton
East Lothian, Scotland

ISBN 1 86232 184 1

British Library Cataloguing-in-Publication Data
A catalogue record is available
on request from the British Library

Typeset by Hewer Text Ltd, Edinburgh
Printed and bound by Bell & Bain Ltd, Glasgow

Contents

Acknowledgements

The origin of this book was a doctoral thesis undertaken at the University of St. Andrews. My acknowledgments then are still applicable today, but I would like to thank those whose help contributed specifically to the completion of this project.

First on the list is Dr. Roger Mason. As a scholar, he continues to be the font of all knowledge (or so he tells me) and a source of inspiration. The time he has invested in me and this book went far beyond the call of duty for an ex-supervisor – and for that I will always be indebted to him. His advice, support and criticism, all of which he gave in abundance, were greatly appreciated and any faults in this book are more than likely because I chose not to listen to him.

The same also applies to Dr. Jane Dawson at the University of Edinburgh. She, too, exceeded her duties as an external examiner. Her patience and understanding were endless, especially during our many phone conversations in which she encouraged me to look at things a little differently and to think through my ideas a little more carefully. Her comments, together with those of Professor John Guy, helped me immeasurably and I can only thank them again for their continued interest and support.

I would also like to thank Thomas Brochard for his French translations, and for the friendship of Jenny Roth, Janet Deatheridge and Pam Cranston, who were always there to keep me full of spirit in more ways than one. But special mention must go to Dr Roland Tanner. He has been a mainstay of support and encouragement over the years, and his very presence helped ease the pain of writing both a thesis and a book. I can only apologise for the number of times his share of the pain seemed greater than mine. Although I hold him in the highest regard as a historian, it is as a friend that I offer him my deepest and sincerest affections.

Finally, acknowledgement must go to my aunt and uncles, Elizabeth and Graeme Ritchie, Robert Mitchell and Ronald Mitchell, who sadly passed away before this book was completed. I can only thank them again for their hospitality and generosity. But it is to my family in Canada that I owe my greatest debt of gratitude. Without the financial and emotional support of my parents, Robert and Doreen, and my sisters, Fiona and Alison, none of this would have been possible. Although words cannot begin to express how truly thankful I am for all they have done, I hope a simple dedication will go some way in conveying my love and affection.

List of Abbreviations

All dates are in New Style and, apart from those listed below, all abbreviations and contractions in the text have been taken from 'List of Abbreviated Titles of the Printed Sources of Scottish History to 1560', *Scottish Historical Review*, supplement (October 1963), pp.vi-xxix.

Adv.MSS	Advocates' Manuscripts
AÉ	Archives de Ministère des Affairs Étrangères, Paris
APC	*Acts of the Privy Council of England,* ed. J.R. Dasent *et al,* New Series, 46 vols. (London, 1890–1964)
BL	British Library, London.
BN	Bibliothèque Nationale, Paris
Ch.	Charter
Cor. Pol.	*Correspondence Politique*
CSP Foreign	*Calendar of State Papers, Foreign Series,* eds. W.B. Turnball and J. Stevenson *et al* (London, 1861–1950)
CSP Ireland	*Calendar of State Papers relating to Ireland of the reigns of Henry III, Edward VI, Mary, and Elizabeth, 1509–1573,* ed. H.C. Hamilton (London, 1860)
CSP Rome	*Calendar of State Papers, relating to English Affairs preserved principally at Rome in the Vatican Archives and Library,* ed. J.M. Rigg (London, 1916)
CSP Spain	*Calendar of Letters, Despatches and State Papers, relating to the negotiations between England and Spain,* ed. J.M. Thomson *et al* (London, 1862–1954)
CSP Venice	*Calendar of State Papers and Manuscripts, relating to English affairs, existing in the Archives and Collections of Venice,* ed. R. Brown *et al* (London, 1867–97)

DNB	*Dictionary of National Biography,* ed. L. Stephen *et al* (London, 1885–1903)
E	Exchequer
EHR	*English Historical Review*
Fo(s)	folio(s)
GD	Gift and Deposit
LPL	Lambeth Palace Library, London
L & P of Henry VIII	*Letters and Papers, Foreign and Domestic, of the reign of Henry VIII,* ed. J.S. Brewer *et al* (London, 1862–1932)
MS(S)	Manuscript(s)
NAS	National Archives of Scotland, Edinburgh
NLS	National Library of Scotland, Edinburgh
Papal Negotiations	*Papal Negotiations with Mary Queen of Scots during her reign in Scotland, 1561–1567,* ed. J.H. Pollen (Scottish History Society, Edinburgh, 1901)
PRO	Public Record Office, London
SP	State Papers
Statutes of the Realm	*The Statutes of the Realm,* ed. A. Luders *et al* (London, 1810–28)

Glossary

Assythment: compensation for loss or injury by payment; reparation, indemnification.

Barratry: the purchase or sale of an ecclesiastical preferment; the crime by an ecclesiastic of the corrupt purchase of benefices.

Bonds (or Bands) of Manrent and Maintenance: contracts promising loyalty, support, protection and service for life or in perpetuity.

Casualty: an incidental item of income or revenue, for example that due from a tenant or vassal in certain contingencies.

Entry: the establishment of an heir as a new vassal with his superior, thereby making his ownership effective.

Escheat: property, possessions or goods taken by foreiture or confiscation – especially falling to the crown; the forteiture of a person's property.

Horn: to outlaw. Literally, the wind instrument used to proclaim one an outlaw. When the king's messenger gave three blasts of the horn, one was officially put to the horn or declared an outlaw.

In Commendam: a benefice given in charge to a cleric or layman to hold until a proper incumbent was provided for it, or bestowed upon a layman or secular ecclesiastic with enjoyment of revenues for life – especially used of a benefice which a bishop or other digniatry was permitted to hold along with his own preferment.

Infeftment: the action or fact of investing with heritable property – the evidence for which is contained in an instrument of sasine.

Justice Ayre: a circuit court held by itinerant judges or officers.

Non-entry: the failure of the heir of a decceased vassal to renew investiture and the feudal casualty due to the immediate superior upon such failure.

Percept: an instrument granting possession of something or conferring a privilege.

Precept of Sasine: an instrument by which the legal ownership of land is transferred.

Propine: gift, tribute.

Sasine: the act of giving possession of feudal property; an instrument proving possession of feudal property.

Stent: an (annual) assessment of the value of property (especially land) for taxation purposes; the amount so fixed paid in tax.

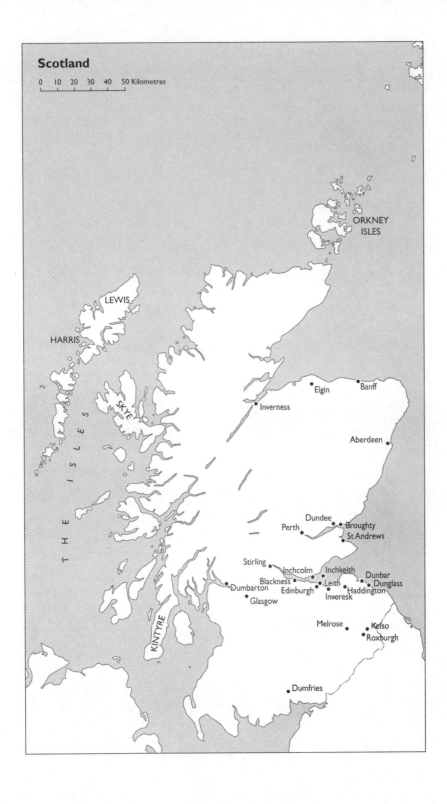

Scotland

0 10 20 30 40 50 Kilometres

ORKNEY
ISLES

LEWIS

HARRIS

SKYE

T H E   I S L E S

KINTYRE

Elgin Banff

Inverness

Aberdeen

Dundee
Perth Broughty
St Andrews

Stirling Inchkeith
Inchcolm Dunbar
Blackness Leith Dunglass
Dumbarton Edinburgh Haddington
Glasgow Inveresk

Melrose Kelso
Roxburgh

Dumfries

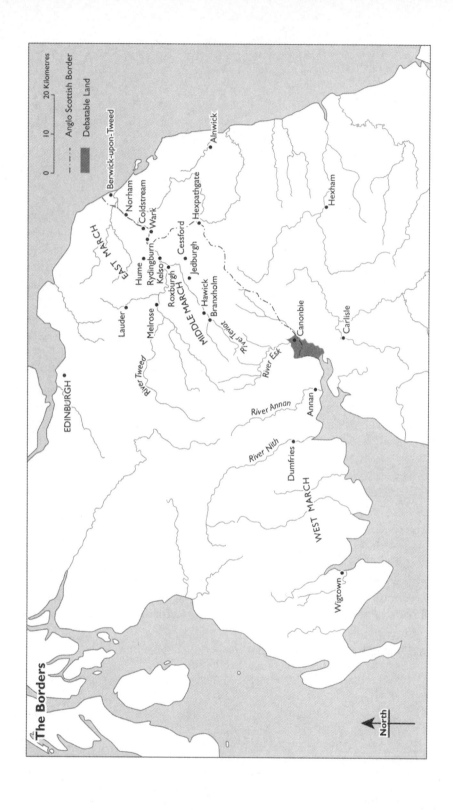

The Borders

Introduction

O n 21 October 1559 the Reformation Rebellion ceased to be a Protestant revolt against Catholicism that was exclusively concerned, at least publicly, with the establishment of the reformed kirk in Scotland. The Lords of the Congregation's 'Act of Suspension' added a nationalist dimension to their rebellion that was now directed specifically against the Queen Regent, Mary of Guise, and the establishment of French power in Scotland.[1] In their act attempting to depose Mary of Guise from the regency, the Lords of the Congregation charged the Queen Regent with the 'interprysed destructioun of thair said commoun-weall, and overthrow of the libertie of thair native cuntree'.[2] She had revealed her true intentions by such acts as building and fortifying strongholds, appointing Frenchmen to key offices of state and, most obviously, by bringing in French troops in August and September 1559. The fact that these troops had arrived in Scotland with their wives and children so soon after Mary, Queen of Scots' husband, François, had succeeded Henri II to become the King of France, was used by the Congregation to infer that Scotland's future as an independent kingdom would be short-lived in the union of the French and Scottish crowns. Such 'enormities' clearly showed that Mary of Guise's true political objective was the 'manifest conqueast of our native rowmes and countree to suppress the commounweall, and libertie of our native countree, [and] to mak us and our posteritie slaves to strangearis for ever'.[3]

Rhetoric such as this typified the propaganda disseminated by the Lords of the Congregation during the Reformation Rebellion.[4] Its

1 Knox, *Works*, I, pp. 444–9 and *History*, I, pp. 251–5; R.A. Mason (ed.), *Knox: On Rebellion* (Cambridge, 1994), pp. 171–4.
2 Knox, *Works*, I, p.444 and *History*, I, p.251; Mason, *Knox: On Rebellion*, p.171.
3 Knox, *Works*, I, p.445 and *History*, I, p.252; Mason, *Knox: On Rebellion*, p.172.
4 For an excellent analysis of the Congregation's propaganda, see R.A. Mason, 'Covenant and Commonweal: the Language of Politics in Reformation Scotland' in N. Macdougall (ed.), *Church, Politics and Society: Scotland, 1408–1929* (Edinburgh, 1983), pp. 97–126.

emphasis on conquest and French domination was designed to play on the xenophobia of the Scots and establish the Congregation as a party of patriots, being the 'borne Counsallouris' of the realm and the 'sworne protectouris and defendaris' of the commonweal.[5] By identifying themselves with freedom, liberty and patriotism, the Congregation not only hoped to secure widespread political support for their 'religious' rebellion, but also, and more importantly, the public and military support of Elizabeth I.

Although it is widely recognised by historians that the Lords of the Congregation engaged in a war of words against Mary of Guise, very little has been done to explore the extent to which their propaganda bore any relation to the facts. The reason for this is symptomatic of a larger problem – neither Mary of Guise nor her political career in Scotland has been the subject of in-depth study or historical analysis. Only two works have been completely devoted to Mary of Guise. Rosalind Marshall's biography[6] is a readable but overly romanticised literary work, while Marianne McKerlie's[7] study is not only dated but devoid of any sophisticated analysis. Any attention Mary of Guise does receive in modern scholarship tends to be in relation to her family in France, Les Guise,[8] her daughter, Mary, Queen of Scots[9] or the Scottish Reformation,[10] and is conventionally used to establish the context of, and pretext for, the Reformation Rebellion of 1559–60. As a result, her political

5 Knox, *Works*, I, p.448 and *History*, I, p.254; Mason, *Knox: On Rebellion*, p.174.
6 R.K. Marshall, *Mary of Guise* (London, 1977).
7 E.M.H. McKerlie, *Mary of Guise-Lorraine, Queen of Scotland* (London, 1931).
8 S. Carroll, *Noble Power during the French Wars of Religion: The Guise Affinity and the Catholic Cause in Normandy* (Cambridge, 1998); J.- M. Constant, *Les Guise* (Paris, 1984); H. Noel Williams, *The Brood of False Lorraine: The House of Guise* (London, 1914); H. Forneron, *Les Ducs de Guise et Leur Epoque* (Paris, 1877); R. de Bouillé, *Histoire des Ducs de Guise* (Paris, 1849); G. de Pimodan, *La Mère des Guises: Antoinette de Bourbon 1494–1583* (Paris, 1925); F.J. Baumgartner, *Henry II: King of France, 1547–1559* (Durham and London, 1988); I. Cloulas, *Henri II* (Paris, 1985).
9 J. Wormald, *Mary, Queen of Scots: A Study in Failure* (London, 1988); G. Donaldson, *All the Queen's Men: Power and Politics in Mary Stewart's Scotland* (London, 1983); A. Fraser, *Mary, Queen of Scots* (London, 1971 edn.); D. Hay Fleming, *Mary, Queen of Scots* (London, 1898 edn.); M. Lee, *James Stewart, Earl of Moray* (New York, 1953).
10 G. Donaldson, *The Scottish Reformation* (Cambridge, 1960); I.B. Cowan, *The Scottish Reformation: Church and Society in sixteenth century Scotland* (London, 1982); M. Lynch, *Edinburgh and the Reformation* (Edinburgh, 1981); F. Bardgett, *Scotland Reformed: The Reformation in Angus and the Mearns* (Edinburgh, 1989); M.H.B. Sanderson, *Ayrshire and the Reformation: People and Change, 1490–1600* (East Linton, 1997).

career in Scotland from 1548 to 1560 has been the victim of selective examination and gross misunderstanding.

The tendency of historians, such as Gordon Donaldson, to read history backwards and examine Mary of Guise's régime within a religious framework has been a convenient way to justify the Lords of the Congregation's rebellion and to account for their ostensible victory. This is largely because modern scholarship is still heavily reliant on partisan sources such as the English State Papers and, in particular, John Knox's version of events contained within his *History of the Reformation in Scotland*. Consequently, the negative imagery surrounding Mary of Guise and her regency has, on the whole, been reinforced and perpetuated over time. While Jenny Wormald and Michael Lynch have gone some way to free Guise of her historiographical stereotype as the defender of Catholicism whose political career climaxed with the Reformation Rebellion,[11] Donaldson's assessment still remains largely unchallenged.[12]

By reading history forwards from the perspective of Mary of Guise herself, however, an entirely new picture develops. A reassessment of the sources traditionally used for this period of Scottish history clearly shows that her political career in Scotland after 1548 must be examined within the wider context of European dynastic politics and, specifically, within the context of the Franco-Scottish alliance of 1548–60. This book, therefore, has expanded the source base to include French and English archival material, largely in the form of diplomatic and state papers held in the French Archives de Ministère des Affaires Étrangères, the English Public Record Office and various manuscript collections in the British Library.[13] These sources reveal that the conventional religious interpretation of Mary of Guise's régime is largely overblown. Dynasticism, not Catholicism, was the overriding characteristic of her political career in Scotland. Mary of Guise emerges as an extremely shrewd and effective politique whose own dynastic interests and those of her daughter took precedence over her personal and religious convictions. It also becomes clear that,

11 J. Wormald, *Court, Kirk, and Community: Scotland, 1470–1625* (Edinburgh, 1981), pp. 109–21 and *Mary, Queen of Scots*, pp. 76–101; Lynch, *Edinburgh and the Reformation*, pp. 68–89.

12 G. Donaldson, *Scotland: James V–James VII* (Edinburgh, 1994 edn.), pp. 63–106 and *All the Queen's Men*, pp. 25, 27–9, 33–4.

13 Some of the material contained within the *Correspondence Politique* and *Mémoires et Documents, Angleterre* series has been printed in Alexandre Teulet (ed.), *Relations Politiques de la France et de l'Espagne avec l'Écosse au XVIe Siècle* (Paris, 1862) and *Papiers d'état, pièces et documents inédits ou peu connus relatifs à l'histoire de l'Ecosse au XVIème Siècle* (Paris, 1852).

[3]

contrary to the assertions of the Lords of the Congregation, Mary of Guise was not solely responsible for the establishment of French power in Scotland. Rather, this process began in 1548 with the signing of the treaty of Haddington and came as a direct result of Henri II's protectorate of Scotland. More importantly, it was a process that was sanctioned and endorsed by the Scottish political élite itself.

This book, therefore, is the first full-scale study of Mary of Guise's political career in Scotland from 1548 to 1560. As such, it is not simply a book about Scotland and its politics during the 1550s, but one that takes an innovative look at the exceedingly important role Scotland played in European politics. While this study does not claim to be definitive or exhaustive, it does examine some fundamental points that modern scholarship has failed to consider. First and foremost is the nature of the Franco-Scottish alliance during the minority of Mary, Queen of Scots. The treaty of Haddington provided for the dynastic union of the French and Scottish crowns with the betrothal of Mary Stewart and François Valois and, more importantly, laid the foundations for a Franco-British empire. Mary Stewart's Catholic claim to the English throne, strengthened by Henry VIII's break with Rome and the repeated failure of Tudor monarchs to secure the line of succession by producing heirs to the throne, made it a very real possibility that she alone could unite the crowns of Scotland, England and Ireland under one Catholic crown. Marriage to the Scottish Queen, therefore, came with the prospect of controlling the entire British Isles and it was this imperial opportunity, which Mary Stewart's dynastic position provided Henri II through marriage to his son, that was the prime motivating factor behind his Scottish policy as a whole.

The possible realisation of Valois notions of a Franco-British empire was not the only advantage the treaty of Haddington afforded Henri. On a more immediate and practical level, it created a protectoral relationship between the 'auld allies'. Henri became the 'Protector' of Scotland, and Scotland a 'protectorate' of France, and it was this relationship that justified and facilitated the establishment of French power in Scotland prior to the union of the crowns in 1558. Specifically, Henri's protection of Scotland and its queen enabled him to maintain a permanent military foothold in a kingdom that served as the backdoor to England, assume control over Scottish diplomacy and direct its foreign policy. But it was his control of the Scottish government through his appointment of Mary of Guise to the regency that was the final and, arguably, most important part of the process establishing French power in Scotland.

Mary of Guise's ascent to power was in no way certain after Mary

Stewart left Scotland to become an absentee monarch in 1548. Indeed, it was commonly presumed that Guise would accompany her daughter to France now that the young Queen of Scots' future seemed so secure. Guise, though, was committed to seeing the Anglo-Scottish conflict brought to an end, and only when peace had been formally contracted in the treaty of Boulogne in 1550 did she feel the time was right to return to her native France for good.

Mary of Guise's celebrated trip to France in 1550–1 is one of the most misunderstood periods of her political career. Questions surrounding the *real* reason why she went to France and, more importantly, the reason why she returned to Scotland in 1551 have never been fully or adequately explored. The answers to these questions are found in the future government of Scotland. In 1548, and in return for a French pension, the Duchy of Châtelherault and a host of other financial inducements, the Earl of Arran agreed to resign as regent at the end of Mary, Queen of Scots' minority. But because Mary was an absentee monarch living in France, a regent was still required in Scotland during her majority. The big question was who? It should not be automatically presumed that Mary of Guise wanted the job or was even at the top of the list to succeed Arran as regent. Everyone expected Mary of Guise to stay in France. Why would she even want to return to Scotland when her children, her family and a life of luxury were all waiting for her at home? The main reason why Mary of Guise returned to Scotland was because the Scots wanted her to. Those who had travelled with her to celebrate Henri's triumphant entry into Rouen were adamantly opposed to the idea of a French gentleman acting as a viceroy and they wanted Mary of Guise to return for the 'executioun of justice and [the] ordouring of the cuntre'.[14] Yet, while the Scots may have had a say in who they wanted to govern during Mary, Queen of Scots' minority, the decision ultimately lay with Henri as the 'Protector' of Scotland. As soon as Mary entered into her twelfth year in December 1553, Henri informed Arran (now the Duc de Châtelherault) that his tenure as regent was over and that his successor would be the Queen Dowager.[15] The establishment of French power was completed on 12 April 1554 when Mary of Guise officially became the Queen Regent of Scotland.

Mary of Guise's regency was dominated by international considerations and this book is the first study to place her régime within the wider context of Euro-British dynastic politics. The Anglo-Imperial

14 *RPC*, I, p.90; *CSP Foreign, 1547–1553*, 225, p.61.
15 NLS, Adv.MSS, 33.1.9, f.1r-v.

dynastic alliance that was forged with Mary Tudor's marriage to Philip of Spain brought the Habsburg-Valois conflict to the Anglo-Scottish Border and Guise's administration was, consequently, overwhelmingly concerned with matters of defence and national security. The Tudor-Habsburg threat also highlighted the need for domestic stability and, in particular, law and order. While this was particularly true of the Borders and Highlands, the general aims of Guise's policy were to effect a strong, yet personal monarchy throughout all of Scotland. To do this, Guise implemented traditional Stewart policies dating back to 1424 that aimed to reassert royal power and advance the interests of the crown at the expense of local jurisdictions. In attacking the vested regional interests of the nobility and local magnates, these policies were very ambitious and extremely difficult to enforce – even for a Stewart king. But this task was even harder for Mary of Guise. Not only did she run the risk of criticism simply on the grounds of her gender and nationality, but also because she was a regent with extraordinary vice-regal powers whose term of office was for an unlimited period of time. What was acceptable for a sovereign was less acceptable for a regent – especially for one who was trying to act like an adult Stewart monarch. A few feathers were bound to be ruffled amongst the ruling élite. Their activities had gone virtually unchecked by central government since the death of James V in 1542 and Mary of Guise did meet with some opposition. Parliament rejected her tax reassessment scheme in 1556, which would have provided emergency funds for her defensive policies, and throughout much of 1557 Mary of Guise was consciously estranged from her subjects. But given the number of criticisms that could have been levied against her, the opposition she did encounter was surprisingly muted and was motivated by noble self-interest rather than as an attempt to prevent the 'conquest' of Scotland by France.

For many members of the Scottish political community, though, the international situation ultimately highlighted the need for Mary, Queen of Scots' marriage. The Scots were increasingly reluctant to finance the Queen Regent's defensive policies simply on account of Henri's foreign policy or, for that matter, on the strength of a protectoral alliance. England's declaration of war against France and entry into the Habsburg-Valois conflict in June 1557 was the catalyst that resulted in the marriage of Mary, Queen of Scots to the Dauphin of France in April 1558. The Franco-Scottish dynastic alliance marked the fulfilment of Mary of Guise's dynastic policies, while the Three Estates' consent to grant the crown matrimonial to the Dauphin brought Henri one step closer to realising his imperial ambitions. The death of Mary Tudor in November 1558 and the dubious legality of the accession of her Protestant half–sister, Elizabeth, saw the launch of a vigorous campaign on the part of the French King to advance the Catholic claim of Mary Stewart to the English throne, which by virtue of the crown matrimonial was also that of her husband, François.

Finally, this book reassesses Mary of Guise's religious policy and refines the traditional view that Guise needed to conciliate her Protestant subjects in order to achieve her dynastic objectives.[16] This interpretation, while not entirely inaccurate, is nevertheless limited in scope and, therefore, misleading. It implies, erroneously, that all Protestants were diametrically opposed to the Valois-Stewart marriage and fails to take into consideration the other political, social and economic factors that determined attitudes to the Franco-Scottish dynastic alliance. Mary of Guise's policy of conciliation was not aimed exclusively at those with reforming sympathies, but at the Scottish political élite as a whole. During the period 1548–51, for example, French patronage was distributed by Guise to Scots of all religious and political persuasions, and during her regency Protestants enjoyed key offices of state alongside their Catholic peers.

Examining Mary of Guise's political career within a religious framework also places undue emphasis on the importance of the reform movement in shaping Guise's policies. Religion was not a predominant concern for Mary of Guise and it took a back seat to the more pressing concerns of securing her daughter's marriage to the Dauphin, defence and national security. This is not to say, however, that she was oblivious to the fact that the Church was in need of internal reform or that the reform movement had amongst its ranks some very powerful and influential members of the nobility.[17] She was a shrewd politician who knew that the alienation of certain sectors of the political community would lead to unnecessary disaffection and dissension. By nature, she was also neither a Catholic zealot nor an advocate of religious persecution, and so it was very

16 See, for example, Donaldson, *All the Queen's Men*, pp. 25, 27–9 and *James V-James VII*, pp. 79–80, 89; and Wormald, *Court, Kirk and Community*, pp. 102, 114–5.
17 During the 1540s and 1550s Protestantism in Scotland was a small and localised movement that was by no means popular. It did, however, have a few high-ranking supporters such as the Earl of Glencairn and the Earl of Argyll. J. Wormald, "Princes' in the Scottish Reformation', in Macdougall, *Church, Politics and Society*, pp. 65–84, and *Court, Kirk and Community*, p.102; I.B. Cowan, *Regional Aspects of the Scottish Reformation* (Historical Association Pamphlet, 1978), pp. 5–38.

much in keeping with her character to assume a tolerant position towards the reform movement and its adherents. This inclusive and accommodating position assured her Protestant subjects that they would not be excluded or marginalised on account of their faith and that the reform movement was not necessarily incompatible with her dynastic policies. Because of this, leading Protestants like the Earl of Argyll, Lord James Stewart and John, Erskine of Dun, were extensively involved in every aspect of Mary, Queen of Scots' marriage to the Dauphin and the union of the French and Scottish Catholic crowns.

But Mary of Guise was also a pragmatic politique who was not above altering her religious policy if international considerations made such a change necessary for the protection and/or advancement of her dynastic interests. This was certainly the case in 1558–9, when the dubious legality of Elizabeth Tudor's accession forced Guise to issue a religious proclamation ordering the return of all Scots to the ancient faith in order to increase Mary Stewart's chances of being recognised as the true and legitimate Queen of England. The fact that this alteration of policy came just months after the Three Estates had ratified Mary, Queen of Scots' marriage contract and granted the crown matrimonial to the Dauphin has reinforced the view that Mary of Guise's policy of religious toleration was always intended to be a short-term measure, dependent on the successful completion of her dynastic policies.

It was because of Mary of Guise's politique position in matters of religion and the support Scotland's reformers gave to the Franco-Scottish dynastic alliance that the Queen Regent viewed the professed motives of the Congregation's rebellion in 1559–60 with such great suspicion. This book outlines the course of events up to and including the outbreak of the Reformation Rebellion and, for the first time, charts the various reactions and responses of the French and Scottish governments to the civil unrest in Scotland. For her part, Mary of Guise consistently maintained that the Congregation's rebellion was not a revolt of conscience, but a rebellion against established authority. Throughout 1559 Guise's suspicions were gradually confirmed by the Congregation's actions – most notably, the defection of Châtelherault to assume the nominal leadership of the Congregation with his son, James, 3rd earl of Arran, and their subsequent 'Act of Suspension' deposing Mary of Guise from the regency. While the Queen Regent had the ideological, constitutional and legal edge over the Congregation throughout most of 1559, the formal intervention of England in the conflict in 1560 and, more decisively, the failure of

France to respond to this intervention with adequate military rein-forcements, irrevocably weakened the foundations of Mary of Guise's administration. Only with her death in June 1560 would its collapse be complete.

1

Something about Mary:
the Treaty of Haddington and the
Founding of a Franco-British Empire

L ike her daughter, Mary of Guise's importance in sixteenth-century Europe lay not so much in what she did as in who she was. In her forty-five years, she was no less than a Duchess, a Queen Consort, a Regent and, most famously of all perhaps, a Queen Mother. Yet none of these public personae accurately captures the essence of Mary of Guise or, for that matter, identifies the driving force behind her actions. In a life of ever-changing roles and circumstances, the only constant in Mary's life was the fact that, above all else, she was a Guise. Born on 20 November 1515 to Claude de Guise and Antoinette de Bourbon, Mary was the eldest child of the first generation of the House of Guise, a scion of the princely House of Lorraine and, arguably, the most powerful dynasty in sixteenth-century France.[1] This prestigious lineage not only served as the foundation for Mary of Guise's own dynastic importance, but also as the motive for her family's overriding dynastic ambition and for her career in Scotland as a dynastic politique.

Dynasticism was central to the prestige of Les Guise in France and throughout Europe as a whole. The Princes of Lorraine, an independent duchy on the Franco-Imperial border, boasted Charlemagne and the Carolingian Kings of France as ancestors. The arms of a host of royal houses also bore the heraldic insignia of Lorraine. Those of Hungary, Naples, Jerusalem, Aragon, Anjou, Gueldres, Flanders and Bar were all represented, while the Princes themselves preferred to be styled as the 'Kings of Sicily'. When Mary's grandfather, René II of Lorraine, stipulated that his second son, Claude, become a naturalised Frenchman in 1506, the prestige of the newly created House of

---

1 For the ancestry of the House of Guise and its establishment in France, see Bouille, *Histoire des Ducs de Guise*, I, pp. 1–72; Forneron, *Les Ducs de Guise*, I, pp. 1–37; Constant, *Les Guise*, pp. 20–2; Pimodan, *La mère des Guises*, pp. 1–98; Carroll, *Noble Power during the French Wars of Religion*, pp. 14–25; Marshall, *Mary of Guise*, pp. 15–39.

Guise was virtually instantaneous.[2] Claude took possession of Lorraine's extensive landholdings in France, including Guise, Aumale, Mayenne, Joinville, Elboeuf and Harcourt and, aided by his family's notoriety on the battlefield and reputation as exceptional ecclesiastics and statesmen, soon became a prestigious and powerful member of the French Court – despite the status of Les Guise as foreigners.[3] For Mary of Guise, this prestige secured her a marriage, firstly, to Louis d'Orléans, duc de Longueville, and, secondly, to James V of Scotland. The significance of these marriages lay not only in their obvious stature, but also in the fact that, having been originally destined for a cloistered life, Mary's religious convictions were to take a back seat to Guise dynastic ambition.

Up until the age of fourteen, Mary received an intense Christian education from her exceptionally devout paternal grandmother, Philippa de Gueldres.[4] Following the death of her husband René II in 1508, Philippa was drawn into a life of holy simplicity. She entered the Convent of Pont-au-Mousson on 15 December 1519 and, despite objections from her family and a papal dispensation excusing her from all forms of austerity on account of her noble standing, lived as a Poor Clare for twenty-seven years.[5] Under the tutelage of her grandmother, Mary became fully immersed in the ascetic life of a Poor Clare. She was expected to attend all religious ceremonies and partake in more menial tasks such as cooking, cleaning and gardening. Although it is not known when Mary entered the Convent to begin her education, her experience at Pont-au-Mousson during her formative years must have had a profound influence on her personal faith. But it is impossible to determine the extent of these convictions based solely on her religious policy in Scotland. Throughout her regency, Mary would display extraordinary tolerance towards the reform movement and her Protestant subjects.

Mary's life as a Poor Clare, however, was brought to an abrupt end when her uncle, Antoine I, decided that she was better suited to a life

2 Bouillé, *Histoire des Ducs de Guise*, I, pp. 45–9.
3 For more on the Guise ecclesiastics, see J. Baker, 'The House of Guise and the church, *c.* 1550–1558' (unpublished DPhil thesis, University of Oxford, 1995); H.O. Evennett, *The Cardinal of Lorraine and the Council of Trent: A Study in the Counter-Reformation* (Cambridge, 1930); J. Bergin, 'The decline and fall of the House of Guise as an ecclesiastical dynasty', *Historical Journal*, 5 (1982), pp. 782–803.
4 Interestingly, Philippa was also the first cousin of James III of Scotland. For a more in-depth discussion of Mary's childhood and education, see Marshall, *Mary of Guise*, pp. 19–32.
5 *Ibid*, pp. 21–2; McKerlie, *Mary of Guise Lorraine*, p.22.

at Court. The Duc de Lorraine's decision to withdraw his niece from the Convent at Pont-au-Mousson set an important precedent for Mary's future political career in Scotland. Although their father had established Les Guise as the protectors of Catholicism by suppressing the Lutheran-inspired peasant revolts in Lorraine,[6] this was a role that Mary and her brothers, François (the future Duc de Guise) and Charles (the future Cardinal de Lorraine), were ultimately willing to forego when it came to the defence and advancement of their dynastic interests.[7]

Mary made the transition from cloister to court with great ease. She had been graced with intelligence, wit and an abundance of natural charm which, together with her prestigious lineage, made her an extremely popular figure at the French Court. François I was so taken

6 In 1525 the socio-political effects of Lutheranism in Germany took the form of peasant revolts against the Holy Roman Emperor, Charles V. Lorraine was also invaded and Antoine I appealed to his brother for French military intervention. The Regency Council in France, however, forbade Claude to use a national army to defend an independent duchy. But on the advice of his staunchly Catholic mother, Philippa de Gueldres, Claude ignored the Regency Council's order and led an expeditionary force into Lorraine. Successful in his mission, Claude 'fut félicité par le pape [Clement VII] et le Parlement de Paris. Il apparut alors auréolé du titre de défenseur du catholicism et de l'ordre social, ce qui plaisait au peuple parisien don't la sensibilité religieuse était vive [was thanked by the Pope and the Parlement of Paris. He thus appeared glorified by the title of defender of Catholicism and of social order, which pleased the Parisian people with its keen religious sensibility]'. From this point on, Claude de Guise was regarded by Catholics as a Christian hero and was dubbed the 'protector of the faith'. To the Protestants, he was known simply as the 'Great Butcher'. Constant, *Les Guise*, p.21; Cloulas, *Henri II*, p.62; Bouillé, *Histoire des Ducs de Guise*, I, pp. 62–5, 79–84; Marshall, *Mary of Guise*, pp. 28–9.

7 François and Charles de Guise are traditionally associated with ultra-orthodox Catholicism and religious persecution during the reign of François II. However, Stuart Carroll has shown that the negative imagery surrounding their administration is largely due to unfavourable Protestant sources and that, in actuality, there was very little difference between Henri's and François' policies. 'The Guise', he argues, 'were conventional in pursuing family interests rather than devoting themselves to a simple religious ideology. Far from altering the designs of the dead king, the Guise showed themselves to be highly conservative. Their policies did not herald the dawn of a new era. They implemented the policies of Henri and his most trusted and faithful friend Anne de Montmorency in maintaining a viable peace with Spain while at the same time pursuing French dynastic claims in Scotland. At home religious persecution was to be intensified, as Henri II had intended.' See Carroll, *Noble Power during the French Wars of Religion*, p.91, and especially his chapter 'Faction, religious schism and dynastic strategy, 1558–1562', pp. 89–115.

with her that he took a direct hand in instigating and arranging Mary's first marriage to the hereditary Grand Chamberlain of France, Louis, duc de Longueville.[8] The marriage was the event of the season, and the entire French Court flocked to the Royal Palace of the Louvre to witness the ceremony on 4 August 1534. Although shortlived, the marriage was happy and fruitful. Louis and Mary had two sons together: François, born at Amiens on 30 October 1535, and Louis, at Châteaudun on 4 August 1537.[9] While pregnant with her second son, though, Mary would suffer the first of many tragic deaths that marred her personal happiness – that of her husband on 9 June 1537.[10] Mary's sorrow was compounded shortly thereafter by the death of her son, Louis, who died within his first year of infancy.

François I wasted no time in playing matchmaker again with Mary. Even in widowhood Mary was a young, wealthy and extremely attractive marital prospect.[11] This time the proposed match was with the French King's also recently widowed son-in-law, James V, who was in the market for a new French bride following the death of François' eldest daughter, Madeleine.[12] Needless to say, the Dowager Duchess of Longueville found the Queenship of Scotland a less than appealing prospect. Marriage to the King of Scots would mean separation from her family and son, François, who would be obliged to remain behind as the new Duc de Longueville and Grand Chamberlain, as well as abandoning a life of luxury in her beloved France. The only other prospect in the offing, however, was even less appealing. Mary had no intention of becoming Henry VIII's next 'victim', rebuffing his marital overtures by claiming that her neck was far too small.[13] Even so, it took a considerable amount of persuasion from both François and James, who wrote a personal letter pleading for her hand, for Mary to relent and agree to marry the Stewart King.[14]

---

8 Marshall, *Mary of Guise*, p.35.
9 *Ibid*, pp. 32–6; Pimodan, *La mère des Guises*, pp. 56–60.
10 *Ibid*, p.65.
11 For the terms of Mary's marriage contract to the Duc de Longueville and her jointure, see *ibid*, p.60; *James V Letters*, pp. 340–1; and Marshall, *Mary of Guise*, p.36.
12 James and Madeleine were married at Notre Dame on 1 January 1537. The marriage lasted only seven months. Madeleine fell ill before leaving France and, just six weeks following her arrival in Scotland, died on 7 July 1538. *James V Letters*, pp. 333–4, 340–1; *TA*, VII, p.181; J. Cameron, *James V: The Personal Rule 1528–1542*, edited by N. Macdougall (East Linton, 1998), p.133.
13 *L & P of Henry VIII*, II, p.150; Marshall, *Mary of Guise*, p.47; Fraser, *Mary Queen of Scots*, p.26.
14 Marshall, *Mary of Guise*, pp. 51–3; S. Zweig, *The Queen of Scots*, translated by C. & E. Paul (London, 1935), pp. 1–2.

The royal marriage was officially contracted and signed before the French Court at Lyon in January 1538, having been negotiated by David Beaton (the future Cardinal and Archbishop of St. Andrews), François I and Mary's father, Claude.[15] The terms of the contract were extremely favourable to both James and Mary. The King of Scots would receive a dowry of 150,000 *livres*, 70,000 *livres* of which was generously gifted by François himself.[16] For her part, Mary's portion was equally lucrative. She was gifted Falkland Palace, the castles at Stirling, Dingwall and Threave, the earldoms of Strathearn, Ross, Orkney and Fife, and the lordships of Galloway, Ardmeanach and the Isles. In the event of James' death with issue, Mary was entitled to a third of her dowry and one half if there was no surviving heir. She was also granted financial immunity for all James' debts and, in return for waiving any claim to her husband's possessions, she was allowed to keep all of her own. More importantly, these terms also applied if Mary wished to return to France. She was entitled to take the allocated portion of her dowry, her possessions, and to retain the revenues from her jointures in Scotland.[17] Clearly, this treaty was designed to satisfy two main objectives – to augment James' revenue and to protect the interests of Mary and her family in Scotland.

These terms having been agreed, James V and Mary of Guise were married at the Castle of Châteaudun on 9 May 1538 with Robert, lord Maxwell acting as proxy for the absent Scottish monarch.[18] Scotland's new Queen arrived at St. Andrews in June 1538 and was formally crowned at Holyrood on 22 February 1539.[19] The marriage produced three children in quick succession: James, born at St. Andrews on 22 May 1540, Robert, at Stirling on 24 April 1541, and Mary, at Linlithgow on 8 December 1542. One week after their second son was born, however, tragedy dealt the King and Queen a double blow – the deaths of Prince James and Prince Robert within hours of each other. The premature death of James V on 14 December 1542 meant that the only surviving heir to the Scottish throne was his infant daughter, Mary, who became the Queen of Scotland at the tender age of six days old.[20]

15 Teulet, *Relations*, I, pp. 115–8.
16 Cameron, *James V*, p.261 *n.47*.
17 Teulet, *Relations*, I, pp. 115–8.
18 BN, f. fr. 5467, f.66; Marshall, *Mary of Guise*, p.53.
19 Cameron, *James V*, pp. 263–4; *Diurnal of Occurrents*, p.23. See Marshall, *Mary of Guise*, pp. 55–64, 79–80 for a more detailed account of Guise's arrival, reception and coronation in Scotland.
20 *Ibid*, pp. 86–7. Mary Stewart's coronation was on 9 September 1543.

Mary Stewart's accession to the Scottish throne rendered her a figure of extraordinary dynastic importance in sixteenth-century Europe, leading one historian to describe her aptly as not so much a person as a 'dynastic entity'.[21] But this importance lay not entirely in her Scottish sovereignty and Guisean lineage. Of even greater significance was Mary Stewart's Catholic claim to the English throne. The dynastic problems caused by Henry VIII's break from Rome, coupled with the repeated failure of successive Tudor monarchs to secure the line of succession by producing heirs to the throne, meant that Mary Stewart was uniquely placed to unite the kingdoms of Scotland, England and Ireland under one Catholic crown.

In 1503 the marriage of James IV to Margaret Tudor, eldest daughter of Henry VII, established the Stewarts as heirs apparent to the English throne upon the failure of the main Tudor line. During the reign of Mary, Queen of Scots, the Stewart claim to the English succession was particularly strong for two reasons. Firstly, the infecundity of the Tudors gave credence to the contemporary perception of England as a kingdom ruled by an infertile and weak dynasty. This belief was exemplified by the collective failure of Edward VI, Mary I and Elizabeth I to fulfil their fundamental duty as sovereigns by producing heirs to the throne and securing the line of succession. Significant as it was in its own right, the problem of infertility also served to exacerbate a larger problem that undermined the strength of England's royal house – the controversies surrounding the *order* of succession as a result of Henry VIII's break from Rome, assertion of royal supremacy and divorce from Catherine of Aragon. The dynastic and political ramifications of Henry's ecclesiastical schism not only generated dissent and opposition to the crown within England, but also cast doubt internationally on the legitimacy of the children from his subsequent marriages.

The effect of the Reformation on dynastic and political issues was uncharted territory and destined to become the source of controversy. Yet, irrespective of all the internal turmoil and uncertainty surrounding the succession as a result of Henry VIII's break from Rome, Mary Stewart's Catholic claim to the English throne remained intact and increased in strength with every Tudor sovereign who failed to produce an heir.

Mary Stewart's prestige was further enhanced by her gender. As a

21 M. Merriman, 'Mary, Queen of France', in M. Lynch (ed.), *Mary Stewart: Queen of Three Kingdoms* (Oxford, 1988), p.31.

female sovereign of extraordinary dynastic importance, Mary was a highly prized marriage prospect as notions of British imperialism could be entertained and potentially realised through marriage to the Scottish Queen. At no time was this more true than during the first eight years of her minority when the Kings of England and France literally fought for her hand, control of her kingdom and, potentially, sovereignty over the British Isles as a whole. During the 1540s two separate treaties contracted her marriage: the collective treaties of Greenwich in 1543 and the treaty of Haddington in 1548. Both laid the foundations for a British empire, respectively Anglocentric and Francocentric in nature, and both depended entirely on the dynastic claims of Mary Stewart.

As an extension of her own dynasticism, Mary of Guise was naturally keen to protect and advance the dynastic interests of her daughter. These interests not only served as the pretext for Guise's formal entry into factional high politics during Mary's minority in the 1540s, but also for her official political career in Scotland as Queen Regent from 1554 to 1560. The minority was marked by the traditional struggle for power and factional infighting that accompanied any period of regency government, but these problems were exacerbated by additional conflicts over foreign, dynastic and ecclesiastical policy.

The factions that emerged fell loosely into two categories: those that supported an Anglo-Scottish dynastic alliance and sought the reform of the Church along Protestant lines, and those that favoured an alliance with France and sought to maintain the authority of the Catholic Church in Scotland. As this study is primarily concerned with the élite politics of post-1548 Scotland, this crude summary of the divisions within the political community during the first five years of Mary Stewart's minority will suffice to place Mary of Guise firmly in the camp opposed to the pro-reform and pro-English faction.[22] This

22 The national and international politics surrounding the minority and marriage of Mary Stewart during the 1540s is a complex and involved subject which Marcus Merriman has already studied in great detail. I do not wish to repeat his work, only to highlight certain events in order to establish the context of the treaty of Haddington and the Franco-Scottish dynastic alliance as a whole. In addition to Merriman's *The Rough Wooings: Mary Queen of Scots, 1542–1551* (East Linton, 2000), see D. Franklin, *The Scottish Regency of the Earl of Arran: A Study in Failure of Anglo-Scottish Relations, Studies in British History*, Volume 35 (Lewiston, 1995); Marshall, *Mary of Guise*, pp. 108–76; Wormald, *Mary, Queen of Scots*, pp. 43–75; Donaldson, *James V–James VII*, pp. 63–84 and *All the Queen's Men*, pp. 15–26; Sanderson, *Ayrshire and the Reformation*, pp. 48–63; Cowan, *The Scottish Reformation*, pp. 89–104; *Scottish Correspondence*, pp. 1–252.

faction was initially led by James Hamilton, 2nd earl of Arran, whom Parliament appointed Governor on 13 March 1543.[23] The Three Estates also confirmed Arran's position as second person in the realm, thereby recognising his place in the Scottish succession as heir presumptive.[24]

Arran desperately needed this recognition as he was a child of a marriage following a divorce of dubious legality. In 1504 his father, James, 1st Earl of Arran, began divorce proceedings against his first wife, Elizabeth Home, on the grounds that she had already been married. The divorce was pronounced in 1504, but for some unknown reason it was pronounced again in 1510. This mysterious chain of events cast doubt on the validity of the Earl's second marriage to Janet Beaton in 1516 and, by implication, the legitimacy of their children – including the Governor.[25]

The man who was most likely to challenge Arran's legitimacy and claim to the Scottish succession was Matthew Stewart, 4th Earl of Lennox who, like Arran, was a descendant of James II. Lennox's grandmother, Eliz   ᵇ Hamilton, and Arran's father were the children of Prince   , d   ᵍʰter of James II, and her husband, Lord Hamilton.   ᵗᵒ be illegitimate, Lennox was next in lin   .ive to the Scottish throne.

This dynastic rivalry   Lennox feud which, for both parti   political alle-giances on opposite s   en Arran came out in support of   action, Lennox returned from Frar   ᵢ led by Cardinal David Beaton. But   ᵣe both motivated by the advancemer   , and their family's, dynastic interests, loyal   religious cause was precarious at best. Arran cou   to alienate Cardinal Beaton who, as the Archbishop of St. ..   ws, dealt with matters of legitimacy, nor could he ignore the fact that his half-brother, John Hamilton, Commendator of Paisley (the future Archbishop of St. Andrews), had came out in support of Beaton. The pressure exerted by both these men together with Mary of Guise proved too much. In September 1543 Arran capitulated and, having recovered

23 *APS*, II, p.411.
24 *Ibid*, II, p.411. Arran officially became heir presumptive in 1536 following the death of John Stewart, duke of Albany.
25 W.C. Dickinson (ed.), *John Knox's History of the Reformation of Scotland* (Edinburgh, 1949), I, *n.*1, p.49.

from his 'godly fit', became an exponent of the French and Catholic cause. In December 1543 the Three Estates reaffirmed the 'auld alliance' with France, and revoked the anti-heresy laws of the March Parliament and its legislation that had provided for the reading of Scripture in the vernacular and the union of the English and Scottish crowns.[26]

Lennox's response to Arran's *volte face* was predictable – he changed sides and immediately became the champion of the English and reforming cause alongside Archibald Douglas, 6th earl of Angus. Fleeing to England, he consolidated his position by marrying Margaret Douglas, the daughter of Angus and Margaret Tudor, Henry VIII's sister and relict of James IV, at the Palace of St. James in 1544. Needless to say, this was a very advantageous marriage. He had not only become Henry VIII's nephew through marriage, but Lennox's wife stood second only to Mary, Queen of Scots in the English succession should the main Tudor line fail.[27] Lennox had managed to place himself in a strong position in both the English and Scottish successions. His actions, though, had officially made him an enemy of the Scottish government under Arran and, in 1545, he was found guilty of treason. As we shall see, this did not prevent Lennox from pursuing his dynastic ambitions in Scotland. His royal connections in England, moreover, ensured that he remained the natural leader of the English cause and made his intrigues in Scotland all the more threatening.

Mary of Guise, conversely, played a leading role in the campaign to promote the interests of France in Scotland. In doing so, she proved to be a shrewd and effective dynastic politician and, more importantly, was seen as such by the Scottish political élite. As early as June 1544, Guise had made such an impact that a Convention at Stirling called on her to supersede Arran as regent.[28] Although Arran and the Queen Dowager were reconciled soon after, Guise retained a position of authority as head of a sixteen-strong council set up to 'advise' the Governor.[29] This episode was an early yet clear indication as to whom the Scottish political élite ultimately deemed most able when it came to governing the realm.[30]

26 *APS*, II, pp. 431–2, 411–26.
27 Donaldson, *All the Queen's Men*, pp. 16–18.
28 *State Papers, King Henry the Eighth, Correspondence Relative to Scotland and the Borders, 1534–1546* (London, 1836), V (iv), pp. 391–4.
29 Lynch, *Scotland: A New History* (Edinburgh, 1992 edn), p.208; Merriman, *The Rough Wooings*, pp. 157–8.
30 Donaldson, *James V-James VII*, p.70.

In the end Mary of Guise was successful in her primary objective of protecting her daughter's dynastic interests in Scotland. The treaties contracting the marriage of Mary Stewart to Edward Tudor were revoked and, largely on account of England's extremely harsh Scottish policy, the military invasions known as the 'rough wooings', a treaty was then ratified between the 'auld allies' at Haddington on 7 July 1548. This treaty not only provided for the future union of the French and Scottish crowns, but as we shall see, also created a Franco-Scottish protectoral alliance which tied Scotland irrevocably to the interests of France.

* * *

Notions of Anglo-British imperialism did not originate with Mary, Queen of Scots. England had a long tradition of claiming suzerainty over Scotland, and the extension of English sovereignty to include Scotland had been a political objective of many an English king, most notably Edward I.[31] The birth of Mary Stewart merely provided the means through which this imperial vision could be realised dynastically – the peaceful conquest of Scotland through the marriage of Mary, Queen of Scots to Prince Edward Tudor, the future Edward VI. Even the scenario of a Scottish queen regnant marrying the heir to the English throne was not unprecedented. In 1290 the betrothal of Margaret 'Maid of Norway' to Edward Plantagenet (the future Edward II) was contracted and ratified in the treaty of Birgham.

However enticing the idea of a united Britain was to the English, the tumultuous history of Anglo-Scottish relations rendered this prospect less attractive to the Scots. Their struggle to maintain and defend the independence of their kingdom from the seemingly incessant threat of English invasion and/or domination over two and half centuries made them acutely sensitive about matters of sovereignty. There were some Scots, such as James Henrisoun, to whom the idea of Britain was appealing, and even providential.[32] The wave of reformist ideologies sweeping across sixteenth-century Europe had not failed to reach the shores of Scotland, and Henry VIII's break from Rome added a Protestant dimension to the already existing geographical, linguistic and cultural arguments in favour of Anglo-Scottish union which culminated in the treaties of

31 For more on Edward I's Scottish policy, see F.J. Watson, *Under the Hammer: Edward I and Scotland, 1286–1306* (East Linton, 1998).
32 See, for example, James Henrisoun's *An Exhortation to the Scotts*, in J.A.H. Murray (ed.), *The Complaynt of Scotlande* (Early English Text Society, 1872–3), pp. 208–36.

Greenwich.[33] Yet only months after its ratification, the treaty contracting the marriage of Mary Stewart to Edward Tudor was renounced by the Scottish Parliament.[34] The Scots' reluctance to enter into a dynastic alliance with England raises the question of why they were so eager to enter into a similar, if not more intimate, alliance with France in July 1548. The answer lies in the English response to the Scots' refusal to recognise the treaties of Greenwich, which had the adverse affect of driving the Scots into the welcoming arms of France and, ultimately, provided for the dynastic union of the French and Scottish crowns.[35]

The *volte face* of the Scottish government regarding the treaties of Greenwich sparked a reactionary English policy in Scotland. Initially placatory in nature with the use of 'assured Scots', Henry VIII soon changed tactics and, in 1544–5, embarked on an aggressive campaign of 'rough wooing' Scotland into recognition of the treaties that contracted his son and heir's marriage to Mary Stewart.[36] After his

---

33 J.E.A. Dawson, 'Anglo-Scottish protestant culture and integration in sixteenth-century Britain' in S.G. Ellis & S. Barber (eds.), *Conquest and Union: Fashioning a British State, 1485–1725* (London, 1995), pp. 87–114; B.P. Levack, *The formation of the British state: England, Scotland and the union of 1603–1707* (Oxford, 1987); R.A. Mason, 'The Scottish Reformation and the origins of Anglo-British imperialism', in Mason (ed.), *Scots and Britons: Scottish Political Thought and the Union of 1603* (Cambridge, 1994), pp. 161–86, and 'Kingship, nobility and Anglo-Scottish union: John Mair's *History of Greater Britain* (1521)', *Innes Review*, 41 (1990), pp. 182–222; M. Merriman, 'James Henrisoun and 'Great Britain': British Union and the Scottish Commonweal', in R.A. Mason (ed.), *Scotland and England, 1286–1815* (Edinburgh, 1987); and A.H. Williamson, 'Scotland, Antichrist and the invention of Great Britain', in J. Dwyer *et al* (eds.), *New Perspectives on the politics and culture of early modern Scotland* (Edinburgh, 1982), pp. 34–58.
34 11 December 1543, *APS*, II, pp. 431–2.
35 This is the crux of Marcus Merriman's argument in *The Rough Wooings*, pp. 19–20.
36 M. Merriman, 'The assured Scots: Scottish Collaborators with England during the 'Rough Wooing'', *SHR*, xlvii (1968), pp. 10–34. For more on England's Scottish policy during the 1540s, see R.B. Wernham, *Before the Armada: The Growth of English Foreign Policy, 1485–1588* (London, 1966), pp. 149–78; M.L. Bush, *The Government Policy of Protector Somerset* (London, 1975), pp. 7–39; S. Doran, *England and Europe, 1485–1603* (London, 1986), pp. 23–50; J. J. Scarisbrick, *Henry VIII*, pp. 355–83, 424–57; Donaldson, *James V–James VII*, pp. 27–9, 63–94; D.M. Head, 'Henry VIII's Scottish Policy: a Reassessment', *Innes Review*, lxi (1982), pp. 14–24; J.B. Paul, 'Edinburgh in 1544 and Hertford's Invasion', *SHR*, viii (1911), pp. 113–31; and, especially, Merriman, *The Rough Wooings*, pp. 111–28, 137–63, 218–91, 'The assured Scots', pp. 10–34, 'The Forts of Eyemouth: Anvils of British Union?', *SHR*, lxvii (1988), pp. 142–55, and 'War and Propaganda during the "Rough Wooing"', *Scottish Tradition*, ix/x (1979–80), pp. 20–30.

death, Henry's Scottish policy was continued by Edward Seymour, duke of Somerset and Lord Protector of England during Edward VI's minority. Believing it to be his 'godly purpose' to 'enjoin the Queen [Mary of Guise] and Council to deliver the young Queen [Mary Stewart] . . . to be suitably nourished and brought up with her husband, as a Queen of England', Somerset launched his military campaign against the Scots in August 1547.[37] The ideological justification for his invasion and subsequent occupation of Scotland was deeply rooted in terms of Anglo-British imperialism. In his *Epistle Exhortatorie* to the Scots (1548), for example, Somerset reasoned that 'as you and wee be annexed and ioyned in one Islande, so no people so like in maner, forme, language, and all condicions . . . should bee, like as twoo brethren of one Islande of greate Britayn', and 'if it wer possible one kyngdome not to be divided in rulers'.[38] Recognising that 'twoo successions cannot concurre and fal into one, by no maner of other meanes, then by mariage, whereby one bloude, one lignage and parentage, is made of twoo, and an indefecible right geuen of bothe to one, without the destruccion and abolishing of either', Somerset stressed that his military objective in Scotland was not to conquer, but simply to 'join in marriage from high to low both the realms, to make of one isle one realm in love, amity, concord, peace, and charity'.[39] The great majority of the Scots, however, found Somerset's declarations of love and amity hard to swallow and saw the English occupation as simply one of conquest.

Central to Somerset's policy was the construction of strategically placed fortresses. The first phase of construction, beginning in September 1547 and lasting until January 1548, resulted in the creation of an English Pale in south-east Scotland.[40] The strongholds erected at Eyemouth, Roxburgh, Home, Inchcolm and Broughty, and later at Lauder, Haddington, Dunglass and Inchkeith, enabled the English to attack Scotland from within and led to the great devastation of the surrounding areas. As Marcus Merriman argues, it was Somerset's military foothold in Scotland and not necessarily the crushing defeat of the Scots at Pinkie Cleugh on 10 September 1547 that 'convinced the Scottish government of the day that England might

37 *CSP Scot.*, I, 50, p.22; P.G.B. McNeill & H.L. MacQueen, *Atlas of Scottish History to 1707* (Edinburgh, 1996), p.127.
38 *The Complaynt of Scotlande*, pp. 239–43.
39 *Ibid*, pp. 239, 241.
40 Merriman, 'The Forts of Eyemouth', pp. 146–7 and *The Rough Wooings*, pp. 246–58, 310–18; H.M. Colvin, *History of the King's Works* (London, 1975), IV, pp. 694–726; *Atlas of Scottish History to 1707*, p.128.

successfully conquer the realm'.[41] For many, however, the battle of
Pinkie, or 'Black Saturday' as it was later dubbed, was a decisive event
that epitomised England's aggressive policy and revealed Somerset's
true objective in Scotland.[42]

The comments of one contemporary observer, Alexander Gor-
don,[43] reveal that Pinkie did little to win favour for the English cause
amongst the Scots:

> . . . we be swa cruelly owrthrawin in this matter we will randyr
> to the Twrk rathyr nor to be onrewangit . . . thocht the
> wysdome off Ingland be extremit greitt, thay gane nocht the
> rycht way to mak unuon off thyr twa realmis. Gyf thay thynk
> to hawe hartlynes, thay suld traist ws moir tendyrly.[44]

More importantly, Pinkie was a catalytic event in terms of the renewal
of the Franco-Scottish alliance. In September 1547 the French ambassador resident in Scotland, Henri Cleutin, seigneur d'Oisel et
Villeparisis, was sent to France with letters and reports from Mary
of Guise and the Scottish Council urgently requesting financial and
military assistance from Henri II.[45] D'Oisel and the King were 'clo-
seted' for three days discussing the situation and the possibility of
French intervention in Scotland. When d'Oisel returned to Scotland
in October, he immediately met with Mary of Guise and Regent Arran
to discuss Henri's response to the Scots' proposal. Although they were
told that the news of Pinkie was the source of 'great displeasure' at the
French Court, Mary of Guise and the Scottish political élite also knew

41 Merriman, 'The Forts of Eyemouth', p.148. This sentiment was also
   expressed by M. de la Chapelle de Biron, treasurer of the French troops
   in Scotland, who reported on 23 March 1548 that '. . . les gens de ce
   pays [Scotland] se ressenttent tant de la perte de la bataille et de la
   crainte qu'ilz ont des fortz que les ennemys tinnent, qu'ilz ne peuvent
   reprandre sans l'ayde du Roy, au moyen de ce qu'ilz ont peu d'artillerie
   et munition, que, sans l'assureance que l'on leur donne du secours du
   Roy, ilz seroient en dangier de bientost prandre l'autre party [the people
   of this country greatly resent losing the battle and the fear of the
   fortresses held by the enemies that they cannot fight again without the
   King's help because they lack artillery and ammunition. Unless they are
   sure of the King's support, they would be in danger of soon rallying to
   the other side]', Teulet, *Relations*, I, p.160.
42 For more on the battle of Pinkie, see Merriman, *The Rough Wooings*, pp.
   233–7; and E. Bonner, 'The French Reactions to the Rough Wooings of
   Mary Queen of Scots', *Journal of the Sydney Society for Scottish History*, 6
   (1998), p.10 *n.*7, for bibliographical references.
43 Brother to George Gordon, 4th earl of Huntly, and postulate of
   Caithness.
44 *Scottish Correspondence*, cli, pp. 213–4.
45 *CSP Scot.*, I, 88, p. 41.

that sympathy alone would not be enough to secure the formal intervention of France in their conflict with England.[46] So, at a Convention at Edinburgh on 16 October 1547, it was decided that a formal appeal be made to the French King for men, money and munition. In return for his help, it was proposed that Henri be granted possession of certain Scottish strongholds and that Mary, Queen of Scots be sent to France 'thair to be keped, quhill sho shuld be mareid at the Kingis pleasour with the Dophine of France'.[47] This offer signalled the complete failure of Somerset's Scottish policy. Instead of coercing the Scots into recognition of the treaties of Greenwich, the 'rough wooings' had had the opposite effect of reducing the Scots to such a state of desperation that they had no choice but to turn to France for help. In doing so, they gave Henri the opportunity to pursue his own dynastic and imperial ambitions within the British Isles.

D'Oisel was off again to France in November to deliver the Scots' formal appeal for French military intervention and the terms under which it would be given.[48] He also carried with him a letter from Arran to Mary of Guise's brother, the Duc d'Aumale, asking that Henri be reminded of his loyalty and faithful service.[49] Arran needed to butter up the King – the purpose of d'Oisel's journey was also to present the terms of Arran's personal support for the Franco-Scottish alliance.

Whilst the decision to entrust Henri with the military security of Scotland and her queen may have come easily to the likes of Mary of Guise, whose dynasticism and daughter's personal safety were directly threatened by the occupying English forces, the Regent of Scotland needed persuading. As the Governor, second person of the realm and heir apparent to the Scottish throne on the failure of the Stewart line, Arran was extremely reluctant to support any alliance that would thwart his own dynastic ambitions and undermine his political position in Scotland. Initially, he had been intent on resolving the conflict with Somerset in order that Mary might then marry his own son and heir, James.[50] The proposal that she become an absentee monarch affianced to the Dauphin of France directly contravened his plans. Moreover, there was also the possibility that such an arrangement

46 *Balcarres Papers*, I, cxxx, p.172; *CSP Spain*, IX, pp. 523–5.
47 Lesley, *History*, pp. 203–4; *CSP Scot.*, I, 78, 81, 86, 88, 92, pp. 37–8, 40, 41–3; *TA*, IX, pp. 127, 15, 4. See also Ninian Cockburn's report in *CSP Scot.*, I, 73, pp. 34–5, for a similar discussion.
48 *TA*, IX, p.115; *CSP Scot.*, I, 88, 92, pp. 41, 42–3.
49 Merriman, *The Rough Wooings*, p.300.
50 *CSP Scot.*, I, 218, p.107; R.K. Hannay, 'The Earl of Arran and Queen Mary', *SHR*, xviii (1921), p.260.

would undermine his position as regent, an office which had served him well in providing for his kinsman and strengthening the power of the House of Hamilton through the nepotistic distribution of patronage and the forging of dynastic alliances.[51] The power and influence wielded by Arran made his support crucial to the success of the proposed alliance. His overriding dynastic and personal ambition, however, rendered him an unreliable political ally whose backing would not be forthcoming unless he felt it was advantageous to provide it. Indeed, it took much more than 'a French gentleman with fair words' to acquire his support.[52]

During November 1547, Mary of Guise and d'Oisel entered into negotiations with Arran. With so much to lose personally, the price of the Regent's support was predictably high, but his terms were nevertheless accepted by Henri at Châtillon on 27 January 1548.[53] In return for a pension of 12,000 *livres*, a French duchy and a French bride for his son James (presumably to compensate for his loss of Mary, Queen of Scots), Arran promised that he would assemble the Estates of Scotland and gain their consent to Mary, Queen of Scots' betrothal to the Dauphin, her removal to France where she would live as an absentee monarch in the protection of the French King, and the delivery of Dunbar and Blackness Castles into French hands. As promised, Arran summoned the Scottish nobility and, at a Convention held at Stirling in February 1548, he publicly endorsed the proposed Franco-Scottish dynastic alliance.[54] His declaration of support was effective. The Convention agreed to Henri's terms for French intervention, but stipulated that Mary would not be sent to France until a formal treaty had been ratified by the Three Estates, and this would only happen when French reinforcements arrived in Scotland to commence their intervention.[55]

---

51 Hannay, 'The Earl of Arran', pp. 258–76 and 'Some Papal Bulls among the Hamilton Papers', *SHR*, xxii (1924), pp. 25–41; E. Finnie, 'The House of Hamilton: Patronage, Politics and the Church in the Reformation Period', *Innes Review*, xxxvi (1985), pp. 3–28; M. Mahoney, 'The Scottish Hierarchy, 1513–1565', in D. MacRoberts (ed.), *Essays on the Scottish Reformation, 1513–1625* (Glasgow, 1962), pp. 51–3; Merriman, *The Rough Wooings*, pp. 27–39; Donaldson, *All the Queen's Men*, pp. 15–7.

52 *CSP Scot.*, I, 67, pp. 30–1.

53 J.A.B. Teulet ed., *Memoire justificatif du Droit qui appartient a M. le duc d'Hamilton de porter le titre de Duc de Chaterlherault* (Paris, 1863), pp. 3–7.

54 *CSP Scot.*, I, 125, 128, pp. 59, 60.

55 The French agreed to this request, but when reinforcements actually arrived in June 1548, the French proved equally reluctant to intervene at full strength until the betrothal contract had been ratified by the Three Estates in Parliament. *CSP Scot.*, I, 281, 283, 284, pp. 139–40; Teulet, *Papiers*, I, p.189 and *Relations*, I, p.221.

In the meantime, Arran was rewarded with letters patent confirming his regency of Scotland during Mary, Queen of Scots' minority and granting him financial immunity for all expenses incurred during that time.[56] In April 1548, by which time Arran had also been invested in the prestigious French chivalric Order of St. Michael, the Duc de Montpensier's eldest daughter was offered to Arran as a bride for his son, James,[57] who had been sent to France as a pledge to ensure Arran's continued and loyal support.[58]

By June, France's intervention in Scotland was in full swing and, accordingly, a Parliament was summoned to convene at the Abbey of Haddington. On 7 July 1548, a treaty was ratified by the Three Estates who, as Mary of Guise commented, were content 'to place all things in the hands of the King'.[59] With the treaty of Haddington formally concluded and the Franco-Scottish alliance firmly in place, Arran finally became the Duc de Châtelherault.[60]

* * *

At its most basic level, the treaty of Haddington was contracted as an immediate response to 'the mortall weiris crudelties depredatiounis and intollerabill iniuris done be our auld enimeis of Ingland aganis our Souerane Lady [Mary, Queen of Scots] . . . hir realme and lieges'.[61] Using the 'auld alliance' as a historical precedent to justify French intervention against England, Henri II pledged to 'reccouer all strenthis Castellis and Fortalices' out of English hands and restore Scotland 'to the auld libertie priuilege and freedome'.[62] Although the treaty was an expression of Henri's regard for the 'ancient lig confederatioun and amitie standand betuix the Realme of France' and Scotland, his offer to assume responsibility for its military security was

---

56 *Balcarres Papers*, II, pp. xxxvi–xxxvii.
57 This marriage never materialised as Mlle. de Montpensier was promised to another. *Balcarres Papers*, II, cli, clxiii, clxviii, pp. 197–8, 245–8, 256–8.
58 *Balcarres Papers*, I, clix–xi, pp. 205–7; *TA*, IX, p.83; *CSP Scot.*, I, 238, pp. 116–7. See also J. Durkan, 'James, Third Earl of Arran: The Hidden Years', *SHR* lxv (1986), pp. 154–66, for a discussion on James' life in France.
59 Teulet, *Papiers*, I, p.680 and *Relations*, I, p.179; *TA*, IX, pp. 183, 108, 197, 207, 214–5, 219–20; Merriman, *Rough Wooings*, p.309.
60 The long process of granting the Duchy of Châtelherault to Arran was completed on 17 June 1549. *APS*, II, pp. 508–10; Merriman, *The Rough Wooings*, p. 310 *n.* 32. Letters of naturalisation for Arran, his heirs and successors were also issued on 8 July 1548. Bonner, 'French Naturalization of the Scots in the Fifteenth and Sixteenth Centuries', *The Historical Journal*, xl/4 (1997), Appendix No.5, pp. 1109–11.
61 *APS*, II, p.481.
62 Bonner, 'Scotland's 'Auld Alliance' with France, 1295–1560', *SHR*, lxxxiv/ 273 (1999), pp. 5–30; *APS*, II, p.481.

not a selfless gesture of goodwill in the name of the 'auld alliance'.[63] In return for French succour, the Scottish political élite had consented to the betrothal of Mary Stewart to François Valois, which was intended to provide for the 'mair perfyte vnion' of Scotland and France.[64] More importantly, this dynastic alliance was also the basis for Henri's vision of a Franco-British empire. The strength of the alliance was further enhanced by the simple fact that, as a direct result of the treaty, Henri not only took the kingdom of Scotland into his personal protection, but also its young queen.

The declared intention of Somerset's invasion of 1547 that Mary Stewart 'be suitably nourished and brought up with her husband, as a Queen of England', had placed the personal safety of the young queen in jeopardy.[65] The Scots responded by taking precautionary measures to deprive Somerset of his prize. Mary was taken into the protective custody of her guardians, Lords Erskine and Livingstone, and was sheltered first at Stirling Castle, then at a secluded priory on the island of Inchmahome in the Lake of Menteith and, finally, at Dumbarton Castle in February 1548.[66] The devastation caused by the occupying English troops, however, brutally demonstrated Somerset's determination to fulfil his dynastic objective. It soon became apparent that Mary, Queen of Scots' safety could not be guaranteed in her own kingdom. It was decided, therefore, that she should leave Scotland to reside in France where she would remain in the personal protection of the French King until her marriage to the Dauphin.[67] Within weeks of the treaty of Haddington's ratification, Mary embarked for France[68] on the galleys that had arrived with the French military reinforcements Henri had, for so long, promised to Mary of Guise.[69] Despite

63 *Aps*, II, p.481.
64 *Ibid*, II, p.481.
65 *CSP Scot.*, I, 50, p.22.
66 Mary would remain at Dumbarton Castle, which had been placed at the disposal of Mary of Guise, until her conveyance to France. Arran retained control of Edinburgh Castle, whilst Henri was entrusted with Dunbar. *CSP Scot.*, I, 147, p.71.
67 *APS*, II, p.481.
68 Lesley, *History*, p.200; *CSP Scot.*, I, 270, 274, 290, 306, 310, pp. 134, 136, 147, 154–5, 157; *APS*, II, p.543; *TA*, IX, pp. 107, 122, 177, 207, 209; *Balcarres Papers*, I, cliv, clv, pp. 200–2. See also W.M. Bryce, 'Mary Stuart's Voyage to France in 1548', *EHR*, xxii (1907), pp. 43–50, for a detailed account of the voyage itself.
69 See 'Letters from Henry II King of France to His Cousin Mary Queen Dowager of Scotland', *Maitland Misc.*, I, 4–7, pp. 214–8 and *Balcarres Papers*, I, cxlv, cxlvi, cxlix, clii, cliv, lxxii, lxiii, pp. 188–90, 195–6, 198–9, 242 for similar assurances of French aid and details of the planned intervention.

Somerset's best efforts, Mary was to 'be suitably nourished and brought up with her husband', not as a Queen of England, but as a Queen of France.

* * *

French military intervention began in earnest on 16 June 1548 with the arrival of a fleet at Leith carrying 6,000 French and foreign troops and munitions.[70] The military objective, as stated in the treaty of Haddington, was to recover all the strongholds in English possession and restore Scotland to 'the auld libertie priuilege and fredome'.[71] Central to the French military campaign was the strengthening of existing Scottish strongholds and the construction of new ones in an attempt to counter the effects of Somerset's own fort-building policy.[72] As promised, Dunbar passed into French hands[73] and, despite financial difficulties, work began immediately to fortify the castle under the direction of Migliorino Ubaldini.[74] The French also set about fortifying and modernising existing strongholds at Leith, Millhaven, Inchgarvie and the castles at Blackness and Stirling, while constructing new ones at Inveresk, Inchkeith and Luffness.[75]

Through their own network of strongholds in Scotland, France's military objective was to over-extend and financially exhaust the English in order to 'isolate the important garrisons and reduce them by either siege or starvation'.[76] Their main target was the principal English stronghold at Haddington. But isolating Haddington proved to be a more difficult task than anticipated. Somerset's intricate network of fortresses had been specifically designed so that strongholds, like Haddington, could be revictualled without hindrance.[77]

70 See Merriman, *The Rough Wooings*, pp. 292–348, for a detailed discussion of France's military intervention as a whole.
71 *APS*, II, p.481.
72 Merriman, *The Rough Wooings*, p.334.
73 5 February 1548, *CSP Scot.*, I, 147, p.71.
74 Dunbar was handed over to the French captain and treasurer of the troops in Scotland, M. de Chapelle, on 18 June 1548. NLS, Adv.MSS, 29.2.3, f.144 and MSS, 2991, f.71; *TA.*, IX, p.445; *CSP Scot.*, I, 147, 228, 257, 265, pp. 71, 111, 125, 131; *CSP Spain*, IX, p.246. In his letter to Mary of Guise from Dunbar on 3 September 1548, Ubaldini reported that the fortification of the castle began on the first day of his arrival, but due to the difficulty in finding sufficient labour, he was unable to commence the fortification of the town itself. For more on Ubaldini and his work in Scotland see Merriman, *The Rough Wooings*, pp. 321–30.
75 *Ibid*, pp. 321–39; Merriman, 'The Forts of Eyemouth', pp. 151–2; Colvin, *King's Works*, IV, p.609 *n.*4.
76 Merriman, *The Rough Wooings*, p.334. This was also Somerset's strategy against the French.
77 *Ibid*, pp. 334–5.

But in 1549 the delivery of provisions *was* hindered and England's position in Scotland irreparably weakened. Ironically, this had nothing to do with France's military intervention, but was rather due to a series of domestic crises in England. Troops and victuals destined for Scotland were retained in England in order to deal with the various uprisings that constituted the 'western rebellion' of 1549. It was because of England's weakened position on a national and international level that Henri felt the time was ripe to refocus his attention on the Continent and intensify his efforts to recapture Boulogne from the English. On 8 August 1549, France officially declared war on England. The combined effects of internal dissension and France's assault on two fronts proved too much for the English. Haddington was abandoned in September 1549 and, in October, Somerset was removed from the Protectorate. Somerset's successor, John Dudley, earl of Warwick and future duke of Northumberland, inherited a financially exhausted and weak administration.[78] Eager to consolidate his position and re-establish order, Warwick moved to end England's conflict with France at Boulogne and in Scotland.[79]

On 18 February 1550, therefore, negotiations for an Anglo-French peace accord began and culminated in the treaty of Boulogne (24 March 1550) – a treaty in which Scotland was comprehended as an ally of France.[80] As the 'Protector' of Scotland, Henri assumed control of Scottish diplomacy, and all matters pertaining to Scotland were represented by the French commissioners at the peace talks. The English still held the strongholds at Roxburgh, Eyemouth, Dunglass, Lauder and Broughty, and while this was the subject of great debate, the treaty of Boulogne was fundamentally an Anglo-French accord. As such, it was not expected to settle all differences between England and Scotland. The major issue was Boulogne and the terms under which it would revert to French possession. Indirectly, however, it did provide for the cessation of Scotland's hostilities with England and paved the way for an exclusively Anglo-Scottish treaty which was eventually contracted at Norham in June 1551.

The treaty of Haddington's significance, therefore, is multi-faceted. On an immediate and practical level, it provided the Scots with French financial and military assistance and a safe haven for their

---

78 For more on Dudley, see D. Loades, *John Dudley, Duke of Northumberland, 1504–1553* (Oxford, 1996) and B.L. Beer, *Northumberland: The Political Career of John Dudley, Earl of Warwick and Duke of Northumberland* (Kent, Ohio, 1973).

79 *CSP Spain*, X, pp. 47, 92–3.

80 *Foedera*, XV, pp. 212–5.

queen, thus preventing Somerset from either conquering Scotland or capturing Mary, Queen of Scots. Dynastically, the treaty provided for the union of the French and Scottish crowns and, on account of Mary's Catholic claim to the English throne, also laid the foundations for a Franco-British empire. But this was not all the treaty of Haddington did. More importantly, the treaty of Haddington established a protectoral alliance between France and Scotland that enabled Henri to assume control of Scottish foreign policy and diplomacy while maintaining a military presence in Scotland after the cessation of hostilities with England. It would also be responsible for Mary of Guise's future political career in Scotland as Queen Regent. With the removal of the English threat, however, the question remained as to whether the Scots would remain favourable to such an intimate Franco-Scottish alliance that gave the French King extraordinary power over their affairs and kingdom. It would seem for the time being that the Scots had no such qualms, but only time would tell if the price of protection against England was too high.

2

The New 'Auld Alliance':
Henri II's Protectorate of Scotland

T he treaty of Haddington's significance is most commonly identified as its betrothal of Mary Stewart to François Valois and, on a more immediate and practical level, its furnishing of men, money and munition to the Scots. However, as will become clear, the treaty of Haddington is also significant in that it created a protectoral alliance between the 'auld allies' which, in turn, justified and facilitated the establishment of French power in Scotland prior to the union of the crowns in 1558. The Three Estates' acceptance of Henri's offer to defend Scotland against England 'and all vthers' now and 'at all necessar tymes to cum', and to 'keip maintain and defend this Realme liegis of the samin liberteis and Lawis thereof', effectively made Henri the 'Protector' of Scotland – and Scotland a protectorate of France.[1]

In this context, the terms 'protector' and 'protectorate' are used not so much in the sense implied by Somerset's title of Lord Protector of England, but more in the modern sense of a less powerful state or territory being protected and largely controlled by a more powerful one. While Henri did not formally assume the title of 'Protector' in relation to Scotland, his extensive use of the language of protection in his correspondence clearly conveys how he saw his role in the Franco-Scottish alliance.

Henri drew no distinction between his protection of Scotland and that of its young queen. Writing to inform the Estates of Scotland that the young Queen, 'my daughter', had arrived safely in France and was with 'the Dauphin her husband', Henri declared that 'in consequence, her Kingdom, her affairs and subjects are with ours the same thing, never to be separated'.[2] Indeed, the Estates' consent to the proposed marital alliance and the solemnity of the ceremony in which it was given were also used to demonstrate how the Scots already

1 *APS*, II, p.481.
2 30 July 1548, M. Belot (ed.), *Lettres et mémoires d'estat des roys, princes, ambassadeurs et autres ministres sous les regnes de François Ier, Henri II et François II par G. Ribier* (Paris, 1666), II, pp. 150–1.

recognised the Dauphin as the King of Scotland.[3] Dynastic arguments such as these were fortified by the residency of Scotland's queen regnant in France. Both François duc de Guise and the Constable of France, Anne de Montmorency, wrote of the French King's desire not to differentiate between his own kingdom and that of Scotland as he regarded 'the little Queen as his own daughter'.[4] Because Mary Stewart was in his protection and affianced to his son and heir, Henri considered it his duty and personal obligation to protect and defend her kingdom as he would his own, for now there was no difference between the two.[5]

The creation of a Franco-Scottish protectoral alliance had a direct and immediate impact in Scotland. During the period 1550–1552, Henri began the process of establishing French power in Scotland that would last until 1560. Henri's perception of Scotland as a 'Kingdom which is under my protection and which I consider as mine' was used to justify this process and, more importantly, was accepted on a national and international level.[6]

Henri II's military intervention in Scotland was never meant to be a

3 Henri wrote to his ambassador resident in England, Odet de Selve, that 'le contract de mariage . . . passe solennellement en Escosse, auant le partement de ladite Reyne, & l'inuestiture & possession des Royaumes, Sceptre & Couronne, baillee & delaissee en la presence, & du consentment des Estats du pays, à mes deputez au profit de mondit Fils, lequel a este en ce faisant reconnu pour Roy d'Escosse [the marriage contract was solemnly approved in Scotland before the Queen's departure, and the investiture and accession of the Kingdom's Sceptre and Crown was granted and assigned with the consent of the attending Estates of the country to my deputies on behalf of my son, who has thus been acknowledged as King of Scotland]'. Ribier, *Lettres et mémoires*, II, p.152. The Imperial ambassador, St. Mauris, also reported that Henri had declared that the 'Parliament of Scotland had agreed to the marriage of the Queen of Scots to his son, and for that reason he had already taken possession of the kingdom, which he intended to keep and govern as his own kingdom'. *CSP Spain*, IX, pp. 336–7.
4 NLS, MSS.2991, fos. 14ᵛ-5ʳ, 9ᵛ-10ʳ; G. Dickinson (ed.), *Mission of Beccarie de Pavie, Baron de Fourquevaux, en Ecosse, 1549* (Oxford, 1948), pp. 12, 9. They also wrote of how 'le Roy a acueur le bien des affaires d'Escosse qui sont les siens propres [the King holds dear Scottish affairs which are his own]'.
5 On 30 July 1548 Henri wrote to de Selve that he regarded, 'la protection, & conseruation dudict Royaume d'Ecosse, comme du mien propre, n'estant a present tous deux qu'vne mesme chose l'vn auec l'autre [the protection and conservation of the said Kingdom of Scotland as if my own, both of them being now a single thing, the one with the other]'. Ribier, *Lettres et mémoires*, II, p.152.
6 AÉ, *Cor. Pol.*, Angleterre, VIII, f.103ᵛ; D.L. Potter (ed.), 'Documents concerning the negotiation of the Anglo-French treaty of March 1550', *Camden Miscellany*, xxviii/29 (1984), 47, p.134.

short-term arrangement that would end with the cessation of hostilities with England. Rather, he was commissioned by the Three Estates in Parliament to defend Scotland against England and all others, in liberty and freedom 'at all necessar tymes to cum'.[7] As the 'Protector' of Scotland, Henri was able to justify his intervention in Scotland in 1548 and maintain a legitimate military position within the archipelago after the cessation of hostilities in 1550. By the same token he was also able to assume control of Scotland's diplomatic affairs and, by implication, her foreign policy. These two defining characteristics of French power,[8] and the protectoral arguments used to justify its establishment, are effectively demonstrated in Scotland's comprehension within the treaty of Boulogne; the *rapprochement* between the Scots and Charles V; and the extensive involvement of France in the negotiations for the Anglo-Scottish treaty of Norham.

* * *

Dynastic and imperial considerations unquestionably motivated Henri II to intervene in Scotland in 1548. But these considerations were only potential returns on his military and financial investment and ultimately depended on the marriage of Mary Stewart to François Valois. To suggest that Henri was motivated by dynastic and imperial ambitions alone is a narrow interpretation of events – especially since it was a very real possibility that these prospects would not materialise. The incentive for Henri's intervention in Scotland must be seen in the wider European context as part of his territorial quest to recover Boulogne, neutralise England, and redress the balance of power that was then in Charles V's favour.

Captured by Henry VIII in 1544, 'Boulogne had dominated French policy towards England in the last years of François I and the first of Henri II'.[9] Henry VIII's determination to hold on to Boulogne prompted François I to launch an attack on the Isle of Wight and

---

7 *APS*, II, p.481.

8 Another feature was the introduction and circulation of French currency in Scotland. This, however, seems to have been a less popular aspect of the establishment of French power owing to the refusal of some Scots to accept French coins as legal tender. Having been examined by the auditors of the Exchequer in July 1550 and authorised as legal currency on 7 August, increasingly harsh penalties were prescribed by the Privy Council for those who refused to accept French coins – including escheat and death. In the end the obstinacy of the Scots prevailed and the Privy Council was forced to issue a prohibition on the importation of certain French coins on 16 November 1551. *RPC*, I, pp. 104–5, 106, 108–9, 109–11.

9 D.L. Potter, 'The Treaty of Boulogne and European Diplomacy, 1549–50', *Bulletin of the Institute of Historical Research*, lv (1982), pp. 50–1.

Seaford in July 1545 in the hope of forcibly weakening the English King's resolve. Stalemate rather than surrender led to negotiations for an Anglo-French peace, and the resulting treaty of Ardres (7 June 1546) provided for the return of Boulogne in 1554, but only upon receipt of two million crowns. Less than satisfactory from a French perspective, it comes as no surprise that the reconquest of Boulogne continued to be a military objective upon the accession of Henri II in 1547. While the Habsburg-Valois rivalry restrained Henri from taking any overt military action against the English for fear of recrimination by Charles V, the Scots' timely appeal for French aid and the ensuing treaty of Hadding-ton presented Henri with the ideal opportunity to confront England directly and legitimately as the 'Protector' of Scotland. French military intervention in Scotland would not only serve to divert English attention from the Continent and deplete resources that otherwise would have been used to maintain and fortify Boulogne, but also provided Henri with the opportunity to cash in on the long-term dynastic and imperial rewards that an alliance with Scotland had to offer.

By July 1549 it was clear that Charles V was not prepared to assist the English in their defence of Boulogne.[10] The door had effectively been left open for Henri to declare war against England in August and commence his military campaign. Despite having taken many of the forts surrounding Boulogne, such as Ambleteuse, Henri's military campaign to take Boulogne itself had ultimately failed.[11] French forces were impeded by adverse weather conditions and what D.L. Potter describes as 'a certain improvisation in the late planning of the campaign'.[12] For England, a series of domestic crises culminating in the collapse of Somerset's protectorate in October 1549 and the debilitating effects of a confrontation with France on two fronts made the overtures for peace as welcome as they were to the French.[13] Just six months after war had been declared, negotiations for an Anglo-French peace accord began in earnest on 18 February 1550.[14]

---

10 *CSP Foreign, 1547–1553*, 160, p.36; Potter, 'Treaty of Boulogne', p.51. Paget was despatched to the Imperial Court at Brussels to ask for assistance against the French in June 1549. See also Charles' letter to Van der Delft on 26 July 1549 in *CSP Spain*, IX, pp. 411–2.

11 *CSP Foreign, 1547–1553*, 196, p.46. See also W.K. Jordan (ed.), *The Chronicle and Political Papers of King Edward VI* (London, 1966), p.13; Cloulas, *Henri II*, pp. 268–9; and Baumgartner, *Henry II*, pp. 141–3.

12 Potter, 'Documents', p.59.

13 Between 1545 and 1550 England's war expenses totalled £3,491,472, approximately £603,900 of which was for their military campaign in Scotland. BL, Harley MSS, 353.28, fos. 90–102; PRO, SP10/15/11.

14 Potter, 'Treaty of Boulogne', pp. 51–65 and 'Documents', pp. 58–180.

Although the treaty of Boulogne was fundamentally concerned with engineering a *rapprochement* between England and France, Scotland nevertheless figured prominently in the negotiations. Scotland was represented by Henri's negotiating commissioners: François de Montmorency, Seigneur de Rochepot, Gaspard de Coligny, Seigneur de Chatillon, André Guillart, Seigneur de Mortier, and Guillaume Bochetel, Seigneur de Sassy.[15] The French King's primary aim was to settle the financial terms under which the English would relinquish Boulogne. By 2 March 1550 he was 'wonderfully delighted' that his offer of 400,000 *écus d'or soleil* and the reservation of England's pension rights were considered reasonable by the English.[16] In order to consolidate the resumption of friendly relations with England and, at the strong urging of Antonio Guidotti,[17] mediator of the negotiations, Henri also proposed the marriage of his eldest daughter, Elisabeth, to Edward VI.[18] Seen by the French commissioners as 'the greatest and most honourable [thing] that we have in our instruction', the acceptance of this proposal would bring to an end England's persistent, albeit futile, demand for the recognition of the treaties of Greenwich and facilitate the promotion of French interests at the English Court.[19] On a more immediate and practical level, *rapprochement* with England, with or without a dynastic alliance, would ensure England's neutrality in the inevitable renewal of the Habsburg-Valois conflict for European supremacy. In this respect, the Franco-Scottish alliance of 1548 and the subsequent establishment of French military power in Scotland placed Henri in a strong position within the archipelago to enforce England's neutrality or, if need be, to check English involvement and/or ambitions on the Continent. But as long as England had a military foothold in Scotland, France's strategic position was undermined and Scotland's national security threatened. Henri's secondary objective during the negotiations, therefore, was the relinquishment of all strongholds held by the English in Scotland.

England's military position in Scotland was a very contentious issue

---

15 Potter, 'Documents', 1, pp. 74–5.

16 AÉ, *Cor. Pol.*, Angleterre, VIII, f.101ʳ; Potter, 'Documents', 47, p.129.

17 A Florentine merchant, Antonio Guidotti was a naturalised Englishman with influential contacts at the French court. *Ibid*, p.85 *n*.1 and 'Treaty of Boulogne', pp. 57–8.

18 AÉ, *Cor. Pol.*, Angleterre, II, f.287ᵛ and VIII, f.107; Potter, 'Documents', 2, 27, pp. 81, 103. For more on the Tudor-Valois marriage negotiations, see *CSP Foreign, 1547–1553*, 347, 351, 387, 411, pp. 107–8, 109, 133, 150; BL, Harley MSS, 353.33, fos. 110–1 and 353.34, fos. 112–3.

19 AÉ, *Cor. Pol.* Angleterre, VIII, f.107; Potter, 'Documents', 27, p.103.

during the negotiations. But this could not be, and was not, effectively dealt with in the treaty of Boulogne itself because it brought into question specific Anglo-Scottish boundary disputes. The contentious issue at hand was the fate of the English strongholds located at Roxburgh, Eyemouth, Broughty, Lauder and Dunglass. Henri's position on the matter was clear from the outset: every stronghold that had been conquered and occupied by the English since Henry VIII's invasion was to be relinquished and returned to the Scots.[20] The English commissioners, however, had been given explicit instructions to hold on to all English strongholds in Scotland and, only as a last resort, to surrender the lesser forts at Lauder, Dunglass and Broughty.[21] By late February the English had done just that,[22] but they were determined to reserve the English King's title to Scotland and retain Roxburgh and Eyemouth, claiming that they constituted 'their ancient boundaries and borders'.[23] This proved to be as unacceptable to Henri as it was to Mary of Guise, who wrote that 'it would be a great tragedy if they could still hold on to one stronghold in this kingdom'.[24]

In response to these claims, Henri was quick to establish and assert his position as 'Protector' of Scotland. Because Scotland was in his protection and, therefore, a kingdom of his own, 'it would be sensible to leave them with nothing out of what they had seized after the last wars'.[25] As Eyemouth and Roxburgh had been taken since the last war, Henri flatly rejected the claims that they constituted England's ancient border and similarly declined the offer of Broughty.[26] Henri

---

20 AÉ, *Cor. Pol.* Angleterre, II, f. 287ʳ; Potter, 'Documents', 2, p.80.
21 BL, Cotton MSS, Caligula E.iv, fos. 285ʳ, 278ʳ, Harley MSS, 36.12, fos. 54–5, 55–6 and Lansdowne MSS, 2.33, fos. 81–3; Potter, 'Documents', p.129 n.2.
22 AÉ, *Cor. Pol.* Angleterre, VIII, f.101ʳ; Potter, 'Documents', 47, p.129. Henri wrote to his commissioners that the English commissioners 'ont accorde de me rendre Boulogne et tous les fortz qu'ilz on alentour et pareillement trois paces [*sic*] qu'ilz ont en Escosse, scavoir est: Donglas, Bourtierac et Ladres, retenans a eulx Roxbourg et Aymond [have agreed to give me back Boulogne and all the surrounding strongholds as well as three fortified towns they have in Scotland, that is to say: Dunglass, Broughty Craig, and Lauder, while retaining Roxburgh and Eyemouth for themselves]'.
23 BL, Harley MSS, 36.11, fos. 52–3 and Cotton MSS, Caligula E.iv, f.282ʳ; Potter, 'Documents', p.138 n.1.
24 Mary of Guise to François, duc de Guise, 26 February 1550, J.-P. Micharde et J.-P.-P. Poujolat (eds)., *Mémoires-Journaux de François de Lorraine, duc d'Aumale et de Guise, 1547 à 1563* (Paris, 1854), p.8.
25 AÉ, *Cor. Pol.*, Angleterre, VIII, f.102ʳ; Potter, 'Documents', 47, p.131.
26 AÉ, *Cor. Pol.*, Angleterre, VIII, f.102ʳ; Potter, 'Documents', 47, pp. 131–2.

thus sent his commissioners back to the negotiating table to demand the return of Eyemouth and Roxburgh and, while they were at it, a reduction in the price of Boulogne.[27] The English, however, were equally determined to retain Roxburgh and Eyemouth, even to the point of temporarily suspending the negotiations, as their position in Scotland was the only leverage they had against the French.[28] Scotland had been reduced to nothing more than a bargaining tool with which both sides haggled over the price of Boulogne. As a result, the fate of Scotland's strongholds had yet to be determined when peace between England and France was finally contracted on 24 March 1550.[29] In order to address this question and other issues pertaining to Scotland's military security and diplomatic affairs, Henri despatched François de Seguenville-Fumel, sieur de Thor, to Scotland.[30]

As the Scottish political community would learn from Fumel, the treaty of Boulogne provided for a less than conclusive and rather confusing settlement of the question of the English-held fortifications in Scotland.[31] Much to the displeasure of Mary of Guise, Eyemouth and Roxburgh were still held by the English even though they had agreed to surrender the lesser forts of Lauder and Dunglass to do so.[32] There was a chance, though, that Eyemouth and Roxburgh could be reclaimed by the Scots because England's possession of them was conditional. If the Scots were able to retake Lauder and Dunglass before the publication of the peace, or officially requested that they be demolished, the English would also be constrained to demolish Roxburgh and Eyemouth.[33] The fate of all four strongholds, therefore, needed to be determined by the Scots – but not before Henri took steps to ensure that their decision was in accordance with his own.[34]

At the time of Fumel's mission to Scotland, Henri had already made up his mind on the course of action that should be taken. In his opinion, all four forts should be demolished as Dunglass and Lauder

---

27 AÉ, *Cor. Pol.*, Angleterre, VIII, fos. 103ʳ-4ʳ; Potter, 'Documents', 47, pp. 133–4.

28 BL, Cotton MSS, Caligula E.iv, f.282ʳ; Potter, 'Documents', p.138 *n*.1.

29 *Foedera*, XV, pp. 211–7; NAS, SP7/40.

30 M. Wood (ed.), 'Instructions to the French Ambassador, 30 March 1550', *SHR*, xxvi (1947), pp. 154–67.

31 Fumel arrived in Scotland in mid-April and addressed the Privy Council on 22 April 1550. *TA*, IX, pp. 393, 397; *RPC*, I, p.86.

32 Micharde et Poujolat, *Mémoires-Journaux*, pp. 8, 31.

33 Wood, 'Instructions', p.160; AÉ, *Cor. Pol.* Angleterre, II, fos. 293ᵛ-4ʳ, 366ᵛ-7ʳ; Potter, 'Documents', 51, p.142.

34 Potter, 'Documents', 52, pp. 144–6.

could always be rebuilt 'to establish a barrier there against the English, to stop them from ever crossing in to the said country [of Scotland]'.[35] To ensure that he got his own way, Henri instructed Fumel to discuss the matter with Mary of Guise, d'Oisel and Paul de Termes, lieutenant-general of the French forces in Scotland, before consulting Châtelherault (Arran). If it was deemed appropriate that the Regent and his council should be consulted, *i.e.* if it was felt that they would reach a similar decision, only then was Fumel to discuss it with them following the advice of the Queen Dowager and her French advisers.[36] The same procedure also applied to Henri's enquiry as to the number of French troops needed in Scotland now that the Anglo-Scottish conflict had ended.

Henri was anxious to reduce his expenditure in this new reign of peace. D'Oisel, de Termes and Mary of Guise were asked to determine how many French garrisons were still required for the security of Scotland, and whether it was feasible to withdraw the *lansquenets* and light horse if he left the *gens d'armes*.[37] Henri was clearly intent on maintaining his military position in Scotland. The most expedient way of cutting his costs would surely have been the complete withdrawal of all French troops. But it is the way in which Henri discreetly assumed control of Scotland's military affairs that is of greater significance. His insistence that matters of military security be discussed with Mary of Guise and her French advisers before consulting Châtelherault demonstrates how the latter's position as regent was being undermined. Châtelherault was only being consulted as a formality. While it appeared as if Châtelherault was the one in control, the real decisions were being made by Henri and his French agents in Scotland. This was a shrewd piece of manipulation by the French King. Whilst reassuring Châtelherault of his position and authority as regent, Henri was simultaneously able to exert his will in order to ensure that the interests of France were being served in Scotland.

In the end it was deemed appropriate that Châtelherault be consulted on these matters of national security and, on 22 April 1550, the Scottish Privy Council issued a formal reply to Henri.[38] With respect to the English-held fortifications in Scotland, it was the opinion of Mary of Guise, Châtelherault and his Council, 'that the fortis of Lauder, Dunglas, Roxburgh, and Aymouth, be all cassin

35 Wood, 'Instructions', pp. 160–1.
36 Ibid, p.161.
37 Ibid, p.165. *Lansquenets* were German infantrymen used as mercenaries.
38 *RPC*, I, pp. 86–93.

doun', finally putting an end to the matter.[39] After England's consent to surrender these strongholds had been received,[40] preparations were soon made for 'the essegeing of forttis within Scotland presentlie in the handis of oure auld inemeis of Ingland'.[41] With oxen, 'pikis, schulis and mattokis', the Scots descended on Lauder and Dunglass to cast down their walls and transfer their artillery and munitions respectively to Home Castle and Dunbar.[42] Even though their demolition had been completed by July 1550, the English nominally retained Eyemouth and Roxburgh until all the boundary disputes were settled in the treaty of Norham (June 1551).[43]

While several of Scotland's strongholds had been allocated for demolition in 1550, France continued to invest in her programme of fortress modernisation that began in 1548.[44] Engineers such as Camillo Marini were sent to plan, and repair, Scotland's border and coastal fortifications.[45] On 8 November 1550, for example, orders were issued to build a fort 'about the toun and castell of Dunbar for strenthing and fortificatioun of the same and resisting of sik danger and inconvenientis as may hereafter follow'.[46] The following March d'Oisel, Châtelherault and Marini also proposed that a fort at Jedburgh would be ideal for defending and enforcing the peace on the Border.[47] Despite complaints that not enough money was being sent from France to carry out the desired renovations,[48] work on Scotland's strongholds was conducted at such a pace that the English ambassador resident in France, Sir John Mason, felt compelled to report that all this activity was distasteful to the Scots, who thought that it was meant for the keeping of them and not for the defence of the country.[49] In

---

39 *RPC*, I, p.90.
40 *APC*, II, p.429.
41 *TA*, IX, p.396.
42 *Ibid*, IX, pp. 421, 423–4.
43 *RPC*, I, p.99; *APC*, III, pp. 47, 97, 171; *CSP Foreign, 1547–1553*, 215, 221, pp. 48, 50; *CSP Scot*, I, 371, p.185; *Foedera*, XV, pp. 265–71.
44 Merriman, 'The Forts of Eyemouth', p.151; Colvin, *King's Works*, IV, p.609 n.4.
45 *CSP Foreign, 1547–1553*, 248, p.59; *Balcarres Papers*, II, lxvi, pp. 92–3.
46 *ADCP*, p.606.
47 15 March 1551, *Balcarres Papers*, II, lxvi, pp. 92–3.
48 In his letter to Mary of Guise, Camillo Marini complained that the 3,000 *livres* Henri sent for the repair of Scotland's border fortifications was insufficient. *Ibid*, II, lxvi, pp. 92–3.
49 18 March 1551, *CSP Foreign, 1547–1553*, 305, p.79. See also *Balcarres Papers*, II, cxxvii, pp. 185–6, for the work that was to begin diligently at Dunbar in December 1553. This was undoubtedly a response to Mary Tudor's accession, the arrival of her consort, Philip of Spain, and the work being done on the English side of the Border, most notably at Berwick.

the light of the Scots' reaction to Henri's enquiries about the reduction of his expenditure in Scotland, however, the accuracy of Mason's
statement is questionable and was more than likely intended to
reassure his English audience.

With a view to 'sparing the Kingis expense in tyme of pece', the
Privy Council proposed that the forts at Inchcolm, Inchgarvie,
Broughty (Balgillo), Montrose and Luffness (Aberlady) also be
demolished.[50] While the Scots proposed certain cost-cutting measures, they also requested that the strongholds at Dunbar, Blackness,
Inveresk, Inchkeith and Broughty Castle be fortified and garrisoned
with French troops. The strategic positions of Inchkeith and Broughty
at the entrances to the Firths of Forth and Tay made this request a
particular necessity, as was the maintenance of Home Castle because
of its close proximity to the Borders.[51] England was still clearly
regarded as a threat to national security, and the stipulation that
1,000 footmen remain in Scotland to garrison the strongholds of the
realm is testimony to the Scots' predominant concern with matters of
defence at the time.[52] It has been estimated that, by December 1550,
d'Oisel was commanding a force of 1,100 French soldiers in Scotland.[53]

Once the fate of the English held fortifications in Scotland and
other matters of military security had been determined, Thomas,
Master of Erskine, was despatched to England on 24 April 1550 with a
commission to 'ratifie, afferme, and appreve . . . the comprehensioun
of Hir Grace and hir realme of Scotland' in the treaty of Boulogne.[54]
The ratification of Scotland's comprehension was formalised on 15
May 1550.[55] From England, Erskine then proceeded to France to
present the Scots' reply to Henri's memorial and to pledge their
continued support for the Franco-Scottish dynastic alliance.[56] Echo-
ing the French King's wish 'to see one day, one's son be married with
one of the most virtuous princesses', the Scots also expressed their

50 *RPC*, I, pp. 90, 119.
51 *Ibid*, I, p.90.
52 *Ibid*, I, p.90.
53 M. Merriman, 'The Struggle for the Marriage of Mary Queen of Scots:
   English and French Intervention in Scotland, 1543–1550' (unpublished
   PhD Thesis, University of London, 1974), p.324. See also R.S. Rait (ed.),
   'Muster-Roll of the French Garrison at Dunbar', *SHS Misc.*, II, pp. 105–
   13. At this point in time, Henri felt that Dunbar should be garrisoned
   with 93 French soldiers.
54 *TA*, IX, pp. 393, 394, 397; *RPC*, I, p.87; Wood, 'Instructions', pp. 159–60.
55 NAS, SP6/49; BL, Cotton MSS, Caligula B.vii, fos. 405, 406, 414, 418–20
   and B.viii, fos. 279–80; *CSP Spain*, X, pp. 91, 98, 168.
56 *RPC*, I, pp. 86–93.

hope that 'be hir [Mary Stewart's] birth, mak his Hienes to be callit the gudschir of ane of the maist victorious princes in the warld and Kyng to ryng lang prosperouslie abufe baith the realmes'.[57] Their formal recognition that Henri was 'the sure and onlie defendar and releiff, under God, of all this realme' also confirmed and reinforced the protectoral relationship that existed between France and Scotland.[58]

By placing the military security of Scotland in the hands of Henri, recognising him as 'Protector' and asking for continued intervention after the cessation of hostilities with England, the Scottish political élite willingly abetted the establishment of French military power in Scotland prior to a projected union of the crowns. Of even greater importance, the establishment of this power was neither forced nor the result of military conquest. But were the Scots in any position to refuse?

The very fact that Henri asked the Scots to determine what, if any, French forces were needed in Scotland is noteworthy. Having expressed the wish to reduce his expenditure, he could have stopped all military and financial aid completely. Likewise, the Scottish political community could have requested the immediate removal of all foreign troops and the complete cessation of French military and financial intervention. Instead, the Privy Council issued Henri with certain conditions that would take a considerable amount of time to satisfy, if at all. Firstly, it was stipulated that 'gif it be the Kingis pleasour to tak away his army here', enough troops were to remain until a final and perfect peace was concluded with England and sure knowledge was had of peace with Charles V.[59] If these objectives were not attainable, Henri's 'imperial dewite . . . oblisit [him] to defend pupillis, that he will grant support of men, munitioun, and sic thair reasonabill help as he may spair'.[60] As we shall see, securing an enduring Scoto-Imperial peace and 'ane honorabill peax of the King of Ingland' was no mean feat – nor, for that matter, was the Scots' second demand.[61] The Privy Council also looked to the French, and in particular Mary of Guise, for help in pacifying their country internally. Once peace had been established on an international level, it was requested that 'sik ordour sall be takyn for executioun of justice and ordouring of the cuntre be the avise of the Quenis

57 Wood, 'Instructions', p.163; *RPC,* I, p.88.
58 *Ibid,* I, p.87.
59 *Ibid,* I, p.93.
60 *Ibid,* I, p.93.
61 *Ibid,* I, pp. 90, 93.

Grace [Mary of Guise], . . . quharewith the King sall have caus to be contentit, and sall be advertist thairof in dew tyme.'[62] The Scottish political élite was in no hurry to see the back of the French.

* * *

Diplomatic control was another feature of the establishment of French power in Scotland. As in matters of military security, control of Scotland's diplomatic affairs, and, by implication, her foreign policy, was considered by Henri to fall within his jurisdiction as 'Protector' of Scotland. Using what was fast becoming his catchphrase that Scotland 'as a kingdom in my protection I consider as mine', Henri was able to justify his eclipse of Châtelherault's authority in the realm of diplomacy.[63] More importantly, the Scottish political community's acceptance of this justification sanctioned the French King's authority in the realm of diplomacy. Two occasions in particular demonstrate Henri's assumption of control of Scotland's diplomatic affairs during the period 1550–1552: the negotiations that culminated in the treaty of Binche in 1550 and the treaty of Norham in 1551.

The volatile and particularly hostile nature of Scoto-Imperial relations in 1550 provided Henri with the ideal opportunity to assert and exercise his diplomatic authority. Fumel had also been instructed by the French King to rebuke Châtelherault for making peace overtures to Charles V without his knowledge or consent.[64] Indeed, Henri found it 'very strange' that the Governor should dare to take such an independent course of action given that Scotland was in his protection, and when negotiations should have been conducted by one of his ambassadors resident with the Emperor.[65] To soften the blow of Henri's assumption of diplomatic control and, of course, to further bind Châtelherault to the interests of France, the Regent was also told that, because of the King's satisfaction with his work in recovering the strongholds held by the English, certain steps had been taken to grant legatine powers to the Regent's half-brother, John, the archbishop of St Andrews.[66] The prospect of a Hamilton controlling the dispensation of all ecclesiastical benefices and offices in Scotland, save bish-

---

62 *RPC*, I, p.90.
63 Wood, 'Instructions', p.163; AÉ, *Cor. Pol.*, Angleterre, VIII, f.103ᵛ; Potter, 'Documents', 47, p.131.
64 NLS, MSS.2991, fos. 72ᵛ-3; *Fourquevaux Mission*, pp. 27–8.
65 Originally, Fumel was instructed to state that Henri found Châtelherault's actions 'quite bad', but this was later modified to 'peculiar'. Wood, 'Instructions', p.163 *n.c*; *RPC*, I, p.89.
66 Wood, 'Instructions', pp. 163–4; *RPC*, I, p.89; Micharde et Poujolat, *Mémoires-Journaux*, p.7; Ribier, *Lettres et mémoires*, II, p.272; *Balcarres Papers*, II, li, pp. 67–70.

oprics, was a very alluring prospect and no doubt the reason behind Châtelherault's rapid submission. The Regent beseeched Henri to 'send his ambassadouris towart the Empriour to procurer ane peax . . . always referring the tyme to his Majesteis discretion', and implored the King to continue the efforts made on behalf of his brother at the Papal Court.[67]

Any peace negotiations between the Scots and Charles V, however, were destined to be fraught with difficulty whoever was at the helm. Henri's first task was to admonish Mary of Guise and Châtelherault for 'the great damage some of their subjects still inflict on the emperor's at sea', and to order the cessation of these maritime violations.[68] The Scots could not afford to have an enemy in the person of Charles V. The Scottish political élite's immediate response to this demand was, at best, half-hearted. Thomas Erskine was commissioned 'to putt inhibitioun to the capitanis, maisteris, and awnaris . . . that nane of thame tak upon hand to mak were upon the Empouris subjectis', but only if he happened to come across any Scottish warships while in France.[69] The Scots' apprehension was justified. Previous peace treaties contracted at Antwerp in 1545 and Edinburgh in 1546, for example, had served only to inaugurate periods of rampant piracy.[70] And while the Privy Council was more than happy for the 'maist Christine King to trete ane peax betuix the Empriour and us', they were also adamant that *their* conditions for peace must be satisfied because the continual violation of the peace by the Emperor and his Flemish subjects, who, in the taking of a great number of Scottish ships 'at the desyre of Ingland', had caused 'grete hurt and damp-nages of the liegis of this realme'.[71]

By 6 July 1550 the Scots' misgivings seemed to be vindicated by the 'gret enormiteis dalie done' within Scotland's 'awin watteris and firthis . . . be the schippis of Holland, Flussing, and uthiris the Lawlandis of Flandaris, subjectis to the Empriour'.[72] An order issued by the Privy Council licensing the launch of Scottish warships for the 'stanching thairof' effectively disregarded Henri's command to cease

---

67 *RPC*, I, pp. 89, 91–2; Finnie, 'The House of Hamilton', pp. 8–9; Mahoney, 'The Scottish Hierarchy', pp. 51–3.
68 Wood, 'Instructions', p.162.
69 *RPC*, I, p.87.
70 M.P. Rooseboom, *The Scottish Staple in the Netherlands* (The Hague, 1910), pp. 68–9.
71 *RPC*, I, pp. 89, 91–3.
72 *Ibid*, I, p.104. Specifically, d'Oisel had alleged that from 4 July to 24 July 1550 the Emperor's 'ships had committed several outrages on the Scots at sea, and behaved with inhuman cruelty'. *CSP Spain*, X, p. 157.

all confrontation with the Emperor's subjects.[73] This hiccup in the resumption of friendly relations was further exacerbated by the confusion and distrust caused by France's involvement in the negotiations and, ultimately, her alliance with Scotland.

The confusion surrounded a letter from Mary of Guise and Châtelherault empowering Sebastian de l'Aubespine, Abbé of Bassefontaine, the French ambassador at Brussels, to conclude a treaty on the Scots' behalf with Mary, Queen Dowager of Hungary, Regent of the Netherlands and Charles V's sister.[74] As with all letters of empowerment, this letter was scrutinised by the legalistic eye of the Imperialists, and several discrepancies were found to forestall the negotiations. It was discovered that, in reality, de l'Aubespine did not have the power to conclude a truce because he was not, as the letter clearly stipulated, the King of France's ambassador resident to Charles V. This was M. de Marillac. The proposed duration of the truce, which was to last until May 1551, was also questioned and rejected by the Imperialists on the grounds that it was 'so long a term that one can only take it the real object of the truce is to put off a peace, and make sure that all your [Charles V's] warships shall be disarmed in the meantime, in order to make war again in the spring if the French feel like it'.[75] Finally, issue was taken with the Scottish government's wish to comprehend the Queen of Scots' 'abettors, confederates and friends'. This clause immediately raised alarm bells in the Imperial camp as to Henri's true intentions. The Queen Dowager of Hungary astutely remarked that:

> It looks very much as if they [the Scots] wished to include
> the King of France, so that if we were hereafter to break with
> the Scots, they might claim that we were also breaking with
> the King of France. This point is of importance, and we must
> be careful to have it cleared up if we really treat with the
> Scots: namely, whether or no war with one country would
> mean war with the other.[76]

Although de l'Aubespine stressed that Henri was merely 'anxious to have the truce concluded in order to stop hostilities', the doubts raised by Mary of Hungary do merit some consideration of the implications of Henri's protectorate of Scotland.[77]

---

73 *RPC*, I, p.104; *CSP Spain*, X, p.157.
74 See *ibid*, X, pp. 157–61, for the Queen Dowager of Hungary's discussion of this letter and analysis of its contents.
75 *Ibid*, X, p.158.
76 *Ibid*, X, p.158.
77 *Ibid*, X, p.159.

The comprehension of France in any treaty contracted between Scotland and Charles V had serious repercussions in the wider context of the Habsburg-Valois struggle for European supremacy. Something as slight as a shipping infraction, for instance, would constitute a violation of the peace and justify French reprisals against the Emperor, thus legitimately renewing the conflict. As an ally of France, Scotland would automatically be drawn into the conflict and *vice versa*. Moreover, France's alliance with, and military position in, Scotland could be used to divert Imperial attention and resources from the focus of the Habsburg-Valois conflict in Italy by intrigues at sea. As in matters of military security, Henri's assumed control of Scottish diplomacy, while ostensibly for the purpose of defence and, therefore, within his jurisdiction as 'Protector' of Scotland, also provided him with the means to manipulate events and pursue his ambitions *offensively* on the Continent. The concerns raised by the Queen Dowager of Hungary are indicative of Henri's advantageous position in Scotland – a position that could be exploited equally for defensive and offensive purposes.

In the end, the potential problems surrounding France's involvement in the Scoto-Imperial negotiations were simply avoided. On 23 August 1550 Mary of Hungary empowered her commissioners to negotiate only with the envoys of Scotland, making no reference to the French King's Imperial ambassador.[78] Mary of Guise and Châtelherault duly responded to this request and, on 8 September 1550, commissioned Thomas Erskine to proceed to Flanders in order to negotiate the accord.[79] Left to their own devices, though, both parties could agree on nothing more than a truce. Only when France intervened were the differences between Scotland and the Low Countries finally resolved in a treaty signed at Binche on 15 December 1550.[80]

The treaty of Binche, also comprehending Henri II and Edward VI, sought to usher in a new era of peace between Scotland and

---

78 23 August 1550, *CSP Spain*, X, p.167. The Imperial commissioners were Count de Reuil, M. de Praet, Charles, Count de Lalaing, Charles, Seigneur de Berlaymont, Jehan de St. Mauris, Seigneur de Montbarey, and Viglius de Zwichem.

79 8 September 1550, *Ibid*, X, p.174; *CSP Scot.*, I, 370, p.184.

80 *Foedera*, XV, p.265; *CSP Spain*, X, pp. 197–201; *CSP Scot.*, I, 374, p.186; Teulet, *Papiers*, I, pp. 229 237 and *Relations*, I, p.250; Rooseboom, *The Scottish Staple*, pp. 69–71. Thomas Erskine arrived in France at the conclusion of the peace on 30 December 1550. *CSP Foreign, 1547–1553*, 270, p.65.

the Low Countries.[81] This was to be achieved through the abolition of piracy and a mutual agreement to help each other in times of war. The treaty also provided for the free passage and entry into each other's territories (eradicating the need for safe conducts), the alleviation of trade restrictions for merchants who paid the appropriate customs and duties, and full and immediate compensation for crimes committed by the subjects of one kingdom against the other. Violators of the treaty were to be branded as robbers and pirates. Finally, and in what must be seen as a victory for the Queen Dowager of Hungary in the negotiations, it was stipulated that any action seen to be contrary to the basic tenor of the treaty was not to be considered a breach of the peace and, thus, a pretext for war.[82]

Although the terms of the treaty had been concluded, 'certan small differens' arose over its ratification by the Scots.[83] Charles V wanted two ratified versions of the peace: one in the Queen's name, to which her great seal alone should be affixed, and the other with the Queen's seals followed by the Regent's and those of the Council and Estates.[84] The reasoning behind this unusual and seemingly pedantic request was the ratification of the treaty of Binche by the Estates of Scotland who, it was claimed, had no written power to do so. The Three Estates' lack of authority could, technically speaking, be used to repudiate the treaty by rendering it invalid, although it was considered most unlikely that the Scots themselves would think to use this as a reason. But there was the possibility that the Scots could be 'influenced and egged on by their neighbours', no doubt a reference to France, who knew that the absence of power was a point taken very seriously by the Imperialists.[85] So, in June 1550, Matthew Strick was sent to Scotland as the Imperial envoy to receive the two ratifications that Henri's 'imbassadour now in Flanderis [de l'Aube-spine] hes grantit tharto'.[86] Once again, France had assumed control and directed Scottish diplomacy. Although the Scottish nobility complied and granted the two ratifications, they nevertheless felt it necessary to respond to the inference that their authority was

---

81 The treaty also comprehended the King of Denmark and Norway, the King of the Romans, Hungary and Bohemia, and the Estates of the Roman Empire. *Foedera*, XV, p.265; Rooseboom, *The Scottish Staple*, p.71.
82 *Foedera*, XV, p.265; Teulet, *Papiers*, I, pp. 239–48; Rooseboom, *The Scottish Staple*, pp. 70–1.
83 *Scottish Correspondence*, ccxxxix, p.354.
84 *CSP Spain*, X, p.337; *Scottish Correspondence*, ccxxxix, p.354.
85 *CSP Spain*, X, p.338.
86 *Scottish Correspondence*, ccxxxix, p.354.

insufficient.[87] Because 'they did not treat separately, and will not ratify separately', both ratifications were identical and both were written in the name of *Maria Regina Scotorum*.[88]

While the treaty of Binche is significant in itself as a peace treaty, the predominant role played by Henri in the resumption of friendly Scoto-Imperial relations is of greater significance. Fumel's instructions, and the answers given by the Privy Council in response to Henri's memorial, clearly indicate that peace with Charles V was an objective for both Châtelherault and the French King. Why, then, was Henri so adamant that he should control the negotiations when the Regent had already made overtures of peace? To ensure that the terms of the treaty were compatible with French interests is one obvious answer. The insistence that France be comprehended in the treaty as an abettor, confederate and friend of Scotland was also a means by which Henri could prevent Châtelherault from pursuing independent policies on the Continent that might conflict with, or undermine, those of France. Control of Scotland's diplomatic relations ensured that her foreign policy was aligned with that of France. Unity in policy symbolised and conveyed strength, and this was of crucial importance when dealing with the English. The negotiations that culminated in the treaty of Norham reveal the extent to which Henri would become involved, and direct, Scotland's relations with England as its 'Protector'.[89]

* * *

As an Anglo-French accord the treaty of Boulogne did not settle the disputes that pertained specifically to England and Scotland. Although progress had been made regarding the English-held fortifications in Scotland, of which Roxburgh and Eyemouth had been fully dismantled under the supervision of Sir Robert Bowes by 11 July 1550, there were still aspects of the Anglo-Scottish war that needed to be settled in order for peace be finally concluded.[90] As stated in the preamble to the treaty of Norham, certain questions and controversies needed to be handled in a friendly manner, ordered and ended, lest

---

87 A meeting of the Scottish nobility was scheduled for 22 June 1550 to mend the 'certan small differens' that existed over the ratification of the treaty of Binche. *Scottish Correspondence*, ccxxxix, p.354.
88 *CSP Spain*, X, p.337.
89 For an overview of the negotiations for the treaty of Norham from an English perspective, see P.G. Boscher, 'English provincial government and its relationship with central government, 1550–70' (unpublished PhD Thesis, University of Durham, 1985), pp. 117–33.
90 *CSP Foreign, 1547–1553*, 215, 220, 224, pp. 48, 50, 51; *RPC*, I, p.99; *APC*, III, pp. 47, 97, 171.

great jeopardy ensue.[91] The main issues of contention concerned the boundaries between England and Scotland, particularly in the Debatable Land, the detention and delivery of captives and pledges, the administration and execution of justice for the piracies, spoils and 'attemptates' done to the subjects of both kingdoms, and the hospitable and friendly reception of merchant ships and subjects in each kingdom.[92] Exclusive as these matters were to England and Scotland, Henri nevertheless took an active and predominant role through his ambassador resident in England, Sieur de Chemault and, more significantly, through his diplomatic envoy, Louis de Saint Gelais, Sieur de Lansac.

It became apparent almost immediately after the ratification of the treaty of Boulogne that these problems were in urgent need of resolution. In response to the daily and continual incursions made against the Scots by the English troops still garrisoned at Roxburgh and Eyemouth, the Scottish Privy Council ordered 'all and sindry' to apprehend and imprison anyone who emerged from these fortifications without licence and/or who, it was thought, intended to inflict harm on Scotland or its lieges.[93] The urgency of the situation was brought to the fore with the detention of Alexander Gordon, archbishop of Glasgow, who was caught travelling through England without a safe conduct.[94] The English considered the Archbishop of Glasgow to be a legitimate prisoner because England 'had no peace with Scotland such that they [the Scots] might pass [through] our country'.[95] Although the Archbishop was deemed a 'prisoner of good price', his ransom being set at 20,000 crowns, Edward VI nevertheless consented to Henri's demand that the Scottish prelate be liberated in view of the Anglo-French peace that had lately been concluded.[96] Yet, despite the English King's concession, there still existed a mutual distrust between the 'auld enemies'. Boundary disputes still continued to exacerbate tensions on the Border.

---

91 *Foedera*, XV, p.265; W. Nicolson, *Leges Marchiarum: Or, The Border-Laws* (London, 1714), pp. 56–7.
92 *Foedera*, XV, p.265; Nicolson, *Leges Marchiarum*, p.57.
93 22 May 1550, *RPC*, I, pp. 99–100.
94 *CSP Foreign, 1547–1553*, 221, p.50; *APC*, III, p.62; Jordan, *Chronicle*, p.38.
95 *Ibid*, p.38; *APC*, III, p.62.
96 Teulet, *Papiers*, I, pp. 218, 220–1 and *Relations*, I, pp. 242–3; *CSP Foreign, 1547–1553*, 235, p.54. Henri's diplomatic intervention is interesting given that it was reported by Sir John Mason on 20 July that 'the King refused to interfere for the Archbishop of Glasgow, who must "stand to folly". Henri later thanked Edward for the 'enlargement of the Archbishop of Glasgow'. *Ibid*, 224, 238, pp. 51, 55.

In July 1550 the English Council received word from William, Lord Dacre, Warden of the West March, that his opposite number in Scotland, Robert, Lord Maxwell, had assembled a sizeable Franco-Scottish force and was planning to invade the Debatable Land in order to pursue certain fugitives.[97] The fugitives in question were the Grahams, a family whom Edward VI confessed to be 'yielded to me'.[98] The Council immediately warned the French Ambassador that if Maxwell carried out his invasion, it would be considered a breach of the treaty of Boulogne.[99] Chemault flatly rejected this line of argument. The Debatable Land was not English-held territory and the Scottish Privy Council had expressly prohibited any Borderer from taking it 'upoun hand to ryde in Ingland or to make ony perturbatioun thairintill under the pane of tresoun'.[100] A raid into the Debatable Land was not an invasion of England and, as such, was not a contravention of the peace.

Clearly this boundary dispute was not going to be settled without formal negotiation, but the English Council still took steps to defend the Debatable Land as if it was their own. If the Scots forcibly entered the Debatable Land, Dacre was instructed to fight back and then to 'reason the matter with the Scottes, why they shulde entre upon the Debatable Grounde, knowing it to have been in the Kinges possession these many yeres'.[101] Dacre was also directed to entreat 'the Graymes,

---

97 Sir John Mason reported '2,000 Scots and 400 or 500 Frenchmen', while M. de Chemault wrote to Henri on 15 August 1550 that 'la Reine, mon cousin le Gouverneur d'Ecosse et le sieur de Termes faisoient marcher vers la terre debatable quatre ensignes de gens de pied [the Queen, my cousin the Governor and sieur de Termes intend to march four ensigns of footmen towards the debatable land]'. *CSP Foreign, 1547–1553*, 232, p.53; Teulet, *Papiers*, I, p.217, and *Relations*, I, p.239.

98 *APC*, III, pp. 104–5, 108–9; *CSP Foreign, 1547–1553*, 230, 232, pp. 52–3; Teulet, *Papiers*, I, pp. 222–3, *Relations*, I, p.244; Jordan, *Chronicle*, p.44. Banished from Scotland c.1516, the Grahams eventually settled in the Debatable Land on the English side of the Esk. Through a string of advantageous marriages with other Scottish Border families, such as the Armstrongs, their occupation of evacuated properties and the extensive tracts of land granted to them by the English Crown, the Graham network spread and eventually crossed over onto the Scottish side of the Debatable Land at Canonbie. As we shall see, the subversive activity of the Grahams against the Scots was the source of much contention in Anglo-Scottish relations. W. Mackay Mackenzie, 'The Debatable Land', *SHR*, xxx (1951), pp. 109–25.

99 Teulet, *Relations*, I, pp. 246–7; J. Nicolson and R. Burn, *The History and Antiquities of the Counties of Westmorland and Cumberland* (London, 1777), I, pp. lxxv, lxxvii, lxxix-xxx.

100 *CSP Foreign, 1547–1553*, 230, pp. 52–3; *RPC*, I, p.86.

101 14 & 21 August 1550, *APC*, III, pp. 104, 108–9. On 3 September, the Warden of the East March for England, Sir Robert Bowes, had been ordered to supply 'ccc hacquebutiers . . . to the Lord Dacres if he write for theim'. *Ibid*, III, p.119.

enhabitauntes there, as amyablie as he might, to kepe them still the Kinges Majesties good subjectes as they have been before.'[102] This was of particular importance as the Grahams had threatened to switch allegiance if England failed to protect them against Maxwell. The prospect of having the Grahams as hostile neighbours was something the English did not want – as the Scots could well testify.[103] So, in order to avoid this situation altogether, the English Council demanded that the French King send an envoy to Scotland to deal with the situation and arrest the enterprise.[104]

Henri had already been informed of the events on the Scottish Border.[105] The French King's response reveals that Maxwell had not embarked on an independent course of action, but that 'the Queen [Mary of Guise], my cousin the Governor of Scotland and sieur de Termes had four ensigns of infantrymen advancing towards the debatable land'.[106] In an attempt to ease the escalating tensions, Henri issued a formal statement explaining Maxwell's movements on the Border. The purpose of the Scoto-French march was not to invade England, but to pursue the troublemakers who were threatening the *neutrality* of the Debatable Land. Refusing to recognise England's claims to the disputed territory, Henri asserted that the Debatable Land had always been neutral and Chemault was to remind the English Council of this point and of the treaty of Boulogne's stipulation that all things were to return to the *status quo ante bellum*. But, recognising the signs of a potentially explosive situation, Henri also instructed Châtelherault and d'Oisel to re-establish order on the Border, if that was possible, and to leave the settling of Border disputes to the appointed Scottish and English commissioners.[107] On 26 August, Sir John Mason confirmed Henri's wish to resolve this affair amicably and reported that the French King 'would issue immediate orders for the prevention of such in future'.[108]

It soon became apparent that Scotland's comprehension in the treaty of Boulogne was riddled with ambiguity. Although the potentially damaging situation of Maxwell's assembly on the Scottish frontier had lessened for the time being, diplomatic tensions soon flared up again during Thomas, Master of Erskine's visit to England in

---

102 *APC*, III, p.105.
103 Nicolson and Burn, *History and Antiquities*, I, p.lxxv.
104 18 August 1550, *CSP Foreign, 1547–1553*, 230, pp. 52–3; Teulet, *Papiers*, I, p.222 and *Relations*, I, p.244.
105 Teulet, *Papiers*, I, p.222 and *Relations*, I, p.244.
106 Teulet, *Papiers*, I, p.217 and *Relations*, I, p.239.
107 Teulet, *Papiers*, I, p.218 and *Relations*, I, p.239.
108 *CSP Foreign, 1547–1553*, 232, p.53.

September 1550. After presenting various letters to Edward VI, Erskine raised what was fast becoming the main concern for the Scots – namely, that 'syns the realme of Scotlande was comprehended in the Treatie, the Quene and Counsaill there desired to knowe wheather the Kinges Highnes and Counsaill ment thei shulde enjoie their olde lymites in like maner as thei did before the last warres'.[109] Specifically, 'their olde lymites' referred to Edrington, also known as Cawe Mill, which was occupied by the English, and the fishing rights to half of the River Tweed.[110] The English Council's reply was less than amenable. Although they declared that their primary concern was the 'continewance of thamytie withe Fraunce' and of Scotland's comprehension therein, the English Council claimed that the Scots had 'required divers thinges more than resonable, which wee oughte not to satisfie, and therfore if thei seeke redresse of any thinge (as we thinke thei have no cause), than lett the French Kinge by his Ministers declare it, and we shall accordinglie make him aunswere whith [*sic*] whom the Treatie hathe been concluded, and not with them'.[111] As Erskine was en route to France, the Council referred him to the French King for an explanation of the treaty.[112] Ironically, the English Council's insistence that France represent Scotland's interests served only to strengthen Henri's position as 'Protector' by legitimising his control over Scotland's diplomatic affairs and, inadvertently, contributing to the establishment of French power in Scotland.

While diplomatic tensions could be masked by polite words at the English Court, the same was not as easily done on the Borders themselves. The threat of vigilante retribution and physical confrontation loomed over the meetings between the Wardens of the West Marches. In October 1550, for instance, Dacre's refusal to provide restitution for the crimes committed by the English against the Scots led to a riotous outbreak which was largely instigated by Maxwell. Upon hearing of Maxwell's role in the disturbance, d'Oisel strongly advised him to conduct himself in a friendly manner towards the English so as not to give them occasion to cause trouble. It would also enable Henri and Edward to resolve the differences between England and Scotland. Instead, he was to do everything by the book, inform Dacre of any problems and not let the hounds loose if the English

109 28 September 1550, *APC*, III, p.132.
110 The land and house at Edrington were located six miles north-west of Berwick.
111 *Ibid*, III, pp. 132, 134; *CSP Foreign, 1547–1553*, 242, p.56. The Scots also laid claim to Thriepland in the Middle March.
112 *Ibid*, 242, p.56.

should irritate him.[113] Henri was similarly displeased with news of this incident. The source of his displeasure, however, was not Maxwell, but England's Border officials. 'The ministers of the King of England on the Scottish Border', he wrote, 'do not follow the soft approach that they usually claim to do in every respect south of the border because they try to differentiate themselves from the situation in the debatable land and yet retain possession over it, which worryingly, we are ready to allow them, if they resort to such ways.' He subsequently ordered Chemault to demand that, in future, they behave graciously and reasonably.[114]

Yet, despite these apparent setbacks, Henri was still pleased with the progress being made on Scotland's diplomatic front. Under his direction a Scoto-Imperial peace had been concluded at Binche and a settlement with England seemed imminent. In December 1550 he confidently expressed his optimism by stating that 'my subjects will immediately be given such good provision, they will have occasion to remain satisfied'.[115] The realisation of such a sentiment, however, greatly depended on the success of his envoy, Sr. de Lansac, on his mission to Scotland.

* * *

In January 1551 Henri complied with the English demands for French diplomatic intervention and sent Lansac to the English Court to present the French King's demands on behalf of the Scots. Feeling it necessary to dispel any English fears of possible ulterior motives, Henri informed his ambassador that 'the only reason I send him over there is to try to pacify the disagreement between the English and the Scots, of which I really want to see an end, and [to see] that the Queen of Scots gets what clearly belongs to her'.[116] Chemault then proceeded to the English Court to request that the 'gentleman whom the French King hathe sent hither may see and speake withe the Kingis Majestie', and to continue the diplomatic pressure being applied to the English to respond to the main questions of the Anglo-Scottish debate – questions which 'had been divers tymes asked and never fullie aunswered'.[117] Chemault was feebly informed that Dacre had already been sent north where he was to make a full answer on the neutrality of the Debatable Land upon his

113 Teulet, *Papiers*, I, p.226 and *Relations*, I, p.247. See also BL, Harley MSS, 34.14, fos. 57–9.
114 26 November 1550, Teulet, *Papiers*, I, p.227 and *Relations*, I, p.248.
115 21 December 1550, Teulet, *Papiers*, I, p.228 and *Relations*, I, p.249.
116 Henri II to M. de Chemault, 23 January 1551, Teulet, *Papiers*, I, p.207 and *Relations*, I, p.251. See also *CSP Foreign, 1547–1553*, 282, pp. 68–9.
117 29 January 1551, *APC*, III, p.203.

arrival.[118] Lansac, though, was granted an audience and, on 1 February 1551, he formally presented Henri II's demands to the English Council.[119]

The French King's demands were, to say the least, predictable. They had already been voiced many times by Erskine and Chemault on behalf of Mary of Guise and Châtelherault. Henri's primary objective was the full restoration of what he considered to be Scotland's proper patrimony. As in the negotiations for the treaty of Boulogne over the fate of Roxburgh and Eyemouth, Henri thought it unreasonable that the English should claim Edrington, fishing rights to the Tweed and the Debatable Land as their own, considering that they had been held only *since* the war, and he appealed to Edward VI on a personal level to ensure their restitution. Henri used Scotland's comprehension in the treaty as a confederate of France to justify his diplomatic intervention and informed Edward that, because Scotland was in his protection, he would be constrained to assist and defend the Scots in this quarrel – a quarrel that he considered to be just.[120] This point was not lost on the English. They reported that:

> . . . forasmuche as he [Henri] had taken the protection of
> the Scottish Quene, considering that Scotlande was
> comprehended, he coulde no lesse do then to desire the
> King his goode brother to restore Edrington, fyssheng in
> Twede and other like limites, with the newtrall estate of the
> Debateable Grounde, in like maner as every thing was before
> the beginneng of the last warres.[121]

The French King also demanded the immediate payment of ransoms for English prisoners who had already been released, the restitution of the five Scottish ships taken since the peace, full and free traffic at sea and on land, open intercourse between the two kingdoms and, finally, the release of the Scottish hostages who had been taken at Solway Moss. The last was particularly important since the English prisoners taken at St. Andrews had already been liberated.[122]

---

118 *APC*, III, p.203.
119 *Ibid*, III, pp. 204–5.
120 Teulet, *Papiers*, I, pp. 208–9 and *Relations*, I, pp. 251–3.
121 *APC*, III, p.204.
122 Teulet, *Papiers*, I, pp. 210–1 and *Relations*, I, pp. 253–4; *APC*, III, p.205;
    Jordan, *Chronicle*, pp. 51–2. See Teulet, *Papiers*, I, pp. 211–2 and *Relations*,
    I, pp. 255–6, for a list of Scots taken prisoner at Solway Moss, which
    included two of Glencairn's sons, and of English prisoners released since
    the peace. The payment of ransoms, the return of prisoners, hostages
    and Scottish ships had been topics of great debate since June 1550. *CSP
    Foreign, 1547–1553*, 215, 221, 224, pp. 48, 50, 51; Teulet, *Papiers*, I, pp.
    221–4 and *Relations*, I, pp. 241–5; *APC*, III, pp. 114, 116–7.

On the whole, the English Council's response to Henri's demands was conciliatory. They agreed to the liberation of all Scottish ships not belonging to pirates and the immediate payment of all outstanding ransoms.[123] But, once again, the Council claimed that the Scots had solicited the French King to demand far too much and, had it not been for Henri's desire to maintain amicable relations with England, he would have refused to do so.[124] This was particularly true with respect to his demands for the restoration of Scotland's old limits and frontiers and the *full* liberty of traffic through England, which met with some, albeit superficial, resistance. They argued, for example, that Edrington, fishing rights to the Tweed and the Debatable Land had all originally belonged to Henry VIII and, having been inherited by his son upon his death, were, consequently, not subject to restitution. It was thus deemed 'laufull for the Kinges Majestie to enjoie and keepe not only Edrington, with other thinges that he keepeth not within that realme, having had the same in his possession long before the last Treatie'.[125] To demonstrate England's commitment to the peace, however, the Council declared that an envoy would be sent to Henri to give a fuller answer on this matter, with which Henri 'oughte to be contented'.[126]

Sir William Pickering was the chosen envoy who, in the words of Edward VI, was 'to declare that, although I had [the] right in the aforesaid places yet I was content to forbear them under conditions to be agreed on by commissioners on both sides'.[127] Pickering was also to give Henri a fuller answer regarding the full liberty of traffic through England. While the Council had declared that 'all Scottishe shippes which arr driven in by tempest or that come by necessitie, shall have libertie to goo agayne', they felt that they could not consent to the 'further libertie of trafficque'.[128] The detention of the Archbishop of Glasgow for not having the proper travel documentation in July 1550 was just one telling example of the underlying distrust the English had of the Franco-Scottish alliance. Another and more revealing example was the Council's refusal to allow Maxwell to pass through England on his return journey from France in February 1551.

---

123 *APC*, III, p.212; Teulet, *Papiers*, I, pp. 214–5 and *Relations*, I, pp. 257–8;
    Balcarres Papers, II, lxiv, pp. 88–91.
124 Teulet, *Papiers*, I, p.213 and *Relations*, I, p.256.
125 *APC*, III, p.211.
126 *Ibid*, III, pp. 211–2; *CSP Foreign, 1547–1553*, 290, p.73.
127 Jordan, *Chronicle*, p.53.
128 *APC*, III, p.212.

The free passage of the French and Scots through England was a matter of great concern to the Council now that Scotland had been 'made Frenche, and bicause it appeareth the libertie therof shulde muche advaunce the French affaires and hinder our owne'.[129] Maxwell's safe conduct was denied on the pretence that 'the realme had been so chargded withe the furnyssheng of those that syns the Peace concluded had thus passed to and from, that wee could not convenyently and lenger supporte it'.[130] The great influx of applications for safe conducts from Scots who had travelled to France with Mary of Guise and now wished to return no doubt added an element of truth to the Council's refusal.[131] But their refusal was more than likely owing to the timing of Maxwell's application. It directly coincided with the great invasion scare of Ireland by France, and the receipt of a related report from Sir Robert Bowes and the Captain of Berwick that Châtelherault, with all the French troops in Scotland and a complement of Scottish ships, was planning to attack Berwick under the pretence of punishing thieves in Liddesdale.[132] Henri's reaction to the English Council's refusal left him 'highly irritated', and this according to Sir John Mason, was further 'fomented by the Queen of Scots [Mary of Guise] and her house . . . who desireth as much our subversion, if it lay in her power, as she desireth the preservation of herself'.[133] Ironically, the Council's attempt to hinder the return of Maxwell backfired. Forced to travel by sea, Maxwell returned to Scotland in just three days and was able to join Châtelherault and d'Oisel at the justice ayre at Jedburgh in accordance with the Queen Dowager's instructions.[134] The intimacy of the Franco-Scottish alliance, which the English themselves re-

129 3 February 1551, *APC*, III, p.205.
130 *Ibid*, III, p.206.
131 Among the applicants wishing to return to Scotland in February 1551 were Sir Hugh Campbell of Loudon, his son Matthew and both their wives, Hugh Kennedy, Ninian Cranston and Sir James Douglas of Drumlanrig. *CSP Foreign, 1547–1553*, 280, 281, 283, pp. 68–9.
132 17 February 1551, *CSP Foreign, 1547–1553*, 291, p.73.
133 23 February 1551, *ibid*, 295, p.75.
134 *Scottish Correspondence*, ccxxxiv, pp. 344–5; *CSP Foreign, 1547–1553*, 305, pp. 78–9; *TA*, IX, pp. 473–4; *RSS*, IV, 1145–58, pp. 185–6. Two musters had been called for this justice ayre on 24 February and 4 March 1551, and were supported by a French military force under d'Oisel. A bond was also signed on 26 March 1551 by Châtelherault and other Border nobles, pledging themselves to keep good rule within their bounds and to bring offenders to justice despite the remission of many crimes against their households, tenants and servants. *CSP Scot.*, I, 369, p.184.

cognised and feared, made French intrigues in Ireland at this time a matter of great concern.[135]

* * *

Tudor Irish policy, particularly Henry VIII's Kingship Act of 1541 and the creation of an English Pale in Ireland, left in its wake many disaffected Irish chieftains. One such individual was Cahir O'Connor who, in 1548, mounted an unsuccessful revolt against the English that ended with the confiscation of the O'Connor and O'More lands and many executions.[136] These events led some disaffected Irish gentlemen to appeal for French aid. Henri was not unaware of Irish antagonism towards England and recognised that intervention, or political intrigues at the very least, would serve to distract the English from the Continent.

In 1548 Henri sent Beccarie de Pavie, Baron de Fourquevaux, on an exploratory mission to Ireland.[137] Fourquevaux's visit to Ireland began in October 1549 and lasted approximately three months.[138] Accompanied by Robert Wauchop, 'the blind bishop', and Jean de Monluc, Fourquevaux met with the Irish princes and noblemen who were 'willing to cast aff the yok of England and becom subiect to the King of France, provyding that he wald procure the Paipes gift of Yreland, and then send to ther help 2000 hacbuters 200 leicht horse men and four canons'.[139] Intervention in Ireland was also favoured by the Earl of Argyll, who offered to lead a subsidised military expedition there, and d'Oisel, who not only provided a military strategy for Argyll's proposed campaign, but also the justification. England had received Ireland on condition that they maintain the rights and authority of the Apostolic Church. If this was violated, Ireland would automatically revert to Papal suzerainty.[140]

When Monluc and Fourquevaux returned to Scotland in January

135 D.L. Potter, 'French Intrigue in Ireland during the Reign of Henri II, 1547–1559', *International History Review*, v (1983), pp. 159–80; *Fourquevaux Mission*, pp. 1–36; J.E.A. Dawson, 'Two Kingdoms or Three?: Ireland in Anglo-Scottish Relations in the Middle of the Sixteenth Century', in Mason (ed.), *Scotland and England*, pp. 113–38; W. Palmer, *The Problem of Ireland in Tudor Foreign Policy, 1485–1603* (Woodbridge, Suffolk, 1994), pp. 15–88; C. Brady, 'The Decline of the Irish Kingdom', in Greengrass (ed.), *Conquest and Coalescence*, pp. 94–115.
136 Potter, 'French Intrigue in Ireland', p.161.
137 NLS, MSS.2991, fos. 7, 29, 43, 49.
138 Teulet, *Papiers*, I, pp. 707, 711.
139 NLS, MSS.2991, f.49; James Melville, *Memoirs of His Own Life by Sir James Melville of Halhill* (Edinburgh, 1827), pp. 9–12; *CSP Ireland, 1509–1573*, p.107; *Maitland Miscellany*, I, 11, pp. 220–1.
140 NLS, MSS.2991, fos. 74^v-6^v; *Fourquevaux Mission*, pp. 30–4.

1550, they immediately proceeded to France in order to present Henri with various propositions from Ireland, the basic tenor of which was that, in return for French military and financial aid, a number of the Irish gentry were prepared to accept French sovereignty.[141] Should he agree, Henri would then be provided with a loyal and obedient following in yet another strategic position within the Atlantic archipelago. But would such an investment yield the French King the same short- and long-term returns as it did in Scotland? Henri clearly did not think so, but in order to exploit his advantageous position in Ireland at the time, he conveniently took his time telling this to the Irish.

Henri ended his Irish intrigues secretly in April 1550. One of Fumel's tasks in Scotland was to order Fourquevaux and Monluc to stop their dealings in Ireland.[142] But it would not be until April 1551 that the Irish envoy, George Paris, was officially told that the French King would not be providing military aid to the Irish malcontents.[143] Paris, an Anglo-Irish gentleman who had links with the O'Connors and represented other disaffected Irishmen such as McWilliam, visited France in 1550 and 1551 to try and persuade Henri to intervene on their behalf against the English.[144] Needless to say, these meetings were of great concern to the English ambassador, Sir John Mason. He filed alarming reports of 'this' Paris, who sought to annoy the King and his realm by serving as 'a common post between the wild Irish and the French'.[145] Mason also informed the Council that the letters presented by Paris bragged that the 'whole nobility of Ireland from the highest to the lowest, had conspired to rid themselves from the yoke of England'. In the light of this discovery, Mason felt obliged to voice his opinion that 'We have, these many years past, wasted there [in Ireland] great sums of money by piecemeal, which, if it had been spent together, might have bred more quietness than we have at this present'. He also thought that 'These *Wildbeasts* would be hunted aforce, and at the beginning should so be

---

141 Melville, *Memoirs*, p.12; Teulet, *Papiers*, I, pp. 716–8.
142 Wood, 'Instructions', pp. 166–7.
143 *CSP Foreign, 1547–1553*, 320, 324, 327, pp. 89–90, 92, 95; P.F. Tytler, *England under the reigns of Edward VI and Mary* (London, 1839), I, pp. 351–3.
144 Paris' mission to France in June 1550, for instance, was to present Henri with letters of credence from McWilliam. *CSP Foreign, 1547–1553*, 217, p.48; Tytler, *Edward VI and Mary*, I, pp. 291–2; Potter, 'French Intrigues in Ireland', pp. 169–70.
145 Tytler, *Edward VI and Mary*, I, pp. 292, 301; *CSP Foreign, 1547–1553*, 217, 218, pp. 48, 49.

bearded, before the whole herd run together'.[146] The gravity of the situation was brought home when Mason reported in October that there had been much talk at the French Court, especially since the coming of the Scots, that Ireland was theirs whenever the King wished. A similar report was sent in December and stated that Paris himself 'doubteth not to see the French King shortly to bear the crown of Ireland'.[147]

Reports such as these, together with those informing the Council of the great warlike preparations being made in France, led to the invasion scare of January and February 1551.[148] Because 'the Frenchmen did go about practice in Ireland', major preparations were promptly made by the English Council. Admiral Winter was to command a small fleet of four ships, Lord Cobham was appointed to take charge of the military preparations, St. Leger was ordered to repair to the southern parts of Ireland with force, Sir James Croft was despatched to Ireland with John Roberts to begin fortifications, John Parker was commanded to victual his forts at Knockfergus and Olderfleet to resist the Scots who planned to attack from the Western Isles, and Osbert Mountford, a dealer in bread grains, was commanded to provide victuals for the ships embarking for Ireland.[149] Interestingly, preparations were also made for Berwick and the northern parts of England, where it was feared a simultaneous attack would be launched by Châtelherault, his French military entourage and its naval complement that had converged at Jedburgh.[150] The crisis peaked when it was reported that sixteen ships of a large French fleet destined for Scotland, and laden with victuals and munitions, had perished on the Irish coast.[151] Given this course of events, it comes as no surprise that the English were anxious to appease the French regarding Scotland – despite their pretences to the contrary. In reality, England was in no position to press her claims in Scotland and had no choice but to capitulate to the French.

---

146 29 June 1550, Tytler, *Edward VI and Mary*, I, pp. 301–3.
147 In December 1550 George Paris returned to Ireland with the French King's replies to the letters he presented from McWilliam and other Irish malcontents. *CSP Foreign, 1547–1553*, 247, 264, pp. 58, 63.
148 30 December 1550, *Ibid*, 270, p.65.
149 Jordan, *Chronicle*, pp. 51–2; *APC*, III, pp. 195, 204–5; *CSP Ireland, 1509–1573*, pp. 110–2.
150 Jordan, *Chronicle*, p.52; *CSP Foreign, 1547–1553*, 291, 295, 305, pp. 73, 75, 78–9; *Scottish Correspondence*, ccxxxiv, p.344; *TA*, IX, pp. 473–4; *RSS*, IV, 1145–58, pp. 185–6.
151 Jordan, *Chronicle*, pp. 54–5; *CSP Ireland, 1509–1573*, p.112; *CSP Foreign, 1547–1553*, 305, pp. 78–9.

This was the real reason why Sir William Pickering was sent to France in February 1551.

Pickering's primary objective in France was to reach an amicable settlement with Henri of all the remaining differences between England and Scotland.[152] In this he was successful, but only because Edward was willing to relinquish what he considered to be his rightful claims to Edrington, the fishing of the Tweed and his private use of Debatable Land in the West Marches, Roxburgh and Eyemouth – despite these having been taken through conquest.[153] Edward's 'kind gesture', however, was only an attempt to retain some degree of English prestige during the negotiations with France. In a private letter to Sir Richard Morsine (England's ambassador to Charles V) the Council admitted that none of these things was really worth keeping and, more importantly, that since the last wars, English soldiers had held Edrington, the Scots had been forbidden from fishing on the Tweed, and wasteland common to both realms in the Debatable Land had been privately held by the English.[154] Finally, the French King was told that Edward was willing to liberate the Scottish prisoners taken at Solway Moss and that the use of English ports by Scottish merchants and ships would revert to customary practices.[155]

These proposals ultimately proved acceptable to Henri, who summoned Mary of Guise, then at Châteaudun, for consultation before replying to the English King on 17 March 1551.[156] Henri simultaneously despatched Lansac and Thomas, Master of Erskine, back to England as his commissioners to discuss these proposals and other Anglo-Scottish Border disputes, and to work with the French ambassador, Chemault, in getting the official negotiations underway.[157] The involvement and influence of the French in Anglo-Scottish affairs did not wane once these negotiations began. As Henri's representative, Lansac played a prominent role during the formal negotiations and

---

152 BL, Harley MSS, 297.5, fos. 31–5 and 353.27, fos. 86–9; *CSP Foreign, 1547–1553*, 290, 292, p.73. In this, Sir William Pickering was to work with Sir John Mason, whom he succeeded as ambassador in April 1551. *Ibid*, 318, p.87; Jordan, *Chronicle*, p.156.
153 *CSP Foreign, 1547–1553*, 314, p.83; *CSP Scot.*, I, 371, p.185.
154 6 April 1551, *CSP Foreign, 1547–1553*, 314, p.83.
155 *Ibid*, 314, p.83.
156 *Ibid*, 301, 305, pp. 77–8.
157 *Ibid*, 303–5, pp. 78–9. On 5 April 1551, for example, Lansac and Chemault presented the names of the Scottish commissioners who were to take part in the discussions preceding the formal negotiations. They were named as either Robert Reid, bishop of Orkney, or David Paniter, bishop of Ross, and Patrick, Master of Ruthven. Teulet, *Papiers*, I, p.215 and *Relations*, I, p.258; *APC*, III, pp. 250–1; Jordan, *Chronicle*, p.57.

was supported by other loyal supporters of the French cause: Thomas Erskine, Maxwell, Sir Robert Carnegy of Kinnaird and Robert Reid, bishop of Orkney.[158] To counter this Franco-Scottish delegation were Edward's representatives: Sir Robert Bowes, Sir Leonard Beckwith, Sir Thomas Challoner and Richard Sampson, bishop of Lichfield and Coventry.[159] Despite some initial communication problems on the part of the English commissioners, who allegedly lacked the proper instructions to accord what Pickering and Mason had agreed with Henri, the negotiations eventually began on Monday, 1 June 1551, and ended nine days later with the formal conclusion of the treaty of Norham.[160]

The articles of the treaty of Norham did not contain any surprises.[161] It was agreed that the English would relinquish all their holdings and 'claims' in Scotland. The limits, bounds and borders of both kingdoms were to revert to their original state as they were prior to the war; the Debatable ground between the West Marches was to revert to its accustomed state and use by subjects of both realms; Edrington was to be restored to the Queen of Scots, the English garrison there being evacuated, in addition to the fishing rights of the Tweed, from Berwick to Rydingburn.[162] The treaty also provided for the expedient delivery of all captives and pledges, and laid down explicit regulations for merchant traffic and the issuing of safe conducts.[163] Years of war had clearly had devastating effects on the Border. The considerable amount of attention devoted to Border Law and the administration and execution of justice in the treaty reflects the urgent need felt by both parties to impose law and order there.[164] The treaty called for the delivery and punishment of murderers, thieves, rebels and other evil-doers by the Wardens of the Marches and their deputies at the Days of Truce according to Border Law. Malefactors who had sought refuge in the other kingdom were to be

---

158 Teulet, *Papiers*, I, p.215 and *Relations*, I, p.258; *APC*, III, pp. 252–3; *Foedera*, XV, pp. 263–4.

159 Teulet, *Papiers*, I, p.215 and *Relations*, I, p.258; Jordan, *Chronicle*, pp. 57–8; *CSP Foreign, 1547–1553*, 318, p.87.

160 *Ibid*, 356, p.111; BL, Harley MSS, 297.5, fos. 36–9; Teulet, *Papiers*, I, p.230 and *Relations*, I, p.271; *Foedera*, XV, pp. 265–72; Nicolson, *Leges Marchiarum*, pp. 56–71; *CSP Scot.*, I, 375, p.186. The treaty of Norham was ratified by Edward VI and Mary, Queen of Scots on 30 June and 14 August 1551 respectively. *Ibid*, I, 367–7, 379, pp. 186–7; *Foedera*, XV, p.273.

161 *Ibid*, XV, pp. 265–72; Nicolson, *Leges Marchiarum*, pp. 56–71.

162 *Foedera*, XV, pp. 265–6; Nicolson, *Leges Marchiarum*, pp. 58–60.

163 *Foedera*, XV, pp. 266, 268–70; Nicolson, *Leges Marchiarum*, pp. 60, 65–70.

164 *Foedera*, XV, pp. 266–8; Nicolson, *Leges Marchiarum*, pp. 60–5.

returned to the appropriate Warden and tried in the place of the crime. Acts of revenge or retribution by an injured party were also discouraged through the annulment of the injured party's cause.

Despite these provisions, the treaty of Norham was far from conclusive. The exact division of the Debatable Land still needed to be determined and was deferred to a later date due to the sensitivity of the subject. Lawlessness, violence and disorder on both sides of, and across, the Anglo-Scottish border continued, as did the almost incessant assembly of Border commissions attempting to resolve these problems. Indeed, Border disputes were the most prominent and consistent feature of Anglo-Scottish relations during the 1550s and, arguably, the bane of Mary of Guise's relations with England. As we shall see, these disputes assumed great significance with the accession of Mary Tudor and, in particular, after her marriage to Philip of Spain. The Borders became the *loci* not only of political intrigue and heightened tensions, but also where Valois and Habsburg power met head on. The immediate task at hand, however, was to restore amicable relations between the 'auld enemies' in an exclusive Anglo-Scottish peace accord. In this, the treaty of Norham succeeded – albeit precariously.

The prominent role played by Henri in achieving this is beyond question. Archbishop Hamilton commented that 'be the kyngis mageste lawboris all the boundis of Scotland is als fre as thai war in ony of ouris days . . . and gud redres and justice on the bordouris'.[165] Henri's participation in the treaty of Norham was typical of his behaviour between 1550 and 1552. He had consistently sought to consolidate his position as 'Protector' of Scotland and to establish French power in Scotland by his close personal involvement in its government and diplomacy. The extent to which he had been successful is highlighted by England's insistence on dealing directly with France. By 1552 he had eradicated the effects of the English occupation of 1547–50 and established peace on Scotland's behalf. He was, therefore, able to turn his personal attention elsewhere while ensuring that French intervention continued in the person of Mary of Guise.

165 14 June 1551, *Scottish Correspondence*, ccxxxix, p.353.

3

Mary of Guise's Ascent to Power

W hile Henri II's protection justified and facilitated the establishment of French power in Scotland, the realisation of the
dynastic provisions contained within the treaty of Haddington was
crucial to its ultimate and long-term success. This, in turn, depended
on the Scottish political élite remaining favourable to the proposed
dynastic alliance and to the idea of Franco-Scottish union. The Three
Estates' renunciation of the treaties of Greenwich, however, demonstrated all too clearly that a ratified betrothal contract was in no way a
guarantee that the marriage itself would actually occur. The question
facing Henri, therefore, was how to ensure that it did – for only in the
person of Mary Stewart could his vision of a Franco-British empire
become a reality. It is within this wider context of European dynastic
politics that Mary of Guise emerged as a leading figure intent on
securing the marriage of her daughter to the Dauphin François and
irrevocably binding Scotland to the interests of France. The year Mary
of Guise spent in France in 1550 constituted the watershed in her
political career.[1] Her return to Scotland in 1551 marked the beginning of her campaign to assume control of her daughter's kingdom,
supplant Châtelherault as Regent upon his stipulated resignation, and
fulfil the dynastic and imperial objectives common to the houses of
Guise and Valois.

Mary of Guise's return to France is the most misunderstood event of
her political career. This is largely due to the tendency of historians to
presume that, because Guise eventually returned to Scotland to
assume the regency in 1554, the main purpose of her trip was to
promote her own political ambitions. But the failure of historians to
explain adequately why Guise should wish to return to Scotland, given
her daughter's situation in 1550, has resulted in weak and unconvin-

1 If Sir John Mason's report of 10 September 1550 is accurate, Mary of
Guise embarked for France at the port of Leith on Saturday, 6
September 1550, and returned to the British mainland at Portsmouth on
22 October 1551. *CSP Foreign, 1547–1553*, 237, 477, pp. 54–5, 190; *APC*,
III, p.364; C.R. Cheney (ed.), *Handbook of Dates* (London, 1991), Table
16, pp. 114–5.

cing analyses. One reason for this is that modern historians have accepted, uncritically, the explanations offered by near-contemporary historians. In his *Historie and Cronicles of Scotland (c.1578)*, for example, Robert Lindsay of Pitscottie contends that Guise 'passit haistalie to France, and tuik certane of the nobillis of Scottland witht hir and thair procurit at the king of France and hir dochteris hand that scho might have the governance in the realme of Scotland thair to be as regent thairof'.[2] Similarly, John Lesley wrote in his *History of Scotland (1573)* that the principal purpose of Guise's visit was 'to prepair and fynd all moyens, be the quhilkis sho mycht obtane the governement of the realme of Scotlande and be regent thairof'.[3] But according to this exponent of the Catholic and Marian cause, this was not the only reason for her journey. Guise also went to visit 'the Quene hir dochter' and to 'congratulat and rejoise' with Henri in the fact that, as Mary was now living in France, Scotland was 'moir subject and bound . . . as a province joynit unto France be mariage'.[4] At the other end of the political and religious spectrum, John Knox focused on 'diverse of the nobilitie baronis and gentillmen of ecclesiasticall estait' who accompanied Guise to France and her 'promisses that thei should be richely rewarded for thare good service'.[5] Knox implies that she did so for political purposes, '. . . for schortly after hir returnyng, was the Governour deposed of the governement, . . . and she maid Regent'.[6]

For their part, modern historians diverge only slightly over the 'political' objective of Mary of Guise's trip. Rosalind Marshall, Antonia Fraser, Patrick Fraser Tytler and David Hay Fleming all contend that the primary purpose was to gain Henri's approval for her designs to supplant Châtelherault as Regent,[7] while Marianne McKerlie is some-

2 Pitscottie, *Historie*, II, p.112. Although he was a contemporary of Guise, Pitscottie's *Historie* should not be taken as an example of historical accuracy. Citing his kinsman and noted reformer, Patrick, 6th lord Lindsay of Byres, as one of his influences, it comes as no surprise that his *Historie* unabashedly reflects his Protestant bias.
3 Lesley, *History*, pp. 234–5. John Lesley, bishop of Ross, was an apologist for Mary, Queen of Scots and his *History* clearly conveys his Catholic sympathies.
4 *Ibid*, p.234.
5 Knox, *Works*, I, pp. 241–2 and *History*, I, p.116.
6 Knox, *Works*, I, p.242 and *History*, I, p.116. Considering the author and the subject of his work, the history of the Scottish Reformation, it comes as no surprise that John Knox paints Guise in a less than favourable light.
7 P.F. Tytler, *History of Scotland* (Edinburgh, 1842), VI, pp. 50–1; Fleming, *Mary Queen of Scots*, p.16; Fraser, *Mary Queen of Scots*, p.77; Marshall, *Mary of Guise*, p.182.

what ambiguous in her statement that in order to conciliate the Scots, the French King 'did all in his power to promote the assumption of the Regency by the Queen Dowager on her return to Scotland'.[8] Financial exigencies have also been cited as a motive. Marshall argues that Guise needed to augment her revenue and replenish her empty coffers to restore Scotland's prosperity, while Fraser asserts that she needed the money to buy the political support of her Scottish travel companions.[9] But it is Gordon Donaldson's contention that Mary of Guise's trip was fundamentally 'a brain-washing expedition', whereby Henri bought the former pillars of the English and reforming cause with French pensions, that has been commonly accepted and adopted by historians such as Marcus Merriman and Michael Lynch.[10] By inference, Donaldson also presumes that Guise had every intention of returning to Scotland to serve as Henri's principal agent and promoter of the French cause.

There thus appears to be a general consensus that Mary of Guise went to France with political designs to oust Châtelherault from the regency. But are these interpretations accurate? Is it not possible that hindsight has provided historians with a convenient explanation of the purpose of Guise's trip and, more importantly, why she returned at all? Did Mary have any motive to return? Is it possible that Mary of Guise returned to France with no political agenda and with no intention of ever again returning to Scotland?

When news spread that Mary, Queen of Scots was leaving Scotland to become an absentee monarch, it was commonly assumed that Mary of Guise would accompany her daughter to France.[11] It was a shock to almost everyone, including her family in France and the French King, that the Queen Dowager chose to stay in Scotland in order to see the Anglo-Scottish hostilities brought to an end. In a revealing letter to her brothers informing them that the French galleys were ready to transport 'the Queen your niece', Guise wrote that 'The King will

---

8 McKerlie, *Mary of Guise-Lorraine*, p.147.

9 Marshall, *Mary of Guise*, p.182; Fraser, *Mary Queen of Scots*, pp. 76–7.

10 It is unclear whether Donaldson has coined this phrase himself or is using a contemporary description of Guise's trip in *All the Queen's Men*, pp. 25–7, 106 and *James V-James VII*, p.80. Marcus Merriman agrees with Donaldson in that Mary of Guise went to France not only 'to see her daughter, but also to expose to a band of accompanying Scotsmen both their young queen and the power and the glory that was the France of her future husband'. Merriman, 'Mary, Queen of France', p.36; Lynch, *Scotland: A New History*, p.208.

11 See, for example, *CSP Spain*, IX, pp. 290, 571; *CSP Venice*, V, 544, p.230; and *CSP Scot.*, I, 274, 306, 336, pp. 136, 155, 169, for reports that Guise was to accompany, or had accompanied, Mary to France.

never consider me a liar, even though it seems to me that, personally, I have not been very well treated, but I will not give up doing whatever will be in my power'.[12] Similarly in 1550, when asked if she intended to stay in Scotland much longer, Guise responded in reference to the war that, 'I am not ready to leave here for a long time'.[13] Mary of Guise's commitment to the war effort is not entirely surprising. She had been instrumental in gaining Arran's support for the proposed dynastic alliance,[14] and her constant pleas for financial and military aid were largely responsible for France's intervention as a whole.[15] After the arrival of French reinforcements on 16 June 1548, Guise's interest in the war effort intensified. She took an active role in military affairs and, during her tour of the various military camps, roused the allied troops with words of inspiration.[16]

Yet, despite this extensive and personal involvement in Scotland's military affairs, Mary of Guise was intent on returning to France after the cessation of hostilities. Indeed, there is no plausible explanation of why she would want to stay in Scotland when her daughter's future in France seemed so secure. Mary, Queen of Scots was already living in her future husband's kingdom as an absentee monarch and was destined to become the Queen of France. Guise's prior involvement in Scottish politics, particularly in her struggle for power during the 1540s, was inextricably associated with the future welfare and authority of her daughter who, at that time, was still in Scotland.[17] If, like the treaties of Greenwich, the treaty of Haddington had stipulated that Mary remain in Scotland until the time of her marriage, only then would the argument that Guise had political designs in Scotland at the time of her trip to France acquire some degree of credibility. There are too many discrepancies and unanswered questions found in these arguments that cast doubt over the presumed 'political' objective of Guise's trip to France and, more importantly, the reason for her return to Scotland. What is certain is that Mary of Guise's sojourn

12 Mary of Guise to the Duc d'Aumale and Cardinal de Guise, 25 June 1548, Teulet, *Papiers*, I, pp. 674–6 and *Relations*, I, pp. 173–5.
13 Mary of Guise to Mlle. de Fourquevaux, 14 February 1550, NLS, MSS.2991, f.27.
14 *CSP Scot.*, I, 73, 92, pp. 34–5, 42–3; *TA*, IX, pp. 127, 15, 4.
15 See, for example, Teulet, *Papiers*, I, pp. 674–6, 680–1, 694–7 and *Relations*, I, pp. 173–5, 179–80, 192–5; *Balcarres Papers*, I, cxlv, cxlvi, cxlix, lxxii, pp. 188–9, 189–90, 195–6, 242; *Maitland Miscellany*, I, 5–7, pp. 215–8.
16 *Histoire de la guerre d'Ecosse, pendant les campagnes 1548 et 1549 par Jean de Beaugué* (Maitland Club, 1830), pp. 37–8, 126–33; Teulet, *Papiers*, I, p.188 and *Relations*, I, pp. 220–1; Lesley, *History*, pp. 212, 228.
17 See, for example, Marshall, *Mary of Guise*, pp. 89–153; Donaldson, *James V–James VII*, pp. 63–71; and *Scottish Correspondence*, pp. 1–252.

requires more investigation before any attempt to understand the reason for her return to Scotland in 1551 can begin.

* * *

There is no doubt that Mary of Guise returned to France to be reunited with her family. It had been two years since she had said goodbye to her daughter at Dumbarton and a staggering twelve years since she had last seen her son, François, and other members of her immediate family.[18] This was also the official reason cited by Henri II. In his letter to Edward VI requesting a safe conduct for Mary of Guise, the French King stressed that the purpose of the Queen Dowager's voyage was only 'to visit us and the Queen of Scots our little daughter'.[19] But the purpose of Mary of Guise's return was also celebratory in nature. She arrived just in time to witness Henri II's triumphant entry into Rouen and, judging by the grandeur conferred upon her there and upon her arrival at Dieppe, Mary of Guise's own homecoming was clearly intended to play a large part in the celebrations.

Henri II was determined to make Mary of Guise's homecoming an occasion to remember. Prior to her departure, Montmorency informed the Queen Dowager that, because of Henri's immense satisfaction with her management of Scottish affairs, 'you will be very welcome and find a company which will greet and meet you with all the honour and happiness one could imagine'.[20] Indeed, it was even reported by the English ambassador in France that Guise's 'service in Scotland is so highly taken here . . . she is in this Court made a goddess'.[21] Accordingly, François, duc de Guise and 'the flower of the nobility' congregated at Dieppe in August 1550 to await the arrival of Henri's esteemed guest and future godmother to his son, Louis.[22] But the days passed without any sign of the fleet carrying Mary of Guise. The day of the royal

18 Mary of Guise did receive a fleeting visit from her younger brother, Claude duc d'Aumale, who had been sent to England as a pledge for the treaty of Boulogne in April 1550.

19 23 July 1550, Teulet, *Papiers*, I, p.234 and *Relations*, I, pp. 237–8. See also Teulet, *Papiers*, I, p.235 and *Relations*, I, pp. 238–9; *ADCP*, pp. 605–6; *APC*, III, pp. 95–6, 101–2; and Jordan, *Chronicle*, p.43, for letters authorising Guise's safe conduct and the French galleys sent to transport her, and for details of Guise's proposed passage through England.

20 *Balcarres Papers*, II, li, p.71. See also NAS, SP13/70 for Henri's letter to Guise dated 4 September 1550, in which he writes how eagerly he awaits her arrival, and NLS, MSS, 3112, f.1, for the lodging arrangements he made for her and Mary, Queen of Scots for his entry into Rouen on 1 October 1550.

21 The words of Sir John Mason in a letter dated at Blois, 23 February 1551, *CSP Foreign, 1547–1553*, 295, p.75.

22 *Ibid*, 232, p.53; NLS, Adv.MSS, 19.1.25, f.6.

christening was postponed to allow for her late arrival,[23] but as the month wore on, the non-appearance of Mary of Guise was fast becoming a source of great concern at the French Court, 'lest recent storms should have driven her to the coast of Flanders'.[24] Fortunately, the reason for Guise's tardiness was nothing sinister. A domestic dispute between some of her travelling companions had simply delayed her departure until Saturday, 6 September.[25]

Mary of Guise finally arrived at Dieppe on 19 September 1550. There 'sho was honorable receaved' by her brother and his noble entourage, which included her 15-year-old son, François.[26] From Dieppe she made her way to Rouen where, six days later, she was 'received with much honour' at the French Court.[27] Henri, in particular, welcomed Guise 'with gret effectione and fawour, shawin alswell to all the nobill men that was with hir and to hir self'.[28] It was in

---

23 On 28 August 1550 Mason reported that, 'The christening is to be on Sunday next'. *CSP Foreign, 1547–1553*, 233, p.53.

24 *Ibid*, 232–3, 237, pp. 53, 57.

25 The altercation surrounded Huntly's arrest of William Mackintosh of Dunnachtane, a Highland chief whom he had charged with conspiracy against his life. According to Lesley, Huntly's subsequent forfeiture of Mackintosh's lands, in which he acted as the judge of his cause as the lieutenant-general of the north, sparked a bitter reaction from Gilbert, 3rd earl of Cassillis, Maxwell, Sir George Douglas of Pittendreich and Sir James Douglas of Drumlanrig. Given the high-profile nature of the dispute, Guise could not proceed to France until the feud between several of her travelling companions was settled. It was because of this that she decided to intervene. A truce was arranged whereby both sides agreed to restore Mackintosh's lands to his son and heir. As a mark of their truce, which was to last for the duration of their trip to France, each one 'uthalden his hand to the Quenis Grace, moder to our Soverane Lady, quhais Grace tuk every manis hand thair upoun'. Having achieved an albeit fragile state of accord between her travelling companions on 5 September, Mary of Guise was finally ready to depart for France and set sail the next day. For Huntly, however, the issue was not closed. Lesley reports that after he departed for France, the Countess of Huntly ordered the execution of Mackintosh on her husband's orders. This, in turn, led to retribution and the murder of Huntly's agent and sheriff-deputy, Lachlan Mackintosh, on 30 September 1551. Attempts were also made on Huntly's life. After his return to Scotland, Huntly complained to Guise 'off the greit tresone and dyssait devyssit for my slayng'. Although Huntly does not identify those who were planning to assassinate him specifically, he was more than likely alluding to associates of the Clan Mackintosh. As we shall see in Chapter 6, this prolonged feud contributed to Huntly's disgrace in 1554. *RPC*, I, p.107; Lesley, *History*, pp. 235, 381; *Scottish Correspondence*, ccliv, p.381 *n.1*; Marshall, *Mary of Guise*, p.185; A.M. Mackintosh, *The Mackintoshes and Clan Chattan* (Edinburgh, 1903), pp. 128–40; *CSP Foreign, 1547–1553*, 237, pp. 54–5.

26 NLS, Adv.MSS, 19.1.25, f.6.

27 Guise arrived at Rouen on 25 September 1550. Tytler, *Edward VI and Mary*, I, p.327; *CSP Foreign, 1547–1553*, 244, p.56.

28 Lesley, *History*, p.236.

this dramatic setting that Mary of Guise was finally and publicly reunited with her daughter Mary. Although Guise ended up missing Louis' baptism, she did arrive in time to participate in what was ostensibly the main purpose of her journey – Henri's triumphant entry into Rouen on 1 October 1550.[29]

Unlike his previous entries at Lyons (1548) and Paris (1549), for example, Henri's entry into the Norman capital was more than a typical Renaissance fête celebrating his accession and sovereignty.[30] It was also a vainglorious display of his accomplishments and a confident expression of things yet to come. Unsurprisingly, his recent recovery of Boulogne and emancipation of Scotland from the English were flaunted unabashedly as great 'military' victories. Following the ceremonious procession of Rouen's townspeople and local officials, a military parade with elaborate floats depicted Henri's 'conquest' of Boulogne.[31] This ostentatious display included replicas of the forts of Boulogne and the spoils, such as ammunition and prisoners of war, taken from the English during Henri's military campaign of August 1549.[32] This pretence of military victory did not escape comment from the English ambassador, Sir John Mason, who was overheard as saying that 'if it [Boulogne] had cost them nothing they might have had a triumph with good reason'.[33]

But the recovery of Boulogne was not the only cause for celebration; so, too, was France's successful intervention in Scotland. Another

29 Tytler, *Edward VI and Mary*, I, pp. 325–6; *CSP Foreign, 1547–1553*, 244, p.56; *CSP Spain*, X, pp. 181–2. For more on Henri's entry into Rouen, see Cloulas, *Henri II*, pp. 271–94; Merriman, 'Mary, Queen of France', pp. 35–41, and *The Rough Wooings*, pp. 25–39; M.B. McGowan, 'Form and themes in Henri II's entry in Rouen', *Renaissance Drama*, i (1968), pp. 199–252; and M. Wintroub, 'Civilizing the Savage and Making a King: The Royal Entry Festival of Henri II (Rouen, 1550)', *Sixteenth Century Journal*, xxix/2 (1998), pp. 465–94.

30 See, for example, I.D. MacFarlane (ed.), *The Entry of Henri II into Paris, 16 June 1549* (Binghampton, New York, 1982).

31 The Imperial ambassador, Simon Renard, reported that 'The townspeople made a good show; some were on horseback, and three ensigns of foot-soldiers equipped at their expense were present and took part in it. The clergy came first, then the burgesses, followed by the judges and the admiralty. The Rouen bailiffs and their officers, the tax collectors for the province, the officials of the parliament, . . . followed in the succession'. *CSP Spain*, X, p.181; Cloulas, *Henri II*, pp. 276–8.

32 Simon Renard also reported that 'The last triumph were the forts of Boulogne; and with it the spoils taken from the English, ammunition and similar things, as a sign and symbol of the conquest of Boulogne'. *CSP Spain*, X, pp. 181–2; Cloulas, *Henri II*, pp. 278–83; Merriman, 'Mary, Queen of France', pp. 36–9.

33 *CSP Spain*, X, pp. 182–3.

military procession saw soldiers in Roman costume carrying banners signifying the Scottish strongholds defended and 'recovered by the French forces', followed by a chariot on which a winged Fortune held an Imperial crown over a laurelled figure clad in armour representing Henri.[34] Directly behind this symbolic chariot rode the two figures who were destined to play a large part in the realisation of Henri's imperial ambitions: the Dauphin of France and Mary, Queen of Scots.[35]

Henri's entry into Rouen, therefore, was also a celebration of the treaty of Haddington and a bold statement of his imperial objective for a Franco-British empire. Just days before his entry, Henri wrote:

> . . . j'ai pacife le Royaume d'Ecosse que ie tiens & possede auec tel commandement & obeissance que j'ai en France, ausquels deux Royaumes, j'en ay joint & vny vn autre, qui est Angleterre, dont par vne perpetuelle vnion, alliance & confederation, ie puis disposer, comme de moy-mesme, du Roy, de ses Subjets, & de ses facultez; de sorte que lesdits trois Royaumes ensemble se peuuent maintenant estimer vne mesme Monarchie [I have pacified the Kingdom of Scotland which I hold and possess with the same power and authority as I have in France, two kingdoms to which I have linked and united another, namely England, which by a perpetual union, alliance and confederation I can use as myself: the king, his subjects and his wealth so that the said three kingdoms together can now be deemed a single monarchy].[36]

The success of the French King's plan for 'a single monarchy', however, ultimately depended on the marriage of Mary Stewart to

34 McGowan, 'Forms and themes in Henri II's entry into Rouen', pp. 213–4; Merriman, 'Mary, Queen of France', p.38.
35 It should be noted that Henri's imperial ambitions extended beyond his vision of a Franco-British empire. An elaborate performance was staged at the Rouen entry depicting France's projected victory over Portugal in Brazil. *CSP Spain*, X, p.182; Tytler, *Edward VI and Mary*, I, p.326; A.H. Williamson, 'Scots, Indians and the Empire: the Scottish Politics of Civilization, 1519–1609', *Past and Present*, 150 (1996), pp. 46–83; Wintroub, 'Civilizing the Savage', pp. 465–71; Cloulas, *Henri II*, pp. 283–8; Merriman, 'Mary, Queen of France', pp. 38–9.
36 Henri II to the Grand Sultan of Constantinople, 27 September 1550, Ribier, *Lettres et mémoires*, II, p.288. See also the Cardinal of Ferrara's letter concerning Henri's alleged designs against the English, in which he writes that, 'estimant que quand vour seriz joints & vnis ensemble; qu'il vous seroit plus aise d'obtenir l'vn de l'autre quelque grace qu'autrement [considering that when you would be joined and united together, it would be easier for you to get some favour from one another than in another way]'. *Ibid*, II, p.250.

François Valois and, in the interim, on a Scottish government favourable to an intimate Franco-Scottish alliance brought about by the proposed union of the crowns. In 1550 the question remained of how this was to be achieved most effectively. Although the Scottish political élite had expressed their desire for the continued protection of the French King in April, this did not guard against the possibility that they could renege on the betrothal contract if, at a later date perhaps, they no longer felt the need for French protection.[37] In this respect, the Rouen entry may also be seen as an elaborate exercise in public relations directed at the Scots who were in attendance with Mary of Guise. The lavishness of Henri's entry into Rouen exposed them to the grandeur of France and, by inference, to the benefits of a dynastic alliance. This message was accentuated by the prominence of Mary, Queen of Scots in the procession. Her position *alongside* the Dauphin, her future husband, was a recognition of her own sovereignty and projected an image of equality in the union of the crowns. The Scots could not fail to be impressed. Even the English and Imperial ambassadors were compelled to report that Henri's entry was so imposing, 'brave and so rich, . . . the like . . . hath not been seen'.[38]

But can such imagery and exposure to lavish ostentation be seen as an attempt to 'brainwash' the Scots? More to the point, was Mary of Guise's trip to France with a large retinue of Scottish notables intended to be 'a brainwashing expedition' whereby Henri could buy their support with French pensions? Historians have used the composition of Mary of Guise's retinue to suggest that it was, but closer examination suggests otherwise.

Issue must first be taken with the term 'brainwashing', which implies a mental and physical imposition on, if not complete control over, passive victims. One would be hard pushed to describe the Scots as either passive or victims. Some credit must also be given to Henri II and Mary of Guise. They needed only to refer to the inability of the English to keep the 'assured Scots' assured during the 1540s to realise that it would take significantly more than a one-off trip to France to secure the Scots' long-term and unwavering support. The prevalent use of the term 'brainwashing', moreover, implies that *all* the Scots who accompanied Mary of Guise to France were opposed to the Franco-Scottish alliance. Surely Guise also wanted to be surrounded by friends at an event that celebrated the failure of England's Scottish

---

37 *RPC*, I, pp. 86–93.
38 Tytler, *Edward VI and Mary*, I, pp. 325–6; *CSP Foreign, 1547–1553*, 244, p.56; *CSP Spain*, X, pp. 181–3.

policy. Unfortunately, Gordon Donaldson has exaggerated these misconceptions by placing undue emphasis on those Scots in Guise's retinue with reforming and/or anglophile sympathies.

The biggest hole in Donaldson's argument is that by relying on an extremely limited source base, he has failed to consider all the Scots who were in, or travelled to, France during Guise's visit. In *All the Queen's Men*, he presents as a complete list only those who are mentioned in the *Register of the Privy Seal*, as being the 'persons who accompanied Mary of Guise to France on her 'brainwashing expedition' in 1550'.[39] Secondly, he has made no attempt to consider the political and religious loyalties of those who did *not* go to France, or whether these individuals were also the recipients of French patronage. And finally, Donaldson has completely disregarded the fact that French patronage had been distributed to the Scots since 1548. Needless to say, these oversights have resulted in an inaccurate and misguided analysis of the factors underlying Mary of Guise's return to France. By taking into account these oversights, it soon becomes apparent that the argument highlighting the positive correlation between those Scots with anglophile or reformist inclinations and those who received French patronage is grossly over-simplified.

There is no doubt that Mary of Guise's retinue was as grand in its composition as it was diverse. As Appendix A shows, those Scots who travelled to France included great nobles, such as the Earls of Cassillis, Glencairn, Huntly, Marischal, Sutherland, and Lords Erskine, Fleming, Home, Maxwell and Somerville, as well as men of lesser status, such as Mr. John Douglas, parson of Newlands, Mr. David Henderson, vicar of Rossie, and the monks of Pittenweem Priory. There were also many lairds in attendance, such as Sir Hugh Campbell of Loudon, Sir George Douglas of Pittendreich, Sir James Douglas of Drumlanrig and Sir William Murray of Tullibardine, in addition to James V's illegitimate sons, Lords James, John and Robert. Other visitors to France included John Spottiswoode, William Lauder of Haltoun, and repre-

---

39 *RSS*, IV, 879, 880, 882, 883, 887, 893, pp. 146–9; Donaldson, *All the Queen's Men*, Appendix C, p.160. In *James V – James VII*, p.80, Donaldson also makes reference to those Scots listed in Knox's *Works*, I, pp. 241–2 and *History*, I, p.116. After by examining a wider range of sources, however, it soon becomes obvious how many more Scots accompanied Guise to France or joined her later – not to mention the large number of Scots who were already there. Safe conducts, correspondence, ambassadorial reports and receipts contained in *CSP Foreign, 1547–1553*, *CSP Scot.*, I, *APC, Scottish Correspondence, Balcarres Papers*, II, *RPC, RMS, RSS*, and NLS, Adv.MSS, 29.2.5 all contain references to these individuals which have been compiled in the Appendix.

sentatives of the ecclesiastical estate, such as Robert Stewart, bishop elect of Caithness, Andrew Durie, bishop of Galloway, and John Roull, prior of Pittenweem and Blantyre. But one must not forget the countless other Scots in France, such as students, merchants, soldiers and servants, who may also have joined in the celebrations at Rouen or attended the same pageants and fêtes as Mary of Guise and Mary, Queen of Scots throughout their French progress.[40] What is certain, and what Appendix A only begins to demonstrate, is that there were far more Scots in France during Mary of Guise's trip than has previously been thought.

Just as the composition of those Scots in France was diverse in terms of social status, so too were their religious and political sympathies. Representatives from all across the religious and political divide seem to have been present. Mary of Guise's entourage included committed reformers, such as the Earls of Glencairn and Marischal; faithful adherents of the established Church, such as the earls of Huntly and Sutherland; and those who may be described as reforming Catholics, the most notable of whom were John Winram, subprior of St. Andrews, and Henry Sinclair, dean of Glasgow.[41] The religious sympathies of others are less certain. While many were ostensibly still Catholics, it is difficult to gauge the effects of the reform movement on particular individuals in 1550, let alone prove the sincerity of their religious convictions. Future membership in the Lords of the Congregation is, similarly, an unreliable indicator of Protestant inclinations in 1550 – widespread support for their rebellion came only when France failed to respond adequately to England's military intervention on the side of the Congregation in February 1560.

Using political activities as a gauge of religious sympathies is equally questionable. Due to the ever-changing political scene in Scotland during the 1540s, political allegiances were not always consistent with religious convictions. Glencairn, Cassillis, Marischal, Sir Hugh Campbell of Loudon, Sir George Douglas of Pittendreich and Lord Maxwell, for example, had all been 'assured Scots' and/or were noted as having secret dealings with the English during the 'rough wooings'. Publicly, though, these Protestant anglophiles opposed Somerset on political

---

40 See Lesley, *History*, pp. 236–7, for an itinerary of Guise's movements after Rouen.

41 I am extremely grateful to Linda Dunbar, whose research on John Winram reveals that, in 1550, he was fundamentally concerned about reforming the Church from within. L.J. Dunbar, 'John Winram *c.*1492–1582: A Study of his life and his role in the pre and post-Reformation Scottish Church' (unpublished PhD Thesis, University of Edinburgh, 1998), pp. 26–55.

grounds, while others resented the aggressiveness of Somerset's campaign and defended their kingdom against the English occupying forces. But, once again, it is necessary to point out the loyal supporters of the Crown and friends of Mary of Guise who were also in France – the most notable of were the Gordon contingency, including Huntly, Sutherland and James Ogilvy of Deskford and Findlater. There was also Sir Robert Carnegy of Kinnaird, John Beaton of Creich, John Sempill of Fowlwood and the Lords Erskine, Fleming, Home and Somerville, all of whom were either ardent supporters of the French and Catholic cause or just decidedly anti-English. From this brief analysis, it becomes clear that a large proportion of Scots who were in France during Mary of Guise's visit were neither anglophiles nor zealous reformers in need of 'brainwashing'. While it is true that, as an exercise in public relations, Guise's trip promoted the Franco-Scottish alliance by exposing the Scots to the grandeur of France, particularly at Henri's entry into Rouen, Mary of Guise had been actively and effectively securing the support of the Scots since 1548.

In fact, it was Mary of Guise's shrewd and effective distribution of patronage that procured the greatest support for the Franco-Scottish alliance. Guise had seen first hand how offers of French gold and titles were instrumental in securing the political support of Arran for an alliance that directly contravened his own dynastic and personal ambitions. Henry, lord Methven confirmed the important role patronage played in gaining the support of the Scottish nobility as a whole:

> The lordis that is greit men and uther lordis and barronis to
> be Cherisit fawvorable wyth your graic and wyth all the
> prynsipall men of gud quhay that cummis out of France heyr,
> for the nater of this pepill is of this realm; first to be gentillie
> don to, and that tha persaif luf and gudnes in the kingis
> graice of France. And als this realm is pwyr and the greit
> men can na way beyr greit exspens of thar awn leving. All
> greit men in this realm has, and utheris efter thair greis has,
> folkis to sarve tham in thair awn bowndis but ony mone bot
> allanerly gud tretyng and greit houss to be haldin of daly
> exspens ordynar of meyt and drynk; bot to remayn lang out
> of thair awn boundis apon thair awn exspenssis thai ma na
> way do the samyn wythout tha be suppleyit and helpit be
> substance.[42]

42 *Scottish Correspondence*, clxxii, p.242.

The accuracy of Methven's description of the Scottish nobility, and how best to treat them, is effectively demonstrated by Patrick, earl of Bothwell whose loyalties during Somerset's occupation were highly suspect.[43] In a letter to the Queen Dowager, Bothwell, reminded her of the 2,000 crowns promised to him, but as yet not received. Knowing that Guise wanted him and Huntly to embark on a northern expedition, he shrewdly pointed out that he had 'nocht at this tym money to mak my furnessingis as afferis me to do', and humbly requested that she 'support me with this said money quhilk my servand suld have ressavit in Frans, that I may ordour me tweching my passage according to your grace will'.[44] In other words, no money – no service. Although Bothwell had a valid point in that money was desperately needed to finance military campaigns, his comments nevertheless reflect the advantageous position the Scots found themselves in as pawns in the game of European dynastic politics. Money was being thrown at the Scots by both England and France in the hope of procuring support for their respective causes. Given that they were the objects of an international bidding war, the allegiance of the Scots ultimately came at a price.

The years 1548–1549, therefore, witnessed an active campaign by Mary of Guise and Henri to consolidate existing support and secure new support for the Franco-Scottish alliance through the distribution of patronage.[45] Methven's advice seems to have been well heeded by Guise, who was undoubtedly already aware of the importanance of patronage for the success of France's military and dynastic objectives

43 During the early 1540s Bothwell was an ardent supporter of Mary of Guise and the French cause, staunchly opposing the English alliance and reformed doctrines. But a year after he apprehended the reformed preacher, George Wishart, in 1546, Bothwell's name appeared on the list of Scots who had bound themselves to Henry VIII and, in 1549, he signed a bond of fealty to Edward VI. Charged with treason in 1550, Bothwell fled Scotland and did not return until Mary of Guise allowed him to return in 1553. She subsequently granted him a remission for his treasonous activities and appointed him Lord High Admiral and Lieutenant of the Borders during her regency. *Scottish Correspondence*, cxlv, cxlvii, ccxxiv, pp. 205–6, 207, 320, 321; *CSP Scot.*, I, 92, 353–5, pp. 42, 178; *APC*, II, p.318 and III, p.92; *TA*, IX, pp. 414, 430; AÉ, *Cor. Pol.*, Angleterre, XIII, f.31ʳ; Teulet, *Papiers*, I, p.269 and *Relations*, I, p.279.
44 *Scottish Correspondence*, cxcv, p.284. See also Kerr and Macdowall's letter beseeching Guise to 'fynd sum lywing for ws in Scotland' in return, it is implied, for their loyal support and service. *Ibid*, ccviii, p.299.
45 This policy was reported on extensively by the Imperial ambassador, St. Mauris, who informed Charles V of Henri's intent to bestow pensions and titles on the Scots in order to 'nourish their affection for France and turn them from friendship or understanding with the English'. *CSP Spain*, IX, pp. 302–4, 312, 361, 573.

in Scotland. She was quite forthright in reminding Henri of his financial obligations and, in particular, of the necessity to ' entreti-enne les seigneurs de ce pays et leur donner des penssions pour les attirer de plus en plus a luy faire service'.[46] As a result, Scots of all religious and political persuasions who were thought to give the best service received the 'luf and all gudnes in the kingis graice of France', predominantly in the form of annual pensions and/or cash gifts.[47] The Earl of Angus and his anglophile brother, Sir George Douglas of Pittendreich, for example, received pensions of 2,500 *francs* and 1,000 crowns,[48] while the decidedly anti-English Border laird, Sir Walter Scott of Buccleuch and Branxholme, was granted a pension of 400 crowns.[49] The Homes were also beneficiaries. John Home of Colden-knowes and Patrick Home of Broomhouse each received 500 *écus*,[50] and in return for relinquishing Home Castle to the French for the duration of the war, pensions of 2,000 *francs* and 500 *écus* were dispensed to Lord Home and his son, Alexander, who, as a cavalry captain, also received 100 light horse.[51]

Bonds of manrent and maintenance were also means through

---

46 25 February 1549, NLS, MSS.2991, f.67[v]; *Fourquevaux Mission*, p.18.

47 NLS, MSS.2991, f.67[v]; *Fourquevaux Mission*, p.18. Due to the scarcity of sources, tracing the annual payments of these French pensions has, on the whole, been a fruitless task. Similarly, the receipts for payments that are available, such as those contained in NLS, Adv.MSS, 29.2.5, tend not to specify whether the cash received was an annual payment of a pension or a one-off cash gift.

48 NAS, E34/14/5–6. In 1514 Archibald, 6th earl of Angus, famously married his second wife, Margaret Tudor, elder sister of Henry VIII and relict of James IV. Although his allegiances often wavered, Angus was consistent in his animosity towards Arran. He led the pro-English/reform faction with Lennox in the early 1540s, but fought for Scotland against Somerset, commanding the defeated army at Pinkie. His younger brother, conversely, was a staunch anglophile and was regarded as the leader of the English party in Scotland during the 1540s. Sir George's refusal to take part physically in Henry VIII's 'Rough Wooing' of Scotland, however, was not looked upon kindly by the English. They laid waste to his lands and took many members of his family captive, including his wife. He subsequently became a loyal servant of Mary of Guise.

49 *Ibid*, SP13/14/12. A prominent Border laird, Sir Walter Scott of Buccleuch strongly opposed the Tudor-Stewart marriage and actively defended his kingdom against Somerset, despite suffering badly at the hands of the English. Scott was murdered in 1552 by partisans of his traditional enemies, the Kerrs of Cessford.

50 1 July 1549, NLS, Adv.MSS, 29.2.5, f.121.

51 *Ibid*, MSS.2991, fos. 67[v]-8[r] and Adv.MSS, 29.2.5, f.123; *Fourquevaux Mission*, p.18. Guise's memo regarding the relinquishment of Home Castle and its furniture is dated 29 February 1549; Alexander's receipt for 500 *écus* is dated 1 July 1549.

which Mary of Guise granted pensions to Scots.[52] Although many of these bonds have been lost, it is nevertheless significant that the majority of those entered into with the Queen Dowager date to the period 1548–1549 and, in what were usually only personal declarations of loyalty and service, contain financial provisions. Consistent with Guise's policy of patronage as a whole, royal bonds of manrent and maintenance were entered into with Scots of all religious and political persuasions – including committed reformers such as George Meldrum of Fyvie[53] and John Erskine of Dun,[54] and faithful adherents of the Crown and Church such as Robert Carnegy of Kinnaird,[55] Sir Walter Scott of Buccleuch and Branxholme,[56] his son and heir, William of Kirkurd [Kirkhope],[57] the Earl of Huntly[58] and his younger brother, Alexander Gordon, the postulate of Caithness.[59] Of these, Carnegy was granted an annual pension of £100, Dun a pension of 500 crowns per annum (in addition to a ruby and diamond for his relinquishing Montrose Castle), Sir Walter Scott of Kirkurd the annual fees formerly received by the late John Melville of Raith,

52 For more on this topic see J. Wormald, *Lords and Men in Scotland: Bonds of Manrent, 1442–1603* (Edinburgh, 1985), especially pp. 168–373, for a comprehensive list of 'Bonds and Contracts of Manrent of Maintenance'.

53 14 March 1549, NAS, SP13/65. George Meldrum of Fyvie was a noted reformer and anglophile, although he did fight for Scotland at the battle of Ancrum (1545).

54 30 September 1549, *ibid*, SP13/68. A reformer whose political allegiances were not always consistent with his religious convictions, John Erskine of Dun opposed Somerset during his occupation of Scotland as the Constable of Montrose. For this and his surrender of Montrose Castle to the French, he received the heartfelt thanks of Mary of Guise (*Spalding Misc.*, IV, pp. 48–51).

55 14 April 1548, NAS, SP13/59. A loyal servant of the Crown, Carnegy entered into his bond with Guise in return for an annual payment of £100 from the rents and duties of Orkney and Shetland.

56 13 August 1548, NAS, SP13/61; Fraser, *Buccleuch*, II, pp. 187–8.

57 14 March 1549, NAS, SP13/65, 66; Fraser, *Buccleuch*, II, p.195.

58 14 April 1548, NAS, SP13/58. While being held in Newcastle after being taken prisoner at Pinkie, Huntly was promised that the French King would pay his ransom and award him the 'order of France [St. Michael]'. He was also promised an annual pension of £2,000 and investiture in one of the earldoms of Orkney, Ross or Moray, and provision for his kin and followers. By 13 February 1549 he had been made a knight of the Order of St. Michael (confirmed during his trip to France in 1550–1 and giving rise to his nickname 'Cock o' the North') and had been granted the lands and earldom of Moray. The following May, Huntly also received a charter for the hereditary bailiary of all the lands in the bishopric of Aberdeen. *RMS*, IV, 299, 319, 366, pp. 71, 75, 84.

59 17 January 1548, NAS, SP13/55. For a survey of Alexander Gordon's ecclesiastical career, see G. Donaldson, *Reformed by Bishops: Galloway, Orkney and Caithness* (Edinburgh, 1987), pp. 1–18, 54–5.

and Alexander Gordon an annual pension of £200 Scots.[60] In addition to her bond of manrent, Guise also entered into an obligation with Gordon to compensate him for his renunciation of the bishopric of Caithness in favour of Robert Stewart on 13 April 1548, and to ensure that he 'perpetually remain his [Henri's] loyal servant and subject'.[61] As such, he was promised another benefice of the same calibre with an annual revenue of 500 merks Scots in either France or Scotland, an annual pension of 1,000 *livres* that Guise was to obtain from Henri and, in the interim, a pension of 400 *livres tournois* from the French King.

The effectiveness of bonds of manrent and pensions in binding the Scots to the interests of France, however, was limited. Patrick, lord Gray, for example, entered into his bond of manrent with Guise just weeks after he had sworn allegiance to 'take the King's [Edward VI's] part in his godly purpose'.[62] The 500 merks he received as an annual pension merely lined his pockets rather than persuading him to abandon the English cause. On the other hand, Guise's bond of manrent with the earl of Sutherland was decisive in securing his support for the French cause.[63] Traditionally, Sutherland's religious and political sympathies were staunchly Catholic and anti-English. A clash with Huntly over the tacks of Moray, however, made him consider switching allegiance, if only to force a favourable decision over the disputed earldom.[64] In his letter assuring Guise of Sutherland's loyalty, Methven hinted that his stepson's fealty was conditional on her granting 'the takkis of Mwrray . . . to the erll of Sotherland nor

---

60 NAS, SP13/59, 68 and E34/15/5; Fraser, *Buccleuch*, II, p.170.
61 NAS, SP13/55; Teulet, *Papiers*, I, pp. 662–3; NLS, MSS.2991, f.68; *Fourquevaux* Mission, pp. 18–9; *Scottish Correspondence*, clxi-ii, clxxi, pp. 227–9, 239–40. Gordon entered into a bond of manrent with Guise on 17 January 1548 and an obligation on 14 April 1548.
62 26 March 1548, *CSP Scot.*, I, 148, pp. 71–2; NAS, SP13/56. Gray was a noted anglophile and reformer, who pledged himself to promote the Tudor-Stewart marriage and surrender Broughty Castle to the English. Two weeks after the battle of Pinkie, in which he did not fight, the said castle was relinquished to the English. *CSP Scot.*, I, 4, 129, 141, pp. 2, 60–1, 66.
63 20 February 1549, NAS, SP13/63.
64 *Scottish Correspondence*, clxvi, clxx, ccxvlii, ccxvliii, pp. 234, 237–9, 365–7; Fraser, *Sutherland*, I, pp. 106–7 and III, pp. 110–3; *ADCP*, p.615. Although fragile, Mary of Guise's resolution of the Huntly-Sutherland dispute over Moray in 1552 is a prime example of her political acumen and ability to use land and ecclesiastical disputes to her political advantage. By satisfying both parties in the feud, Guise ensured that both Huntly and Sutherland remained in her service as opposed to one of them supporting Châtelherault out of disaffection.

till ony utheris'.[65] Such a decision would also, of course, be characteristic of Guise's 'greit wisdom . . . don evir for the commoun weill
persever'.[66] Methven's warning was further substantiated by reports
that, despite his ostensible displays of loyal service,[67] Sutherland was
actually 'of good mind to the King's [Edward VI] godly purpose . . .
beand honestly entyrtaynit'.[68] Mary of Guise's bond of manrent, in
which Sutherland was granted tenancy in the earldom of Ross, was a
direct response to his alleged wavering loyalties.[69] Whether Sutherland's temporary lapse of faith was genuine or simply a ruse for
personal gain, Guise's bond nevertheless succeeded in its objective
and secured his steadfast support for the French cause.

Despite the example of Lord Gray, Mary of Guise considered the
distribution of French pensions to be an effective and necessary policy
– albeit an expensive one. She initially covered the costs personally,
but in 1549 informed Henri that she could no longer afford to do so.
In her request for financial assistance, Guise revealed that a total of
'XXV thousand *francs* per year' was needed 'to be handed out to these
people who will be able to serve him best'.[70] The combined total of the
pensions subsequently granted to the Queen Dowager (10,000 *francs*),
Arran (6,000 *francs*) and Huntly (6,000 *francs*) suggests that they were
intended for redistribution as opposed to personal gain.[71] But offers
of French gold were not the only means of maintaining or procuring

65 1 June [1548], *Scottish Correspondence*, clxx, pp. 237–8.
66 *Ibid*, clxx, p.238.
67 In the same letter, for example, Methven informed Guise that Sutherland
    'has promyttit to do his utir delygens in thay partis for gud rewill and
    concord, and to cause all the folkis be in armour and wappines and to
    sarve the auttorite', and later reported on 17 July 1548 that, 'This day the
    erle Sotherland and the northtland folk departis of Edinbrogh to the
    camp, – xvj^c men, and, as tha say, ma is cummand'. *Ibid*, clxx, clxxvii, pp.
    238, 251.
68 28 August 1548, *CSP Scot.*, I, 323, p.163. In addition to Sutherland, Lord
    Gray cited Atholl, Crawford, Marischal, Rothes and Errol as potential
    supporters of the English cause and, therefore, suitable candidates for
    bribery.
69 20 February 1549, NAS, SP13/63; Fraser, *Sutherland Book*, III, p.107.
70 NLS, MSS.2991, f.67^v; *Fourquevaux Mission*, p.18. Fourquevaux agreed that
    'XXV ou trente mils escuz [XXV or thirty thousand crowns]' was needed
    from Henri, 'pour faire presentz aux seigneurs descosse tels que ladite
    dame [Guise] ly dira. Et ce faisant tout le Royaulme marchera arme a sa
    faveur et la devotion desdits seigneurs sera tout plus encline au service et
    bien du Roy [to be given to the Scottish lords as required by the said
    lady. By doing so, the whole kingdom will march behind him in arms
    and the said lords' devotion will be all the more favourable to the service
    and good of the King]'. NLS, MSS.2991, f.78v; *Fourquevaux Mission*, p.36.
71 BN, MSS.f.fr.18153, fos. 66–8; *Fourquevaux Mission*, p.18 *n*.1.

support for the Franco-Scottish alliance. The resources of France extended beyond the monetary to include the titular, and both Henri and Mary of Guise were astute enough to realise the importance and effectiveness of benefices and preferments.

The offer to Arran of a French duchy and investiture in the Order of St. Michael is the best example of how effective titles and honours were in securing support, or at least a resigned acceptance of the Franco-Scottish alliance.[72] Arran's sons were also beneficiaries. In 1548 Master James Hamilton was assigned a post in Guyenne worth 10,000 *francs* a year and 50 lances in an attempt to keep Arran 'well in hand, firm in his own devotion, and willing to foster it among the other Scottish lords'.[73] For his part, Arran was quick to take advantage of Henri's generosity and asked that he send two of his sons 'to school in Paris and the oldest son to serve the King'.[74] But Guise recognised that this was also a policy that needed to be extended to other Scots. In February 1549, Henri was told again that by bestowing French titles on 'some principal earls and lords . . . they will be more loyal and devoted servants to him'. Guise then proceeded to nominate the Earls of Cassillis, Erroll and Marischal, Lord Home and Sir George Douglas of Pittendreich for honours, in addition to the Earls of Angus, Argyll and Huntly, 'the three knights of the order [of St. Michael]'.[75] Mary of Guise's recommendations were taken seriously. Shortly after one such recommendation, one of Lord Erskine's sons was provided to Cambuskenneth Abbey.[76]

Huntly, in particular, seems to have been earmarked for special recognition. Guise wanted Henri expressly to know of 'the behaviour of the said lord huntly as regards every aspect of his service and that it will be very good if the King pleases to treat him well from now'.[77] Similarly she had not forgotten her obligation to Huntly's brother, and Mary of Guise implored Henri to provide Alexander Gordon with some 'benefice to give him means to support himself and continue to serve him as he had begun'.[78] But the French King did not need

---

72 Following the ratification of the treaty of Haddington, Arran, his heirs and successors were also issued with letters of naturalisation. Bonner, 'French Naturalization of the Scots', pp. 1109–11.

73 *CSP Spain*, IX, pp. 303–4. As we have already seen, Master James was also promised the hand of the Duc de Montpensier's eldest daughter in 1548.

74 NLS, MSS.2991, f.74^r; *Fourquevaux Mission*, p.29.

75 NLS, MSS.2991, f.67^v; NAS, E34/14/5; *Fourquevaux Mission*, p.18 *n*.b; Knox, *History*, I, p.103 and *Works*, I, p.217; *RMS*, IV, 299, 366, pp. 71, 84.

76 NLS, MSS.2991, f.68^v; NAS, SP2/4, f.321; *Fourquevaux Mission*, p.20.

77 NLS, MSS.2991, f.68^r; *Fourquevaux Mission*, p.18.

78 NLS, MSS.2991, f.68^r; *Fourquevaux Mission*, pp. 18–9.

reminding. He had already taken steps to compensate Gordon for the loss of Caithness with the archbishopric of Glasgow. Alexander Gordon's subsequent provision to the see of Glasgow on 5 March 1550, however, would prove to be as controversial as it was short-lived.[79]

Upon the death of Gavin Dunbar on 30 April 1547, the vacancy of the prized western see of Glasgow became the source of great contention. No sooner had the bishopric become vacant than the Governor nominated his half-brother, James, dean of Brechin. But this recommendation was flatly rejected on the grounds that the Council of Trent had prescribed lawful birth as a prerequisite for all episcopal appointments.[80] James Hamilton's rejection, however, had less to do with his illegitimacy than with Châtelherault's exploitation of the right of nomination as regent.[81] The papacy had become increasingly wary of Châtelherault's nepotistic recommendations – especially since a Hamilton was already the Archbishop of St. Andrews. Hamiltons holding the two most important ecclesiastical offices in Scotland was simply too much power concentrated in one family and, on 5 March 1550, the see of Glasgow went instead to Alexander Gordon.[82] Needless to say, Châtelherault was far from pleased. Apart from having his own plans thwarted, Châtelherault was particularly upset because he had not recommended Gordon for the post. As regent and representative of the crown, it was his right to nominate individuals to vacant ecclesiastical offices.[83] In the case of Alexander Gordon, his right of nomination had not only been eclipsed, but was also sanctioned by the papacy:

> La Royne d'Escosse, soubsage, avec le Gouverneur du
> royaulme aultrefoys et nagueres traictantz des matieres
> concernantz le faict dudict royaulme et les libertez
> parcydevant a luy donnes par plusieurs papes, le tout par le
> conseil et consentement des trois estats d'ecelle, se sont
> trouvez and trouvent grandement blessez et preiudiciez

79 *HBC*, p.313. For discussions of the controversy surrounding Gordon's provision to the see of Glasgow, see Hannay, 'Some Papal Bulls', pp. 25–41, especially pp. 32–5, and S*cottish Correspondence*, pp. 325–33.

80 Hannay, 'Some Papal Bulls', p.34.

81 Finnie, 'The House of Hamilton', pp. 8–17; Mahoney, 'The Scottish Hierarchy', pp. 52–3.

82 *HBC*, p.313.

83 The right of nomination was clarified in the indult of 20 April 1487, whereby a king (or regent) had eight months to nominate an individual to important benefices such as bishoprics. See N. Macdougall, *James III: A Political Study* (Edinburgh, 1982), p.229.

d'une telle quelle dicts provision de la personne d'un quidict Alexandre Gordoun a l'eglise de Glasgo, faicte par Notre Sainct Pere le pape [The Queen of Scots, a minor, with the Governor of the kingdom, formerly and of late dealing with matters relating to the actions of the said kingdom and freedoms previously granted to him by several popes, all this being done through the advice and consent of her Three Estates, have found and find themselves highly offended and harmed by some provision of Alexander Gordon at the church of Glasgow, granted by Our Holy Father the Pope].[84]

Châtelherault did not lightly accept being snubbed. His immediate response was to place Gordon on a charge of barratry and to lodge a formal protest with Pope Julius III, requesting that an inquiry be launched to investigate the events surrounding Gordon's appointment.[85]

The French King seems to have been the principal agent behind Gordon's unorthodox provision to Glasgow. In this, he was naturally supported by Les Guise and the papacy, but had also written to Châtelherault 'for his consent of Glasquha'.[86] The Queen Dowager, conversely, was in a difficult position. She could not publicly support Gordon's claim for fear of antagonising Châtelherault and directly challenging his authority as Governor. Although Gordon was keen to have Guise's unqualified support, he was nevertheless mindful of her situation. He reassured her that 'I put nocht zour grace to pain in this mater in aventeur my lord governor suld think zour grace did him tort, and I salbe laitht to gyff my lord governor occasion but to do zour grace service as partenis him'.[87] And, in what must be seen as a clear indication that his provision to Glasgow was the result of French intrigue, Gordon pledged that:

> . . . gyff God pleis put me in that rome, I salbe als necessair and sedabill to the werk of zour grace as any of may estait borne in ony of the realmes. I sek bot ane lyf and to haif the moyance to serve zour grace and my natife princes zour

84 *Balcarres Papers*, II, 1, pp. 68–9.
85 In his letter to the Queen Dowager dated at Peebles, 14 June (1551), Archbishop Hamilton reports that Gordon '. . . is cumit and stollying this benefice [Glasgow] and tharfor declarit ane barratour in this cuntre'. *Scottish Correspondence*, ccxxxix, p.352; Hannay, 'Some Papal Bulls', pp. 34–5.
86 *Balcarres Papers*, II, Appendix B, ii, pp. 309–10.
87 *Ibid*, II, p.309.

grace dochter, and that I wer provydit therein, sall all I haif done be dischergit as the King and zour grace plessis.[88]

Yet, despite the high esteem in which both Henri and Mary of Guise held Gordon,[89] they were nevertheless reluctant to take steps to resolve the controversy surrounding his provision to Glasgow.[90] Because of this, the papacy had no choice but to rule in Châtelherault's favour and uphold his objections to Gordon's nomination. In a series of papal bulls dated 4 September 1551, James Beaton, the abbot of Arbroath, was provided to the archbishopric of Glasgow, while Gordon received the titular archbishopric of Athens, Inchaffray *in commendam* and other emoluments in Scotland, doubtless in compensation for his loss of Caithness and Glasgow.[91]

The cessation of hostilities with England did not witness the end of the distribution of patronage, but saw its continuation. Mary of Guise's celebratory return to France provided Henri with an ideal opportunity to reinforce a policy that had been successfully implemented for the past two years and was not, as the Venetian ambassador, Daniel Barbaro, alleged, the sole purpose of her trip.[92] In his report on England, he claimed that 'the Queen Dowager, having gone to France, taking with her the chief nobility of Scotland, the King bought them completely; so that in France there is neither Scottish duke, nor lord, nor prelate, nor lady, nor dame, but who is munificently bribed by the most Christian King'.[93] Barbaro's observations and interpreta-

88 *Balcarres Papers*, II, p.309.
89 *Scottish Correspondence*, ccxxxix, pp. 352–4. Archbishop Hamilton particularly objected to the favour shown by Henri and the Queen Dowager to Alexander Gordon, despite the latter's charge of barratry. This, he complained, had led to rumours that 'the kyngis mageste and your grace is nocht contentit with my lord [Governor] in na sort, . . . for the kyngis mageste hes gevin to the said master Alexander the respeck to ane abbacy and hes relevit his pension and bakoris and hes don na thyng on the wther twart Glasg[o]w'. See also *Balcarres Papers*, II, p.309, where Gordon thanks Guise for the gracious reception he received from her family in France.
90 See, for example, *Scottish Correspondence*, ccxxvii, ccxxxvii, ccxxxix, pp. 323–4, 349, 352–4, in which James Beaton, abbot of Arbroath, Huntly and Archbishop Hamilton all wonder what Guise and Henri have decided to do about Gordon's provision to Glasgow. Beaton had a particular interest in the outcome of the Glasgow controversy as he had been gifted the temporalities of the archbishopric on 6 January 1550. *RSS*, IV, 533, pp. 89–90.
91 Hannay, 'Some Papal Bulls', p.35; *HBC*, p.313.
92 *CSP Venice*, V, 703, pp. 338–362; *APC*, III, p.111.
93 *CSP Venice*, V, 703, p.361.

tion of events are not entirely accurate. Firstly, there were many Scots of note who did *not* accompany Guise to France and, more importantly, who had been recipients of French patronage during 1548–49. The most obvious example of this is, of course, Châtelherault. Someone had to stay and govern the realm, although it was reported that d'Oisel wielded almost sovereign authority during the Queen Dowager's absence.[94] Other recipients in this category included the Earls of Angus and Argyll, Sir Walter Scott of Buccleuch and John Erskine of Dun.[95] An examination of the patronage that was distributed in France reveals further inconsistencies in the argument that Guise went to France so that Henri could buy the Scots off completely.

Commenting on the distribution of patronage in France, Knox wrote that 'What thei [the Scots] receaved we can nott tell; but few maid ruse at thare returnyng'.[96] While it is impossible to determine what every member of Guise's retinue received in the form of patronage, if anything at all, it is certain that this policy was continued in France and, more importantly, was not aimed exclusively at pro-Protestant, pro-English Scots. Moreover, several of them had already profited from the 'luf and all gudnes in the kingis graice of France' prior to their journey.[97] Cassillis, Huntly, Marischal, Fleming, Lord James Stewart, commendator of Kelso and Melrose, James Ogilvy of Deskford, Gavin Hamilton, commendator of Kilwinning Abbey, John Beaton of Creich and Patrick, Master of Ruthven, all received gifts of money in France.[98]

Nominations to ecclesiastical offices were also on offer in France. Lord John Stewart, commendator of Coldingham, for example, was recommended to the 'abbacie of Flawgeny [Flavigny]' and his half-brother, Lord James, commendator of St. Andrews, to another.[99] Indeed, the strong contingent of James V's bastard sons in France suggests that they were selected for support in particular. Rumours of Lord James' double dealings with England may also have played their part – especially if he influenced the political and religious loyalties of

---

94 *CSP Spain*, X, p.559.
95 NAS, E34/14/5, E34/15/5, SP13/14/12 and SP13/68; NLS, MSS.2991, f.67ᵛ; *Fourquevaux Mission*, p.18; *RMS*, IV, 299, 366, pp. 71, 84.
96 Knox, *Works*, I, p.242 and *History*, I, p.116.
97 See Appendix A. Patronage was also distributed by the Scottish government in the form of gifts of escheat, non-entry and grants of Crown land etc.
98 NLS, Adv.MSS, 29.2.5, fos. 143, 146, 140, 142, 138, 136, 150, 148, 151; *Scottish Correspondence*, ccxxxv, pp. 345–7.
99 *Ibid*, ccxxxiii, p.343; Donaldson, *James V–James VII*, p.80.

his half-brothers.[100] In addition to their pensions and ecclesiastical nominations, both Lord James and Lord John were granted letters of legitimation on 7 February 1551.[101] But the example of Lord John's nomination to Flavigny highlights another feature of Guise's policy of distributing patronage – the granting of 'empty promises'. Indeed, Guise would later be forced to rely on this technique during her negotiations with the Congregation in the hope that she could buy enough time for reinforcements to arrive from France. This is not to say that all of her promises were empty from the outset, but there is some evidence to substantiate Sir John Mason's rather exaggerated claim that this was a deliberate policy to keep the Scots impoverished with 'the intent that, being brought to extreme need, they may be compelled upon hope of relief, like slaves to hang upon the Queen'.[102] Lord John Stewart is a case in point. Despite having been nominated for the ecclesiastical office, Lord John found he could not come into possession of the abbacy of Flavigny because the

> . . . sowme is gret that I man gif for my bullis . . . and it is
> nocht wnknawne to your grace [Guise] that I have gottin na
> proffet of my benefice in Scotland sen the begynnyng of the
> weiris. And be ressone that I can nocht gett possesioun of the
> benefice that the kyngis grace hes vouchasit apoun me ther
> will na bancquier tak on hand to furnis the prowisioun of my
> bullis, for I have na othir way to recompence the bringis
> hayme of my provisioun bot allanerlie the dewtie of my said
> benefice. Heirfor I beseik your grace to laubour affectuousslie
> at this tymethat I may have ane commissioun of the kyngis
> grace to put me in possessioun, otherwayis I will gett na
> credett of na bancqueir for the expeditioun of my bullis for I
> have na othir esperance bot in your grace alanerlie.[103]

Just as the English ambassador had described, Lord John was completely dependent on the help of Guise and Henri to escape a predicament that they themselves had created, perhaps unintentionally. In such a state of desperation, Lord John had no choice but to remain loyal to those who had the power to determine his fate.

---

100 Along with other noted agents such as Bothwell and the zealous reformers, John Cockburn, laird of Ormiston, and James Henrisoun, Lord James received several payments from the English during the period 1550–1552. *APC*, III, pp. 103, 347 and IV, pp. 103, 190.
101 *RMS*, IV, 565, p.125; *RSS*, IV, 1064, p.174.
102 Tytler, *Edward VI and Mary*, I, pp. 354–5.
103 *Scottish Correspondence*, ccxxxiii, p.343.

To all intents and purposes, the continuation of this policy during 1550–1551 seemed to be effective in securing support for the French cause – at least in the short term. In return for his pension of 2,400 *francs*, for example, Glencairn promised Guise that 'Quhat service your grace plesis comman me vith in Scotland let me be advertyst and it salbe reddy don vith sic gud vill as I am able to do'.[104] Maxwell is another case in point. Upon hearing the news that, in addition to the 'xij hunder frankis, . . . ye [Guise] appontid to gewe me', he was to receive 'viij^c frankis mair' and 'be ane of the gentilmen in the [ki]ngis chalmer,' Maxwell was not only 'mair adettid to serve [the] king and you,' but also 'redy to serve . . . quhair it sall pleis the king or you to command me . . . for I sall reserwe nathing to my parte bot only my allagence to quene my soverane'.[105] Mary of Guise soon took advantage of Maxwell's offer of ready service and, in February 1551, sent him back to Scotland on a special mission to join Châtelherault and d'Oisel on the Borders, where tensions with England were mounting.

Time would tell how effective patronage would be in securing and maintaining long-term support for the proposed dynastic alliance. Glencairn, for example, was the first magnate of significance to support the Congregation's rebellion openly and militarily in May 1559, and was followed soon after by Argyll and Lord James Stewart. In the meantime, offers of French pensions, titles and offices were eagerly accepted by the Scottish nobles who profited immensely from their position as pawns in the game of European dynastic politics. It was exactly because of their position as pawns that the Scots could afford to change their loyalties if the price was right. If patronage was going to be an effective policy, therefore, it needed to be a continuous and long-term endeavour. The fact that French patronage had pre-dominantly taken the form of annual pensions was one way of providing for this, but actually making these yearly payments was another matter altogether. Lord Home's pension of 2,000 *livres*, for example, was in arrears by 1556.[106] When it had been determined that she would return to Scotland, Mary of Guise was adamant (even to the point of falling out with Henri) that she had with her a considerable sum of money presumably for this purpose.[107] Because of this, her trip to France cannot be seen as a one-off attempt to buy the Scots, but

104 *Scottish Correspondence*, ccxxxvi, pp. 347–8.
105 *Ibid*, ccxxxviii, pp. 349–51.
106 'MSS of the Duke of Athole and Earl of Home', *HMC Twelfth Report*, Appendix viii, p.184.
107 *CSP Foreign, 1547–1553*, 305, 341, pp. 79, 103.

rather as the continuation of a policy that had been implemented since 1548 and would continue after 1551.

But could the distribution of patronage alone, or a trip whereby a select group of Scots were exposed to the splendours of France, ensure the long-term support of the Scots to the French cause or guarantee that the Franco-Scottish union of the crowns would become a reality? What was also needed in Scotland was an administration that was willing not only to promote, but to act in the interests of France and, more importantly, secure the marriage of Mary, Queen of Scots to the Dauphin. It was questionable whether Châtelherault could be relied upon to act in such a capacity. Matters pertaining to the government of Scotland, therefore, were of extreme importance to Henri if his imperial objectives had any chance of being realised. In this respect Mary of Guise's trip to France might better be regarded as a 'brainstorming' rather than a 'brainwashing' expedition. Now that the Anglo-Scottish hostilities had ceased, it was necessary not only to decide on French policy in Scotland , but also to determine who was best able to implement it.

* * *

By early September 1550 it was clear that Scottish affairs of state were going to be a major topic of discussion with the arrival of Mary of Guise in France. When asked about the liberation of the Scots who had been taken at the siege of St. Andrews Castle (30 July 1547),[108] Henri responded that 'he would defer the question of their full liberty till the arrival of the Queen Dowager, when that and all matters connected with Scotland should be adjusted'.[109] There was much

108 E. Bonner, 'The Recovery of St. Andrews Castle in 1547: French Naval Policy and Diplomacy in the British Isles', *EHR*, cxi (June 1996), pp. 578–98; C. Edington, 'John Knox and the Castilians: A Crucible of Reforming Opinion?', in R.A. Mason (ed.), *John Knox and the British Reformations* (Aldershot, 1998), pp. 29–50.

109 *CSP Foreign, 1547–1553*, 238, p.55. At the urging of Mary of Guise, Henri released the 'Castilians' who had been transported to prison in France on 7 July 1550. In the words of Knox, they were shortly thereafter 'called to Scotland, thare peax proclamed, and thei thame selfis restored to thare landis, in dyspite of thare ennemies. And that was done in hatterent of the Duck, becaus that then France begane to thrist to have the regiment of Scotland in thare awin handis . . . Thare rested a number of commoun servandis yitt in the galayes, who war all delivered upoun the contract of peace that was maid betuix France and England, after the tackin of Bullon [Boulogne]; and so was the haill cumpany sett at libertie'. Knox, *Works*, I, p.233 and *History*, I, p.111. The release of all the hostages and prisoners was a lengthy process and, although the treaty of Boulogne had stipulated their liberation, it was still an issue that had to be specifically addressed in the negotiations for the Anglo-Scottish treaty of Norham. For additional references to the release of the 'Castilians' at this time, see *CSP Foreign, 1547–1553*, 215, 221, 224, 314, pp. 48, 50–1, 83–4; *APC*, III, pp. 95, 205; and Jordan, *Chronicle*, p.38.

'adjustment' needed with respect to Scotland. Châtelherault had agreed to resign his regency when Mary, Queen of Scots reached her age of majority, and the question at hand was who was going to replace him and, as it would later emerge, when. The question of government in Scotland, therefore, was the subject of intense debate during Guise's visit as, indeed, she had expected it to be.[110] Henri and his ministers had been eager to hear Guise's thoughts and proposals on the matter as early as May 1550. In his flattering letter to Guise, Montmorency wrote:

> Quant au surplus des affaires dela [Scotland], il est
> impossible de mieulx les acheminer que vous faictes, dont
> ledict Seigneur [Henri] a grant contentement, les voyant
> disposees pour venir au poinct qu'il desire et s'asseure qu,
> avant vostre partement de la pour venir icy, vous y
> pourvoyerex de sorte que vous en serez tous deux en
> repos; . . . M'asseurant que au retour de Sieur de Bresze,
> mous scaurons la deliberation que vous aurez sur ce prinse
> [As to the rest of the affairs there, it is impossible to handle
> them better than you do, with which the said Lord is greatly
> content, seeing them so organised that he wants and trusts
> that, before you leave from there to come here, you will see
> to it so that you will both put your mind at rest; . . . trusting
> that once Sieur de Brézé is back, we will know your decision
> concerning that matter].[111]

Whether Guise's proposals included standing for the regency herself is unknown, but the matter soon became the subject of great debate in France.

According to Lesley, discussions pertaining to the government of Scotland took place at Blois, where the French Court, including 'the Quene of Scotlande and the Quene douarier hir moder, and the nobill men of Scotlande', took up residence for the winter season after Henri's entry into Chartres on 20 November 1550.[112] At this time, Lesley contends that:

> the Quene douarier did oppin the caus of hir cuming into
> France to the King and his secreit counsallouris, be the
> adwyse of the duike of Guise and Cardinall of Lorane hir
> brethir, principallie for advancing of hir to the goverement

110 *CSP Foreign, 1547–1553*, 255, p.61.
111 *Balcarres Papers*, II, li, pp. 70–1.
112 Lesley, *History*, pp. 236–7; McKerlie, *Mary of Guise-Lorraine*, pp. 146–7.

of the realme of Scotland, quhilk was thocht verrey guid, and
approved by the King and his counsall, quha referrit the
ordering and dres of the hoill matter principallie to the
Quene hir self, specialie quhat was to be observed to draw
the governement of the realme furth of the Duik of
Chattillirailt handis without ony tumult.[113]

At Caudebec on 3 November 1550, Sir John Mason reported that
there had been 'great consolation [sic] as to Scotland, the French
desiring to keep the Queen Dowager in France, and to appoint a
Frenchman there, to which the Scots will not agree'.[114] Clearly, Mary
of Guise was not the prime candidate to succeed Châtelherault as
Regent, nor was it she to whom the idea of a French gentleman acting
as viceroy was anathema – it was opposed by the Scots themselves. The
Scottish political élite's preference for Mary of Guise may be owing to
the fact that they had recently looked to her, and not Châtelherault,
for the 'execution of justice and [the] ordouring of the cuntre'.[115] But
it probably had more to do with the fact that Mary, Queen of Scots'
majority would witness an unprecendented situation in Scotland.
Never before had there been a need for a permanent Regent, whose
tenure of office in an absentee monarchy would be unlimited and
whose position, therefore, would assume far more political and regal
significance than that of previous Regents. As Queen Dowager and
Queen Mother, Mary of Guise was a familiar and respected figure in
Scotland, who had also established herself in recent years as a direct
channel to the resources of France.

Mary of Guise's political acumen had, similarly, not gone unnoticed
in France. Upon his arrival in Scotland, for example, the French
captain M. de la Chapelle de Biron commented that:

> . . . sans le bon ordre et conduicte que y mect la Royne le
> tout yroit mal. Maiz en ma vie ne congeux prince ne
> princesse, veu ces affaires, s'i scavoir mieulx gouverner. Elle

---

113 Lesley, *History*, p.237. Similarly, Lindsay contends that Guise lobbied for
   the government of the realm, 'because scho saw the realme nocht weill
   gydit at that tyme, ffor scho saw nothing bot awarice and gredienes in
   the place of Iustice, nor nothing sought ffor the weillfair of the realme
   nor for the profeit of hir dochter that was to succeid thairto. The king of
   France and consall heirand this grantit immedeatlie to hir desyre, that is
   to say [to] be regent of Scotland and he to tak on him to satisfie the
   governour ffor his goode will and tyttill thairof and that he did schortlie'.
   Pitscottie, *Historie*, II, pp. 112–3.
114 *CSP Foreign, 1547–1553*, 255, p.61.
115 *RPC*, I, p.90.

est bien aymee en ce pays et y a beaucoup de gentilzhommes qui m'ont dict que, si se n'estoit pour l'amour d'elle, ne feroient aucune chose pour monsieur le Gouverneur [without the good order and leadership established here by the Queen, everything would go wrong. But, in my life, I have never know either a prince or princess who knows how to govern better. She is well liked in this country and has many gentlemen here who told me that were it not for their liking for her, they would do nothing for the Governor].[116]

From a French perspective, Guise dynastic ambition was synonymous with Henri's imperial objectives. This, in addition to Mary of Guise's maternal dynastic instincts – to protect and advance Mary, Queen of Scots' rights and claims – would ensure that the Queen Dowager would serve French interests if she returned to Scotland. The Scots' apparent preference for Mary of Guise, moreover, would theoretically render them more amenable to the implementation of Franco-centric policies by her as opposed to a French stranger, who might be seen as an adverse symbol of French hegemony. This was something d'Oisel had come to understand first hand. Despite having been 'left in charge' by Henri during the Queen Dowager's absence, d'Oisel considered the return of Guise to be imperative for the ultimate success of Henri's objectives.[117] Guise's absence, he declared, 'will not bear any fruit at all but, on the contrary, will be highly prejudicial to the interests of the King and her own, which are the same thing'.[118] For all parties concerned, therefore, Mary of Guise emerged as the best candidate to return to Scotland to assume the regency from Châtelherault. Yet, there were still inherent problems with Mary of Guise's candidacy. She would be open to criticism, and potential opposition, simply because she was French, and the fact that she was to govern during her daughter's majority in an almost viceregal capacity meant that feathers would be ruffled amongst Scotland's ruling élite – not least because she was a woman. But given the alternatives, she was still the best choice – if only because she was the lesser of two evils by far.

The decision surrounding Mary of Guise's return to Scotland was probably made at Blois in February 1551. On 23 February, Sir John Mason reported disparagingly that:

116 Teulet, *Papiers*, I, pp. 659–60. For similar comments on Guise's management of Scottish affairs, see *Balcarres Papers*, I, cxxxv, cxlv, lxiii, pp. 179, 188–9, 239 and II, li, pp. 70–1; and *Maitland Misc.*, I, 4, pp. 214–5.
117 *Balcarres Papers*, II, xlix, p.66; *CSP Spain*, X, p.339.
118 *Balcarres Papers*, II, lvii, p.79.

The Scottish Queen desireth as much our subversion, if it lay
in her power, as she desireth the preservation of herself,
whose service in Scotland is so highly taken here, as she is in
this Court made a goddess. Mons. de Guise and M. d'Aumale,
and the Cardinal of Lorraine, partly at her egging, and partly
upon an ambitious desire to make their house great, be no
hindrance of her malicious desire.[119]

Such noteworthy praise had not been afforded to Guise since her
arrival in France, and the fact that Mason felt it necessary to comment
on it, albeit negatively, meant that something was afoot. Mary of Guise,
however, refused to return to Scotland without some form of personal
compensation and a guarantee that her administration would be
supported financially by Henri. So, in March 1551, Guise received
an annual pension of 50,000 *francs* for the maintenance of her estate,
and 50,000 *francs* 'more to bestow as she shall see cause'.[120] But, by
May, things had started to go wrong. It was almost with glee that Sir
John Mason reported that 'The Dowager of Scotland maketh all this
Court weary of her, from the high to the low, such an importunate
beggar she is for herself and her chosen friends. The King would fain
be rid of her'.[121] The cause of this ill feeling was money. Henri wanted
Guise to return to Scotland 'upon a promise of payment', while the
Queen Dowager insisted that she 'have the money with her'.[122] Guise
knew all too well the importance of money in procuring and retaining
the support of the Scots. She was astute enough to realise that the
mere promise of money would have a limiting effect in achieving her
dynastic and political objectives, let alone pay the annual instalments
of the French pensions she and Henri had been so free in distributing
throughout 1548 and 1549.[123]

Despite the wishful thinking of Sir John Mason, the spat between
Henri and Mary of Guise did not result in a permanent rift.[124] The
Queen Dowager and her Scottish entourage remained the honoured

119 *CSP Foreign, 1547–1553*, 295, p.75.
120 18 March 1551, *ibid*, 305, p.79.
121 *Ibid*, 341, p.103.
122 *Ibid*, 341, p.103.
123 NLS, MSS.2991, fos. 67ᵛ, 78ᵛ; *Fourquevaux Mission*, pp. 18, 36.
124 Mary of Guise's trip to France is an area that requires much more
    investigation, especially in French archives. The sources I have consulted
    for this book do not reveal whether Guise actually left with the promised
    50,000 *francs* or not. In the French King's accounts for 1554 it is recorded
    that an annual payment of 60,000 *livres* was granted 'to the Queen of
    Scots', but it is unclear whether this is a reference to Mary, Queen of Scots
    or her mother. Bouillé, *Ducs de Guise*, II, Appendix vi, p.592.

guests of Henri and spent the following spring and summer travelling around France with the Court, visiting such places as Tours, Angers and Nantes.[125] Only at the end of her sojourn did Guise part company with Henri so that she could visit her family at Joinville before she embarked on her journey back to Scotland in September 1551.[126]

* * *

While Mary of Guise's return to France had been a time of joyous celebration, her return to Scotland was marred by personal tragedy. No sooner had an assassination plot been uncovered to poison Mary, Queen of Scots in April 1551, than Guise's son fell grievously ill.[127] Fortunately, François had been escorting his mother to Dieppe when he became sick, and Mary was able to care for him personally at Amiens. However, her personal ministrations and bedside vigil could not save her son – François died in her arms that September.[128] Despite her grief and personal loss, Mary of Guise had committed herself to rule Scotland on her daughter's behalf and she had no choice but to leave France and her family. Almost immediately following François' internment, Mary made her way to Dieppe to await passage across the Channel to England.

The decision to return to Scotland through England was a shrewd political move by the Queen Dowager – though reports of Flemish ships along the coast and the desire to avoid a long and potentially rough sea voyage also made this decision a practical one.[129] A 'state' visit through England would provide her with an ideal opportunity to launch her political campaign officially and promote herself as a force on the international stage. Her visit also served the interests of France. The Habsburg-Valois rivalry was on the verge of erupting into a full-scale war in Italy, and Henri was particularly concerned to maintain favourable Anglo-French relations in the hope that England would remain a neutral party in the conflict.

Landing at Portsmouth on 22 October 1551, Mary of Guise officially began her royal progress through England.[130] As in France, she was honourably received and lavishly entertained by

---

125 Lesley, *History*, p.239.
126 *CSP Foreign, 1547–1553*, 449, p.174; *APC*, III, pp. 364, 397; Jordan, *Chronicle*, pp. 80, 84, 89; Lesley, *History*, pp. 239–40.
127 Teulet, *Papiers*, I, pp. 249–60 and *Relations*, I, pp. 260–70; *CSP Foreign, 1547–1553*, 332, 371, pp. 97–8, 121; Jordan, *Chronicle*, p.62. For more on his plot to poison the Queen, see Merriman, 'James Henrisoun', pp. 100–1
128 NLS, Adv.MSS, 29.2.1, f.90; Marshall, *Mary of Guise*, pp. 191–2.
129 Pimodan, *La Mère des Guises*, p.143.
130 *CSP Foreign, 1547–1553*, 477, pp. 190–1; Jordan, *Chronicle*, p.89.

the flower of the English nobility. Upon hearing that she had arrived, Edward VI immediately issued orders for the 'honourable entertainment' of the Queen Dowager, who was not only to be greeted by members of English nobility, but escorted all the way to the Border.[131] The likes of the Dukes of Northumberland and Suffolk, the Earls of Warwick and Wiltshire, the Marquis and Marchioness of Northampton, the Countess of Lennox and a plethora of other ladies and gentlemen were all on hand to welcome Guise who, on 4 November, 'was most honourably and princely received and welcomed by the King's Majesty' at Westminster.[132] That evening, she dined with Edward, who took great pains to record the most banal details of the banquet, down to the serving staff and number of sewers (two).[133] 'After dinner, when she had heard some music,' Edward noted that he then 'brought her to the hall and so she went away' – but not before receiving a diamond ring and two nags as a gift from the king the next day. Unfortunately, Edward's journal gives no indication of whether affairs of state were discussed, but based on the elaborate reception Mary of Guise received throughout her journey, and the composition of the party which escorted her from Portsmouth to Berwick, the Queen Dowager was deemed a very important guest.

Mary of Guise finally returned to Scotland in late 1551. Met by the Earl of Bothwell, Lord Home 'and utheris barronis apoun the bordouris', she was immediately conveyed to Edinburgh, 'quhair the Governour receaved hir with gret honour and fawour'.[134] But for Châtelherault, the return of the Queen Dowager was anything but a cause for celebration; it marked the beginning of the end of his political career. Rumours had already begun to circulate that measures were being taken in France 'to prevein the tyme of the governouris office afore the quenis cuming to perfite age'.[135] Although Châtelherault denounced such rumours publicly, the fact that he felt it necessary to remind Henri and Guise of their 'promis and appoyntment' indicates a man on the defensive.[136] This is further substantiated by his intention to send 'the Abbé [de Villouin] towards his Majesty, to ascertain his intentions regarding the administration of the

131 BL, Harley MSS, 290.2, fos. 6–8; *CSP Foreign, 1547–1553*, 477, pp. 190–1; Jordan, *Chronicle*, pp. 89–94.
132 *CSP Foreign, 1547–1553*, 477, pp. 190–1.
133 Jordan, *Chronicle*, pp. 93–4.
134 Lesley, *History*, pp. 240–1.
135 *Scottish Correspondence*, ccxxxiv, p.344; *CSP Spain*, X, pp. 339–40.
136 *Scottish Correspondence*, ccxxxiv, p.345.

country after the Queen's minority expires'.[137] While the return of Mary of Guise clearly revealed who was designated to succeed Châtelherault as Regent, it was less clear when this transfer of power would actually occur, as Mary, Queen of Scots' 'perfect age' was conveniently brought into question by the French. But reports that Châtelherault had openly declared that 'while he lived there should be no other Regent in Scotland than he', indicated that it was not only a question of when, but if Châtelherault would resign as regent at all.[138]

The Parlement of Paris considered Mary, Queen of Scots' age of majority at the request of the French King.[139] Specifically, Henri wanted to know whether it was during or upon completion of her twelfth year. After examining many historical and legal precedents, the Parlement of Paris determined that at any time *during* her twelfth year, Mary, Queen of Scots could officially assume control of the government of Scotland, and her kingdom be 'administered by the advice and counsel of such people who will be chosen to that end according to King's good pleasure'.[140] With this piece of legislation behind him, Henri could insist that Mary of Guise assume the regency as early as 8 December 1553, the date of her daughter's eleventh birthday and one year earlier than Châtelherault's anticipated date of resignation. But the question of when Guise should actually assume the regency remained a matter of great debate at the French Court.[141] In d'Oisel's opinion, Henri and Guise's brothers were 'rather too enthusiastic to realise and promote the task in question'.[142] The Cardinal de Lorraine, in particular, seems to have been pushing

---

137 *CSP Spain*, X, p.585. In response to this news, Mary of Guise advised Châtelherault to 'put off the Abbé de Villouin's journey until a more suitable season', while d'Oisel reminded him that it was his duty 'to endeavour to enable his Majesty to rest secure and tranquil. In the meantime he might be sure he would have to do with a King so good, sincere and virtuous that as long as the Regent should serve him and the Queen Dowager loyally, he might confidently look forward to great favour and advancement'. If Châtelherault persisted, Guise and d'Oisel assured Henri that they would do their best to dissuade him and/or delay Villouin's departure in order to give the King time to act accordingly. This report, dated at Falkland, 6 October 1552, was intercepted by the Imperialists. *Ibid*, X, pp. 586–7.

138 *Ibid*, X, p.586.

139 Teulet, *Papiers*, I, pp. 261–6 and *Relations*, I, pp. 274–8.

140 Teulet, *Papiers*, I, p.261 and *Relations*, I, p.274.

141 8 August 1553, *Balcarres Papers*, II, Appendix A, pp. 302–6.

142 *Ibid*, II, p.304. The Guise were in a position to push for their sister's advance because of the Duc de Guise's recent military victory in capturing the Three Bishoprics of Lorraine (Metz, Toul and Verdun) for the French King.

hardest for his sister to assume the regency during Mary, Queen of Scots' eleventh year. Because of 'the Governor's ill-will towards her', the Cardinal argued that Châtelherault should be deposed immediately before he had the chance to fortify himself with friends.[143] D'Oisel disagreed and the matter was ultimately left to Guise's discretion, who was to report on Châtelherault's activities so that Henri and his ministers could better assess the situation and supply her with reinforcements if necessary.[144]

Mary of Guise duly complied and sent two reports, prompting Henri and his ministers to meet once again to discuss the timing of the Queen Dowager's assumption of the regency.[145] By 30 November 1553 the decision to proceed had been made. Montmorency wrote to Mary of Guise that 'as I see it, now is the appropriate time and opportunity to see through what we have been waiting and hoping for so much'.[146] The decision to act had no doubt been prompted by Guise's suspicion that Châtelherault was intriguing with the English to prevent her from assuming the reins of power. Voicing her suspicions to the French ambassador in England, Sr. de Noailles, Mary wrote that '. . . the Commissioners sent by our Governor to solve the affairs concerning our borders are negotiating well. Yet I find their stay too long which makes me suspect some intrigue, thus I will hasten to know the truth'.[147] The Queen Dowager now shared her brother's belief that Châtelherault must be removed from power as soon as possible.

So, just four days after Mary, Queen of Scots' eleventh birthday, Henri wrote to Châtelherault informing him that 'my daughter has come of age this present month of December to enjoy these her rights and also to take control here over the [administration] and government of the said Kingdom [Scotland]'.[148] Thanking him for his good works as Regent, which has been to the satisfaction of the Queen, 'my little daughter,' Henri hoped Châtelherault would be content with Mary's recommendation that he be 'lieutenant general under the said lady, her mother Regent', and with his own offers that d'Oisel was to present on his behalf.[149] Unsurprisingly, Henri's offers were largely designed to appeal to Châtelherault's greed.

On 19 February 1554 Châtelherault formally agreed to resign the

143 *Balcarres Papers*, II, Appendix A, p.304.
144 *Ibid*, II, pp. 304–5.
145 31 October 1553, *ibid*, II, cxx, pp. 174–6. Mary of Guise's reports were dated 15 September and 25 September 1553.
146 30 November 1553, *ibid*, II, cxxv, pp. 181–2.
147 AÉ, *Cor. Pol.*, Angleterre, XII, fos. 123^r, 108, 139.
148 12 December 1553, NLS, Adv.MSS, 33.1.9, f.1^r.
149 *Ibid*, 33.1.9, f.1^{r-v}.

regency in favour of Mary of Guise.[150] In a private contract with Guise, Châtelherault was promised all monies owing to the crown and a discharge of all goods intromitted since the death of James V. His position as second person in the realm was guaranteed in the event that Mary, Queen of Scots should die without issue, in which event it was promised that all the castles and forts in French possession would be returned and the Hamilton claim to the Scottish succession safeguarded. Châtelherault was also absolved from 'ony maner of cryme of quhatsumevir gretnis' during his regency and was to receive a formal declaration that he had faithfully performed his duty as regent in Parliament. For his part, Châtelherault agreed that his resignation of the regency was 'of his awin free will' and that Edinburgh Castle would be immediately handed over to Lord Erskine for the use of Mary of Guise.[151]

Securing Châtelherault's capitulation, however, had been a gruelling task for d'Oisel, who reported that it took two days to reach a settlement that even resembled 'the intention of the King'. But, 'with the help of God, this Princess' [Mary of Guise] leadership, and also the fact that the said Governor has seen and knows all the Lords of this Kingdom, both spiritual and temporal, who accompany us here and remain firm and steadfast, we have finally won the victory to the great regret of the said Governor'.[152] The true extent of France's victory was realised on Thursday, 12 April 1554 when Mary of Guise was formally invested in the office of regent.[153] Following the ceremonial resignation of Châtelherault, the transfer of power was completed when d'Oisel placed the crown of Scotland on the Queen Dowager's head and handed her the sceptre and sword of state.[154]

* * *

As in matters of diplomacy and military security, Henri's protectorate of Scotland enabled him to control Scotland's government. His appointment of Mary of Guise to the regency effectively completed the process of establishing French power in Scotland, which was to be

---

150 *ADCP*, pp. 630–2. See also *ibid*, pp. 629–30, for the Three Estates' bond with Châtelherault, registered at Edinburgh, 20 February 1554, stipulating the terms of his resignation.

151 On 5 March 1554 d'Oisel reported that Edinburgh Castle had been delivered as promised on 3 February 1554. AÉ, *Cor. Pol.*, Angleterre, IX, fos. 273, 277 and XII, f.322.

152 21 February 1554, *ibid*, XII, fos. 321–2, 333 and IX, f.258.

153 *Ibid*, XII, f.379. See *Balcarres Papers*, II, cxxxvii, cxxxix, cxl, pp. 200–7, for letters of congratulation from Guise's mother, Antoinette de Bourbon, and her brothers, the Cardinal de Lorraine and Duc de Guise.

154 Marshall, *Mary of Guise*, p.198; AÉ, *Cor. Pol.*, Angleterre, XII, f.379.

consolidated by the marriage of Mary Stewart to François Valois four years later. It should not necessarily be presumed, however, that Mary of Guise always aspired to become regent. Had it not been for her past political experiences in Scotland and the Scots' professed affection for her, there is a very real possibility that Mary of Guise would not have returned to Scotland at all in 1551. But the integral role she *did* play in securing French military and financial intervention and Scottish support for the proposed dynastic alliance, most notably through the effective distribution of patronage, had rendered her the best candidate to ensure that the interests of France would be served in Scotland, and the best candidate in the eyes of many Scots. Mary of Guise's assumption of the regency, 'to the great satisfaction of all the Estates', was crucial to the realisation of Guise dynastic ambition and, more importantly, Henri's vision of a Franco-British empire.[155] This sentiment was summed up by Noailles, who, in wishing Mary of Guise good fortune during her regency, hoped that her new government would be so strong that 'I may be able to see the whole island obedient to you soon'.[156] But as we shall see, Mary of Guise's administration would be continually affected by the international scene and, in particular, by events in England – no more so than during the reign of Mary Tudor.

155 AÉ, *Cor. Pol.*, Angleterre, XII, f.398.
156 Noailles to Mary of Guise, 27 April 1554, *ibid*, IX, f.321.

4

In Defence of the Realm: Mary
Tudor and the Anglo-Imperial Threat

The accession of Mary Tudor in 1553 and her subsequent marriage to Philip of Spain (the future Philip II) in 1554 inaugurated a period of renewed tension and intense suspicion between the 'auld enemies'. Through the forging of dynastic alliances England and Scotland had become inextricably, although not officially, involved in the Habsburg-Valois conflict which now met head-to-head on the Anglo-Scottish Border. The struggle for power on the Continent had now evolved into a quest for supremacy in the British Isles. On a more immediate level, fears of an Anglo-Imperial invasion of 'Valois' Scotland dictated that matters of defence become a top priority – especially on the Borders. Throughout Mary Tudor's reign, therefore, matters of national security assumed great significance and became the predominant concern for Mary of Guise.

* * *

Mary Tudor's overthrow of Lady Jane Grey as Queen of England in July 1553 was a political, dynastic and imperial disaster for Henri II. As the cousin of Charles V, Mary Tudor's natural affinity with the Habsburgs made the prospect of an Anglo-Imperial alliance a very real possibility. In such a situation the best Henri could hope for was England's neutrality in the Habsburg-Valois conflict. When rumours began to circulate that a marriage with Philip of Spain was on the cards for the English Queen, however, Henri's hopes quickly diminished. The prospect of an Anglo-Imperial dynastic alliance would mean complete encirclement by the enemy. As the French Ambassador resident in England, Antoine de Noailles, foresaw, this scenario spelled certain disaster for France. Henri would be engaged in a simultaneous and perpetual war with both his traditional enemies.[1]

---

1 On 6/7 September 1553 Noailles wrote to Henri that, 'la chose me semble estre d'une extreme importance, estimant que ce soit pour vous et les vostres une perpetuelle guerre estans tous vos anciens et presens ennemis joincts ensemble pour estre aprez si fortz [the affair seems to me to be extremely important, thinking that it would be a perpetual war for you and your men as all your former and current enemies would be united together to be strong enough afterwards]'. AÉ, *Cor. Pol.*, Angleterre, XII, fos. 61^r-2^v; L'Abbé de Vertot, *Ambassades de MM. de Noailles en Angleterre* (Leiden, 1763), II, pp. 144–5.

But the potential military force that an Anglo-Imperial alliance could muster was not the only way in which Mary Tudor's accession and marriage to Philip threatened France. From a dynastic point of view, it also prevented the immediate realisation of Henri's vision of a Franco-British Empire.

The imperial opportunities that the Franco-Scottish alliance afforded Henri were the cause of great concern at the Imperial Court, at no time more so than on the eve of Edward VI's death and during the short reign of Queen Jane. When, in the spring of 1553, it was clear that Edward was not going to survive his latest bout of pulmonary tuberculosis, steps were taken to prevent his Catholic half-sister, Mary, from succeeding to the throne. There was just one snag: to do so would directly contravene the terms of Henry VIII's 'Third Act of Succession'. To overcome this constitutional obstacle, the order of succession was dictated in a 'device for the succession'.[2] Bypassing the Tudor line in favour of the Suffolks, the descendants of Henry VIII's *younger* sister, Mary, Edward stipulated that the succession would pass to 'the Lady Fraunceses heires masles, if she haue any such issu befor my death', and then to 'the Lady Jane'.[3] Because Frances, duchess of Suffolk had no male heirs, her eldest daughter, Lady Jane Grey, officially became Edward's successor. No mention was made of either Mary or Elizabeth Tudor and, on 21 June, letters patent were issued confirming their illegitimacy.[4]

News of the 'Device' sparked alarm in the Imperial camp. It was feared that 'if the Princess [Mary] and Elizabeth are excluded, the King of France may claim a right to the Crown through Scotland' on the grounds that Mary Stewart was a descendant of Henry VIII's *elder* sister, Margaret.[5] If the terms of the 'Device' were upheld and Lady Jane did succeed Edward as Queen of England, the way was then clear for Henri to advance the superior claims of Mary Stewart to the English throne by right of descent. In 1553, therefore, the realisation of Henri's imperial objectives depended on the enthronement and

---

2 Inner Temple, Petyt MSS, 538/47, fos. 317[r-v]; J.G. Nichols (ed.), *The chronicle of Queen Jane and two years of Queen Mary* (Camden Society, 48, 1850), pp. 89–90. The terms of the 'Device' were also included in Edward's last will and testament. I am extremely grateful to Alan Bryson for his help and advice on the 'Device' and the reign of Edward VI as a whole.

3 Inner Temple, Petyt MSS, 538/47, f.317[r].

4 *CSP Spain*, XI, p.82; Guy, *Tudor England*, p.226.

5 *CSP Spain*, XI, pp. 54–5, 98. See also *ibid*, XI, pp. 90, 96–7, 99, 101–2, 104, 115–17, 157, 188, 301–2 for additional reports on the intrigues of France concerning the English succession and the advancement of Mary Stewart's claim.

sustained queenship of Lady Jane Grey. In other words, Henri needed Lady Jane Grey to stay on the throne long enough so that she could then be replaced by Mary, Queen of Scots.

Following the death of Edward VI on 6 July 1553, the Imperial Court was inundated with reports detailing the intrigues of France against Mary Tudor in support of Queen Jane. Charles V was repeatedly warned that the French 'were carrying on intrigues for the purpose of stirring up trouble in England and discord between that kingdom and your Majesty', their object being 'to gain a foothold in England for their own ends and to the advantage of the Queen of Scotland and that of her affianced spouse, the Dauphin of France'.[6] Northumberland's delay in proclaiming Lady Jane as Queen of England, however, would prove disastrous to Henri and any hopes he had for a Franco-British empire at this time.[7] Why Northumberland waited three days before making his announcement is uncertain, but his delay enabled Mary Tudor to rally enough popular and military support to overthrow Queen Jane, bring an abrupt end to her nine-day reign, and quash Henri's imperial ambitions in the process.[8]

Needless to say, Mary's accession was viewed ominously by the French. Protocol, however, dictated that publicly a more favourable reception be given to England's new Queen. Both Henri and Mary of Guise sent letters of commendation, congratulating Mary on her accession and reciprocating her professions of friendship, 'good will and disposition to peace'.[9] But beneath this veneer of amity lay a deep-rooted suspicion that emanated from the dynastic alliances forged by both Queens on the Continent. The threat that Mary Stewart's betrothal to François Valois posed to England's national security, for example, was used by Imperial propagandists to foster support in England for a Spanish marriage.[10] For

6 *CSP Spain*, XI, p.85.
7 Northumberland had also failed to secure Parliamentary support for the 'Device', the legitimacy of which was dubious anyway because it was uncertain whether a minor could make a will let alone determine the succession, and because it was a privilege granted only to Henry VIII in the first 'Act of Succession'. 1534: 25 Henry VIII, c.22, *Statutes of the Realm*, III, pp. 471–4; Loades, *Mary Tudor*, pp. 15–6.
8 Lady Jane Grey was executed on 12 February 1554.
9 *CSP Scot.*, I, 398, p.192; *CSP Foreign, 1553–1558*, 12, 66, pp. 6, 23–4.
10 See, for example, *CSP Spain*, XI, pp. 334–5, 340–1, 409–11. Interestingly, the Franco-Scottish dynastic alliance was also used by those opposed to the Spanish marriage to demonstrate the inherent dangers of a queen regnant marrying a foreigner. Grounds for opposition also lay in the possible reaction of France to the Spanish marriage. Stephen Gardiner, bishop of Winchester, for example, feared that the French would conspire with England's Protestant community to place Elizabeth Tudor on the throne or, in the worst possible scenario, incite them to declare war. *Ibid*, XI, pp. 332–7.

the French, Mary Tudor's determination to wed Philip of Spain was viewed as an inevitable precursor of war. As such, French fears that Scotland would be the obvious target of an Anglo-Imperial invasion prompted Henri to take defensive measures there.

By 7 December 1553 the English Council and the Council of State for the Low Countries had approved the terms of the marriage treaty between Mary and Philip.[11] While Henri 'expressed his pleasure that her Majesty desired a continuance of the amity', his fears that Mary Tudor's marriage would bring Spanish troops to England for the sole purpose of invading Scotland prompted him to take steps to ensure that Scotland was in a state of readiness.[12] D'Oisel, who had been serving in the French campaigns on the Continent,[13] was immediately despatched back to Scotland on a renewed commission to serve as Henri's lieutenant-general.[14] The purpose of his return was the source of much speculation among foreign observers, while the reports simultaneously and deliberately leaked out of the French Court claiming that the Vidâme de Chartres was also being sent to Scotland with a large number of troops, did little to allay suspicions that France itself was preparing for war against England.[15] Although there was nothing behind these rumours, except the hope that they would deter Mary from actively joining the Habsburg-Valois conflict on the side of the Imperialists, one aspect of d'Oisel's commission did concern the militarisation of Scotland. He was to co-ordinate the mobilisation of troops and, with Mary of Guise, ensure that Scotland was prepared to implement the King's will if necessary. It was in expectation of Henri's request for military support that Guise went to Edinburgh in March 1554 to oversee the fortification of its castle and to prepare for the reduction of French troops on the Border should they be required elsewhere.[16]

---

11 *CSP Spain*, XI, pp. 397–8; *CSP Foreign, 1553–1558*, 193, p.77; Loades, *Mary Tudor*, p.73. The Council of State for the Low Countries actually approved the draft treaty on 27 November 1553, two days after it was submitted. For discussions on the marriage negotiations and the Spanish marriage in general, see *ibid*, pp. 57–95, and M.J. Rodríguez-Salgado, *The Changing Face of Empire: Charles V, Philip II and Habsburg Authority, 1551–1559* (Cambridge, 1988), pp. 79–85.
12 *CSP Foreign, 1553–1558*, 66, 131, 144(i), pp. 23–4, 46–7, 55.
13 D'Oisel returned to France in February 1552. *APS*, II, p.489; *CSP Scot.*, I, 389, p.189; *CSP Spain*, XI, pp. 160, 173; AÉ, *Cor. Pol.*, Angleterre, IX, fos. 60–2^r.
14 *CSP Scot.*, I, 402, 403, p.194; *CSP Foreign, 1553–1558*, 115, p.43; AÉ, *Cor. Pol.*, Angleterre, IX, f.112^r.
15 *CSP Foreign, 1553–1558*, 115, 131, 170, pp. 43, 46–7, 55, 58, 66–7; AÉ, *Cor. Pol.*, Angleterre, XII, f.139^r.
16 8 March 1554, *ibid*, IX, f.150^r.

Another reason for d'Oisel's return was to initiate proceedings for the formal transfer of power from Châtelherault to Mary of Guise, arguably Henri's most significant response to Mary Tudor's dynastic policy. As we have already seen, the decision to begin proceedings for Guise's assumption of the regency was made by 30 November 1553, by which time a draft of the marriage treaty between Mary and Philip had been submitted for approval to the respective councils of England and the Low Countries.[17] Although the Spanish marriage was never cited as the specific reason, the timing of this decision cannot be regarded as mere coincidence.[18] Henri's declaration of 12 December 1553 also seems to confirm this. His pronouncement that Mary, Queen of Scots had reached her perfect age came just five days after the English Council approved the terms of the marriage treaty.[19] Given this chain of events, Mary of Guise's assumption of the regency cannot be viewed purely from a Scottish perspective. Taking the wider context of British and European dynastic politics into consideration, it becomes clear that her own accession was a direct response to that of Mary Tudor and the Anglo-Imperial dynastic alliance.

Other events in England also contributed to the sense of urgency surrounding Mary of Guise's assumption of the regency. In October 1553 Noailles reported that the Earl of Lennox was intriguing to secure the government of Scotland for himself.[20] Lennox's strong claim to the Scottish succession naturally made such reports alarming in themselves, but it was his wife's connections in Scotland and England that made this danger all the more immediate. Not only did Margaret Douglas enjoy an extremely privileged position at the English court as Mary Tudor's best friend, but she also had access to Scotland's most powerful magnates through her father, the Earl of Angus. Lennox was not above exploiting his wife's Scottish connections to achieve his political objective. Mary of Guise had been warned that the Countess of Lennox was planning to visit her father in the hope that Angus would then rally support amongst his friends for Lennox's designs in Scotland.[21] Surprisingly, and despite all indications to the contrary, Noailles was certain that the English Queen was not involved in this plot. The Countess of Lennox might very well be the Queen's principal favourite, but such favour did not naturally extend to her husband. Moreover, by

17 *Balcarres Papers*, II, cxxv, pp. 181–2.
18 *Ibid*, II, Appendix A, pp. 302–6; AÉ, *Cor. Pol.*, Angleterre, IX, fos. 150–1 and XII, fos. 192, 221, 252–4.
19 12 December 1553, NLS, Adv.MSS, 33.1.9, f.1^{r}.
20 AÉ, *Cor. Pol.*, Angleterre, XII, fos. 88–9^{r} and IX, f.83.
21 *Ibid*, XII, f.88^{v}.

supporting an enterprise that would inevitably be regarded as an overture of war against the Scots, Mary would be endangering her plans to re-establish Catholicism in England, a priority for both the English Queen and her Chancellor, Stephen Gardiner.[22]

Noailles, however, was naïve in his assumptions. Lennox *was* acting with the consent, and on the advice, of Mary Tudor and her Council.[23] But the fact that Lennox was able to do so was solely down to Mary of Guise, who handed this opportunity to the English on a platter. In her quest to weaken Châtelherault's power base prior to her assumption of the regency, Guise had apparently written to Lennox offering to restore his lands in Scotland 'and show him treatment befitting his rank' in return for his political support against Châtelherault.[24] It was only a matter of time before Guise's letter reached the inner sanctum of the English Court. Queen Mary and her Council subsequently decided that, because of Lennox's particularly strong claim to the Scottish succession, he should:

> draw near to the Scottish border and reply that, if they will treat him better there than in the past, he will very willingly return to his country on account of his natural affection for it and because he does not find himself welcome in England. This he will say in order to have a grievance, and if he is encouraged he will cross over to Scotland and secretly enter into communication with the Regent [Châtelherault] against the Dowager, with a view not only to driving her from the country, but to making himself King if possible and throwing Scottish affairs into confusion. If he is able to do this, the Queen will help him with money to the best of her ability.[25]

It was also hoped that money would be forthcoming from Spain so that Mary 'would be able to follow up the said intrigue, and would make ready to aid your Majesty [Charles V] and his Highness [Philip] against the French'.[26]

The proposed intrigues of Lennox in Scotland may offer some explanation why Henri, the Cardinal de Lorraine and the Duc de Guise were extremely anxious to declare Mary, Queen of Scots of age in her eleventh year. Châtelherault's ill-will towards Mary of Guise was no secret.[27] His

---

22 AÉ, *Cor. Pol.*, Angleterre, XII, f.88ᵛ.
23 Simon Renard to Charles V, 3 April 1554, *CSP Spain*, XII, pp. 204–5.
24 AÉ, *Cor. Pol.*, Angleterre, XII, p.204.
25 *Ibid*, XII, p.204.
26 *CSP Spain*, XII, pp. 204–5.
27 *Balcarres Papers*, II, p.304.

declaration that 'while he lived there should be no other Regent in Scotland than he' fuelled French fears that he would come to some sort of arrangement with the English and/or the Imperialists in order to safeguard his position in Scotland.[28] But it was only when Mary of Guise began to suspect in September 1553 that Châtelherault was indeed dealing with the English that the decision was made to begin proceedings to remove him from power. It is uncertain whether Châtelherault's suspected intrigues involved Lennox at this time. Although the nature of the Hamilton-Lennox rivalry would render such a prospect unlikely, Châtelherault's overriding personal ambition would not have made an alliance with even his arch-enemy impossible if it provided him with the opportunity to retain his power and position in Scotland. As for the Countess of Lennox, she never did make the journey north. After Mary of Guise became Queen Regent in April 1554, the English Queen suddenly found the Countess's presence at Court indispensable.[29] Despite this setback, Lennox never lost sight of his dream to become the 'master' of Scotland. Throughout 1554 and 1555 reports continued to flow out of England detailing his movements and suspected intrigues in Scotland.[30]

In what was fast becoming a game of strike and counter-strike, the marriage treaty between Mary Tudor and Philip of Spain was formally ratified by the English Parliament on 28 April 1554, just weeks after Mary of Guise became Queen Regent.[31] This, together with Philip's arrival in England the following July, meant that the Habsburg-Valois powers now met on the Anglo-Scottish border. A period of increased suspicion and mounting tensions between the 'auld enemies' had begun anew. The predominant concern for both sides was the fear of invasion, and this prompted Henri II, Guise and d'Oisel to implement more tangible defensive measures in Scotland.

In August 1554 all indications suggested that Philip was preparing to launch an attack against Scotland. D'Oisel was worried. Scotland was ill prepared to withstand an invasion, let alone provide Henri with 'good service' should he require it.[32] D'Oisel attributed this specifically to the lack of justice and inadequate defences on the Border which, he argued, provided Philip not only with the opportunity, but also a virtually free passage into Scotland.[33] In this, d'Oisel strongly disagreed

28 CSP Spain, X, p.586; Balcarres Papers, II, p.304; AÉ, Cor. Pol., Angleterre, XII, fos. 108, 123ʳ, 139.
29 Noailles to Mary of Guise, 24 December 1554, ibid, XII, f.108ᵛ.
30 See, for example, ibid, XII, f.206ʳ and IX, fos. 184, 239ᵛ, 335ᵛ-8ʳ.
31 CSP Foreign, 1553–1558, 193, p.77.
32 D'Oisel to Noailles, 22 August 1554, AÉ, Cor. Pol., Angleterre, IX, f.253ʳ.
33 Ibid, IX, f.253ʳ.

with Noailles who was pushing for Scotland's formal entry into the Habsburg-Valois conflict.[34] Scotland's entry would make little difference to the war effort because it could offer little more than the Scots who were already serving in France. Rather, French troops were needed in Scotland to fortify and reduce the Border to good obedience.[35] Fortunately for d'Oisel, the French King still did not think it was necessary for the Scots to declare war against Charles V.

* * *

The Habsburg-Valois conflict had re-erupted on 15 January 1552 when Henri II, having successfully secured an alliance with the German Lutheran Princes of the Holy Roman Empire, felt in a strong enough position to declare war against Charles V.[36] Like his alliance with the Scots, Henri's treaty with Charles' disgruntled Protestant subjects was largely protectoral. In return for financial assistance, the French King was granted the right to possess, govern and protect the Imperial towns of Cambrai, Toul, Metz and Verdun as the defender of German liberties.[37]

Henri's declaration of war, however, seriously threatened the Scoto-Imperial peace contracted at Binche just two weeks earlier. France's comprehension in this treaty placed the Scots in a very precarious position. Did this mean that they, too, were at war with Charles? Henri initially thought so and wrote to the Three Estates asking them 'to declair thame selffis and tak his part according to the tennour of the auld treatys'.[38] But the Scots, war weary from seven long years of

---

34 AÉ, *Cor. Pol.*, Angleterre, IX, fos. 342–3ʳ.

35 *Ibid*, IX, f.343ʳ.

36 Baumgartner, *Henry II*, pp. 146–57; Rodríguez-Salgado, *The Changing Face of Empire*, pp. 41–72; Jean-Daniel Pariset, *Relations entre la France et l'Allemagne au milieu du seizième siècle* (Strasbourg, 1983), pp. 84–114 and 'France et les princes allemands', *Francia*, 10 (1980), pp. 259–81; Cloulas, *Les Guise*, pp. 25–8; R.J. Knecht, *French Renaissance Monarchy: Francis I and Henry II* (London, 1984), pp. 44–5. See also *Balcarres Papers*, II, lxxxi, lxxxiv, lxxxv, xc, xci, xciii, xciv, xcvii, xcviii, cxvii, cxxxix, cliv-vi, clxxvii, pp. 111–3, 115–6, 116–8, 122–4, 124–5, 126–8, 128–9, 131–3, 133–6, 168–70, 203–5, 229–35, 267, for the continuous stream of reports keeping Guise up to date on the progress of the war on the Continent.

37 Baumgartner, *Henry II*, pp. 147–8.

38 *RPC*, I, p.120. See also *Balcarres Papers*, II, lxxvi, pp. 105–6, for Montmorency's letter to Mary of Guise on 31 December 1551: 'vous priant, Madame, donne ordre suivant ce qui vous a este demrnierement escript que voz subjectz et vaisseaulx se mectent en mer pour courir sus et endommaigner ceulx de l'empereur, qui sont et doynent estre vos enemys aussi bien que les nostres [begging you, Madam, to give order as has lately been described to you so that your subjects and vessels set sail to attack and damage the emperor's, who are and must be your enemies as well]'.

hostile relations with England, hoped to convince the French King otherwise by pointing out the 'incommodite [that] may cum to this realm gif the peax with Emperour beis brokin; quhat harme may be done thairthrou to the said Emperour, his enemy; and quhat chargeis his Majestie salbe constranit to entere in to on this side in caise the Emperour put ony greit force to thir seyis'.[39] Yet, despite their reluctance, the Scottish political élite still recognised Henri's ultimate authority as 'protector' of Scotland:

> bot gif alwayis his Majestie persistis and abidis at that poynt, that he will haif decaratioun of weir maid to the Emperour in naim and behalf of this realme, in that cais thair salbe send to the Emperour ane sufficient personaig to gif up the samyn peax, and declair unto him that this realme can nocht remane at freyndschip with him, he standand at inmymite with the said maist Cristin King of France, maist anciant and maist speciale freynd unto the Quenis Grace our Soverane Lady, and this hir realme.[40]

The extent to which Henri's protectorate of Scotland was *not* an exercise in absolute power is demonstrated by the fact that he did take into consideration the feelings of the Scottish political community. In June 1552 Mary of Guise was informed that 'the King does not think that, for the time being, war should be declared between the Scots and the emperor, so that you can live more at ease'.[41] This is not to say, however, that the Scots were not expected to contribute to the war effort in some other way.

In November 1552 the Privy Council issued a stent for 'ane certane number of fitmen be resit and upliftit of this realme, to be send in France for the support of the maist Christinet Kyng'.[42] For every 40 merks of land (including crown, temporal and church lands), one footman was to be raised and 'weill furnischit, cled in new hoise, and ane new doublett of canves at the lest, with a jack of plett, steilbonet, splent slevis, of mailyie of plait, withe ane speir of six elne lang'.[43] Similarly, the burghs were to provide 300 hackbutters adequately furnished with 'powldir flask, morsing hornis, and all uthair geir belanging thairto', the Borders and Lowlands were to raise 400 horsemen, and two ensigns of footmen were to be raised from

39 *RPC*, I, p.120.
40 *Ibid*, I, p.120.
41 *Warrender Papers*, xxix, p.22; *Balcarres Papers*, II, lxxxviii, pp. 120–1.
42 *RPC*, I, pp. 129–31.
43 *Ibid*, I, pp. 129–30.

Huntly's lieutenantry in the Highlands.[44] So eager were some Scots to support Henri's military campaign that a number of those who attended the Convention of Estates at Edinburgh on 12 December 1552 volunteered out of their own 'fre will and benevolence' to raise even more horsemen – albeit at the King's expense. Those who did not attend the Convention were also given the opportunity to show their 'benevolence' to the French cause. They were 'taxt be the remanent to furnis horsmen like as utheris thair nychbouris hes done'.[45] Cassillis was appointed to command the Scottish army on the Continent as Lieutenant-General, while Patrick, lord Ruthven was made 'Coronet of the futmen'.[46]

Despite its reluctance to enter the Habsburg-Valois conflict formally, Scotland's contribution to Henri's military campaign was considerable. Approximately 3,000 Scottish soldiers were sent to fight on the Continent.[47] When Philip of Spain arrived in England, however, circumstances and priorities changed. Rumours that Spanish troops were being sent to Berwick precipitated Henri's decision to redeploy men in Scotland in order to replenish d'Oisel's few remaining French companies and to reinforce the Scots.[48] By the end of February 1555, six bands of 'Scottishe footemen . . . with a force also of dyvers other Frenchemen, bothe fotemen and horssemen', numbering about 3–4,000, had arrived in Scotland.[49]

For d'Oisel, the arrival of reinforcements could not have come soon enough. His commission to place Scotland in a state of readiness had been seriously undermined by the number of men (French and Scottish) committed to the war effort on the Continent. Equally detrimental was the lack of resources to maintain the French soldiers serving in Scotland and the irregularity with which these payments

44 The Privy Council re-issued this order on 6 December 1552. Commissioners were also appointed to oversee the 'rolling' of all the Scottish troops who were being sent to France. RPC, I, pp. 131, 132, 134, 136–7.

45 Ibid, I, pp. 134–5.

46 Ibid, I, p.135. See also ibid, I, pp. 135–6, for a list of 55 other notables who went to serve in France, including Cassillis' brother, Archibald, Sir Hew Kennedy of Girvanmains, Ruthven's brother, James, and the Laird of Kinnaird, who were exempted from any legal proceedings against them during their absence.

47 See also BL, Harley MSS, 353.41, fos. 125–6; AÉ, Cor. Pol., Angleterre, IX, f.61; Balcarres Papers, II, cxvi, pp. 164–8, CSP Spain, XI, pp. 2–3, 5, 13, for additional references to Scots serving in the French campaigns.

48 AÉ, Cor. Pol., Angleterre, IX, fos. 302, 316–8, 320, 329, 332–5, 373; PRO, SP15/7/33; CSP Foreign, 1553–1558, 307, 307i, 316, 356, 356i, pp. 146–7, 151–2, 166; APC, V, pp. 91, 94, 95, 98; CSP Venice, IV, p.12.

49 APC, V, pp. 94, 95; AÉ, Cor. Pol., Angleterre, IX, fos. 325^{v}-6^{r}, 373^{r}.

came from France, if they came at all. The non-arrival of the banker, Timothy Cagnioli, with the 'frainchemans money', for example, forced d'Oisel to find the money elsewhere.[50] Having to borrow money from the Scots was something about which he complained bitterly to Noailles: 'I have damaged and exhausted all my friends' resources trying to secure finances for the maintenance of our troops as well as for all other necessities'.[51] Fortunately, d'Oisel had many 'friends' in Edinburgh and 'nuchtbouris of this toun' who were willing to lend him the money, and from them he received £1,000 'for sik effaris'.[52]

But d'Oisel had no greater friend than Mary of Guise who, once again, was forced to shoulder much of the financial burden involved in the establishment of French power in Scotland while waiting for funds to arrive from France. Although she committed her personal resources to this purpose, such as agreeing to pay the unpaid balance of d'Oisel's loan, she was also now in a position to allocate funds from the public purse as Queen Regent.[53] The French captain, Galliard, for example, received regular payments of £75 from the Lord High Treasurer 'for [the] supporting of certane horsmen Franchmen in Annand',[54] and it was not uncommon for the government to step in and cover the costs of supplying the French troops with bread.[55] The Queen Regent also relied on the private sector to victual the French troops serving in Scotland. Throughout 1555 numerous proclamations were issued to the inhabitants of Lasswade, Musselburgh, Fisherrow, Preston, Inveresk, Dalkeith, Newbattle, Jedburgh and Dunbar, ordering them 'to cause provisioun be maid for thair [the Frenchmen] vivers . . . and to provide thair lugeingis'.[56] Collectively, however, the Scots' greatest contribution went towards Mary of Guise's fort-building and modernising policy.

As with the redeployment of troops in Scotland, the urgency surrounding the construction and fortification of Scotland's strong-

---

50 NAS, SP13/76/61.
51 AÉ, *Cor. Pol.*, Angleterre, IX, f.357ʳ.
52 *Edinburgh Burgh Recs.*, pp. 206–7, 214–5, 215–6. As Michael Lynch points out, Edinburgh's merchants acted as moneylenders to the Crown. This soon became a source of tension within the burgh, as these voluntary loans soon became forced exactions under the threat of imprisonment. Lynch, *Edinburgh and the Reformation*, pp. 71–2.
53 Guise, for instance, granted two other obligations on 16 and 17 May 1555. *Edinburgh Burgh Recs.*, pp. 215, 226.
54 *TA*, X, pp. 241, 263, 265, 268, 270, 272, 275, 277, 281, 284, 287.
55 *Ibid*, X, pp. 287, 295.
56 *Ibid*, X, pp. 281, 291, 297.

holds came in response to Philip of Spain's indisposition to peace in late 1554 and early 1555.[57] In February 1555, Noailles wrote urgently to Mary of Guise and Henri warning them of Scotland's 'impending subservience' at the hands of the Imperialists, if, as the French ambassador suspected, they attacked France and its outposts next season (the summer of 1555).[58] In such an eventuality, the French King's protection of Scotland could not be guaranteed because he would more than likely be preoccupied on the Continent.[59] It was thus imperative that Guise fortify Scotland's strongholds and prepare for war while she still had the time. Edinburgh Castle, 'the heart and best place of the Kingdom', Leith and Dunbar Castle, reportedly in a bad state of repair, were all considered by Noailles to be integral to Scotland's defence.[60] More importantly, these places were ideal locations from which Henri could launch an attack or declare war against England if the need arose.[61]

The English were only too well aware of the advantageous position Henri enjoyed within the archipelago as a result of the establishment of French military power in Scotland. Noailles wrote that, if the English

congoissent quelque grand advantage soit du couste d'Escosse ou de France pour se declairer a la Guerre, Ils ne faudront point de le prendre, mais aussi Je ne fais doubte que silz voyent que les villes de vostre Royaulme qui sont a leur teste & voisines de Calais, soient en bon estat comme Bouloigne, Ardres, Montreuith & Dorlan, Ils se pourront facilement refroidir ayant este aussi Sire pourveu aux affaires d'Escosse, comme il vous a pleu tres bien & prudemment considerer, d'y avoir envoye les souldatz, qui sont comme il s'entend icy desja arrivez & qui ont este cause de mettre ceulx cy en quelque soubcon & jalousie

[know that there is some great advantage [to be gained] either on the Scottish or the French side to declare war, they will not fail to take it; yet I also remain confident that if they see the towns of your kingdom, which they control and are near Calais in good condition, like Boulogne, Ardres,

57 AÉ, *Cor. Pol.*, Angleterre, IX, fos. 302, 316–8, 320, 332–5, 347^r, 370 and XII, fos. 336–7.
58 *Ibid*, IX, f. 370 and XII, fos. 336–7.
59 *Ibid*, IX, f.370^v.
60 *Ibid*, XII, f.337^r.
61 *Ibid*, XII, f.336^v. See also *ibid*, IX, fos. 370, 377–8^r, 398–9 and XII, fos. 306–7; Teulet, *Papiers*, I, p.721; PRO, SP15/7/35.

Montreuil-sur-Mer, and Dorlan, they might easily lose heart,
Sir, having also provided for Scottish affairs, as it has been
very satisfactory to you and was cautiously considered to have
sent soldiers there, who have, as is rumoured here, already
arrived and have been responsible for making them
somewhat suspicious and jealous].[62]

Mary of Guise did not need to be told of the importance of fortifying
her strongholds and securing Scotland's frontiers at this particular
time. Her brother, François, had proffered similar advice even before
Philip arrived in England:

> je scaiche que estes dame pour governer le royaume et
> disposer de toutes choses non seullement en paix mais en
> guerre et y pourveoir ainsi qu'avez bien et saigement faict par
> le passe, suyvant ce qu'il vous a pleu me commander, que le
> temps qui est doulx et paisible requiert que vostre frontiere
> soyt plus forte qu'elle n'a este jusques icy, de sorte que vosv
> voysins ne puissent vous venir veoir si a leur ayse et qu'il y ayt
> quellque place qui les arreste

> [I know that [you] are a lady to rule the country and
> organise everything not only in peacetime but also in wartime
> and to provide for it, as you did well and skilfully in the past,
> following what you were pleased to order me [to do], and
> this sweet and peaceful time calls for your frontier to be
> stronger than what it has been until now so that your
> neighbours will not be able to come and see you so easily
> and that there be some fortresses to stop them].[63]

Having secured some money in January 1555 for this purpose, Mary of
Guise set about repairing, fortifying and victualling Scotland's existing
strongholds and constructing new ones on the Border – the most
notable of which was planned at Kelso.[64] By March 1555, however, the
Kelso enterprise had suffered a serious setback and seemed doomed
to failure. The non-arrival of engineers from France threatened to
ruin it even before it began and prevented essential repairs from
being carried out at Dunbar and Leith. Progress was further hindered

---

62 AÉ, *Cor. Pol.*, Angleterre, XII, fos. 336^v-7^r.

63 27 May 1554, *Balcarres Papers*, II, cl, pp. 220–2.

64 *RPC*, XIV, p.13; *Edinburgh Burgh Recs.*, II, pp. 214–5; *Aberdeen Council
Register*, pp. 209–10, 215–6, 298, 299; PRO, SP15/7/35; *CSP Spain*, XIII,
p.145; Teulet, *Papiers*, I, p.721; AÉ, *Cor. Pol.*, Angleterre, IX, fos. 377–8^r,
398–9.

by the shortage of workmen, whom d'Oisel contended had been promised, but had not yet arrived.[65]

The greatest problem was, and would continue to be, a lack of money to finance the works. D'Oisel was left with the difficult task of trying to explain to his colleagues why significant advances had not been made to place Scotland in a state of surety and good defence. In his letters to Noailles and the Duc de Guise, d'Oisel stressed that while both he and Mary of Guise knew what needed to be done, it was more a question of means than will. Although they had advised that the Queen Regent

... ne laisser perdre une seule heure de temps a bien fortiffier ses places et les munir de vivres, me commandant vous dire, sur ce propos, que selon la puissance et les moyens qu'elle en pourra avoir, elle y fera user de toute l'extreme diligence que faire ce pourra ... Ce que je solliciteray soigneusement et aultant que je congnois en estre besoing; mays nous avons souvent l'argent en ce païs plus a loysir et avec plus de difficulte que on ne pense et que l'occasion d'un tel service, qui est l'advancement des places, ne le requiere. Ce qui procedde entierement des moiens qui n'y sont pas et non de faulte de bonne vollunte en cest endroict.

[should not lose a single hour in strengthening her fortresses well and providing them with victuals, commanding me to say to you, in that case, that according to the strength and means available, she will do so as hastily as she can Which I will carefully encourage for I know it to be necessary; but in this country, we often have money in a more possible manner and with more difficulties than we think of and that the occasion of such a duty, which is the favouring of the fortresses, requires it. This is entirely due to unavailable resources rather than a lack of willingness in that respect].[66]

In the meantime the Queen Regent laboured tirelessly to fortify her daughter's kingdom with what resources she could muster. In March 1555, for instance, Guise was forced to requisition funds for the repair of Inchkeith that d'Oisel hoped would enable him to begin similar work at Dunbar soon after.[67] But with the Three Estates' rejection of

---

65 Teulet, *Papiers*, I, p.721.
66 *Ibid*, I, p.721; AÉ, *Cor. Pol.*, Angleterre, IX, fos. 398–9.
67 Teulet, *Papiers*, I, p.721; PRO, 3/31/22, f.41; *CSP Spain*, XII, p.43.

Guise's tax reassessment scheme in 1556,[68] the delays at Kelso and the extraordinary expenses involved in the maintenance of d'Oisel's standing force of light horse on the Border, all building activity became concentrated on the strongholds at Annan and, in particular, Langholm.[69] Despite these efforts, very little progress had been made by January 1557. Scotland was still ill prepared for war and did not have one 'good fortress to defend itself and withstand a siege'.[70]

But even if the Scots had approved her tax reassessment scheme of May 1556, which would have provided her with emergency funds to finance her defensive policies, Mary of Guise would not have enough troops to garrison the forts she would then have had been able to build. Following the Franco-Imperial truce of Vaucelles in February 1556, the majority of the troops that had been sent to Scotland in 1555 were redeployed on the Continent, leaving Scotland almost destitute of armed forces. Those that did remain were primarily concerned with reducing the Border to obedience and pursuing thieves and rebels. So few were the number of Frenchmen serving in Scotland that the Border was actually garrisoned and policed by an itinerant regiment of light horse and a small number of foot soldiers.[71] So while peace may have come temporarily to the Continent, the Borders still needed to be fortified against England and pacified for domestic tranquillity. The scarcity of armed forces only served to undermine Guise's continual efforts to defend, police and implement good rule on the Border.[72] Contrary to her later reputation, Mary of Guise's government in Scotland was characterised less by French domination than by an inability to implement French policy because of chronic underfunding.

Nevertheless, the presence of French troops on the Border, the little work that was being done on Scotland's strongholds and the discovery of the Kelso enterprise were enough to raise alarm in England and contribute to the mounting tensions and increased

---

68 See Chapter 5.
69 AÉ, *Mémoires et Documents*, Angleterre, XV, fos. 7ʳ⁻ᵛ, 10ᵛ; *Papal Negotiations*, pp. 428–9; LPL, Talbot MSS, 3194, fos. 336–7; *APC*, V, p.280; Colvin, *King's Works*, IV, p.609 *n*.4. In 1556, the work at Langholm cost the crown £453 15s 1d. Up until 1558, this seems to be the only place where a significant amount of money was spent. *TA*, XI, p.409.
70 AÉ, *Mémoires et Documents*, Angleterre, XV, fos. 8ᵛ, 10ᵛ; *Papal Negotiations*, p.429.
71 AÉ, *Mémoires et Documents*, Angleterre, XV, fos. 9ᵛ, 10ʳ⁻11ᵛ; *Papal Negotiations*, p. 430.
72 AÉ, *Mémoires et Documents*, Angleterre, XV, fos. 7ᵛ, 8ᵛ, 9ᵛ, 10ᵛ; *Papal Negotiations*, pp. 428–9.

suspicions that prevailed throughout the period 1554–1556.[73] Philip promised the English Council that for every fort Mary of Guise built on the Border he would build three and forever continue the rumours that the Spanish were being sent to Berwick.[74] Verbal threats such as these were backed up by orders for the interception of all communication passing through England between Scotland and France; the fortification and victualling of Berwick, Wark and Norham; and placing the Border on one hour's notice for the defence of the kingdom.[75] The Border, however, was not Mary Tudor's only concern; she was equally worried about Franco-Scottish intrigues in Ireland.

* * *

Mary Tudor had every reason to be suspicious of French subversive activity. France's alliance with Scotland provided a conduit through which intrigues could be conducted, and ready access to Mary's own discontented subjects to whom her dynastic and religious policies were equally anathema. As a traditional hotbed of unrest, Ireland was the next logical and susceptible target for foreign intrigue, and Mary's accession inaugurated a period of renewed insurgent activity in Ireland and reports that the French King had 'incited them thereto'.[76]

Although Mary had little, if any, concern for Irish political affairs *per se*, the revolts that had accompanied her accession gave rise to her suspicions of French complicity.[77] These suspicions were fuelled by reports that the Irish revolts had involved a number of Scots and by rumours that France was planning an invasion of Ireland. In October and November 1553, two possibly related rumours were circulating to this effect. One concerned the imminent execution of

> a plan conceived some time ago for making an attack on
> Ireland to seize two places that might be converted into two

73 AÉ, *Cor. Pol.*, Angleterre, IX, f.377ʳ; PRO, 3/31/32, f.41; *CSP Spain*, XII, p.43.
74 AÉ, *Cor. Pol.*, Angleterre, IX, f.347ᵛ. See *ibid*, IX, fos. 302, 316, 320, 332 and 342 for references to rumours of Spanish activity on the Border.
75 PRO, SP11/3/31, 12/93/18, LPL, Talbot MSS, 3194, fos. 39, 43 47; *APC*, IV, pp. 397, 411 and V, pp. 6, 7, 14, 15.
76 *CSP Foreign, 1553–1558*, 66, pp. 23–4.
77 C. Brady, 'Court, Castle and Country: the framework of government in Tudor Ireland', in C. Brady & R Gillespie (eds.), *Native and Newcomers: Essays on the making of Irish Colonial Society, 1534–1641*, p.31. Ireland did not even warrant a mention on Mary Tudor's list of political priorities for her administration, but the revolts there, which were being 'kept alive by the French and the Scots', did figure in Simon Renard's list of problems facing the Queen alongside matters of religion and crown magnate relations. *CSP Spain*, XI, p.335.

roomy harbours, able to hold one thousand ships and more. With these ports in their hands, the French might harm England, aid Scotland, and prevent, or at least render difficult, your Majesty's [Charles V] subjects' fisheries, commerce and carrying trade.[78]

The second was that the Grand Prior of France (Guise's younger brother, François) was being sent to Ireland with 60 gentlemen and a great number of soldiers 'to assist the Wild Irish against the Queen' and foster the troubles in Ireland that they themselves had started.[79] Henri took great pains to dispel these rumours and refute the allegations that he was behind the sedition in Ireland. 'As for the incursions of the Scots in Ireland, and the report spread that he incited them thereto', the English Council was informed that the French King 'took God to witness that he never thought of such a thing. For knowing her Majesty's desire of peace with her neighbours, he should do all he could to assist her against such as might go about to molest her'.[80]

Publicly, of course, Mary and her Council never *really* thought that the rumours were true or that Henri was *actually* behind the troubles in Ireland.[81] But the fact that some Scots had been cited as participants in the insurgent activity did raise the question of whether their involvement had been sanctioned by the Scottish government or, given her obvious French connections, were the subversive work of Mary of Guise.

Although Henri was assured that Mary Tudor 'did not believe that these disturbances were done by the privy maintenance of the Scottish rulers, but reckoned such a report to be untruly spread by those light savage people', the French King was nevertheless compelled to defend Guise publicly. The English Queen was reassured that the 'Queen Dowager of Scotland is as glad of her Majesty's accession as any may be, and equally desirous of peace'.[82] As for the Scots who participated in the revolts, blame was specifically attributed to 'les Sauvages', presumably a

78 *CSP Spain*, XI, p.261.
79 AÉ, *Cor. Pol.*, Angleterre, IX, fos. 96, 97^r, X, fos. 114–5^r, 116^r and XII, f.98; *CSP Spain*, XI, pp. 358–9, 401; *CSP Foreign, 1553–1558*, 66, pp. 23–4.
80 *Ibid, 1553–1558*, 66, pp. 23–4. Noailles was also instructed to convey these assurances with haste and proffer a possible explanation for the origin of these rumours – namely that the Grand Prior was actually en route to Malta via Corsica, not Ireland. AÉ, *Cor. Pol.*, Angleterre, IX, fos. 96, 97^r, X, fos. 114–5^r, 116^r and XII, f.103^r. For more on Malta and Corsica, see Tytler, *Edward VI and Mary*, II, pp. 250–3, 255.
81 AÉ, *Cor. Pol.*, Angleterre, XII, fos. 108^r, 114^r.
82 *CSP Foreign, 1553–1558*, 66, pp. 23–4.

reference to the redshanks and gallowglasses of the Western Isles who, as Jane Dawson notes, 'provided the backbone of the fighting forces of the Gaelic chieftains and were the basis of their successful resistance to the English'.[83] But was the activity of these mercenaries an exercise in intrigue and, if so, at whose instigation?

The answer to the first question is more than likely 'No'. The government in Edinburgh had very little control over the mercenary trade to Ireland and even less control over the activities of the MacDonalds there – a situation which the English found completely foreign and incomprehensible. This is not to say that intrigues in Ireland had not been considered. Noailles, for one, strongly advocated a policy of intrigue in Ireland as part of an overall attempt to sway English public opinion against the Tudor-Habsburg dynastic alliance. In October 1553 he suggested to Mary of Guise that, owing to the discontent brewing in certain sectors of English society over Mary Tudor's marital intentions, the time was right to fan the flames of discord in Ireland.[84] There is no evidence to suggest, however, that Guise heeded the French ambassador's advice. Then again, did she really need to when the Scots were already causing the English Queen so much aggravation? All that could be done to allay English fears was to ply Mary with fair words. Reassuring her that the Scots who had travelled to Ireland to participate in the revolts were savages and exiled Scots of bad reputation, it was actually claimed that Mary of Guise wanted them placed in the English Queen's hands so that they would then receive the punishment they deserved.[85]

Similarly, in 1556, Scottish insurgent activity in Ireland was the source of contention between the 'auld enemies'. In November 1555 Archibald Campbell, Master of Argyll and Lord Lorne, led his first independent military expedition to Ireland in order to assist Calvagh O'Donnell in his quest to overthrow his father, Manus O'Donnell of Tyrconnell.[86] On 1

---

83 Dawson, 'Two Kingdoms or Three?', p.115.
84 AÉ, *Cor. Pol.*, Angleterre, XII, f.89[r]. In December 1553, Sir James Croft, former deputy of Ireland (1551–1552) and one of the conspirators behind Wyatt's rebellion, offered 'susciter infinis Troubles en Angleterre et Irlande [to create endless troubles in England and Ireland]' on behalf of the French King. Nothing came of this offer. *Ibid*, XI, f.111[r].
85 *Ibid*, XII, fos. 108[r], 114[r-v].
86 BL, Lansdowne MSS, 155.153, f.374[r]; NLS, Adv.MSS, 34.1.11, f.110[v]; *CSP Scot.*, I, 410, p.196. The 4th Earl of Argyll promised O'Donnell military support in a contract dated 13 July 1555. See J. Mackechnie, 'Treaty Between Argyll and O'Donnell', *Scottish Gaelic Studies*, vii (1953), pp. 94–102; *Highland Papers*, IV, pp. 212–6. I am extremely grateful to Jane Dawson for her advice on this matter and for providing me with some background information on Lord Lorne, who is the subject of her forthcoming work on the 5th Earl of Argyll.

November 1555 Calvagh, Lorne and his expeditionary force of High-land troops invaded Donegal and, together with the MacDonalds, succeeded in capturing Manus O'Donnell, while also taking possession of several castles, killing and imprisoning many Irish subjects, and generally laying waste to an area of approximately 60 square miles.[87] Needless to say, the insurgent activity of such a large number of Scots brought a rapid response from Mary Tudor. Sir Thomas Challoner was immediately sent to Scotland in February 1556 to seek redress from the Queen Regent. He was also commissioned to discover, by whatever means possible, 'what practises they [the Scots] haue with France, and . . . what their meaninge is in the matter of Ireland'.[88]

Challoner's instructions clearly reveal the English government's incredulity that Lord Lorne's expedition was staged without the involvement of the Scottish government. Their suspicions were raised by the fact that Lorne had 'sondrie good vessells well furnished for the warres' *and* 'divers great peeces of ordennce of brasse', which did not seem to be 'the furniture of a comon subiect', but ordnance that was 'more than like to have comen from some greater power than themselues'.[89] Although Mary of Guise was aware of the naval pre-parations being made by Argyll, she did not authorise, sanction or furnish Lord Lorne's expedition to Ireland.[90] On the contrary, Guise tried to stop the expedition by sending explicit instructions to Argyll on 8 October 1555 'nocht to pas in Irland'.[91] Whether Argyll received Guise's instructions too late to prevent his son's departure or whether he simply chose to ignore them is unknown. What this episode does reveal, however, is the lack of control the Scottish government had over the activities of certain Scots in Ireland and Scotland who, more often than not, and despite appearances to the contrary, acted independently of the crown.

* * *

Mary Tudor had every reason to be suspicious of Franco-Scottish intrigues in England as well as Ireland. The complicity of the French in Wyatt's ill-fated rebellion in January-February 1554 was no secret. Both Noailles and d'Oisel had been in communication with the

---

87 BL, Lansdowne MSS, 155.153, f.373[r-v]; NLS, Adv.MSS, 34.1.11, f.110[v]; *CSP Scot.*, I, 410, p.196; *CSP Foreign, 1553–1558*, 486, p.213.

88 See BL, Lansdowne MSS, 155.153, fos. 373–5[r]; NLS, Adv.MSS, 34.1.11, fos. 110–1; and *CSP Foreign, 1553–1558*, 410, p.196, for Challoner's complete set of instructions.

89 BL, Lansdowne MSS, 155.153, f.374[r]; NLS, Adv.MSS, 34.1.11, f.100[v].

90 *TA*, X, p. 287; *RPC*, XIV, p.14. Mary of Guise had commissioned the Earls of Argyll and Atholl to pass into the Western Isles on 27 June 1555.

91 *Ibid*, X, p. 298.

leaders of the conspirators who planned to oppose their Queen's dynastic policy through a series of revolts in Devon, Leicestershire, Kent and the Welsh borders in March 1554.[92] Part of d'Oisel's commission upon returning to Scotland in January 1554 was to reiterate Henri's willingness to back the conspiracy on condition that the rebellion received enough public support to guarantee success.[93] By the time d'Oisel had returned to the archipelago, all indications suggested that public opinion was against the marriage. As early as December 1553 Noailles wrote optimistically to Mary of Guise that 'I think she [Mary Tudor] is more Spanish than English and that she has a long-standing hatred against her own nation, by which she is not deceived at all since her subjects have no best wishes for her'.[94] While the Queen Regent sincerely hoped that the Anglo-Scottish peace would continue, she nevertheless shared the belief that Mary Tudor's marriage to Philip of Spain would prove disastrous. Writing to Noailles in December 1553, Guise commented: 'As for the marriage of your Queen, I cannot think but the country would be very displeased if she gets married abroad, and one will have to see the end of it'.[95] In this, Guise was of the same mind as d'Oisel, the Duc de Guise and the Cardinal de Lorraine, who believed that the Habsburg threat emanating from England could only be countered by a pro-active policy.[96]

92 Edward Courtenay, earl of Devonshire, Sir James Croft, Sir Peter Carew, Sir Edward Rogers and Sir Thomas Wyatt. E.H. Harbison, *Rival Ambassadors at the Court of Queen Mary* (Princeton, 1940), pp. 109–36, especially pp. 120–5; Loades, *Two Tudor Conspiracies* (Cambridge, 1965), pp. 12–88; Wernham, *Before the Armada*, pp. 208–20.

93 On 23 November 1553 Henri instructed d'Oisel that, 'si vous voyez que ce soit a bon essient que leschoses s'eschauffassent et que la dicte Royne se resolvent a prendre pour mary le deict Prince d'Espaigne, aussi qu'il y ait apparence que ledict de Courtenay soit dispose et ait moyen de brouiller les cartes vour pourrez encoures plus asseurement dire que vous estes bien que pour ung si grand bien audit Royaulme [England], Je ne voudrois pas luy desnier ma faveur, ny-aux aultres seigneurs qui cognoissant le mal que cella peut amener a leur Royaulme si vouldroient opposer [if you see that things get truly heated and that the said Queen decides to take the said Prince of Spain as a husband, and also that it seems likely that the said Courtney would be willing and able to confuse the issue, you could assert even more assuredly that you are certain help will come to the Kingdom [England], I would not like to refuse my favour to him nor the other lords, who knowing the evil it would bring to their country would want to oppose it]'. AÉ, *Cor. Pol.*, Angleterre, IX, f.99; Harbison, *Rival Ambassadors*, pp. 115–6.

94 24 December 1553, AÉ, *Cor. Pol.*, Angleterre, IX, f.106; Harbison, *Rival Ambassadors*, p.119.

95 7 December 1553, AÉ, *Cor. Pol.*, Angleterre, XII, f.123^r.

96 *Ibid*, IX, fos. 142, 143, 148, 21, 185.

The aggressive stance that Henri was willing to take in England in November 1553 can be attributed to the influence of Les Guise, who took advantage of Montmorency's sick leave from Court to promote their interventionist policy over the Constable's favoured and precautionary course of action – diplomacy.[97]

It was during his week's sojourn in London that d'Oisel became directly involved in the anti-Marian conspiracy. In an attempt to translate public sentiment into effective action, d'Oisel worked closely with the conspirators and all but promised them that if the enterprise was to go ahead as planned, men, money and munitions would be forthcoming from France.[98] But by the time Henri had finally made the decision to support the English rebels on 26 January 1554, it was too late.[99] When his messenger reached London with the news, the rebellion had already been and gone. Details of the conspiracy had reached the ears of Mary. Reports that she and her Council were working to break up the enterprise forced the conspirators to act prematurely and, as it turned out, unsuccessfully.[100]

The collapse of Wyatt's rebellion on 7 February 1554, however, did nothing to quell anti-Marian sentiment, reduce opposition to the Anglo-Imperial alliance or put an end to French intrigues in England.[101] The English exiles who fled to France to escape persecution continued to plot against Mary and to look to Henri for support in their quest to overthrow the English government by armed insurrection.[102] Fears of armed insurrection and foreign invasion were also kept alive by French intrigues emanating from Scotland.

---

97 AÉ, *Cor. Pol.*, Angleterre, IX, f. 90; Harbison, *Rival Ambassadors*, pp. 115–20.

98 Neither d'Oisel nor Noailles had been authorised to give an official promise of aid at this time. They were simply to encourage the conspirators with the prospect of French military and financial assistance. But according to Croft and Wyatt's confession, d'Oisel had promised them men, money and munitions. AÉ, *Cor. Pol.*, Angleterre, IX, fos. 114–5, 273ᵛ-4; Tytler, *Edward VI and Mary*, II, p.306; Harbison, *Rival Ambassadors*, pp. 122–4.

99 AÉ, *Cor. Pol.*, Angleterre, XII, fos. 156–7ʳ.

100 For details of the rebellion, see *ibid*, IX, f.118 and XII, fos. 167ᵛ-9; Loades, *Mary Tudor*, pp. 81–2; Harbison, *Rival Ambassadors*, pp. 125–36; Wernham, *Before the Armada*, pp. 215–6.

101 See, for example, Noailles' comments to d'Oisel on 21 February 1554 in AÉ, *Cor. Pol.*, Angleterre, XII, fos. 172–3ʳ. Nothing substantial came of these plots. Henry Dudley's plan to lead a revolt in England and, later, to take Calais, was abandoned because details of the plot had been leaked, while Thomas Stafford's invasion of England led only to a brief occupation of Scarborough Castle. Loades, *Two Tudor Conspiracies*, pp. 151–75; Wernham, *Before the Armada*, p.231.

102 Loades, *Two Tudor Conspiracies*, pp. 151–75.

Throughout 1554 various plots were concocted to cause problems for Mary Tudor on the Anglo-Scottish Border. One such conspirator was Mark Antony (Mario Antonio Erzio), a servant of Courtenay, who 'fled' to Scotland in January 1554 on the pretence that he was dissatisfied in his patron's employ.[103] On the face of it, Scotland was a logical place for Antony to flit to because he was married to a Scot, but the fact that he was also one of Noailles' agents and an acquaintance of d'Oisel caused more than one eyebrow to be raised in London.[104] It did not take long before the English Council's suspicions proved correct and reports filtered through that Antony was indeed plotting at Berwick.[105] Contemporaneous with these reports were d'Oisel's own communiqués to Noailles in which he described the practices of a gentleman 'who was a friend of mine and a great ally on the Border' to enlist the services of various English officials, such as Lords Wharton and Dacre.[106] It is quite possible that this particular gentleman was Antony, who was sent by Noailles and used by d'Oisel to rally the support of the gentlemen of the North against the Spanish marriage and 'to help themselves in their cause, to maintain and preserve their freedom, and to avoid carefully falling into that poor servitude which the Emperor and the said Prince [Philip] want to put them'.[107] Orders for Antony's arrest were consequently issued and, by 10 March, he had been captured and scheduled to be interrogated by Dacre.[108] The Council's request that a transcript of Antony's interrogation be returned to them 'with speede' is perhaps indicative of the seriousness with which they viewed the threat that French intrigues posed to Mary's administration on the Anglo-Scottish Border.

Philip's anticipated arrival in England sparked a renewed attempt to stir up trouble on the Border by soliciting the Percys of Northumberland to 'raise ane commotioun and insurrectioun of the leigis of England' against Mary Tudor and her authority.[109] This plot is of particular significance not simply because Scotland served as a conduit for French intrigues in England, but because it was instigated by, and directly involved, the Scots.[110] The principal agent in

103 *CSP Spain*, XII, p.17.
104 AÉ, *Cor. Pol.*, Angleterre, XII, fos. 98^v-9^r.
105 *CSP Spain*, XII, p.17.
106 AÉ, *Cor. Pol.*, Angleterre, IX, fos. 142, 148; Tytler, *Edward VI and Mary*, II, p.307.
107 Noailles to d'Oisel, 22 January 1554, AÉ, *Cor. Pol.*, Angleterre, IX, f.121.
108 *APC*, IV, pp. 382, 408.
109 *RPC*, XIV, p.126.
110 *CSP Spain*, XII, pp. 221–2; *CSP Foreign, 1553–1558*, 199, pp. 80–1; AÉ, *Cor. Pol.*, Angleterre, IX, f.185^v.

this enterprise was a servant of Bothwell, John Pringle. While travelling through England as part of the Bishop of Ross's retinue, Pringle made contact with Henry Percy, a staunch opponent of the Spanish marriage, and offered him 'great pensions, rewards, prerogatives and armed support to start trouble near the Scottish border'.[111] But before anything could come of this association, Pringle was arrested and detained in English custody on 16 April 1554.[112] When it came to pointing the finger and assigning blame, Pringle left no holds barred. The French King, the Queen Regent, d'Oisel, Bothwell and the Bishop of Ross were all named as the chief devisers of the plot, upon whose instructions Pringle claimed he was acting.[113]

For their part, Guise and d'Oisel denied that they 'motionit tresown or conspirasy aganis ony Prince', and implored Mary Tudor to 'haif na sic conssait of ws that we suld haif committit sic chargis to sic as James Hoppringill [Pringle] . . . for he had nowther lettre nor credit of ws to nane within hir realme, and, gif we had bene evill myndit, we culd haif gottin mony hiear consalis to haif set furth the samin nor be this Hoppringill'.[114] Privately they shifted the blame onto Bothwell, whose record of treasonable dealings with England rendered him a less than trustworthy ally. According to d'Oisel, Bothwell was the one who had devised this plot and proposed it to the Queen Regent in the hope that he could weasel his way back into her favour. If he was allowed to return to either Scotland or France, Bothwell assured Guise that he would then have the means to do her service as he was a man who had many friends in the North of England. Naturally Guise's interest was aroused by such talk, but she was determined not to show it in front of Bothwell. Instead, she chose to let him know her long-held opinion of him – that he was a 'weak and indolent man and is not one to organise good intrigues'.[115] It was presumably at this point that Guise took charge of the affair and began working out the finer details of the conspiracy. As for Pringle, he remained in English custody until 14 February 1555, when he was 'delyvered out of the Kinges Benche, and was ordered by the Lords within tenne dayes after his delyverie to tary

---

111 *CSP Spain*, XII, p.221; AÉ, *Cor. Pol.*, Angleterre, IX, f.185ᵛ.
112 *Ibid*, IX, f.165.
113 *CSP Spain*, XII, pp. 221–2; *CSP Foreign, 1553–1558*, 199, pp. 80–1; AÉ, *Cor. Pol.*, IX, Angleterre, f.185ᵛ.
114 *RPC*, XIV, pp. 126–7. Quinten Kennedy, the abbot of Crossraguel and Cassillis' brother, was sent to convey Guise's denial to the English Queen. *Ibid*, XIV, pp.126–7; AÉ, *Cor. Pol.*, Angleterre, IX, fos. 184, 197, 198–9.
115 *Ibid*, IX, f.185ᵛ.

no lenger within the realme, but to departe the same at his further peril'.[116]

Ultimately failing in their objective of preventing the Spanish marriage, Franco-Scottish intrigues succeeded only in heightening the tensions within the archipelago that climaxed in the summer of 1555. Never before during Mary Tudor's reign had Scotland and England been so close to becoming directly involved in the Habsburg-Valois conflict as enemies. What threatened to tip the balance between war and peace, however, had nothing directly to do with either of the Habsburg-Valois powers. Rather, the potential catalyst came from a somewhat surprising source, Christian III of Denmark.

In June and July 1555, reports that great naval and military preparations were being made by the King of Denmark for a descent on Scotland sent shock waves throughout the British Isles. The reason for this widespread alarm was the uncertain purpose of Christian III's naval expedition and, more importantly, whether Scotland or England was the Danish King's intended target.[117] Rumour and supposition gave both sides cause for worry. For the Scots, rumours that Charles V had furnished the Danish King's naval expedition with munition seemed to confirm reports that Scotland was the intended target.[118] The lack of intelligence coming out of France also served to substantiate and fuel Scottish fears. The failure of Henri and Montmorency to respond to the repeated requests of d'Oisel and Noailles for news, particularly with respect to the state of Franco-Danish relations, left them to presume that Christian was no longer observing the peace with France and that Scotland was, indeed, the focus of his attention.[119] As to the purpose of Christian's expedition, Mary of Guise and d'Oisel first thought that he intended to reclaim Orkney and Shetland as Danish territory. If this was indeed the case, the remoteness of these isles and the absence of any armed forces there made them extremely vulnerable and ready for the taking. If, however, the Danish made their descent on St. Andrews or Leith, as later reports suggested,[120] the chances of fending them off

---

116 *APC*, V, p.97; PRO, 3/31/33. Despite the fact that Pringle had also implicated the Bishop of Ross in the conspiracy, the latter escaped with only a warning, 'although such dishonourable dealing might by law have justified the detention of the Bishop'. *CSP Foreign, 1553–1558*, 199, pp. 80–1; *CSP Spain*, XII, p.222.

117 For a brief summary of Scotland and England's diplomatic relations with Denmark, see Merriman, *Rough Wooings*, pp. 171–7.

118 AÉ, *Cor. Pol.*, Angleterre, IX, fos. 468–72.

119 *Ibid*, IX, fos. 468–72, 476^r, 480–1, 482^r, 488^r, 489, 490, 493.

120 *Ibid*, IX, fos. 482^r, 486, 490, 492, 501–2, 503^r; St. Andrews University Library, Special Collections, msDA784.7, ms4347.

with the combined forces of France and Scotland were greatly improved.[121] Although Christian had written to the Queen Regent assuring her that the only purpose of his naval expedition was to suppress piracy round his shores, alarming reports continued to stream in that the Danish army was planning to make a descent on Scotland, and neither Guise nor d'Oisel was prepared to take any chances.[122] A force was assembled and deployed to Shetland and Orkney, where several ships were stationed to act, it was hoped as a deterrent.[123] Steps were also taken to secure and reinforce the Borders. Being 'weill bodin in feir of weir', Mary of Guise ordered two musters to meet at Dumfries in July and August for the purpose of 'repressing the West Bordouris'.[124] So well fortified was Dumfries in the summer of 1555 that even Lord Conyers felt compelled to comment that 'the Danishe fleete shold moch inquier of the state and streneth of this towne'.[125]

The English were similarly unenlightened as to Christian III's real intentions, and just as worried.[126] Another rumour circulating at the time, and one personally favoured by d'Oisel, was that the Danish King intended to use Scotland as a back door to England in order to provide Princess Elizabeth and England's Protestants with military support against Mary and Philip.[127] Once again, the conspicuous absence of any news from France left room for speculation. Could Henri's silence be interpreted as a sign of his complicity?[128] The nature and extent of French intrigues in England left no doubt as to Henri's true feelings for Mary Tudor and, as no word had come from France intimating that the Franco-Danish peace had broken down, Christian's expedition could be

---

121 AÉ, *Cor. Pol.*, Angleterre, IX, f.471[r].
122 12 July 1555, NAS, SP13/77. Noailles wrote to Montmorency that the rumours of a Danish invasion were 'si chaud en Escosse que mesmes la royne regente et ledict Sr DOisel auoient pourveu acequils auoient cognu estre necessaire ne scachant qu penser pour vn temps comme ils ne font encores ainsy que le roy et vous pourrez veoir par la lettre que ledict Sr DOisel men a escrite [so hot in Scotland that even the Queen Regent and the said Sieur d'Oisel had done everything they deemed necessary, not knowing what to think for a while and still do not as the king and you will be able to see, thanks to the letter written to me by the said Sieur d'Oisel]'. AÉ, *Cor. Pol.*, Angleterre, IX, f.493[r].
123 *Ibid*, IX, fos. 480–1; LPL, Talbot MSS, 3194, f.75[r].
124 *RPC*, XIV, pp. 13–4, 162–3; AÉ, *Cor. Pol.*, IX, fos. 501–2, 503[r]; St. Andrews University Library, Special Collections, msDA784.7, ms4347; LPL, Talbot MSS, 3194, f.107; *TA*, X, pp. 259–61; *RSS*, IV, 3038–9, 3155, pp. 534, 557.
125 LPL, Talbot MSS, 3194, f.107.
126 *APC*, V, p.160; LPL, Talbot MSS, 3194, fos. 75[r], 125[r].
127 AÉ, *Cor. Pol.*, Angleterre, IX, fos. 465, 480–1.
128 *Ibid*, IX, fos. 480–1.

seen as yet another Valois attempt to stir up trouble in England. As a result, orders were issued by the English Council to the Wardens of the Marches 'to learne by thier best espialles what tyme the shippes of Denmarke cam into scotland, and to what port they intend, and what is said to be their meanyng', while the Earl of Shrewsbury, the newly appointed Lord President of the Council of the North, was sent north with orders to place the Borders in readiness to fight at one hour's notice.[129]

In the end, the Danish threat came to nothing and Scotland and England were spared formal entry into the Habsburg-Valois conflict. No descent was made on St. Andrews or Leith, nor was there an attempt to take the Shetland and Orkney Isles. In fact, there was not even a single sighting of the King of Denmark's navy anywhere along Scotland's north or east coastlines.[130] On 21 August 1555 a Danish envoy arrived in Scotland with letters of explanation from Christian III to Mary of Guise. According to these, naval and military preparations were made in response to a rumour that Henri was plotting, with the support of the Scots, to oust Christian from his throne in favour of Charles III, duc de Lorraine and Mary of Guise's second cousin.[131] As this rumour was circulating at a time when several thousand of his subjects were already in revolt against him, the Danish King felt it necessary to assemble his forces and deal with a particular gentleman named 'Pillard', who had apparently already made several naval descents on Denmark in the name of France and Scotland.[132] Upon hearing these explanations, the Danish envoy was assured by Guise that 'today there is not a single Scottish warship at sea' – the naval fleet sent to the Orkney and Shetland Isles in July presumably having been recalled. The Dane then made the curious observation that neither

129 *APC*, V, p.160; AÉ, *Cor. Pol.*, Angleterre, IX, fos. 465, 490, 493. For Shrewsbury's appointment, see *RPC*, XIV, pp. 159–62.
130 AÉ, *Cor. Pol.*, Angleterre, IX, fos. 501–2, 503ʳ.
131 Although technically an independent duchy, Lorraine had been governed by a French regent, Nicolas de Vaudémont, duc de Mercoeur, since 1552. Vaudémont was the Duc de Lorraine's uncle and Mary of Guise's first cousin. He supplanted his pro-Habsburg sister-in-law, Christina, Duchesse de Lorraine and Charles V's niece, as regent after Henri persuaded her to resign her post, send her son to reside at the French Court and consent to the latter's marriage with the French King's daughter, Claude. This, in addition to Henri's successful capture of the Three Bishoprics of Lorraine, helped to establish and maintain the permanent influence France would have in Lorraine up until its formal annexation in 1766. See Baumgarter, *Henry II*, pp. 150–3, and pp. 146–57, for his discussion on Henri's treaty with the German Princes and his subsequent 'Promenade on the Rhine' in 1551–2.
132 AÉ, *Cor. Pol.*, Angleterre, XII, fos. 417ᵛ-8.

the Scots nor the French[133] had had an ambassador resident in Denmark for about two years, whereas the Emperor had sent one about the same time Christian began to raise his army.[134] Was he suggesting that the Habsburgs were behind these intrigues with the purpose of turning allies into enemies? This is certainly plausible, but the extent or nature of Imperial involvement is unclear and d'Oisel did not elaborate on this point when relating it to Noailles. Nevertheless, the uncharacteristic ignorance of d'Oisel and Noailles about French affairs, especially pertaining to Scotland, together with the Danish envoy's attestations that Christian III 'continues a good and secure friendship with the King our Master, the Queen and the Kingdom of Scotland, and does not pick a quarrel with us at all over the Orkney and Shetland Islands', suggests that both parties were the victims of some sort of foreign intrigue.[135]

Amicable relations having been restored, or rather reconfirmed between France, Scotland and Denmark, the immediate crisis was over. For the time being, Scotland and England had avoided being drawn into the Habsburg-Valois conflict despite all indications to the contrary. In February 1556 the five-year truce of Vaucelles brought a short respite in the Continental wars, taking away at least some of the pressure from the Habsburg and Valois allies within the archipelago. For Mary of Guise, these welcome interludes of peace gave her the opportunity and the time to focus all her attention on the government of Scotland itself, and it is to Guise's domestic policy that we now turn.

133 AÉ, *Cor. Pol.*, Angleterre, XII, f.418ᵛ.
134 *Ibid*, XII, f.418ᵛ.
135 *Ibid*, XII, f.418ᵛ.

5

Mary of Guise and the
Reassertion of Stewart Policy

Although the extremely volatile international situation was her predominant concern, domestic affairs were also of prime importance for Mary of Guise during her regency. The debilitating effects of seven years of 'rough wooing', coupled with a decade of plague and famine, had resulted in widespread dearth, prolific violence and a general state of lawlessness and disorder. Mary Tudor's accession and marriage to Philip of Spain served only to highlight the underlying need for law and order and, in consequence, the importance of restoring stability to the realm through a powerful monarchy and strong central government. The general aims of Mary of Guise's administration and policy in Scotland, therefore, were overwhelmingly concerned with reasserting, consolidating and expanding the authority of the crown and imposing royal justice.

Adhering to the tradition established by her Stewart predecessors, Mary of Guise turned to Parliament to respond to the events that had disrupted Scottish society. Under the Stewarts, the Three Estates in Parliament had become the main forum for discussing and determining matters of national importance, such as taxation, foreign affairs, forfeitures for treason and legislation. On the whole, the legislation enacted during Guise's regency aimed to advance the interests of the crown at the expense of local jurisdictions. By extending royal authority into the localities, Guise was not only shifting the balance of power to the advantage of the crown, but was also making a clear statement about to the role the Second Estate was expected to play in her administration. Magnates such as Châtelherault, Huntly, Argyll, Sutherland and Maxwell were required to enforce, execute and administer the Queen's laws as extensions of royal power, not as autonomous local powers. This was particularly true with respect to the Highlands, Western Isles and Borders, where the assertion of royal power was seen to be of paramount importance for the defence and stability of the realm, and where failure to execute the Queen's will met with fierce recrimination. But Mary of Guise also recognised her own role in asserting and enforcing the authority of the crown. From the time she returned to Scotland in 1551, she took an active interest in affairs of state and was determined to establish a strong, yet personal royal presence. Her progresses to the Borders and Highlands in 1555 and 1556, for instance, were deliberate attempts to impose law, order and royal power through visible displays of force.

But these were not Mary of Guise's only objectives. War had also emptied Scotland's coffers, and the complete absence of any sound fiscal policy during Châtelherault's administration (a problem which was exacerbated by his own personal greed) made the augmentation of crown revenues another priority for the Queen Regent. Again, the pressing matter of finance was inextricably associated with Euro-British dynastic politics. Guise needed money not only to subsidise her defensive policies against the Anglo-Imperial threat from England, but also to finance the establishment and maintenance of her daughter's household in France. Upon becoming regent, Mary of Guise faced many obstacles before she could fulfil her commission for the 'ordouring of the cuntre' and putting the 'realme to ane quyateness'.[1] To help her in this task, she relied on the support and advice of the Frenchmen and Scotsmen who served officially and unofficially on her council.

* * *

Much of the negative imagery surrounding Mary of Guise and her regency in Scotland is based on the allegedly dominant role Frenchmen played in her administration and, in particular, the key offices of state they held to the exclusion of the Scottish nobility. This is largely due to the fact that Mary of Guise's régime is conventionally used to establish the context of, and the pretext for, the Reformation Rebellion. The fact that modern scholarship also tends to be written from the perspective of the Lords of the Congregation and based on sources such as John Knox's *History of the Reformation in Scotland* serves only to reinforce and perpetuate this negative image. The composition of Guise's council is one area where historians have done very little to test the extent to which the Congregation's propaganda bore any relation to the facts. The presence of Frenchmen and, in particular, the 'French officers who had been appointed to the highest offices of the kingdom as keepers of the seals', was one argument used by the Congregation to show that Guise's true objective was the 'interprysed destructioun of thair commoun-weall, and overthrow of the libertie of thair native cuntree, be the meanes of the Quene Regente and certane strangearis her Prevey Counsallouris'.[2] But only

1 *RPC*, I, p.90; *Scottish Correspondence*, ccliii, p.379.
2 *Brosse Missions*, p.150; Knox, *History*, I, p.140 and *Works*, I, pp. 292–3, 444.

three Frenchmen had any formal position of power in Scotland during Guise's regency, and only two of them were actually on her Council, which continued to be dominated by the Scots.

As with any new administration, changes in the composition of the Council inevitably followed Mary of Guise's assumption of the regency. However, this did not entail a complete 'cabinet re-shuffle'. Many of those who comprised Guise's inner circle were veterans of Châtelherault's administration.[3] Huntly, for example, retained his Chancellorship,[4] while James, 4th lord Fleming, and David Paniter, bishop of Ross, both carried on in their respective posts as Royal Chamberlain and Secretary until their deaths in 1558.[5] Sir John Bellenden of Auchnoul also continued to serve as Justice Clerk, as did Alexander Livingston of Donypace as Director of the Chancery.

Yet there were the inevitable changes. Donald Campbell, abbot of Coupar Angus, for example, replaced George Durie, commendator of Dunfermline, as Keeper of the Privy Seal, while James Makgill of Nether Rankeillour replaced Thomas Marjoribanks of Ratho as Clerk Register.[6] The most significant change was the appointment of Gilbert Kennedy, earl of Cassillis, as Lord High Treasurer.[7] Cassillis' appointment is but one example of how Guise continued to use patronage as a means of consolidating political support, which included accommodating those who had Protestant and/or anglophile sympathies. As a noted reformer and ex-'assured Scot', Cassillis had already profited by switching allegiances and abandoning the English cause.[8] His appointment as Lord High Treasurer in 1554 was no doubt an attempt

---

3 For the composition of both Châtelherault and Mary of Guise's councils, see the sederunt and witness lists contained in *RPC*, I, and *RMS*, IV.

4 Appointed on 5 June 1546, Huntly retained this office until his death on 28 October 1562. Annie Cameron suggests that the only reason Huntly retained the Chancellorship was because Guise was not strong enough to oust him. But as we shall see, it seems that Guise was making an example of Huntly in order to assert her authority over the rest of the nobility. *HBC*, p.183; *Scottish Correspondence*, pp. 374–5; Teulet, *Papiers*, I, p.722.

5 Fleming was appointed Chamberlain on 12 November 1553. After his death in December 1558, the office was left vacant until his successor, John, 5th lord Fleming filled the post on 30 June 1565. David Paniter was appointed Secretary on 20 January 1543. Serving in both Arran's and Guise's administrations, he held this post until his death on 1 October 1558 – save for four months in 1543, when Henry Balnaves of Halhill held the office. He was succeeded by William Maitland of Lethington on 4 December 1558. *HBC*, pp. 186, 193.

6 *Ibid*, p.197.

7 *Ibid*, p.188.

8 NLS, Adv.MSS, 29.2.5, fos. 143, 146 and MSS, 2991, f.67ᵛ; *Fourquevaux Mission*, p.18.

by Guise to ensure that his support for the Franco-Scottish dynastic alliance continued – not necessarily because he was a Protestant, but because he was a member of the Scottish political élite. When it came to acquiring and maintaining support for her dynastic policies, Mary of Guise's attempts at conciliation knew no political or religious boundaries. She wanted the support of the entire political community.

The composition of Mary of Guise's Council seems to have changed very little during her regency. The witness lists contained in the *Register of the Great Seal* for this period show the regular attendance of those just mentioned, in addition to the noted reformer, Archibald Campbell, 4th earl of Argyll (until his death in 1558), and John Hamilton, archbishop of St. Andrews. From late 1557 onwards, James Douglas, 4th earl of Morton, a signatory of the First Band of the Congregation, and James Hepburn, 4th earl of Bothwell, were in regular attendance, the latter in his capacity as Lord High Admiral of Scotland. James Beaton, archbishop of Glasgow, William Chisholm, bishop of Dunblane, and Robert Reid, bishop of Orkney and Lord President of the Court of Session, conversely, are recorded as having appeared only once.[9] As with her distribution of patronage, Scots of all religious and political persuasions had representation in Mary of Guise's Council. What these witness lists do not contain, however, are the names of the two Frenchmen who were also members of the Privy Council – Bartholomew de Villemore, Comptroller, and Yves du Rubay, vice-Chancellor.

Villemore was appointed Comptroller on 1 May 1555 and was the receiver-general of all crown revenue.[10] This consisted of the fruits, rents and ordinary revenue from duchies, earldoms and crown lands, plus all the customs duties from burghs and ports.[11] Du Rubay's position as vice-Chancellor was unquestionably the most contentious of all of Mary of Guise's appointments. Du Rubay's possession of the Great Seal meant that a Frenchman possessed and exercised powers traditionally reserved for Scots generally from a leading magnatial family or bishopric.[12] Together, the Chancellorship and the Great Seal were important and prestigious symbols of Scottish sovereignty,

9 Robert Reid died in 1558. *HBC,* p.198; *RMS,* IV, 1221, 1258, 1261, 1269, 1272, 1280–2, 1305, 1315, 1334, 1350, 1356, 1358, 1371–2, 1376–81, 1384–7, pp. 271, 280–1, 283–5, 287–8, 291–2, 293, 296–7, 300, 302, 306–12.
10 *HBC,* p.191.
11 P.G.B. McNeill (ed.), 'Discours Particulier d'Escosse, 1559/60', *The Stair Society Miscellany,* II (1984), pp. 100–1.
12 The events surrounding du Rubay's possession of the Great Seal will be discussed in Chapter 6.

and it is not surprising that du Rubay would later be targeted by the Lords of the Congregation in their patriotic propaganda of 1560. The lack of source material for Guise's domestic administration, however, makes it difficult to come to grips with the machinations of her Council or even to determine how often it met. This may suggest that Council meetings were just a formality and the real business at hand was conducted within the Queen Regent's household. This *was* predominantly French and included such figures as de Villemore and du Rubay.[13]

The most powerful Frenchman in Scotland was neither a member of Mary of Guise's Council nor her household, but Henri II's ambassador resident in Scotland, Henri Cleutin, seigneur d'Oisel et de Villeparisis.[14] He was the real power behind the throne and, as such, played an extraordinary role in Scottish affairs of state – a role, more importantly, that generally went uncriticised by the Scots.

D'Oisel's diplomatic post assumed far greater significance as a result of the Franco-Scottish protectoral alliance and the establishment of French power in Scotland. His appointment as the French King's Lieutenant-General of Scotland at the behest of Mary of Guise in the spring of 1552 essentially placed matters of national security within his jurisdiction.[15] More importantly, d'Oisel was also Mary of Guise's principal adviser and right-hand man. As such, he enjoyed a unique and powerful position within Scotland, enabling him to exert a considerable amount of influence and control over Scottish affairs of state. It was d'Oisel, and not Châtelherault, whom Henri left in charge

13 See Mary of Guise's household accounts in NLS, Adv.MSS, 29.2.5; NAS, E33/4, 5 and E34/12, 14, 17, 18, 20, 21, 25, 26, 27; *TA*, XI, pp. 24–7. On 13 January 1557 the Queen Regent asked Henri to provide du Rubay with some honourable estate in Scotland as a reward for his good service in her household, which he had apparently done at his own expense, and as a means of inducing him to stay in Scotland. AÉ, *Mémoires et Documents*, Angleterre, XV, fos. 9ᵛ-10ʳ; *Papal Negotiations*, p.430.
14 D'Oisel was the French King's ambassador resident in Scotland from 1546 to 1560.
15 In the spring of 1552 Claude de l'Aubespine informed the Queen Dowager that, 'M. d'Oisel s'en est alle satisfaict ainsi que vous desirez, pourveu d'estat gentilhomme de la chambre, establi lieutenant general du Roy par dela, present deux mille excuz et de six cens francz par moys pour son estat, oultre sa pension et, qui est myeulx, avecques la tres bonne grace du Roy comme aussi en est-il tres digne [Monsieur d'Oisel has gone and done as you wished, appointed to the position of gentleman of the chamber, named as the King's lieutenant there, granted two thousand crowns and six hundred francs each month for his position, in addition to his pension and, even better, with the King's good grace as he is highly worthy of it]'. *Balcarres Papers*, II, lxxxiv, lxxxi, pp. 111–3, 115–6.

during Mary of Guise's trip to France in 1550–1551.[16] During the Queen Dowager's absence, he was reported to have 'wielded almost sovereign authority in matters of state and justice'.[17] But it is the overall acceptance of d'Oisel by the Scottish political community that is of greater significance. At no time was d'Oisel the subject of criticism or the target of collective opposition like his compatriot and colleague, du Rubay. Rather, the French Ambassador was a well liked and well respected figure amongst the Scots.[18] When he was recalled for service on the Continent during the Habsburg-Valois conflict in 1552, the Three Estates ordained that a remembrance of d'Oisel's 'guid seruice done in thir partis baith in tyme of peax and weir sould be writtin to the said maist Christin King not allanerlie thankand his grace of the samin bot alswa suppleand to thank and reward the said Monsieure Dosell'.[19]

D'Oisel's direct access to both Mary of Guise and Henri also contributed to his importance and boosted his 'popularity' amongst the Scots. During Huntly's disgrace and imprisonment in Edinburgh Castle, it was d'Oisel to whom he turned for help. 'My lord', he wrote, 'I man mast hartlie dyssyir your lordship be say gud as to contenew in your lawbris for me, and that your lordship wyll tak one yow my part and serwyce to the quenyis grace.'[20] Even the Lords of the Congregation pleaded with the French Ambassador to act on their behalf during the Reformation Rebellion in May 1559, 'requiring of him, that by his wisdome he wold mitigate the Quenis raige, and the raige of the Preastis'.[21] As with Mary of Guise, Knox's opinion of d'Oisel changed drastically after the latter refused to do as the Congregation had asked, but rather chose to suppress their letters 'to the uttermost of thair [the French] power'.[22]

Together, Mary of Guise and d'Oisel were a formidable political team. They not only 'wrolet' [ruled], but were also fortunate that 'allin Scotland obey and lyketh them'.[23] As such, d'Oisel commonly

16 19 May 1550, *Scottish Correspondence*, xlix, pp. 65–7.
17 *CSP Spain*, X, pp. 339, 340.
18 See, for example, Cassillis' remarks upon hearing of d'Oisel's appointment as Lieutenant-General and of his imminent return to Scotland in May 1552: 'I am glaid of the gwd treitment and awansement of monsieur DOisel, and also glaid of his retwirning bayth for the Kengis serwis and weil of this contre'. *Balcarres Papers*, II, ccxlii, p.360.
19 *APS*, II, p.489.
20 4 January 1555, *Scottish Correspondence*, cclxiii, pp. 395–6.
21 Knox, *Works*, I, p.327 and *History*, I, p.166.
22 Knox, *Works*, I, p.329 and *History*, I, p.166.
23 LPL, Talbot MSS, 3194, f.173ʳ. This observation is all the more poignant having come from an Englishman, Sir Thomas Wharton, on 30 October 1555.

received presents alongside the Queen Regent. On 16 December 1555, for instance, the 'prouest baillies and counsale' of Edinburgh thought it expedient 'to propine the Quenis grace with four scoir pundis worth of wyne walx and spycery . . . and xx *li* worth to Monsieur Dosell', while in August 1556 their Aberdeen counterparts ordained that a propine of 'two tonnis of wyne, with spycerie and wax, extending to the sowme of tuenty poundis' be given to the Queen Regent and 'half ane twn of wyne, ane dossain of torchis, and two dossund bustis of scorchettis' be given to d'Oisel.[24] As with any double-act, the death of Mary of Guise in June 1560 marked the end of d'Oisel's diplomatic and military career in Scotland. However, throughout the 1550s he was not only the most influential and, arguably, the most powerful Frenchman in Scotland, but also Mary of Guise's closest ally.

Yet the power and position of Frenchmen in Scotland did not assume any great significance for the Scots themselves until after the marriage of their Queen to the Dauphin in 1558 and the death of Henri II in July 1559. The formal union of the French and Scottish crowns brought into question the traditional role of the Scottish nobles in governing the kingdom. In this respect, Huntly's fall from grace assumed great importance. Although he nominally retained his chancellorship and theoretically remained the most important Scottish minister of state, Huntly's loss of power in favour of a Frenchman had serious implications. It symbolised what could *legitimately* happen to the entire Scottish nobility in the Franco-Scottish union of the crowns – loss of their political authority and control as the natural-born councillors of the realm. Irrespective of their number or how much power they really exercised, the mere presence of Frenchmen on Guise's Council was taken and used by the Congregation as a sign of things to come. This worst-case scenario of French usurpation became a central theme of the Lords of the Congregation's propaganda that was designed to play on Scottish xenophobia and, it was hoped, attract widespread political support for their rebellion against the Queen Regent in 1559–60. Yet, while several Frenchmen did hold important posts in Mary of Guise's administration, the Congregation's propaganda cannot be taken at face value. We must not forget the important offices and positions the Scots themselves occupied. Nor, for that matter, should the influence native Scots had over their Queen Regent be ignored – after all, the realisation of Guise's political

24 *Edinburgh Burgh Recs.*, II, pp. 227, 257; *Aberdeen Council Register*, pp. 300, 298.

and dynastic objectives ultimately depended on their support and official sanction. French domination, then, was always more a fear of things to come in the minds of Franco-sceptics than a reality.

Mary of Guise's immediate concern upon becoming regent, however, was not the realisation of her dynastic objectives, but responding to the events of the past decade that had disrupted Scottish society. To impose some degree of stability, she followed in the footsteps of Stewart kings since 1424 by attempting to restore a powerful monarchy in Scotland.[25] Her administration and policy in Scotland aimed to advance the interests of the crown at the expense of local jurisdictions, pursue royal justice and, ultimately, to assert the authority of the crown throughout the entire kingdom. Guise's policy was hardly revolutionary and entirely in accordance with Scottish tradition.

* * *

Mary of Guise held her first Parliament at Edinburgh on 20 June 1555.[26] This meeting of the Three Estates was extremely productive. A total of forty-one statutes were passed, many of which were re-enactments of statutes from previous reigns. The nature of this legislation gives us a clear insight into the Queen Regent's agenda for the governance of Scotland and the nature of her longer-term programme to impose law and order and extend royal government into the localities. A central feature of the legislation enacted in the Parliament of 1555 reflects Mary of Guise's determination to strengthen the role of the central government, particularly with respect to the administration of the realm. Procedures for the reversion of lands and reversions involving the transfer of gold and silver, the appointment of curators, the warning of tenants to flit, and the nullification of contracts and infeftments were all stringently detailed and outlined.[27]

In most cases Mary looked to the policy of her late husband when seeking inspiration for ways of increasing the power of central government and extending royal power into the localities. The 'greit and mony falsettis daylie done . . . be Notaris' prompted Guise to re-enact James V's statute summoning all notaries, spiritual and temporal, to appear before the Lords of Council for an examination of their

---

25 For more on these monarchs see M. Brown, *James I* (East Linton, 1994); Macdougall, *James IV* (East Linton, 1997); Cameron, *James V*; J.M. Brown, 'The exercise of power', in J.M. Brown (ed.), *Scottish Society in the Fifteenth Century* (London, 1977), pp. 33–65; Wormald, *Court, Kirk, and Community*, pp. 3–26.

26 *APS*, II, pp. 492–501.

27 *Ibid*, II, pp. 492, 493, 494, 495.

protocol books.[28] Years of war with England had allowed the activities of notaries to go unchecked and resulted in lapses in procedure. This was not always a deliberate attempt by the notaries to abuse the system – political necessity often required that protocol be abandoned. One particular phenomenon that was a source of great trouble, and the result of war, was the granting of sasines by some notaries upon precepts not issued by the Chancery, and the reluctance of others to do so. The controversy surrounding the legitimacy of these non-royal precepts needed to be resolved, and Guise duly responded by using and amending legislation of her late husband. James V's act outlining the procedures for the giving of sasines upon precepts issued from the Chancery was accompanied by Guise's declaration that sasines were also to be issued upon precepts 'past furth the Chancellerie', the validity of which was confirmed in a separate statute.[29] Realising, however, that there would be a continued reluctance by some notaries to accept the legality of non-royal precepts, Guise interestingly chose not to punish them, but placed the onus of responsibility on the precept holder to find a bailie who was prepared to issue them with an instrument of sasine. While this may be viewed as being inconsistent with Guise's quest to increase the efficiency of the administration of the realm, it does reveal her ability to adapt when circumstances dictated.

In other areas she was less inclined to compromise. This was particularly true in the case of the burghs, where the effects of war had resulted in great disorder and the 'infinit skaith baith of thair landis and gudis'.[30] In an attempt to address this problem and keep Scotland's Third Estate sweet, the Queen Regent confirmed with the greatest emphasis 'all [the] priuilegeis and actis of Parliament grantit and maid in fauouris of Burrowis Burgessis and Merchandis' by Mary, Queen of Scots' 'maist Nobill progenitouris'.[31] But the problem of disorder within the burghs ran far deeper than this. The choosing of craft deacons, in particular, was a 'rycht dangerous' process that had caused 'greit troubill in Burrowis commotioun and rysing of the Quenis lieges', and the 'making of liggis and bandis amangis tham selfis and betuix Burgh and Burgh'.[32] To prevent such outbreaks occurring in the future, Guise attempted, firstly, to regulate the appointment of craft deacons, by ordaining it as the exclusive re-

---

28 *APS*, II, p.496, 359–60.
29 *Ibid*, II, pp. 493, 497.
30 *Ibid*, II, p.497.
31 *Ibid*, II, p.497.
32 *Ibid*, II, p.497.

sponsibility of the provost, bailies and burgh council; and secondly, they were to ensure that their chosen candidate was 'the mais honest mand of craft of gude conscience', who 'laubour[ed] sufficientlie' and produced 'sufficient stuffe and wark'.[33] Guise had effectively abolished the office of craft deacon and all the privileges craftsmen enjoyed within the burgh. Within a year, however, financial pressures proved too much and the Queen Regent reversed her position by granting a charter nullifying the act of 1555. As Michael Lynch has shown, this was 'a manoeuvre by the regent to extract more revenue out of the burgh rather than, as some have argued, a last stand for catholicism and the French alliance'.[34] At a time when money was desperately needed for the defence of the realm, Guise received an offer of four thousand merks from the craftsmen in return for her *volte face* in policy.[35]

For Guise, though, the more disturbing matter was the making of leagues and the giving and taking of bonds of manrent and main-tenance in the burghs and throughout the entire kingdom.[36] This, she thought, was 'aganis all Law and obedience of subiectis towart thair Princis' and, therefore, deserving of 'greit punischment'.[37] In a sweeping piece of legislation, she took the drastic and ambitious step of nullifying all leagues, bonds of manrent and bonds of maintenance, including those made in the future. Equally ambitious was her decree that 'ony proffeit be lyferent of landis takkis teindis bailliereis or zeirlie payment grantit or geuin for the saidis bandis of manrent [should] returne to the gifaris'.[38] Those who dared to continue in such practices faced imprisonment, 'thair to remane during the Quenis grace will'. Intentional or not, this was a direct attack on the very infrastructure of Scottish society – the localised kin groups and the complex network of alliances that were traditionally forged between these groups and between lords and their dependants. For Guise, therefore, the problem of disorder in Scotland was inextric-ably linked with its localised organisation. To rectify both these 'problems', she sought to eradicate the mechanisms, such as bonds

---

33 *APS*, II, pp. 497–8.
34 Lynch, *Edinburgh and the Reformation*, p.71.
35 *Ibid*, pp. 70–2; *Edinburgh Burgh Recs.*, II, pp. 188–9, 230–2, 234–6, 236.
36 See Wormald, *Lords and Men*, Appendix A, pp. 168–373, for a list of bonds of manrent and maintenance made *c.*1442–1603. According to this list, approximately 164 bonds were entered into from December 1542 to January 1555, while only 23 were contracted following the Parliament of 1555 until the Queen Regent's death in June 1560.
37 *APS*, II, pp. 495, 497.
38 *Ibid*, II, pp. 495–6.

of manrent, that kept power in the localities and prevented the effective exercise of central authority. This was very ambitious legislation and not likely to win Guise many friends – as James I had discovered to his peril. The main difference, though, was that Mary of Guise was a regent trying to act like an adult Stewart monarch. This in itself was bound to put backs up, but, add to it legislation that sought to limit local magnate and noble activity that had gone unchecked for thirteen years, and abolish what was a customary practice and defining characteristic of Scottish society as a whole, meant that it was legislation that was very difficult to enforce and thus of little effect.[39]

But what of the royal bonds of manrent that Guise herself had entered into with numerous Scots during 1548–1551? Are we to presume that these were also rendered null and void, or did the statute only apply to those made between lieges? The preamble, 'it is thocht aganis all Law and obedience of subiectis towart thair Princis in the making of particulare liggis . . . and geuing and taking of bandis of manrent and mantanance', tends to favour the latter interpretation, but the wording of the statute itself makes no such distinction. *All* leagues and *all* bonds of manrent and maintenance were null, and the cited exceptions (heritable bonds and bonds for the asythement of murder) did not include those of the Queen Regent. There are arguments either way for Guise wanting to nullify all leagues and bonds. If she was trying to break the traditional ties between lords and men in the localities, there is no reason why she would want to sever the ties that kept individual lords exclusively bound to her service. As we saw in the last chapter, and as Mary of Guise herself realised, unwavering loyalty came at a price. But by 1555, circumstances had changed. Guise had secured sufficient political support not only for the proposed Franco-Scottish dynastic alliance, but also for her own regency. A semblance of stability coupled with her financial difficulties may have prompted her to 'cut corners' and get out of paying the annual pensions she so often granted in her bonds of manrent with members of the Scottish political élite.

Upon becoming regent, Mary of Guise inherited a financially strapped kingdom. Châtelherault had taken full advantage of the terms of his resignation that absolved him of all financial expenses incurred during his regency, and he left his successor with a deficit of

---

39 Wormald, *Lords and Men*, p.95 and *Court, Kirk, and Community*, pp. 27–40; K.M. Brown, *Bloodfeud in Scotland, 1573–1625* (Edinburgh, 1986), pp. 108–43.

£31,184 12s 6d.[40] As we have already seen, Guise was particularly anxious for ready cash at this time, owing to Mary Tudor's marriage to Philip of Spain and the threat this posed to security on the Scottish Border. At no time since Somerset's occupation of Scotland had the need to construct and fortify strongholds on the Border been more urgent, and the deficit inherited from Châtelherault's administration had deprived Guise of adequate funds to finance this project – thus intensifying the urgency. Added to this were her personal financial problems. In June 1552 the Cardinal de Lorraine had to send Gilbert de Beaucaire, Seigneur de Puiguillon, to Scotland to settle his sister's debts and give her money.[41] War with England had not only been costly for Henri II, but also for Guise, who had to dip regularly into her own purse to pay the wages of French soldiers serving in Scotland in addition to the French pensions awarded to many Scots.[42] This had clearly been a drain on the Queen Regent's resources. The accounts of her treasurer in France, Jacques Girard, reveal that her charges exceeded her yearly household allowance of 10,000 *livres* by 4,000 *livres turnois* in 1549, and peace did not lessen her financial obligations.[43] The establishment of

---

40 *TA*, X, p.216. One need only refer to the *Accounts of the Lord High Treasurer of Scotland* (X) to see the inordinate amount of money Châtelherault spent on himself, his family and friends during the latter years of his governorship – expenses which, significantly, disappear during Mary of Guise's administration. Regular features of the accounts were the monthly 'expensis debursit upoun my lord governour, his graces lady and barnis awne personis'. While these accounts are mainly for clothing, they also contain entries for other extravagances such as the purchase of 'gold to cord ane dosane of napkynnis' (p.18) and 'vj pair of gilt knyffis quhilk Ladye Jene [Châtelherault's daughter] send to gentillwemen of the Courte of France' (p.205). So full are these accounts of payments made to Châtelherault's immediate and extended family and his dependents that it is impossible just to cite a few examples. As James Balfour Paul notes in his introduction to this particular volume, the greed of Châtelherault is evidenced simply by the fact that out of 200 pages relating to the closing years of his regency, approximately 50 are discharges for clothes alone (p.xli).

41 *Warrender Papers*, xxix, p.22.

42 See, for example, NLS, Adv.MSS, 29.2.5, fos. 40, 63–4, 68, 71, for military-related expenses included in Mary of Guise's household accounts. As we have already seen, these payments were over and above those she made to Scots in the form of patronage during 1548–51.

43 NLS, Adv.MSS, 29.2.5, fos. 27, 28, 35–7; NAS, E34/26, 27; *Balcarres Papers*, I, pp. xxvi–xxix. See also NLS, Adv.MSS, 29.2.5, fos. 26, 45–8, 67, 84, 85, 153–4, 157–61; NAS, E33/4–5 and E34/12, 14, 17, 18, 20, 21, 23, 25; *TA*, X, pp. 225, 228, 294, for additional accounts of Mary of Guise's household expenditure rendered by Lieger Chesnieu, Jean Bougouin, Astier, and Lady Livingstone, who was often employed for the 'outtredding of the Quenis grace effaris'.

Mary, Queen of Scots' household in France in 1554 would prove to be yet another financial burden.

Proposals for the establishment of a separate household for Mary Stewart first came from the Cardinal de Lorraine in February 1553. In a letter to his sister, the Cardinal expressed the opinion that since Henri was establishing a separate household for the Dauphin, it was also time for Mary to have the same.[44] Even at this embryonic stage, it was clear that establishing a household was going to be an expensive enterprise. The Cardinal estimated that it would cost at least 55,000 *francs* to set up and 60,000 *francs* if it was to be done well. Added to this was the devastating news that Guise could not expect any assistance from Henri, who said that 'the revenue of the kingdom is so small that he will not be able to keep her [Mary]' – putting even more financial pressure on the Queen Regent.[45] The major problem facing Guise, therefore, was not only how she was going to come up with the necessary funds to establish her daughter's household, but also how to maintain it in years to come.

Mary of Guise's dowry from the Longueville estate was one source of income that was used to finance Mary Stewart's household. The untimely death of François, duc de Longueville, without an heir in 1551 sparked a lengthy dispute over the division of his estate, primarily between his mother, Mary of Guise, his uncle through marriage, Philip of Savoy, duc de Nemours, and Françoise d'Alençon, duchesse de Vendôme, his father's first wife.[46] The terms of the settlement took years to hammer out, and it was not until October 1553 that Jacques Girard wrote to Guise with an estimate of her portion. Although she could expect to receive approximately 32,000 *livres* and another large, unspecified sum from Normandy, the size of the Queen Regent's debts left her very little to work with, if anything at all. Even if she accepted Jacques Girard's generous offer to forego the 7,000 *livres* owing to him, this was no amount of money to begin setting up a household.[47] Yet despite these financial setbacks, Mary, Queen of Scots 'began hir hous' on 1 January 1554, two weeks after having been officially declared of age by the French

44 *Balcarres Papers*, II, ciii, pp. 141–2. See also, *Ibid*, II, ci, pp. 138–9, and A. de Ruble, *La première jeunesse de Marie Stuart, 1542–61* (Paris, 1891), pp. 267–80, for the establishment of the Dauphin's household.

45 *Balcarres Papers*, II, ciii, p.143.

46 Philip of Savoy was the husband of the late Charlotte d'Orléans, sister of François d'Orléans, duc de Longueville, Guise's first husband. See *Balcarres Papers*, II, ciii, cxix, cxxxv, pp. 143–4, 171–4, 195–7, for details of this dispute and the division of the Longueville estate.

47 *Ibid*, II, cxix, cciii, cxxxv, pp. 171–4, 143–4, 195–7.

King.[48] The accounts for her household in 1556 reveal that Guise not only relinquished her personal pension of 20,000 *livres* from Henri to finance her daughter's household, but also her dowry of 13,000 *livres* from her son's estate.[49] A sum of 25,000 *livres* was also to be provided from the crown revenues of Scotland for the same purpose.

Mary of Guise's public and private financial obligations during her regency were, therefore, considerable. Given the sizeable deficit she inherited from Châtelherault's administration and the size of the Scottish government's financial commitment to Mary, Queen of Scots' household, it comes as no surprise that a major concern for Mary of Guise during her regency was the augmentation of crown revenue. This concern is effectively demonstrated by the act of revocation of 1555, which revoked 'all maner of infeftmentis and dispositiounis' made by Châtelherault during his regency and returned them to the crown.[50] Of greater significance, perhaps, was the act's scathing criticism of Châtelherault's conduct that made an act of revocation necessary in the first place. Thus one reads of the 'hurt and detriment' Châtelherault had caused by the granting of 'Crowne landis rentis possessiounis patronageis of benficis and offices', most of which went to Hamiltons and their adherents. But the most controversial attempt by Guise to augment the crown's revenue came in 1556 when a new tax assessment scheme was proposed and subsequently rejected.

On 2 May 1556 the Lords of the Articles submitted to Parliament for approval a proposal for the 'better vplifting of the present taxa-

---

48 NAS, E34/25; *CSP Foreign, 1553–1558*, 131, pp. 46–7; NLS, Adv.MSS, 33.1.9, f.1ʳ. See also NAS, E34/26–27 and *Balcarres Papers*, II, cxxxv, cli, clii, clvii, clviii, clxxx, pp. 195–7, 222–6, 226–7, 235–7, 238–241, 270–5, for additional details of the establishment and maintenance of Mary Stewart's household in France.

49 NAS, E34/26; *Balcarres Papers*, II, pp. li-liii. Mary of Guise received an annual payment of 7,000 *livres* from the Marquis de Rothelin, who served as a guardian to her son, 1,000 *livres* as rent from the estate of Estrepagny, and an annual income of approximately 5,000 *livres* from the estate of Moustenbellay, her dowry and inheritance from her son, the late Duc de Longueville.

50 *APS*, II, pp. 500–1. As with any revocation, those who had benefited from the distribution of crown lands during a minority government were bound to be unhappy about having to give it back. On 9 August 1555, for instance, Henry Balnaves of Halhill wrote to the Queen Regent from Paris to put her 'heighnes in remembrance of sick thingis as ather mycht hurt, or proffeit, hir grace [Mary, Queen of Scots'] patrimonie and privilege of hir majesties crown, or the office quhilk you heighnes presently bearis in hir grace name and authorite'. *Scottish Correspondence*, cclxx, pp. 404–5.

tioun'.[51] On the surface, this was a standard piece of bureaucratic legislation, outlining, for example, the procedures for the submission of tax rolls to the Treasurer and prescribing the information that these rolls should contain. It is with respect to the latter that the Lords of the Articles' proposal was so controversial. For, in addition to a list of 'all landis within the realm', the tax rolls were also to contain the names of every freeholder, feuar, tenant, craftsman, cottar and parishoner 'togidder with the . . . quantitie of their substance & gudis mouable & Inmovabill', so that the 'qualitie of their personis & quantitie of their guidis & landis may be knawn & put In roll'.[52] In essence, the Lords of the Articles were proposing that the rate of taxation be assessed on the value of one's possessions over and above the 'auld extent', which was assessed exclusively on one's lands.[53] This new 'goods tax' met with great opposition in Parliament. For some members of the Three Estates, the prospect of having to inventory their 'estate and substance', as if 'to make their last willes and testamentes', was anathema. For others, the idea that this was to become a perpetual annual tax was grounds for opposition and rejection in itself.[54] Taxation was always an unpopular subject in Parliament, and while Mary of Guise's tax reassessment scheme was entirely justified for the defence of the realm, the response of the Three Estates was traditionally negative and utterly predictable.[55]

There is some question, though, as to whether the Lords of the Articles were actually proposing a perpetual tax. Their failure to stipulate the duration of this new tax assessment scheme does give that impression, yet there is some evidence to suggest that it was actually an attempt by Mary of Guise to raise emergency funds for the construction and fortification of strongholds. In a letter to the Cardinal de Lorraine dated 13 January 1557,[56] she wrote despairingly of her ill-preparedness for war, stating that she had not 'a single good fortress to defend herself and withstand a siege'.[57] This, she claimed,

51 *APS*, II, Appendix 10, pp. 604–5; *RPC*, XIV, p.14.
52 *APS*, II, pp. 604–5.
53 J. Goodare, 'Parliamentary Taxation in Scotland, 1560–1603', *SHR*, lxviii (1989), pp. 23–52; T. Thomson, *Memorial on Old Extent*, J.D. Mackie (ed.) (The Stair Society, 1946).
54 *CSP Scot.*, I, 411, pp. 196–7.
55 Many thanks to Roland Tanner for his help in this matter. For more on the Three Estates' view on taxation, see his *The Late Medieval Scottish Parliament: Politics and the Three Estates 1424–1488* (East Linton, 2001).
56 AÉ, *Mémoires et Documents*, Angleterre, XV, fos. 7–10ʳ; *Papal Negotiations*, pp. 427–33. See also AÉ, *Mémoires et Documents*, Angleterre, XV, fos. 10–11 for a similar letter written by Guise to Constable Montmorency on 13 January 1557.
57 *Ibid*, XV, f.7ᵛ; *Papal Negotiations*, p.428.

was due to the 'extraordinary expenses' involved in maintaining a standing force on the Border to quell 'a great number of thieves and rebels who are destroying the whole country'.[58] Guise cited another reason why funds were not readily available to finance her fort-building policy: Parliament's rejection of the 'goods tax' proposed by the Lords of the Articles.[59] Even though she had the money ready for the construction of new forts for the security of the realm, Guise complained that

> Jaurya esperance que laffaires qui auroit este mis cy aucun au dernier parlement pourrois pour y satisfaire voyans que les grans l'avonts trouvé le meilleur du monde, Mais la commune noblesse et le peuple sous entrez cy vne tels Jalousie que est pour le mectre une perpetuelle taille. [I had hoped that the affair, which had been put before the last Parliament, would have satisfied them, seeing that the great lords had found it as satisfactory as possible. But the commonalty, both the lesser lords and the people, have become so suspicious as to think that it would be a perpetual tax on them].[60]

Clearly the new tax reassessment scheme was not intended to be permanent. If it had been, why would Guise feel the need to state otherwise to her own brother and confidante? On the other hand, if this extra revenue was going be used to finance her fort-building policy, why was this not cited as the reason for the introduction of a goods tax? Mary of Guise's supplications to Rome in 1555, 1556 and 1557, for example, explained that a subsidy of two-tenths of all

---

58 AÉ, *Mémoires et Documents*, Angleterre, XV, fos. 7ʳ-8ʳ; *Papal Negotiations*, p.428. Contrary to what Lesley claims, the 'perpetual tax' was not for the maintenance of a standing army on the Border as this had already been paid for. Lesley, *History*, p.254.

59 This tax was introduced in Parliament on 6 May 1556. On 9 May, Wharton reported to Shrewsbury that ' the noble men was togwetheris at Edinburgh the vjth and was thought then that their parlyament wold contynew vj or vij daies more. The dowager demandyth a grete soume to hir borne of the Realme, which at the fyrst the Lords denied'. On 13 May a second report followed: 'The Scots mayd end of their parliament the ix. The Dowager in hir own person gave thanks to all their bodys of the parlyament And comendyd their consyderacion for the Surety of hyr Realme which she answered was nathir of her self nor of the french. And understandyng hir wyse oppynyons did commend them. And upon Wedynsday befor them breakynd up she in fayr maner tho not well pleased departed'. LPL, Talbot MSS, 3194, fos. 237ʳ, 249ʳ.

60 AÉ, *Mémoires et Documents*, Angleterre, XV, fos. 8ᵛ-9ʳ; *Papal Negotiations*, p.429.

ecclesiastical revenue was needed for 'the fortification of castles and border strongholds and for the repair of them' against England.[61] Similarly, the Privy Council had no problem approving a tax of £20,000 on 22 January 1555, so that 'ane forth [could] be bigged besyde Kelso'.[62] Of this 'grete extent', £10,000 was to be subdivided between 'the Barronis, Landed Men, Temporall Estait, and Burrowis', while the other half was to be paid by the clergy, who seem to have been remiss in their payments. Instead of enforcing the law and putting the offenders to the horn as rebels, Mary of Guise changed tactics and adopted a far more lenient position. In an attempt to induce the clergy to pay their taxes by means of gentle persuasion, the punishment for non-payment was rescinded by Parliament in 1555.[63] Yet beneath Guise's accommodating veneer was a steely determination to collect the revenue owing to her from the First Estate for the Kelso enterprise. It was made perfectly clear that this act was to remain in effect only as long as 'the Lordis of the spiritualitie prouyde and find sum vther sure and ressonabill maner how the samin salbe inbrocht to our Souerane Lady and hir grace payit thairof'.[64]

Money for the defence of the kingdom, therefore, was clearly a priority for Mary of Guise during her regency.[65] This is hardly surprising given the 'cool' relations between Scotland and England during the reign of Mary Tudor. Guise's financial burdens were already weighty enough without the added pressure of war and/or an Anglo-Imperial invasion. The deficit she inherited from Châtel-herault's administration left her with little or nothing for emergency defensive policies, let alone long-term financial commitments such as the establishment and maintenance of Mary, Queen of Scots' household in France. But the augmentation of crown revenue and matters of defence were not the only concerns for Guise – the pursuit of

---

61 *Papal Negotiations*, pp. 3–4, 522–5; Mahoney, 'The Scottish Hierarchy', p.74; Donaldson, *James V-James VII*, p.87.
62 *RPC*, XIV, p.13; *Edinburgh Burgh Recs.*, II, pp. 209–10, 214–5, 215–6; *Aberdeen Council Register*, pp. 298, 299. It was not until 8 June 1556 that the burgh of Aberdeen paid off 'thair haill taxt that the said toune was sett to . . . for the bigging certane forthis vpoun our souerane ladyis bordouris', which amounted to £66.5.0. For additional references to the Kelso enterprise, see AÉ, *Cor. Pol.*, Angleterre, IX, fos. 377–8ʳ, 398–9 and XX, f.222.
63 *APS*, II, p.498.
64 *Ibid*, II, p.498.
65 Schemes to extract money from the church and laity were also submitted to the Queen Regent for her consideration. These included 'Suggestions for augmenting the queen dowagers revenue without grudge, hurt or feiling of the people'. NLS, Adv.MSS, 34.2.17, f.124.

royal justice and the imposition of law and order were equally important.

* * *

Mary of Guise's regency is best characterised by her overwhelming concern for law and order. Central to this was her quest to provide for the effective administration and execution of justice throughout the entire kingdom. In order to achieve this, she naturally turned to Parliament, where legislation was passed to standardise and regulate legal procedures as they pertained to criminal cases. In the Parliament of June 1555, for example, statutes were enacted stipulating the procedures for the issuing of summonses and the time allotted for charges of murder to be processed.[66] Legislation regulating court protocol was also enacted. Those called to underlie the law were required to show up on the day appointed, defendants were asked to bring the testimonies of only their most honest, wise and substantial friends and, of course, their advocates, while the pursuers of the action were allowed the testimonies of four of their friends.[67]

The Parliament of 1555 also passed legislation against specific crimes such as fraud and perjury. In particular, Guise sought to eradicate the problem of perjured witnesses by imposing stiff penalties. Persons who bore false witness or induced witnesses to perjure themselves were to be punished 'be [the] peirsing of thair toungis and escheting of all thair gudis to our Souerane Ladyis vse and declairit neuer to be habill to bruke honour office or dignitite'.[68] They were to receive further punishment at the discretion of the Lords according to the extent of their crime.[69] Another prevalent problem that Guise sought to address was that of retributory justice. Because of the odious crimes of slaughter daily committed within the realm, and in particular, the slaying of parties pursuing and defending their actions, a statute was enacted that outlined the legal procedures if the defendant in a murder case slew the pursuer of the action and *vice versa*.[70] In accordance with her programme to strengthen royal power, Guise's attacks on the 'private' justice of the feud was, ultimately, an attempt to promote the 'public' justice of royal courts.[71]

The nature of this legislation clearly reflects Mary of Guise's

66 *APS*, II, pp. 492–3.
67 *Ibid*, II, p.495.
68 *Ibid*, II, p.497.
69 *Ibid*, II, p.497.
70 *Ibid*, II, pp. 494–5.
71 The distinction between 'private' and 'public' justice is first developed by Jenny Wormald in 'Bloodfeud, Kindred and Government in Early Modern Scotland', *Past and Present*, 87 (1980), pp. 54–97.

[140]

determination to provide for the effective execution of royal justice through the centralisation of Scotland's legal system and standardisation of procedure. But for Guise, it was the administration of justice that was in greatest need of reform. This, she claimed, and not necessarily Scots law itself, was the greatest source of injustice in Scotland.[72] Upon becoming regent, she was determined to rectify the problem by looking to the French legal system as a model for reform. Her request that two French lawyers be sent immediately to Scotland was granted on 24 October 1554, when Montmorency informed her that he was busy finding, 'les deux hommes de robbe longue que avez demander pour le faict et administration de votre justice affin de le vous envoyer incontinent [the two lawyers you requested for the running and administration of your justice so that they may be sent to you immediately]'.[73] Unfortunately, it is not known who these legal envoys were, when they came, or what advice they gave the Queen Regent. Nevertheless, their presence may offer some explanation of to why the administration of justice eventually became a source of discord between Guise and the Scots.

In January 1557 Guise wrote a very revealing letter to the Cardinal de Lorraine in which she confessed that for the first time in her political career she actually felt estranged from her Scottish subjects.[74] According to the Regent, the primary reason for this deterioration in crown-magnate relations was her determination to 'see justice take a straightforward course'.[75] The Scots, she complained, and in particular the great lords, are

> . . . si peu desirent de la Justice quilz sont plustost aise de
> veoir tousiours quelque chose a desmettre qui lempescher, Et
> ne peult on parla demander lay Justice quils ne disent
> Incontinant veult lon ladicte veult changer leur loix . . . Dieu
> scait Monsieur mon frere quelle vie Jay, ce nest peu de chose
> que damener ung peuple nouveau a parfection et nouuelle
> servuitude a eulx qui ont enuy a de voir regnir Justice.

> [so little desirous of justice, that they are, on the contrary,
> always very happy to find some complication which may
> impede it. One cannot talk of [or] demand this justice
> without their instantly saying that one wants to change their

72 *Papal Negotiations*, p.430; AÉ, *Mémoires et Documents*, Angleterre, XV, f.9ᵛ.
73 *Balcarres Papers*, II, clxvi, pp. 251–2.
74 AÉ, *Mémoires et Documents*, Angleterre, XV, f.9ʳ; *Papal Negotiations*, p.430.
75 *Papal Negotiations*, p.430; AÉ, *Mémoires et Documents*, Angleterre, XV, f.9ʳ.

laws . . . God knows, brother mine, what a life I lead. It is no small thing to bring a young nation to a state of perfection, and to an unwonted subservience to those who desire to see justice reign].[76]

But in her desire to see justice reign, Guise confessed that she had been 'a little severe' and the Scots would not tolerate it because

. . . [ils] disent que ce sont les loix dela francais et que leur vieilles loix sont bonnes, la pluspart desquelles sont les plus Injustes du monde, non dicelles mesmes mais cy la manier quilz cy vsent, la qui est cause de tous nostre discord, que le passe toustesfois la plus doulcement que je puis sans biens gaster attendans meilleure saison, et que Je voye au quil plaira adieu de disclose.

[[they] say that these are laws of the French, and that their old laws are good, which for the most part are the greatest injustices in the world, not in themselves, but from the way in which they are administered.][77]

Guise's request for French judicial intervention, coupled with her desire to reform Scotland's legal system, gave the impression, rightly or wrongly, that she wanted to replace Scotland's ancient laws with those of the French. For the Scots, any alteration to their ancient laws and liberties, the cornerstones of their cultural and institutional independence, was a form of sacrilege.

We have already seen how the Scots went to great pains to ensure that their ancient laws and liberties were safeguarded in the treaties of Birgham, Greenwich and Haddington. This was also a stipulation of Mary of Guise's assumption of the regency. The Scots insisted that Guise procure a bond from Henri guaranteeing that 'this realme with all dominiounis and possessiounis tharof or subject tharto and lieges of the samin sall brouke and jois the awld liberteis and privilegeis tharof, and salbe onlie governit . . . be the lawis . . . and consuetudis of this said realme . . . without ony alteratioun or innovatioun'.[78] Any attempt on the part of Guise to reform Scottish law, therefore, was bound to meet with fierce resistance – not least if it was aimed at the

76 AÉ, *Mémoires et Documents*, Angleterre, XV, f.8ʳ; *Papal Negotiations*, p.428.
77 AÉ, *Mémoires et Documents*, Angleterre, XV, f.9ᵛ; *Papal Negotiations*, p.430.
78 *ADCP*, p.630. In the treaty of Haddington, for example, Henri promised that he would '[observe] and [keep] this Relame and liegis thairof in the samin fredome liberteis and Lawis and hes bene in all kingis of Scotlandis tymes bypast'. *APS*, II, p.481.

élite's own exercise of power in the localities. Mary of Guise's unique position of power may also have exacerbated tensions. What was acceptable behaviour for a sovereign was less acceptable for a regent and Guise, whose position as regent was indefinite and unprecedented, was caught somewhere in the middle. She was neither a monarch nor a governor, but a regent in an absentee monarchy with almost viceregal qualities. The political élite's determination to maintain their traditional role in government by resisting any policies that would affect their power and ancient rights and liberties may be viewed as an attempt to come to terms with the unique position in which they, and she, found themselves.

Unsurprisingly, this deterioration in crown-magnate relations was seized upon by the Lords of the Congregation during their rebellion, and Guise was accused of attempting to 'change their laws'.[79] The Scots' opposition to the Queen Regent's legal reforms in 1556–7, however, prevented their implementation and ironically enabled her to deny this charge outright. The Congregation was subsequently told that 'she did not know of a single one that had ever been contravened. And if there had been any innovation, they should state their grievance and lodge a protest'.[80]

* * *

Mary of Guise's domestic policy was motivated by the best of intentions, and continued a Stewart tradition dating back to 1424. It was also combined with a need to deal with the immediate matter of self-defence and law and order. But this went against the selfish local and financial interests of many of the nobility and gentry. The myth of French domination, then, was far more a product of noble self-interest than any attempt by Guise to force French innovation on Scotland.

Mary of Guise's pursuit of royal justice and quest for law and order, however, consisted of far more than the mere formulation of policy. It also meant putting these policies into practice. Justice not only needed to be legislated for, but also duly executed – nowhere more so than on the Borders and in the Highlands and Western Isles of Scotland, the traditional hotspots of lawlessness, violence and disorder. This was no easy task and the international situation that prevailed throughout most of Guise's regency served only to frustrate matters further. The Habsburg-Valois conflict and, more directly, Mary Tudor's marriage to Philip of Spain necessitated that Guise

---

79 *Brosse Missions*, pp. 150, 151.
80 *Ibid*, pp. 152, 153.

focus almost all of her time, energy and resources on matters of national security. This was particularly true of the Anglo-Scottish Border, where the Continental superpowers now met as a result of the dynastic alliances each had forged within the archipelago. Yet, it was precisely because of the international situation that the need for law and order on the Border was the greatest, not only for the security of the realm, but also to maintain what was already a precarious peace between the 'auld enemies'. Moreover, the undue attention Guise was forced to pay to the Borders also frustrated her attempts to deal with the so-called 'Highland problem' – violent insurgent activity that had returned with a vengeance during Mary, Queen of Scots' minority. Both of these areas were earmarked for special recognition in Mary of Guise's quest for law and order, and it is to the Borders, Highlands and Western Isles that we now turn.

6

The Borders, Highlands and Western Isles

S hortly after her assumption of the regency, Mary of Guise
received some advice for the punishment of crime.[1] Written in
response to 'the mone slawchtiris commettit with in this realme', and
for 'the ordour of the bordour quhilk is the maist prencipall thing to
put the realme to ane quyatenes', this memorandum outlined the
social ills that Mary of Guise had been commissioned to cure –
disorder, lawlessness and violence.[2] Nowhere were these problems
more prevalent than on the Anglo-Scottish Border. There,

> the aquentenc at is betwen Scotland and Ingland amangis the
> theifis one bayth the bordouris, to gether with the deidli
> feidis quhilk, . . . beyng nocht weill luket apone, sall ever hald
> your grace in ane bessenes: for your grace man tak respeik to
> ther thingis be your grace self, for your grace knawis the
> natour of the pepell and effectione at is amangis thame,
> throw the quhilk effectione your grace hes knawyng the
> cowmon weill perreche dywiris tymes.[3]

It was generally perceived that the key to a quiet, peaceful and law-
abiding kingdom was the Borders, and 'withowt your grace haif ane
respeik to it, consederane the partecularaty and effection at your
grace knawis in Scotland, it is unabill to be weill'.[4]

One major factor contributing to lawlessness and disorder on the
Border was the continued existence of the Debatable Land in the
West March. According to the terms of the treaty of Norham, the
Debatable Land was to return to the *status quo ante bellum*.[5] As long as
the boundaries and sovereignty of the Debatable Land remained in
dispute, the chances of imposing order there were drastically reduced. Added to this was the refusal of the inhabitants of the

---

1 *Scottish Correspondence*, ccliii, pp. 379–80. It is not known who wrote this
 letter, or when.
2 *Ibid*, ccliii, p.379.
3 *Ibid*, ccliii, p.380.
4 *Ibid*, ccliii, p.380.
5 *Foedera*, XV, pp. 265–6; Nicolson, *Leges Marchiarum*, pp. 58–9.

Debatable Land to evacuate their premises – another stipulation of the treaty of Norham.[6] The Debatable Land was a no man's land and, as such, a safe haven for the less desirable elements of Scottish and English society. As a first step in tackling the problem of disorder on the Border, the Scottish and English governments resolved to evict the inhabitants of the Debatable Land by force – specifically, by burning them out of their homes.[7]

The joint incursion was planned for 10 December 1551 and was to be led by both Wardens of the West March, Lords Maxwell and Conyers.[8] On 26 November proclamations were despatched to Selkirk and Roxburgh charging the inhabitants of those shires to convene at Hawick on 8 December, 'to pas upoune the thevis of the Debatable ground with lord Maxwell'.[9] But by 7 December the English had withdrawn their support for the enterprise. Lord Conyers not only 'refusit to keip the dyat, bot wold haiff the samyn stayit'.[10] The reason for this sudden withdrawal, and the order for Conyers to suspend all communication with the Scots, was the murder of an Armstrong – one of the two main families inhabiting the Debatable Land illegally. The possible repercussions of a military expedition directed against these families sparked fears in the English camp that 'somme greater inconvenience might growe, and thereby the peace and amitie empayred'.[11] Mary of Guise, Châtelherault and the Privy Council, however, had no such qualms and remained fully committed to the enterprise. Maxwell was ordered to proceed as planned, 'provyding alwayis that the said Lord do, nor procure to be done, upoun the severall ground of Ingland that may tend to the ruptor of the peace and violatioun thairof'.[12] On 10 December he set out on his course of destruction, intent not only on the 'birnyng of the Debatable ground', but also the demolition of the inhabitants' homesteads.[13]

Maxwell's raid, however, failed to reduce the Debatable Land to a state of uninhabited neutrality. The Grahams and the Armstrongs, the

6 *Foedera*, XV, p.266; Nicolson, *Leges Marchiarum*, pp. 58–9.
7 *TA*, X, pp. 34, 39–40.
8 *RPC*, I, p.117; *TA*, X, p.34. In November 1551 the logistics of the raid for 'the recovery of the Debaitabill land' were hammered out between Maxwell and a special depute acting for Conyers at Dumfries, where Châtelherault was holding a justice ayre. *RSS*, IV, 1416–1428, pp. 225–7; *TA*, X, p.31.
9 *Ibid*, X, p.34.
10 *RPC*, I, p.117.
11 *APC*, III, pp. 363–4, 430, 443.
12 *RPC*, I, pp. 117–8.
13 Maxwell was accompanied by hackbutters, masons, quarrymen and 'peonaris' who were armed with 'pikkis and mattokkis'. *TA*, X, pp. 39–40.

primary targets of the raid, stood their ground and remained a permanent fixture within the disputed territory. If anything, Maxwell's raid worsened the situation by inaugurating a particularly violent feud between his house and that of the Grahams, several of whom were slaughtered during the Warden's expedition.[14] As a result, lawlessness and disorder continued to plague the Borders and it became patently clear that, in order to rectify the situation, the Debatable Land had to be divided and its boundaries settled once and for all.

Just weeks after Maxwell's raid, the Privy Council described in detail the degenerate state of the Borders on account of the existence of the Debatable Land. It was reported that

> the greit and hevy attemptatis committit upoun our Soverane Ladys pur liegis be thevis and uthairis malefactouris, brokin men, and the diverse murthuris and slauchteris committit be thaim in tyme bigane, and specialie be the inhabitantis [of] the Debatabill land, quha nychtlie, day, and continualie rydis and makis quotidiane reiffis and oppressionis upon the pur; and in likmaner, all evill doaris and faltouris resortis to the said Dabatabill land, and quhatsumever falt thai commit thai ar welcum and ressett be the inhabitantis thairof, and assistis and takis plane part with theif and tratour in thair evill deidis, and na trew man offendit to can get rameid, nor na trespassour can be put to dew punischment; and als understandand that the said Debatabill land and inhabitantis thairof hes bene thir mony yeris the occasioun of weris, and ay hes beine the principall brekaris of the pece, and as yit daylie intendis to do that is in thaim to do the samyn.[15]

They concluded that the only workable solution was that the 'Debatabill land be dividit . . . for the commoun weill of this realme, rest and quitenes of the lieges thairof, and interteneyng of the peax in all tymes to cum'.[16] The English had reached the same conclusion and approached the French ambassador then in London, Claude de Laval, Seigneur de Boisdauphin, to set the wheels in motion.[17] On 20 March 1552 Cassillis, Maxwell, Sir James Douglas of Drumlanrig and John

---

14 *RPC*, I, pp. 117–8, 118–9, 144–6; R.B. Armstrong, *The History of Liddesdale, Eskdale, Ewesdale, Wauchopedale, and the Debateable Land* (Edinburgh, 1833), Appendix liii, pp. xciii-xciv.

15 27 January 1552, *RPC*, I, pp. 118–9.

16 *Ibid*, I, p.119.

17 BL, Cotton MSS, Caligula B.vii, f.490.

Bellenden of Auchnoul were appointed to meet with the negotiating commissioners for England, the Earl of Westmorland, Sir Thomas Palmer and Sir Thomas Challoner, for the equitable division of the Debatable Land.[18]

It had been decided quite early on that the negotiations would not be held in the Debatable Land itself because it was feared that the inhabitants there, 'being affectyoned to their owne pryvate purpose', would prevent the realisation of its division. Cassillis' advice to Mary of Guise, that 'it is best that nain knaw qwhow thir materis standis', was echoed in the English Council's declaration that 'the lesse pryvey the Borderers be made to the devision hereof, the more likely it is the thing shall take place'.[19] The talks were consequently scheduled to take place at Carlisle and Dumfries. Despite these precautionary measures, it was not the reaction of the Grahams or the Armstrongs that threatened to jeopardise the negotiations, but the terms of the settlement itself.

The fate of Canonbie Priory and two stone houses belonging to Sandy Armstrong and Thomas Graham were the major points of contention that eventually broke up the negotiations just weeks after they had begun in May 1551.[20] The Scottish government issued explicit instructions to the negotiating commissioners that 'ye enter nocht to na divisoun of the landis of the Priorye of Cannoby as debatabill'.[21] They were, however, willing to adopt a far more compromising position on the matter of the Graham and Armstrong residences. Ideally, they would have preferred the 'downputting of baith the stane houssis', but the Scottish commissioners were instructed to abandon this point if it proved to be a stumbling block for the division of the Debatable Land as a whole.[22] The English commissioners, conversely, had been issued with far more stringent

18 Richard Maitland of Lethington also became involved in the negotiations and was one of the signatories of the final agreement on 24 September 1552. *RPC*, I, pp. 120–1; *APC*, III, pp. 492–3; *Foedera*, XV, pp. 315, 318–9.
19 *Scottish Correspondence*, cclxii, pp. 359–60; *APC*, III, pp. 491–4.
20 On 22 April 1552 the Scottish Commissioners were ordered to make their way towards the West March to begin the negotiations, but the English Commissioners' initial reluctance to deal with Lord Maxwell, and the dispute over whether the first meeting should be held in Scotland or England, meant that the actual division of the Debatable Land was not discussed until early May. *RPC*, I, pp. 124–5; *Scottish Correspondence*, cclxii, pp. 357–60; BL, Cotton MSS, Caligula B.vii, fos. 461–5; Boscher, 'English provincial government', pp. 137–8.
21 *RPC*, I, p.122. See *ibid*, I, pp. 121–2, for the Scottish commissioners' complete set of instructions.
22 *Ibid*, I, p.122.

instructions.[23] In addition to Black Bank, a strategic location 'by the which there is a strayte and yet a good passage for the entrye or convoye of ordynance owt of Skotland over the water of Esk into England', they were to secure both houses, especially Sandy Armstrong's, and the areas of the Debatable Land in which they stood.[24] The negotiating commissioners had come to the table with a clear conflict of interest.

Cassillis reported as much when he detailed the events of their meeting to Mary of Guise:

> . . . we dessyirrit them [the English commissioners] to mark in the plat, as they wald answ[e]r afoir ther Consel, [qwhat] war ane ressonabil dewision and we swld do the lyik. Sa, madame, they maid ane merk and passit throw ane part of Cannabe and maid al the best land to them and bayth Sande Armestaringis hows and Thome Gramis. Than we dessyirrit to geif them it that they offerit to ws and to tak the toder, qwilk they [cu]ld nocht aggre to, as they said. Than we dewydit it in twa maners and offerit them ther chois, qwhilk they said they mycht nocht accord to, . . . Madame, the caws of wr defference presantly is that [they] exteim Cannabe debatabil, qwhilk we cwld nocht accord onto. Nocht theles, madame, the mater is brocht to ane neir poinct.[25]

Despite the impasse over Canonbie Priory and the English Commissioners' rejection of the Scots' proposal that both sides take one house each, the Queen Dowager was nevertheless heartened by the way the negotiations seemed to be progressing. She was so optimistic that, on 25 May 1552, she told the Duc de Guise that a settlement was imminent.[26] She had either been misinformed or grossly misled. By the time she wrote to her brother, the negotiations had effectively broken down. Once again it would take the intervention of France, in the person of Boisdauphin, to get the negotiations up and running.[27]

The second round of negotiations commenced in June and, making little headway, dragged on through the summer of 1552. While the English had agreed to concede the lands of Canonbie Priory, they had become more determined than ever to possess both the Armstrong

23 BL, Harley MSS, 289.26, fos. 36–8.
24 *Ibid*, 289.26, f.38.
25 8 May [1552], *Scottish Correspondence*, ccxlii, pp. 358–9.
26 *Balcarres Papers*, II, lxxxii, pp. 118–9; Boscher, 'English provincial government', pp. 138–9.
27 *APC*, IV, p.69; PRO, SP10/14/36.

and Graham homesteads. It was not until 16 August that some definite progress was made. Boisdauphin, frustrated by the proceedings, presented the English Council with 'the Scotes last offer towching the particion of the Debatable Land' and finally received Edward VI's assent.[28] A treaty dividing the Debatable Land was concluded on 24 September 1552 and, interestingly, strongly resembled the terms originally proposed by the Scots in April-May 1552.[29] The lands of the Priory of Canonbie *and* the house of Sandy Armstrong fell to Scotland, while the English gained possession of the area dominated by the Grahams. Once again, an Anglo-Scottish treaty had largely been effected by French diplomatic intervention. As P.G. Boscher comments, 'it would be wrong to view the division of the Debatable Land as a product of Anglo-Scottish cooperation; it came about chiefly as a result of French pressure to resolve the controversy once and for all'.[30]

The existence of the Debatable Land, however, was just one factor contributing to the prevalent disorder on the Border. A more serious problem was the general disregard for Border law and the ineffective administration and execution of justice by warden officials on both sides of the Anglo-Scottish divide. The rectification of these problems became an overriding concern for Mary of Guise during her regency. Her extensive involvement in every aspect of Border affairs, from the most trivial task to those more befitting her rank, reflected her determination to fulfil her commission and provide for the 'executioun of justice and ordouring of the cuntre'.[31] The methods she employed to combat disorder and reduce the Border to obedience, moreover, are representative of those she employed throughout all of Scotland.

Mary Tudor's accession, and her expressed desire for peace and the maintenance of law and order, provided Mary of Guise with an ideal opportunity to seek redress for the numerous outrages committed by the English on the Border against the Scots.[32] Antoine de Noailles, the

28 *APC,* IV, pp. 113, 118.
29 *Foedera,* XV, pp. 315–9; *CSP Scot.,* I, 394, p.191, Nicolson, *Leges Marchiarum,* pp. 316–9; *RPC,* I, pp. 121–2; *Scottish Correspondence,* cclxii, pp. 358–9; Boscher, 'English provincial government', p.141. See *Foedera,* XV, pp. 319–20 and 325–6, for Mary, Queen of Scots' ratification of the treaty and Sir John Maxwell of Terregles and John Johnstone's commission to exchange this confirmation with Sir Thomas Dacre and Sir Richard Musgrave, which took place on 15 December 1552.
30 Boscher, 'English provincial government', p.141.
31 *RPC,* I, p.90.
32 Noailles informed Mary of Guise of Mary Tudor's inclination to peace on 6 September 1553. AÉ, *Cor. Pol.,* Angleterre, IX, f.68; *CSP Scot.,* I, 398, p.192.

new French ambassador resident in London, was ordered to present letters from Mary of Guise congratulating the English Queen on her accession and reciprocating her goodwill.[33] More importantly, he was to describe in detail the nature of the outrages committed by the English on the Border, and to 'perswaid the Queen and Counsale to direct Commissioneris . . . to meit ane lyke nomer Commissioneris for Scotland, . . . for redressing of sic attemptatis, stancheing of male-factouris, and ordorying of the Bourdouris, manteinance of the peax and quiet of the liegis of baith the realmes'.[34] If Mary refused to comply, Noailles was further instructed to 'mak the Kyng [Henri] advertisment thairof'. Mary of Guise was fully prepared to use Henri's protectorate of Scotland, and the latent threat of his intervention, to force the English Queen into compliance.[35]

Noailles presented the Queen Dowager's letter on 8 October 1553.[36] From him, the English Queen heard numerous complaints and charges against her Border subjects in great detail. They were accused, for example, of making daily incursions into Scotland for the purpose of 'takand heirschippis of gudis, committand slaulteris and utheris gret crymes and rangis upon the liegis of this realme'.[37] The more serious charge, however, lay in the fact that for these crimes the Scottish Wardens 'can get na redress, quhilk apperis manifestlie to move occasioun of weir betwix the realme, gif haisty remeid be nocht providit and ordour put thair to'.[38] This also applied to the infraction of Lord Home's fishing rights of the Tweed by the Captain of Norham, a matter that the Deputy Warden of the East March for England, Mr. Gray of Chillingham, refused to settle. This was because Chillingham was allegedly involved in criminal activity himself. Chillingham had been accused of making cattle and sheep raids into Scotland with Cuthbert Musgrave, Captain of Harbottle. The Captain of Wark was similarly accused, but with the murder of two Scots 'nocht half ane Scottis myle fra the said metynge place of Roddane burne, and scant tua houris afore the meting of the Wardanis'.[39] These charges reveal the truly lawless state of the Borders. Not only was justice not being executed, but there was also the more serious

---

33 *CSP Scot.*, I, 398, p.192. Châtelherault also sent a letter to Mary Tudor on 25 September 1553, which simply reiterated Guise's message. *Ibid*, I, 398.i, p.192.
34 *RPC*, I, p.149.
35 *Ibid*, I, p.149.
36 *CSP Foreign, 1553–1558*, 53, pp. 17–8; *RPC*, I, pp. 148–51.
37 *Ibid*, I, p.148.
38 *Ibid*, I, p.148.
39 *Ibid*, I, pp. 148–9; *CSP Foreign, 1553–1558*, 53, pp. 17–8.

problem of the responsible officials having a complete disregard for Border law themselves. How could one expect Border law to be observed when the very people who were employed to enforce it, and dispense impartial justice, were themselves engaged in criminal activity?

In response to these allegations, Mary Tudor adopted a non-committal position. She neither admitted nor refuted the charges made against her subjects, but simply acceded to Mary of Guise's request for a meeting of commissioners on the Anglo-Scottish Border.[40] Sir Thomas Cornwallis and Sir Robert Bowes were appointed to meet with the Scottish commissioners, Sir Robert Carnegy of Kinnaird and Sir John Bellenden of Auchnoul, 'to determine all past quarrels, and give order to avoid the like in future'.[41] In late October 1553 the English Commissioners proceeded to Berwick armed with their instructions and a similar list of outrages committed by the Scots against the English.[42]

The result of this meeting of commissioners was an indenture dated 4 December 1553. The indenture was a reassertion and redefinition of Border law and practices, and aimed to provide for the effective administration and execution of justice.[43] It dealt with a wide range of issues from individual disputes, such as Lord Home's fishing rights, to the general backlog of unredressed bills at Days of Truce, and also outlined the correct procedures for the punishment of crime. In cases of murder, for example, Wardens were ordered to observe all points of the law and exact the full penalties because the 'negligent omission of offences in executioun and performing the said treatie and lawis in that poynt hes bene the occasioun of sic greit enormiteis and discordes upone the bordouris of baith the saidis realme'.[44] While the payment of damages remained the customary penalty for arson and assault, the commissioners added a further stipulation that the perpetrators of these crimes were to be delivered to the Warden opposite and 'punissit be him in strait presoun be the space of sex monethis'.[45] The Indenture of 1553, therefore, served as the legal foundation upon which Mary of Guise sought to implement good rule on the Border as Queen Regent.

40 Mary Tudor to Mary of Guise, 13 October 1553, *CSP Scot.*, I, 400, p.193. See also *CSP Foreign, 1553–1558*, 53, pp. 17–8, for the English Council's account of Noailles' audience with Mary and their thoughts on the charges levied by the Scots.
41 *CSP Scot.*, I, 400, p.193; *APC*, IV, p.357; *RPC*, I, p.150.
42 BL, Harley MSS, 289, f.160 and 1757, f.314.
43 *RPC*, XIV, pp. 115–22; Nicolson, *Leges Marchiarum*, pp. 71–83.
44 *RPC*, XIV, pp. 119–20.
45 *Ibid*, XIV, p.120.

During the first three years of her regency, Mary of Guise worked laboriously to see that Border laws were observed and enforced. In May 1554 d'Oisel reported to Noailles that, since her advancement to the regency and despite making a very good start, she had nevertheless been continually prevented from refortifying the Border and providing resources for the good policing and justice of the kingdom, both of which were badly needed.[46] One way she sought to remedy these problems was to take a direct hand in all aspects of Border affairs. As one would expect, she corresponded with Mary Tudor or used the French Ambassador resident in England to voice her complaints and seek redress at the English Court. But she also took the unusual step of regularly writing directly to England's Wardens on routine matters of business that one can only describe as trivial, and certainly not matters with which one would expect a Queen Regent to have concerned herself. In her correspondence with Lord Conyers and Lord Dacre, for example, she discussed the return of fugitives and the delivery of pledges, fought for the release of Scottish subjects who had been illegally detained in England and sought redress for crimes committed against individual Scots. By keeping in constant communication with Dacre and Conyers, Mary of Guise applied a great deal of pressure to the Wardens to enforce and execute Border law. She reinforced this policy by maintaining a high profile in the area.

In the summer of 1554 the Queen Regent made an extensive and prolonged visit to the Border. Her progress was intended to be a visible display of royal power, asserting her authority and that of the crown on a personal level. It also provided her with an opportunity to ensure first hand that justice was being served on both sides of the Anglo-Scottish divide. Informing Dacre of her forthcoming visit, Guise declared that the purpose of her progress was 'nocht only for our pastyme, bot to put ordour amangis sic misreulie peple as wald tend to raise ony truble or disquiet betuix the trew subjectis of thir twa realmes'.[47] She then made the extraordinary move of summoning him to a meeting with Lord Yester, Warden of the Middle March for Scotland, at Hexpethgate on 20 June to dispense the justice that should have been dispensed at an earlier meeting in May.[48] The Queen Regent's scheduled appearance at this conference was to ensure that it was. Her shrewd manipulation of events left Dacre in

---

46 AÉ, *Cor. Pol.*, Angleterre, IX, fos. 185, 232[r].
47 *RPC*, XIV, p.129; AÉ, *Cor. Pol.*, Angleterre, IX, f.232[r].
48 *RPC*, XIV, pp. 128–9.

no position to ignore the Queen Regent's summons or decline her 'invitation' to administer justice without adding to the friction that already existed between the two sides.[49]

The precarious nature of Anglo-Scottish relations in 1554 led the English to view Mary of Guise's visit to the Border with great suspicion. Although she had clearly stated the purpose of her journey to Dacre, an ulterior motive was nevertheless suspected.[50] Conyers was particularly worried. On 6 June 1554 he wrote to Shrewsbury expressing his concern: 'to what purpose hir commyng is, I am not (as yet) suer . . . But whatsoever hir intent is, I thinke (by the grace of god) with the small powre I have to put my self in such arreadyness as for the suddyn (if her purpose so were) that she and hir force sholde be resisted'.[51] As a precautionary measure, Shrewsbury subsequently ordered that all the English Wardens place themselves at one hour's notice for the defence of the Border, 'if nede shall so require'.[52] In the meantime, the Queen Regent's movements were to be watched and reported scrupulously.[53]

The highlight and main purpose of Guise's trip was to attend a justice ayre at Jedburgh in mid-July.[54] The fortnight she spent in the burgh satisfied suspicious English observers that she was genuinely concerned with justice, having 'travelled verie ornestlie to bring hir subiectes unto amytie and love on with an other'.[55] Leaving Jedburgh on 23 July, the royal party, which was also escorted by a company of French light horse under the command of d'Oisel, made its way to Kelso and arrived there that same evening. From Kelso, the Queen Regent and her military entourage then proceeded to Home Castle, Langton, Eyemouth, Dunbar and Haddington respectively.[56] Clearly Guise was determined to cover as much ground as possible during her progress for 'puttand reull vpoun the Bordouris' through a visible display of royal power. She also sought to achieve this by taking hostages as pledges for good behaviour and obedience to the crown.

In accordance with the advice she received for the punishment of crime and for 'the handillyng of the bourdour men',[57] she used her

49 *RPC*, XIV, pp. 130–1.
50 LPL, Talbot MSS, 3194, fos. 43^r, 47^r.
51 *Ibid*, 3194, f.47^r.
52 Conyers to Shrewsbury, 1 July 1554, *ibid*, 3194, f.43^r.
53 *Ibid*, 3194, f.43^r.
54 *RSS*, IV, 2783–90, pp. 481–3; *TA*, X, p.264; LPL, Talbot MSS, 3194, fos. 43^r, 51, 57, 59^r; *RPC*, XIV, p.137.
55 LPL, Talbot MSS, 3194, fos. 51, 59.
56 *Ibid*, 3194, f.59^r.
57 *Scottish Correspondence*, ccliii, pp. 379–80.

royal progress, and the justice ayre at Jedburgh in particular, as an opportunity to take 'plegeis of the clannis and vtheris quhilkis mycht be maist noysum to the peax'.[58] The Scotts and the Kerrs were two clans that fell into this category. The Queen Regent regarded their longstanding feud in the Scottish Middle March, which climaxed on 4 October 1552 with the murder of Sir Walter Scott of Buccleuch, as a 'grit impediment [to the peace] this lang tyme bygaine'.[59] One of her first acts was to summon the principal members of both houses to Edinburgh and enter them into a bond of assurance binding them to the peace.[60] In an attempt to ensure that this and other such bonds were upheld, she took 'dyverse surnames [as] pledges, for the observing and keping of good rule, as the Carres, the Scottis with dyverse others, wherefore there may be knytt frendshipp one with other'.[61] But this policy failed to pacify the Middle March or bind the Kerrs of Cessford permanently to the authority of the crown.

Indeed, Mary of Guise's progress as a whole did little to quell the endemic lawlessness and violence of the Border. International considerations and, more immediately, the Scots' contribution to the Habsburg-Valois conflict undermined her efforts and deprived her of valuable resources needed to reduce the frontier to obedience. In January 1555 d'Oisel complained of this bitterly to Noailles and pleaded that French troops be sent to Scotland 'for the work in hand to re-establish fear and good obedience on our frontiers'.[62] By the summer of 1555, the rapid deterioration of conditions on the Border led d'Oisel to surmise that it was the worst the area had seen for fifty years. The French Lieutenant-General attributed this specifically to the failure of England's Wardens to observe and enforce Border law, and warned that if they did not do something about it soon, Mary of Guise would.[63] The heightened tensions between England and Scotland in 1555 did little to improve the situation and, as d'Oisel predicted, left the Queen Regent with no choice but to implement a decidedly more aggressive Border policy.

Throughout 1555 Mary of Guise attempted to reduce the Borders to obedience through force. In May 1555 she called a muster to support Huntly, Cassillis and Morton in their commission 'to punish and repress certain crimes and Slaughters committed upon the

---

58 Fraser, *Wemyss*, III, pp. 9–10.
59 *RPC*, XIV, p.122.
60 *Ibid*, XIV, pp. 122–3 and I, pp. 152–3.
61 LPL, Talbot MSS, 3194, f.59; *RPC*, I, pp. 153–4.
62 AÉ, *Cor. Pol.*, Angleterre, IX, f.343ʳ.
63 *Ibid*, IX, fos. 468–72.

Borders'.[64] The military objective of this expedition was to invade Lauder and force the Laird of Cessford 'and utheris of this cuntre men his freyndis' to follow the Queen Regent's 'direction anent the ordowring and putting of gude rewll in the cuntre'.[65] In July and August two additional musters were called at Dumfries, where Guise and d'Oisel sought to effect the same on the West Border.[66] But even these military campaigns failed to produce the desired results. The same was also true in 1556, even though changes in the international situation had allowed the Queen Regent to focus her attention exclusively on domestic concerns.

In February 1556 the Habsburg-Valois truce of Vaucelles provided a welcome respite in the Continental wars and enabled Mary of Guise to step up her efforts on the Border. In May she successfully levied a police tax of £4,000 'for [the] furnessing of certane horsemen vpoun the west bordouris', and commissioned Bothwell, her newly appointed Lieutenant-General of the Marches, to lead a military expedition there for the repressing of thieves and traitors – starting at Sandy Armstrong's house.[67] Yet, despite being accompanied by a large number of French and Scottish troops,[68] Bothwell's campaign against the Scottish rebels in July 1556 was disastrous.[69] During the raid approximately eighteen of the Queen Regent's forces were killed and an additional forty taken prisoner – including Bothwell himself.[70]

---

64 Pitcairn, *Trials*, I.i, p.384; *TA*, X, p.264; *Scottish Correspondence*, cclxvi, pp. 400–1. Those who failed to observe the muster and assist Huntly, Cassillis and Morton in their commission were subsequently charged. Pitcairn, *Trials*, I.i, p.384.

65 *Ibid*, I.i, p.384.

66 *TA*, X, pp. 259–61; *RSS*, IV, 3038–9, p.534; *RPC*, XIV, pp. 13–4; AÉ, *Cor. Pol.*, Angleterre, IX, fos. 501–2, 503^r; LPL, Talbot MSS, 3194, f.107; St. Andrews University Library, Special Collections, msDA784.7, ms4347.

67 AÉ, *Cor. Pol.*, Angleterre, XIII, f.31^r; Teulet, *Papiers*, I, p.269 and *Relations*, I, p.279; *RPC*, XIV, p.14; *Aberdeen Council Register*, pp. 296–7.

68 Four hundred Scottish light horse and 'quelque nombre de gens de cheval et de pied de ceulx que le Roy entretient par deçà [a great number of horesmen and infantrymen that the King keeps in our country]' comprised the Queen Regent's forces 'pour réduire en l'obéissance quelques rebelles habitants en icelle frontière [to get the submission of some rebels living on the border]'. AÉ, *Cor. Pol.*, Angleterre, XIII, f.31^r; Teulet, *Papiers*, I, pp. 269–70 and *Relations*, I, p.281.

69 See AÉ, *Cor. Pol.*, Angleterre, IX, fos. 665–8 and XIII, fos. 30^v-33, 45, 47–9; Teulet, *Papiers*, I, pp. 267–77 and *Relations*, I, pp. 279–88; and LPL, Talbot MSS, 3194, fos. 262, 266, for specific details of Bothwell's ill-fated expedition.

70 AÉ, *Cor. Pol.*, Angleterre, XIII, fos. 31-2^r, 49^v; Teulet, *Papiers*, I, pp. 270–1, 276–7 and *Relations*, I, pp. 282–3, 287–8; LPL, Talbot MSS, 3194, f.266.

Even when attacked with force, the endemic lawlessness and violence prevailed and would continue to do so for the remainder of Mary of Guise's regency. But this problem was not exclusive to the Borders. It was also true of the Highlands and Western Isles, where Guise was equally determined to restore law and order after the failure of Châtelherault's Highland policy.

* * *

The untimely death of James V in 1542 inaugurated a period of renewed lawlessness and violence in the Highlands and Western Isles. The semblance of order that the king had managed to impose there prior to his death quickly evaporated under Arran's administration. The factionalism that accompanied Mary Stewart's accession, together with Donald Dubh's attempt to restore the Lordship of the Isles and the intrigues of England during their 'rough wooing' of Scotland, all contributed to the revival of the 'Highland problem'. As in the Borders, Mary of Guise attempted to deal with this problem by providing for the execution of justice, making royal progresses as a visible demonstration of royal power and, ultimately, by extending and asserting the authority of the crown through force. But, as we shall see, much of the 'Highland problem' that Guise was faced with upon becoming regent was a direct result of Châtelherault's ineptitude.

In 1543 Scotland's new regent, James Hamilton, earl of Arran, chose to release the clan chiefs and hostages whom James V had captured and imprisoned during his naval expedition and royal progress to the Highlands and Western Isles in May 1540.[71] Arran's power struggle with Cardinal Beaton, who vehemently opposed his position on reform and dynastic union with England, prompted him to release these prisoners in a deliberate attempt to revive the 'Highland problem' and deprive Beaton of the active support of Huntly and Argyll, the respective Lieutenants of the North and Western Isles. Arran had been unwittingly helped by Donald Dubh, who had escaped from Edinburgh Castle in 1543 and returned to the Isles in an attempt to reclaim his patrimony – the former Lordship of the Isles.

Donald was the grandson of John MacDonald, the last Lord of the Isles, who forfeited the Lordship in 1493 and spent the remaining ten years of his life as a prisoner of the crown.[72] The Lordship of the

71 For an overview of James' Highland policy, see Cameron's 'Daunting the Isles', in *James V*, pp. 228–54.
72 Macdougall, *James IV*, pp. 100, 101.

Isles was a vast territory that included the Hebrides, the western coastline from Lewis to Kintyre, and the earldom of Ross. The sheer size and remoteness of the Lordship made it extremely difficult for the crown to impose and consolidate royal power there, let alone govern it effectively. Even the crown's agents for the region, Huntly and Argyll, found it difficult and often met with hostile resistance for threatening to undermine the Lords' accepted autonomy. Historically, the Lords of the Isles had a precarious relationship with the crown.[73] The willingness and frequency with which they refused to recognise the authority of the crown when it was in their interest to do so, often resulted in their denunciation as rebels, and this made them attractive allies to the English. English intrigues in Scotland often involved the Lords of the Isles, and the threat of a two-pronged attack from across the Border and from the west was one of the main reasons why Stewart Kings from James I actively tried to daunt the Isles into submission – albeit rarely with any long-lasting success. John MacDonald's forfeiture of the earldom of Ross in 1476, for example, came after he was successfully charged with treason for conspiring with Edward IV of England to conquer and divide Scotland. Donald Dubh, who had been born in prison in 1504 and incarcerated as a hostage of the crown until he escaped in 1543, was determined to restore the Lordship of the Isles to its former glory and reclaim what he considered to be his rightful inheritance. However, the revival of Donald's campaign to regain possession of the Lordship of the Isles and the earldom of Ross, ousting Argyll and Huntly in the process, had been hindered by the absence of many of his supporters.[74] Arran's release of these prisoners was a deliberate and open invitation to rebellion.

On an immediate and practical level, Arran's policy produced the desired results. In the summer of 1543 Donald Dubh and his insurgent cohorts launched an attack against Argyll, who was compelled to stay and defend his lands. But in the end it was Arran himself who suffered the devastating effects of this policy. On 3 September 1543 he recovered from his so-called 'godly fit'. Abandoning the reforming and anglophile cause, the Regent reversed his position and aligned himself with Cardinal Beaton and Mary of Guise. Having done so, he then had to try and put an end to the

---

73 For background information on the Lords of the Isles and their relationship with the crown, see R. Andrew MacDonald, *The Kingdom of the Isles, c.1100–c.1136* (East Linton, 1997); and D. Gregory, *The History of the Western Highlands and Isles of Scotland* (London, 1881).

74 *Ibid*, pp. 154–5.

chaos he had unleashed in the Highlands and Isles – a task which was made all the more difficult by the intrigues of his arch-rival Matthew Stewart, earl of Lennox, during Henry VIII's 'rough wooing' of Scotland.

Shortly after the Earl of Hertford began his campaign to 'burn Edinburgh town', sack Leith and ravage the Borders and Lowlands of Scotland in 1544, Lennox embarked on an equally savage naval expedition to the Western Isles.[75] With a fleet of eighteen galleys, Lennox invaded the Isles of Arran and Bute before proceeding to Dumbarton where he planned to deliver its castle to Henry VIII and render it a key English stronghold in Scotland.[76] To achieve his military objective, Lennox was relying on the support of Glencairn, whom he had urged to 'ramayn with in the castal qwel I com haym . . . and kep yowr lordschip self and trest with na man bot with in the sayd plays'.[77] Lennox's fears of disaffection were justified. Glencairn had been secretly reconciled with Mary of Guise and a plot was subsequently devised to capture Lennox upon his return to Dumbarton and foil his attempt to deliver the castle to the English.[78] In his letter of 25 September 1544, Glencairn informed Guise of the 'guid wordes . . . gifand me' by the wife[79] and friends of Lennox's retainer, George Stirling of Glorat, captain of Dumbarton Castle, which were made on behalf of Lennox and 'my lord of Lennax freindis'. Despite these efforts to keep him on side, Glencairn accurately predicted that they 'sall failzie [in] thare entent'.[80] Upon arriving at Dumbarton Castle, Lennox sensed something was wrong and hastily departed for the safety of his ships. When Sir George Douglas of Pittendreich arrived in Dumbarton with a force of 4,000 Scots soon after, Lennox decided to

75 *Hamilton Papers*, II, pp. 325–7; Gregory, *History*, pp. 361–9, 371–2, 379–80.

76 *L &P of Henry VIII*, XIX, ii, p.312.

77 *Scottish Correspondence*, lxxvii, pp. 99–100; *L & P of Henry VIII*, XIX, i, p.809.

78 Gregory, *History*, p.165.

79 Annabel, daughter of Sir William Edmonstone of Duntreath, captain of Doune.

80 *Scottish Correspondence*, lxxxiv, pp. 106–8. On 19 March 1546 the government issued an act of indemnity to George Stirling and discharged him of all the 'diverse and sindrie attemptatis, reiffis, spulyeis, slauchteris, depredationis and uthairis, committit and done be the personis being in the said Castell' when in the possession of Lennox, on the grounds that there were 'utharis that wes principale committeris of the saidis reiffis, spulzeis, and heirschippis' and that, after the flit of Lennox to England, he 'randerit the said Castell to my said Lord Governour'. *RPC*, I, p.66.

make a hasty retreat to the Isle of Bute, only to be attacked by the Earl of Argyll en route.[81]

It was during this conflict with Argyll that Lennox first entered into communication with Donald Dubh, whose own vendetta against Argyll made him a logical choice of ally. On his part, Donald was in favour of any alliance that would help him in his own quest to reclaim his patrimony and he had the active support of many clan chiefs and prominent Islesmen, several of whom had been released from prison by Arran. A military alliance was thus formed. Lennox immediately returned to England to report on these developments and plan for future events, while Donald and his friends were left to continue their attacks against Argyll and Huntly, the bastions of central government in the Highlands and Western Isles.[82] Once again, Arran was to suffer the consequences of his ill-conceived decision to release the clan chiefs and hostages imprisoned by James V in 1540. By 1545 the 'Highland problem' had taken on a distinctly British dimension. The 'gret invasions and persute maid be Donald allegesand him of the Ilis and utheris hieland men his part takaris', was 'nocht alanerly throw thair awine pissance bot also throw the suppli myance and favour of the King of Ingland, talkand gude deid of him and his thairfore, tending to do that is in thame to bring the hale Ilis and ane grete part of the ferme land of this relame to the obesance of the King of Ingland'.[83]

Arran's attempt to counter the effects of this alliance was feeble at best. In June 1545 a proclamation was issued by the Privy Council ordering Donald and his followers to 'desist and ces fra all maner of persewing or invading of our Soverane Ladyis liegis als wele duelland in the Ilis as in the ferme land of this realm, or invading of our Soverane Ladyis liegis to byrn hery slay or distroy ony of thame, or mak ony oppressionis upoun thame, . . . under the pane of tresoun'.[84] The government's threats of legal action and 'thair utir rewyne and distructioun' by 'the hale body of the realm of Scotland with the succour laitly cumin fourth of France' had absolutely no effect in

---

81 In September 1544 Mary of Guise offered Sir George Douglas of Pittendreich a pension of 1,000 crowns in return for his support and service. As has already been mentioned, Sir George and his brother, the Earl of Angus, were the nominal leaders of the English faction in Scotland until they became disgruntled with Henry VIII and Somerset's overly aggressive Scottish policy. *Scottish Correspondence*, lxxxv-lxxxvii, pp. 108–33; Gregory, *History*, pp. 163–7.

82 *Ibid*, pp. 167–8.

83 *RPC*, I, p.4.

84 *Ibid*, I, pp. 4–5.

daunting Donald into submission – it only strengthened his alliance with Lennox.

In July 1545 Donald commissioned two plenipotentaries to negotiate with Lennox the terms of his submission to the English King. These negotiations ultimately proved successful. On 5 August 1545 Donald and the Lords and Barons of his Council, which included such notables at Hector MacLean of Duart, Rory MacLeod of Lewis and Alexander MacLeod of Dunvegan, swore an oath of allegiance to Henry VIII *and* recognised Lennox as the true regent of Scotland and second person in the realm.[85] More importantly, Donald would have the backing of the English in his quest to reclaim the Lordship of the Isles and the earldom of Ross. In return for his military and political support, Henry VIII confirmed Donald's annual pension of 2,000 crowns and agreed to pay the wages of 3,000 Islesmen for two months.[86]

By the time Arran had finally decided to initiate legal proceedings against Lennox and other 'certane genillmen of the Ilis', it was too little, too late.[87] In September 1545 preparations for a large-scale invasion of Scotland from Ireland had already been made.[88] Lennox was to command the expeditionary force of 2,000 Irish soldiers provided by the Earl of Ormond, who was also to participate in the invasion, and 8,000 of Donald's men. However, delay and a certain amount of disorganisation prevented this invasion from becoming a reality. Lennox had been called away to assist Hertford in his military campaign on the Borders and, during his prolonged absence, dissension within the Highland contingency grew over the payment of wages and eventually led to its disbandment.[89] The death of Donald Dubh shortly thereafter, and the selection of John MacDonald of Islay as his successor, served only to intensify the dissension within the Highlands and Western Isles. Lennox's plans for the invasion of Scotland were severely undermined by the disaffection of many clan chiefs, such as the MacLeods of Lewis and Harris, who refused to recognise John of Islay as Lord of the Isles and sought to reconcile themselves with Arran. Lennox and the English party suffered a further blow when, on 18 June 1546, Arran successfully negotiated a truce between Argyll and John of Islay, who renounced his title as Lord of the Isles.[90] But this was not the last the Scottish government

85 Gregory, *History*, pp. 170–1.
86 *Ibid*, pp. 170–4.
87 *APS*, II, pp. 452–4, 456, 459, 464, 468–9.
88 *Scottish Correspondence*, cvii, p.146; *Diurnal of Occurrents*, p.39.
89 Gregory, *History*, p.174.
90 *RPC*, I, p.30; *Scottish Correspondence*, ccxxxix, p.353.

would hear of Lennox or of his intrigues to become 'master' of Scotland.

Reconciliation did not necessarily imply active support for the government. While many Highlanders and Islesmen fought at the battle of Pinkie during the second phase of England's 'rough wooing' under Protector Somerset, many still ignored Arran's summonses to muster out of indifference or fear of arrest. The MacLeods of Lewis, for example, were noticeably absent even though they had been reconciled with the government. The absence of John Moidart, chief of the clan Ranald, and Ewan Allanson of Lochiel, clan chief of Cameron, however, was far more understandable. In his proclamation against 'the grete slauchteris, murthouris, reiffis, and commoun oppressionis, with convocatiounis of our Soverane Ladyis liegis, committit and done be diverse personis', Arran promised that he 'sall newther giff respect nor remissioun, supersedere nor relaxatioun, to an maner of persoun nor personis that sal happin to committit slauchter or mutilatioun, reiff and commoun oppressioun' or those 'personis resettaris and manteinaris of sik rebellis, oppressouris, and malefactouris, bot sall use his Graces authorite aganis thame'.[91] The insurrection of the Clanranald and the Clan Cameron against Huntly and the Frasers of Lovat made them prime targets for prosecution.[92] Needless to say, it was in their best interest to stay out of Arran's way in the comparatively safe haven of the Highlands and remain conspicuously absent from any national campaign that could result in their own internment.

By the time the Anglo-Scottish conflict ended in 1549–50, there was thus a great need to restore order following the chaos that war and Arran's policies had created in the Highlands and Western Isles. Upon returning to Scotland from France in November 1551, Mary of Guise immediately set out to fulfil her commission to 'put the realme to ane quyatenes' even though she had yet to assume power in an official capacity. In what would be the first indication that she would emulate her late husband's Highland policy, Guise and Arran, now

91 *RPC*, I, pp. 59–60, 71. Argyll's name in the sederunt for this meeting of the Privy Council suggests that 'sik rebellis, oppressouris and malefactouris' included the insurgents of the Highlands and Isles, such as the Clanranald and Clan Cameron.

92 Culminating in 1544 at the battle of Lochy, this insurrection resulted in many deaths, including those of Hugh, lord Fraser and his son and heir, Simon. W. MacKay (ed.), *Chronicles of the Frasers: The Wardlaw Manuscript entitled Polichronicon Seu Policratica Temporum, or, The True Genealogy of the Frasers. 916–1674. By Master James Fraser* (SHS, 1905), pp. 134–40; Gregory, *History*, pp. 157–63.

styled Châtelherault, embarked on a progress throughout the Highlands in the summer of 1552.[93] Guise's influence on this expedition
did not escape the notice of contemporary observers. In his *History*, for
example, Lesley wrote that 'the Governour be advyse of the Quene
and nobilitie, determinit to hald justic aris throuch all the partis of the
realme, and that rather for staying of trubles in tymis, nor for rigorous
punishment of anye offences by past; and to that effect, he being
accumpaneit with the Quene and syndre uther nobill men, past in the
north partis of Scotland'.[94] Many commentators have also viewed this
expedition as a self-serving enterprise on the part of the Queen
Dowager, who used it to secure support for her own political ambitions against Châtelherault.[95] This no doubt played a part, but it must
ultimately be regarded as an attempt to deal with the 'Highland
problem' by asserting the authority and will of the crown through a
visible display of royal power.

Upon becoming Queen Regent, Mary of Guise determined to take
an aggressive stance with respect to the 'Highland problem'. This was
to be achieved *not* through French domination, but by implementing
traditional Stewart policy that sought to daunt the Isles into submission through the work of crown agents such as the Earls of Huntly,
Argyll and Sutherland. In June 1554 Guise commissioned Huntly and
Argyll to raise armies, and by land and sea 'to pas with fyre and sword
to the utter extermination of the Clarannald, Donald Gorme [of
Sleat], Macloyde of the Lews, and thair complices, that sends not and
enters thair pledges as they ar chairged'.[96] Guise's vehemence
stemmed from the failure of the Clanranald and Clan Cameron to
render themselves before the crown at a justice ayre held at Inverness
in 1552, despite having been summoned to do so.[97] Huntly and Argyll
were immediately instructed to pursue the Clanranald and Clanca-
meron, but only Argyll succeeded in extracting an explanation for
John Moidart of Clanranald's absence – namely, 'that he wald haif
cumin to the Quenis lawis, and done obeysance, giff my Lord
Governouris lettres and chargeis had cumin to his knawledge befoire
his passing to the Irland'.[98] The Council, having accepted Moidart's
explanation, then gave Argyll until December 1552 to bring John

93 Cameron, *James V*, pp. 245–8.
94 Lesley, *History*, p.243.
95 Marshall, for instance, claims that 'Mary was not solely interested in the
   punishment of the disturbers of the peace. She used the expedition to
   further her own cause'. Marshall, *Mary of Guise*, p.195.
96 *RPC*, XIV, p.12.
97 *Ibid*, I, pp. 125–6.
98 *Ibid*, I, p.126.

Moidart before the Governor and Council so that he could formally offer his submission and obedience to the crown.[99] By September 1553 Huntly had managed to secure the Clanranald's submission. At Ruthven in Badenoch he entered into a contract with John Moidart of Clanranald, his son, Alan, and 'thair kyne, freindis, allys, and pertakaris', whereby the latter agreed to submit to the authority of the crown in return for a general pardon of all their past crimes.[100] Guise's commission of June 1554, however, reveals that John Moidart's submission was not worth the paper it was written on.

Argyll set off on his military expedition for the 'surprissing of the Rebellis of the Ilis' on 12 August 1554. He informed Guise that his army was to pass to Mull, 'quhar James McConnill and McClane wyth ther haill folkis ar convenit and remanis upoun my cuming. And quhen we ar all convenit thaire, sall tak purpos to pas forthwarttis upoun the saidis rebellis'.[101] What happened during Argyll's expedition to the Isles is unknown, but we are to presume that, like Huntly, he failed. Unlike Huntly, however, Argyll was fortunate to have escaped the wrath of Mary of Guise.

The personal price paid by Huntly for failing in his commission to establish order in the Highlands was high. The reason for this is not entirely clear. According to Lesley, the Lowland contingent of Huntly's army refused to serve on foot, and Huntly refused to 'merche with the hieland men onlie, for the lait hattrent that thai had conceaved aganis him for the deithe of McIntoche, and thairfore he returned'.[102] Huntly's failure to carry out his commission resulted in his being summoned before the Queen Regent on 11 October 1554 to explain his actions. It was subsequently 'descerned that he had not used his commission according to his acceptation and dewtie, bot had failzied thairin, and thairfore wes ordaned to be punissed at the Quenis pleasour'.[103] Guise's 'ewyll opponzeone' of Huntly was made manifestly clear by the extent to which she chose to punish the 'Cock o' the

---

99 *RPC*, I, p.126.
100 *Scottish Correspondence*, ccxlviii, pp. 366–7.
101 *Ibid*, cclix, pp. 388–9; *TA*, X, pp. 229, 287.
102 Lesley, *History*, p.251; *Scottish Correspondence*, cclxiii, p.395 *n*.2. Huntly had many enemies in the North, one of them the Clan Mackintosh. At a lieutenant court in Aberdeen in August 1550, Huntly had arbitrarily charged Mackintosh with conspiracy against his life. Although the burgh council overturned this verdict, Mackintosh was nevertheless executed by the Countess of Huntly, allegedly at the instigation of her husband. The Huntly-Mackintosh feud was exacerbated by the murder of Huntly's sheriff-depute on 30 September 1551. This was the same feud that delayed Mary of Guise's trip to France in 1550. See ch.3 *n*.25.
103 *RPC*, XIV, p.13.

North' – she was not going to tolerate such self-serving disregard for her authority from any of her nobles.[104] Huntly was subsequently imprisoned and sentenced to be banished to France (although this was later remitted), received a heavy fine and suffered the revocation of his interests in Orkney and Moray. The most severe punishment, or at least the one with the greatest repercussions, was the passing of the Great Seal to Huntly's vice-Chancellor, du Rubay, which effectively stripped him of any real power as Chancellor.[105]

There is, however, some question as to the real motive behind Mary of Guise's extremely harsh treatment of Huntly. Was this a genuine attempt to assert her authority, or does the nature of Huntly's punishment reveal an ulterior motive? Frenchmen certainly benefited from Huntly's disgrace. Du Rubay exercised a considerable amount of power as Keeper of the Great Seal, and M. de Bonot benefited from the revocation of Huntly's interests in Orkney by being appointed bailie there in March 1555.[106] Guise was also able to satisfy Sutherland's claims similarly, appointing him bailie of Moray on 2 August 1555.[107] Yet the fact that he was restored to favour within a year of his disgrace suggests that Huntly was being used, as d'Oisel had intimated, as an example to the rest of the nobility.[108] It was impossible for Guise to effect a strong monarchy and extend royal government into the localities if powerful nobles disregarded her authority when it served their own interests.

Unlike Huntly and Argyll, Mary of Guise did have some success with the Earl of Sutherland. He managed to capture and imprison Iye du MacKay, lord Reay, who had been wreaking havoc on his lands since Sutherland had accompanied Mary of Guise to France in 1550.[109] By 1554 MacKay's 'mischeif' had not abated. He continued to spoil and molest the lands of Sutherland and, on a recent occasion, had taken 'away certane wemen and gudes'.[110] In July 1554, therefore, Sutherland received a commission to arrest MacKay and reduce the country to obedience. He was to be assisted by his stepfather, Sir Hugh Kennedy of Girvanmains, who sailed from Leith with a naval force

---

104 *Scottish Correspondence*, cclxiii, p.395.
105 Huntly entered into his contract with the Queen Regent at Stirling Castle on 30 March 1555. *Scottish Correspondence*, cclxiv, cclxiii, pp. 396–8, 395–6; Lesley, *History*, p.252; *Diurnal of Occurrents*, p.52.
106 *Scottish Correspondence*, cclxv, pp. 389–9; Lesley, *History*, pp. 256–7.
107 Fraser, *Sutherland*, I, pp. 106–7; *Scottish Correspondence*, p.374.
108 Teulet, *Papiers*, I, p.722.
109 As an 'assured Scot', MacKay had assisted the English in their capture of Haddington in 1548. *Scottish Correspondence*, cclviii, pp. 386–8.
110 *Ibid*, cclviii, pp. 387.

on a command of the Justiciary dated 11 August 1554.[111] Sutherland invaded Strathnaver, successfully captured and demolished the principal MacKay stronghold at Borve and forced Lord Reay's capitulation. By 14 October 1554 Girvanmains informed the Queen Regent that his submission was imminent. On 11 November MacKay formally submitted to the crown and sailed with Girvanmains to Dumbarton Castle, where he was subsequently imprisoned.[112]

In 1555 Mary of Guise renewed her efforts to combat the 'Highland problem'. A process of treason was issued against Rory MacLeod of Lewis and, in June, the earls of Argyll and Atholl were commissioned to pursue rebels, including MacLeod and the Clanranald, and to reduce the Isles to obedience.[113] These expeditions met with limited success. Through Argyll, MacLeod made certain offers to the Privy Council for his submission and was granted a respite, while Atholl succeeded in bringing John Moidart of Clanranald and two of his sons before Mary of Guise to offer their obedience to the crown. In a serious lapse of judgement, however, Guise pardoned the Clanranald for all their past offences and incarcerated them at Perth and Methven Castle, from where they escaped only to resume their insurgent activity in the Highlands.[114] It was presumably because of this that she decided to embark on another royal progress of the Highlands and Isles to pursue royal justice and to daunt the area into submission. Accompanied by such notables as Huntly, Argyll, Atholl, Marischal and the Bishops of Ross and Orkney, Guise's progress of 1556 took her to Inverness, the earldom of Ross, Elgin, Banff and Aberdeen.[115] She held justice ayres in all these places and dispensed 'the most extreme and rigorous punishment'.[116] Emulating her late husband's policy, she 'charged everie ane of the capitanis of the hie landis to bring in the offendaris of thair awin kin, according to the ordour prescribit in King James the Fiftis tyme onder gret panis; quhairthrow mony was entered'.[117] But just when she was starting to make her authority felt and having some success in her pursuit of

111 *Scottish Correspondence*, cclxi, pp. 390–3; *ER*, XVIII, p.584; *TA*, X, p.281.
112 MacKay, *Chronicles of the Frasers*, pp. 142–3.
113 *RPC*, XIV, p.14; *TA*, X, pp. 229, 277, 278, 286, 287; Pitcairn, *Trials*, I.i, p.392.
114 Gregory, *History*, p.185.
115 Lesley, *History*, pp. 256–7; *RMS*, IV, 1095, 1097, 1110, pp. 243, 247; *TA*, X, pp. 308–9, 311–13, 317–9; AÉ, *Cor. Pol.*, Angleterre, XIII, fos. 47–9.
116 Lesley, *History*, pp. 256–7; Pitcairn, *Trials*, I.i, pp. 390–2; AÉ, *Cor. Pol.*, Angleterre, XIII, fos. 49[r-v]; Teulet, *Papiers*, I, p.275 and *Relations*, I, pp. 286–7.
117 Lesley, *History*, p.256.

royal justice, changes in the international situation quickly under-mined her efforts, and prevent us from knowing how effective Mary of Guise's Highland policy would have been in the long term.

The renewal of the Habsburg-Valois conflict in January 1557, and the outbreak of war between England and France the following June, dictated that Mary of Guise focus her attention, once again, on matters of national security and the Border. The Congregation's rebellion of 1559–60 served only to distract her attention further, consuming all of her time and energy during the final years of her administration. It was during periods of neglect such as these that the 'Highland problem' was allowed to fester virtually unchecked. Con-tinuity, time and adequate resources were the essential ingredients for an effective Highland policy. During the fifteenth and sixteenth centuries, however, these ingredients were in short supply. A string of minority governments and the disruptions of war constantly under-mined any efforts to pacify the Highlands and impose royal authority. In this respect, the reign of Mary Queen of Scots and the regency of Mary of Guise were no exception.

* * *

The first years of Mary of Guise's regency were dominated by inter-national considerations. The tensions that arose out of the Habsburg-Valois conflict and, in particular, Mary Tudor's accession and mar-riage to Philip of Spain, forced Guise to focus her attention almost exclusively on matters of defence and national security. These ten-sions also highlighted the need to assert her authority and reduce the kingdom to obedience if law and order had any chance of being imposed and, more importantly, if peaceful relations with England were to have any chance of being maintained. Ironically, these very same tensions undermined the execution of Guise's domestic policy as a whole, which aimed to put the realme 'to ane quyatenes' through a powerful monarchy and strong central government.

Yet, despite these frustrations, Mary of Guise's commitment to the pursuit of royal justice and the ordering of the country did not falter. She even began to make some headway in the Highlands and in her attempts to advance the interests of the crown at the expense of local jurisdictions. The frustrations of 1554–56, however, were just a glimpse of things to come. The Franco-English war of 1557 soon brought dynastic issues to the fore. The Scots were faced with the prospect of entering a war they did not necessarily want or feel they had to fight, and inevitably brought into question the marriage of their own queen.

7

War and Marriage

J ust eleven months after it had been contracted, the five year Habsburg-Valois truce of Vaucelles had completely broken down. By the end of January 1557 Henri and Philip, now the King of Spain and ruler of the Netherlands, were at war.[1] Henri's military alliance with Pope Paul IV, however, presented Philip with some serious problems and rendered him a less than willing participant in the conflict. The religious ramifications of waging war against the papacy would give credence to Pope Paul IV's diatribes accusing both Philip and his father of being heretics and oppressors of the Holy See.[2] Added to this was the more immediate problem of financing the war. Philip naturally turned to his wife for support and travelled to England in March 1557 in the hope of procuring financial and military assistance. As before, the English government remained hostile to the idea of fighting Philip's war and refused to commit resources to the Continental campaign. Yet within a matter of months, the English government had dramatically reversed its position by issuing a formal declaration of war against France on 7 June 1557. Years of French intrigue against the Marian régime had taken their toll, making the English more disposed to war than to peace. The straw that broke the camel's back was Thomas Stafford's capture of Scarborough Castle on 28 April 1557 and the reports that the French had facilitated his invasion. Mary now had the perfect excuse to push her government into supporting Philip in the Habsburg-Valois conflict.[3]

1 For Charles V's abdication and the formal transfer of power to Philip in October 1555, see Rodríguez-Salgado, *The Changing Face of Empire*, pp. 126–32, and pp. 137–252 for the war that was formally declared between France and Spain on 31 January 1557.

2 Pope Paul IV deeply resented Spain's domination of Italy and, in particular, his native Naples.

3 Two French galleys reportedly convoyed Stafford and his expeditionary force from France to England. Noailles, however, knew nothing of this enterprise and recognised the damage it had done with respect to England's neutrality. LPL, Talbot MSS, 3195, f.31; AÉ, *Cor. Pol.*, XIII, fos. 195ᵛ-7; PRO, SP31/3/23, fos. 161–2, 172, 179; *APC*, VI, p.80; Loades, *Two Tudor Conspiracies*, pp. 151–75.

England's declaration of war against France, however, had far wider implications than simply the English joining the Continental wars. The Habsburg-Valois conflict had now officially come to the British Isles, and it would be only a matter of time before Scotland also became involved, directly or indirectly, on behalf of the French. Scotland's inevitable participation was something that Mary of Guise had predicted with a great sense of foreboding when she learned of the Duc de Guise's military expedition to assist Pope Paul IV against the Duke of Alva in Naples in January 1557. Foreseeing that this would lead to a breach of the truce of Vaucelles, Guise wrote to the Cardinal de Lorraine that 'I pray, and shall pray daily, to our Lord from my heart that He will please to send us peace. For I greatly fear that if that good God does not put His hand to it, when once matters come to an open breach on [?your] side, it will be difficult for us to avoid our share'.[4]

War was the last thing Mary of Guise wanted at this particular time. Scotland was in no position to fight a war let alone defend herself against a foreign invasion.[5] This was primarily due to the Scots' reluctance to finance Guise's defensive policies. For many members of the Scottish political élite, the question of Mary Stewart's marriage needed to be settled before they committed any more money for the defence of the realm on account of France's foreign policy.[6] As Guise would later learn, this was one reason why the Three Estates rejected the proposed tax reassessment scheme in May 1556. With the Habsburg-Valois truce now on the verge of collapse, the Scots' refusal to finance Guise's defensive policies made the question of Franco-Scottish dynastic union a matter of political necessity and national security. Explaining this to the powers that be in France, however, was not going to be easy. The only way she could account for Scotland's ill-preparedness and substandard defences was to explain the Scots' position, but in order to do this, Guise had to broach the subject of dynastic union.

Raising the sensitive matter of marriage to the French King without seeming to do so out of self-interest was a very delicate operation, so Guise first turned to her family in France for a more sympathetic audience. Referring to the Three Estates' rejection of the tax-reassessment scheme, the Queen Regent wrote to the Cardinal de Lorraine:

4 *Papal Negotiations*, p.428; AÉ, *Mémoires et Documents*, Angleterre, XV, f.7^v.
5 See *ibid*, XV, fos. 7–11, for Mary of Guise's comments to the Cardinal de Lorraine and Constable Montmorency on the sad state of Scotland's defences.
6 *Ibid*, XV, fos. 7–11.

Et ne fault que je vous celles, ce que aucuns m'ont dict cy
lesdicts cy parlans que Je ne vous refer pour vouloir accelera
et haster les choses, Mais pour vous faire cognoister les
oppinions de ceste nation, Qui fin quils mectoys la charrue
deuans les boeufs Et me trompoys de pense riens aspirer de
deca si au preallable le mariage nestans accomply, Car Ils
estents tousiours cy doubte soubz quil seigneur Ilz debuonts
tomber. Je noseroys mander telles choses au Roy dautant que
lon pourroit estimer que je le disse pour mon affection
particulliere. Dieu scayt ce qui en est.

[Nor must I conceal from you, what some have said to me,
when I spoke to them about it – (I do not refer the matter to
you from a wish to accelerate or hasten it, but in order to
make you acquainted with the temper of this country) – that
it would be putting the cart before the oxen, and deceiving
myself, if I thought of settling anything before the marriage is
accomplished, for they are still doubtful under which lord
they shall fall. I should not venture to write such things to
the king for fear he should imagine I said them from
interested motives, but God knows the truth of the matter].[7]

Guise conjectured that another factor contributing to the Scots'
reluctance to finance her defensive policies was the reported ill health
of Mary, Queen of Scots. Throughout the summer and autumn of
1556 Mary had been afflicted by a string of fevers that the Queen
Regent claimed 'has put many things in doubt' in the minds of the
Scots.[8] If she were married, such doubts would be irrelevant. The
impetus behind Franco-Scottish dynastic union, therefore, came
mainly from the Scottish political élite, whose desire to see their
Queen married sprang from a greater desire for political stability in
the extremely volatile arena of European dynastic politics. While it is
true that for Scots with Protestant sympathies the union of the French
and Scottish Catholic crowns might have been seen as a direct threat
to the reform movement in Scotland and grounds for opposition to
the Valois-Stewart marriage, this was a domestic issue and not a
dynastic one.

7 AÉ, *Mémoires et Documents*, Angleterre, XV, f.9ʳ; *Papal Negotiations*, p.429.
   Mary of Guise does not elaborate on the identity of these Scots who
   wanted the marriage question settled.
8 Fraser, *Mary, Queen of Scots*, pp. 89–90; *Papal Negotiations*, pp. 419–21, 429;
   AÉ, *Mémoires et Documents*, Angleterre, XV, fos. 9ʳ, 10ʳ.

This desire for political stability was also shared by Mary of Guise, whose relationship with her magnates had reached an all-time low by January 1557. For the very first time, Guise was feeling estranged from her subjects. 'Men's minds', she complained, 'have been so changeable, and so in suspense, that those from whom I hoped the most, I have found more estranged that I have ever seen them, not only since I have ruled them, but since I have known Scotland.'[9] She had generated opposition through her taxation, defensive and foreign policies, with the result that random acts of violence were still being carried out against the French soldiers serving on the Border, despite Parliament's act of June 1555 against those 'that rasis murmuris sclanders and seditioun betuix the liegis of this realme and the maist Christin Kingis lieges'.[10] But for Guise, the real source of discord was her determination to see justice take a straightforward course.[11] Her attempts to implement legal reform met with fierce opposition from the Scottish political community, who claimed that she was really trying to replace their old laws with those of the French.[12]

Mary of Guise's political alienation was the result of the problems exclusively associated with her regency. As a Frenchwoman, she was open to criticism on account of her nationality if she implemented unpopular Franco-centric policies. If, on the other hand, she followed in the Stewart tradition and implemented policies directed at the nobility in the localities with a view to strengthening the authority of the crown, she was accused of being a regent with notions of power above her station. What was acceptable for a sovereign was less acceptable for a regent – and the fact that she was a female regent during a majority rule was bound to ruffle a few feathers. All these factors, singularly or collectively, were potential grounds for opposition. By January 1557, Mary of Guise's political position in Scotland had weakened to such an extent that she was finding it increasingly difficult to impose her will and authority. 'Great responsibilities', she would lament, 'are easily undertaken, but not discharged to God's satisfaction without difficulty.'[13] For Mary of Guise, the marriage of Mary, Queen of Scots was just as important for her own political stability as it was for Scotland's magnates. As long as the Franco-Scottish alliance remained in a state of limbo, the implementation of

9 *Papal Negotiations*, p.430; AÉ, *Mémoires et Documents*, Angleterre, XV, f.9[r].
10 PRO, SP 31/3/22, f.19; *APS*, II, pp. 499–500.
11 AÉ, *Mémoires et Documents*, Angleterre, XV, f.9[r]; *Papal Negotiations*, p.430.
12 AÉ, *Mémoires et Documents*, Angleterre, XV, fos. 8[r], 9[r-v]; *Papal Negotiations*, pp. 428, 430.
13 *Ibid*, p.428; AÉ, *Mémoires et Documents*, Angleterre, XV, f.8[r].

her defensive and legal policies would continue to be frustrated. The Franco-Scottish protectoral alliance had run its course and now needed to take on a more definite and concrete form that only dynastic union could bring about.

But Mary of Guise was still faced with the problem of how to broach the subject of marriage with the French King. Even though the Valois-Stewart marriage was also in Henri's imperial interests, it was imperative that he did not think that Mary of Guise wanted it purely for her own 'affection particullier'.[14] As the 'Protector' of Scotland, Henri was the only one who could decide when the marriage would take place, if at all, and for this to happen the marriage had to be seen as politically expedient.[15] There was a faction opposed to the Valois-Stewart marriage at the French Court led by Constable Montmorency, the steadfast rival of Les Guise. He was of the opinion that the Queen of Scots should wed a French duke or prince instead of the Dauphin so that she could return to Scotland with her husband 'to hald ther awen contre in gud obedience'.[16] As Sir James Melville of Halhill recounts, the basis of the Constable's argument was that 'when prencis ar absent, and far af fra ther awen, rewling ther contrees be lieutenantis, maist commonly the subiectis of sic contrees vses to rebell; quhilk gene the subiectis in Scotland did, it wald be hard and coistly to get them reducit'.[17] But in reality, Montmorency's opposition to the marriage had more to do with the extraordinary power and prestige it would give Les Guise at the French Court than with the prospect of civil unrest in Scotland and its financial implication.

Countering the arguments of Montmorency were, as ever, the Duc de Guise and the Cardinal de Lorraine, who predictably extolled the advantages of dynastic union with Scotland. While their own dynastic ambition and the prestige of having their niece as the future Queen of France were, unquestionably, the prime factors behind their support of the Valois-Stewart marriage, the Guise brothers were more subtle in their arguments to Henri. He would hear 'how it wald be baith honorable and proffitable to the crown of France, and that ther wald be revenus anough to mantean garnissons within the contree, to hald the subiectis vnder obedience; bigging ma citadelis, and hauyng the

14 AÉ, *Mémoires et Documents*, Angleterre, XV, f.9^r; *Papal Negotiations*, p.429.
15 We have already seen how Henri made the decision as to when Mary Stewart came of age and who would govern the kingdom during her majority. These precedents, in addition to Guise's deference to Henri on the subject of dynastic union, suggest that he had the final say as to when the marriage of Mary and François would proceed.
16 Melville, *Memoirs*, p.72.
17 *Ibid*, p.72.

haill strenthes in ther handes'.[18] Like their sister, though, they had to tread carefully lest their support for the Valois-Stewart marriage be perceived as merely the self-promotion and aggrandisement of the House of Guise. While the Queen Regent could count on the support of her brothers in France when the time came, her domestic troubles meant that she could not wait for Henri to make the first move. She had to take matters into her own hands and push things along discreetly within the Scottish political community – no mean feat, given her estrangement from the 'great lords' who, she confessed, were 'more difficult to manage than ever'.[19]

So, in late February 1557, Mary of Guise summoned a Convention of her 'lordes lairdes and gentry' to meet at Stirling on 4 March – ostensibly to gain their support for France in the Habsburg-Valois conflict.[20] Guise used the developing international situation to play on the Scots' fears of an English invasion that, she claimed, was inevitable given the nature of the Anglo-Imperial alliance. Her tactics proved successful. At a Parliament held in Edinburgh shortly after the Convention, the Three Estates promised that they would support the French King, but only if the English invaded Scotland.[21] Moreover, by highlighting the threat that Mary Tudor's marriage to Philip of Spain posed to Scotland's national security, a threat which was intensified by the poor state of the kingdom's defences, Guise had shrewdly and simultaneously increased the resolve of the Scots to see the conclusion of their own queen's marriage. So persuasive was she in her arguments that the Three Estates requested that either she, a special envoy, or a delegation of commissioners go to France in order to bring the matter to a 'bon fin'.[22] They even consented to raise a small tax to finance this diplomatic expedition.[23]

The Scots had played directly into her hands. Guise's ruse had worked, but it was not finished. Even though she was hugely relieved, she could not then blow her cover by immediately acceding to the

---

18 Melville, *Memoirs*, p.72.
19 *Papal Negotiations*, p.428; AÉ, *Mémoires et Documents*, Angleterre, XV, f.8ʳ.
20 LPL, Talbot MSS, 3194, fos. 314, 328.
21 *Ibid*, 3194, fos. 314, 328; AÉ, *Mémoires et Documents*, Angleterre, XV, f.12ʳ.
22 AÉ, *Cor. Pol.*, Angleterre, XIII, f.178ᵛ and *Mémoires et Documents*, Angleterre, XV, f.12ᵛ; Teulet, *Papiers*, I, p.283 and *Relations*, I, pp. 293–4.
23 AÉ, *Cor. Pol.*, Angleterre, XIII, f.178ʳ; Teulet, *Papiers*, I, pp. 282–3 and *Relations*, I, pp. 293–4. In December 1557 a tax of £15,000 was levied in response to Henri's formal request that a delegation be sent to France in order to commence the marriage negotiations. *APS*, II, p.504; *RPC*, XIV, p.14.

political community's requests. She had to maintain an aura of composed indifference. So, Guise informed the Scots that she could not possibly make the journey to France because Scotland would more than likely be at war with England and, as for a delegation of commissioners, she would have to think about it. In the meantime, she would write to Henri regarding these developments and seek his advice on the matter.[24]

By her shrewd manipulation of events, Guise was finally in a position to raise the issue of dynastic union directly with Henri without appearing to do so from self-interest. By assuming the role of messenger, she was conveying the wishes not of herself, but of the Scottish political élite. In her letter to Henri dated 29 March 1557,[25] she related how the *Scots*, seeing that they did not have the power to defend their kingdom and because the Queen of England was married to the King of Spain, had come to the conclusion that, 'they cannot be strong enough without a master'.[26] The marriage of their 'mistress' to the Dauphin was crucial for the strength and surety of their realm and, in return for Henri's due consideration of the matter, the Three Estates had consented to support their 'auld ally' militarily in the event of an Anglo-French war. Of greater importance to the Queen Regent herself, was the Three Estates' declaration that 'if it pleases her, she will be able to make use of the kingdom's subjects, whether in peacetime or wartime, like the Kings before the Queen her daughter'.[27] In other words, the Three Estates were not only confirming Mary of Guise's position as regent, but were also acknowledging that, as such, she had sovereign powers akin to the Stewart kings.

The ball was now in Henri's court as to when the Valois-Stewart marriage would proceed. All Mary of Guise could do was wait for word to come from France. The fact that matters had come this far at all,

24 AÉ, *Cor. Pol.*, Angleterre, XIII, f.178ᵛ and *Mémoires et Documents*, Angleterre, XV, f.12ᵛ; Teulet, *Papiers*, I, p.283 and *Relations*, I, pp. 293–4.
25 AÉ, *Mémoires et Documents*, Angleterre, XV, fos. 11ᵛ-3ʳ. Letters of the same date were also written by Guise and d'Oisel to Montmorency and d'Acqs, informing them, and giving details of this Parliament. *Ibid*, XV, fos. 13ᵛ-14 and *Cor. Pol.*, Angleterre, XIII, fos. 177–8; Teulet, *Papiers*, I, pp. 278–84 and *Relations*, I, pp. 290–5.
26 AÉ, *Mémoires et Documents*, Angleterre, XV, f.12ʳ. It is unclear whether 'ung maister' refers specifically to the Dauphin or is a more general reference to Henri, who, in all probability, would rule on behalf of his son as the 'Protector' of Scotland. However, the Scots' suggestion that 'ung maister' would reign superior to their mistress is of interest when considering Parliament's consent to grant the crown matrimonial to François in November 1558.
27 AÉ, *Cor. Pol.*, Angleterre, XIII, f.178ᵛ; Teulet, *Papiers*, I, p.283 and *Relations*, I, p.294.

however, demonstrates the sheer political acumen of the Queen Regent. At a time when she was politically estranged from her magnates, when her position and authority as regent were rocky at best, and when she was continually being frustrated in her attempts to govern the kingdom, she was nevertheless able to manipulate the less than favourable international situation to her own advantage. Henri received assurances of Scottish military support in his conflict with Philip, Guise received political backing for her dynastic policies and, in doing so, regained the support of her nobles for her administration. While greatly lamented by the Queen Regent, the renewal of the Habsburg-Valois conflict had provided her with an opportunity to satisfy her own need, and that of the Scottish political community, for political security while, at the same time, advancing her own dynastic ambitions. For all parties concerned, this stability was inextricably associated with Franco-Scottish dynastic union and the marriage of Mary, Queen of Scots to the Dauphin.

Yet, when all was said and done, neither Mary of Guise nor the Scots wanted a war with England. Both hoped that the peace between the 'auld enemies' would prevail. War with Scotland was similarly the last thing Mary Tudor wanted while simultaneously engaged in a war with France, and she took diplomatic steps to prevent it coming about. In its attempt to neutralise the Scots through diplomacy, however, the English government grossly underestimated the effect its proclamation of war against France would have on the Scots and, more importantly, the loyalty of the Scots to their 'auld ally'.

* * *

The English government attempted to prevent Scotland's formal entry into the Habsburg-Valois conflict and preserve the Anglo-Scottish peace during a meeting of Border Commissioners in June 1557. The Border had still not been reduced to a state of obedience, despite Mary of Guise's best efforts. The endemic problems of lawlessness, violence and disorder continued to strain Anglo-Scottish relations to near breaking point. In January 1557, therefore, the Queen Regent commissioned Sir Robert Carnegy of Kinnaird to present Mary Tudor with a detailed list of Border complaints against the English on her behalf.[28] Carnegy was to be accompanied by the newly appointed French ambassador in London,

---

28 *APC*, VI, p.80. The arrangements for Carnegy's diplomatic mission were finalised in March. AÉ, *Mémoires et Documents*, Angleterre, XV, f.14ᵛ and *Cor. Pol.*, Angleterre, XIII, fos. 146–7, 177–8, 194; Teulet, *Papiers*, I, pp. 278–82 and *Relations*, I, pp. 289–92; LPL, Talbot MSS, 3195, f.17; *Foedera*, XV, pp. 457–8. For copies of Carnegy's instructions, see AÉ, *Cor. Pol.*, Angleterre, IX, fos. 665–8 and *Mémoires et Documents*, Angleterre, XV, fos. 15–20.

François de Noailles, bishop d'Acqs.[29] Apart from being a display of unity and force, seeing the French and Scots together was something that, reportedly, also annoyed the English.[30] Irksome strategies aside, the grievances presented by Carnegy and Noailles were of a very serious nature.

In April 1557 Mary Tudor and her Council heard of the refusal of English Border officials, especially Lords Dacre and Wharton, to hand over certain Scottish fugitives, to provide redress for various crimes committed against the Scots and to dispense justice in general. A case in point was Richard Norton, Captain of Norham. He had still not paid the £20 fine levied against him in the Indenture of 1553 for his illegal occupation of the Tweed.[31] The most serious charge, however, concerned the illegal activities of the Grahams in the West March. None of that surname had been handed over to the Scottish authorities for their numerous acts of pillaging, spoliation, murder and larceny committed during their devastating and frequent incursions into Scotland. Moreover, Wharton and Dacres' refusal to administer and execute justice against them led Mary of Guise to believe that they were deliberately encouraging and supporting the Grahams in their criminal activities against the Scots. Bothwell's disastrous Border expedition in July 1556 was cited as just one example of this behaviour. To all intents and purposes, the conduct of the Grahams and the English Wardens resembled a breach of the peace, which, Guise added, would not be the case if Mary and Philip maintained order on the Border. The Queen Regent demanded redress and warned that she did not know for how much longer she could persuade her subjects to tolerate such outrageous and injurious acts.[32]

In response Mary Tudor consented to a meeting of Border commissioners and, on 25 May 1557, representatives from both England and Scotland were appointed to meet at Carlisle.[33] Scotland was to be represented by Carnegy, Cassillis, the Bishop of Orkney and later, by

---

29 Antoine de Noailles wrote to Mary of Guise on 31 October 1556 to inform her that his brother, François, would be replacing him as ambassador. AÉ, *Cor. Pol.*, Angleterre, XIII, f.63ᵛ.

30 *Ibid*, XIII, f.178ʳ; Teulet, *Papiers*, I, pp. 281–2 and *Relations*, I, pp. 292–3.

31 On 16 December 1556 Richard Norton was summoned before the English Council and 'commaunded againe to cause indelaied restitucion to be made of the xxˡⁱ by the Commissioners in the Borders to paye unto the Scottes, toke upon him to cause the same to be doone out of hand, so as no further matter of complaynte shulde be made thereof hensfourthe'. *APC*, VI, p.30.

32 AÉ, *Cor. Pol.*, Angleterre, IX, fos. 665–8 and *Mémoires et Documents*, Angleterre, XV, fos. 15–20.

33 *Foedera*, XV, pp. 464–5; PRO, SP51/8/12.

James Makgill of Nether Rankeillour, while the Earl of Westmorland, the Bishop of Durham, Robert Hyndman, Chancellor of the Bishopric, and Dr Thomas Martin, President of the Chancery, constituted the English delegation. But for the English, this meeting had far greater significance than the settling of Border grievances. Carnegy's diplomatic mission had coincided with Thomas Stafford's invasion and capture of Scarborough Castle, and the Border Commission would be an ideal opportunity to try and prevent Scotland from entering a conflict they themselves were just about to enter. One way of achieving this, and keeping the peace with Scotland, was England's voluntary reparation of certain 'attemptates' committed against the Scots. However much it wanted to keep the Scots sweet, the English government was still not prepared to satisfy all of Mary of Guise's demands. The English government's continued refusal to hand any of the Grahams over to the Scottish authorities as pledges proved to be a point of contention that would eventually break up the Border Commission in July 1557.

As in 1550, the fear of losing the Grahams as allies was the principal reason for the English government's obstinacy. If they complied and handed the Grahams over as security for compensation, there was the possibility that the Graham family would not be able to pay for their release. The only option that would then be left open to them would be to renounce their affiliation with England and side with the Scots.[34] Given that they were effectively agents of the English crown, this was completely unacceptable. The Scots, however, would not settle for anything less. When it became clear that no headway was going to be made, the English government relented and offered to pay approximately £3000 worth of damages out of the Exchequer.[35] This gesture alone signifies the extent to which the English government was determined to maintain peaceful relations with the Scots in order secure their neutrality in the Habsburg-Valois conflict. But even this offer proved unsatisfactory to the Scots, who were determined to have the matter settled on their own terms and strictly according to Border law.

The Scottish commissioners' inflexibility may be explained by England's formal declaration of war against France on 7 June 1557.[36] From the outset, the English commissioners were acutely

34 LPL, Talbot MSS, 3194, fos. 336–40.
35 Estimates of the compensation due to the Scots ranged from £907 to £3000. *Ibid*, 3195, f.36 and 3194, f.306.
36 AÉ, *Cor. Pol.*, Angleterre, XIII, fos. 225–7. See also *ibid*, XIII, fos. 232^{v}-6^{v}, for Henri's letter of acknowledgement, and fos. 224–5, for a copy of Mary Tudor's letter publicising the war against France.

sensitive to the mood of the Scots – especially after their declaration of war had been proclaimed. On 11 June Thomas Martin filed a report with Mary Tudor describing the reaction of each of the Scottish commissioners to the news.[37] Although they were all appalled by England's breach with France, Martin nevertheless reported that each was of the opinion that this would not affect the Anglo-Scottish peace. Robert Reid, for example, wished only for 'equal restitution on both parts to preserve amity, nothwithstanding the French', while James Makgill saw no reason to break with the English on account of the French. The 'Emperours warres with the French', he claimed, 'empeacheth not owre league and amytie with thEmperour'.[38] But it is Cassillis' response that is most famous. In response to Westmorland's assumption that 'my lord, I thinke hit but foly for us to treate now togyther, we havinge broken with France, and ye beinge French for your lyves', Cassillis stated that 'I am no more French then ye ar a Spanyard', and then proceeded to divulge the movements of French troops in Scotland.[39] While Cassillis' anti-French comments are not surprising in themselves, it would be foolish to suppose that either he or the rest of the Scottish commissioners were being totally honest with their English counterparts. The movements of the French along the Border had never been any secret in England, and the eagerness with which Cassillis was willing to disclose this information seems to be just a little too deliberate, so as to suggest an 'official' leak or, as Boscher contends, a deliberate ruse to allay English suspicions of Scottish intentions.[40]

Even more suggestive are Sir Robert Carnegy's comments upon hearing of Mary Tudor's 'sincere meaning for continuance of the league with Scotland'.[41] While he gave 'his faith of a Christian, and honour of a Scottish knight, that his mistress meant the like', he then added the stipulation, 'As farre as we yet ken'.[42] Even the author of this report had his suspicions as to the Scots' true intentions. Having heard from Cassillis, 'Doe yowe my lordes, what yowre commissions directe ye to, and so wyll we',[43] Martin took the opportunity to study the Scots' commission. On doing so, he found what he hoped was a clerical error. Reading, '*Damus potestatem nostris commissariis audiendi,*

37 *CSP Scot.*, I, 416, pp. 198–9.
38 *Ibid,* I, 416, p.198.
39 *Ibid,* I, 416, p.198.
40 Boscher, 'English provincial government', pp. 260–1; Vertot, *Ambassades,* IV, pp. 317–8.
41 *CSP Scot.*, I, 416, p.198.
42 *Ibid,* I, 416, pp. 198–9.
43 *Ibid,* I, 416, p.199.

tractandi, concordandi, concludendi, et finaliter dissidendi', Martin realised that if this were indeed correct, no agreement would ever be reached because the Scots had not been commissioned to conclude one.[44] The Scottish commissioners had not been instructed to settle finally [*finaliter decidere*], but rather, finally to disagree [*finaliter dissidere*].[45] There was also some suspicion that the Scottish commissioners were employing delaying tactics to give Mary of Guise more time to prepare for war against England. This was a particular fear of Westmorland, who believed that war with Scotland was imminent. The Scottish commissioners' insistence that redress be given for crimes not covered by their commission led Westmorland to 'verely beleve, that they mynd no trueth but to delay and tasle the tyme with us unto they be prepared and redy (if they may) uppon a sudden to work some displeasour unto this realme'.[46] The English Council was inclined to agree, and saw the introduction of new business, especially that which could have been handled by the Wardens themselves, as a sign of the Scots' ill-will: '. . . for if there had byn nowe other things ment by the appointing of the commissioners but the rigoure and extremitie of the lawe then it had byn in vayne to send expresse personages to the borders for the onely doings of that which might well enough have byn don by the wardens'.[47]

The suspicion that the Scots were really preparing for war put a new slant on the English government's offer to compensate the Scots with cash from the Treasury. Dacre, for one, regarded this as a very bad idea given that, in his opinion, 'shortly it will growe to open warr'. The considerable amount of money owing to the Scots for damages, he argued, would enable them to 'get all they might, and then be at libertie to spye their tyme and to make warres uppon us with our owen money'.[48] There was the danger that, in trying to maintain the peace by offering financial restitution, the English would be inadvertently financing the Scottish war effort against them. While the Scottish commissioners' refusal to accept this method of payment ruled out such a possibility, it also meant that a settlement was not going to be reached during this particular Border Commission. So, on 13 July, the commissioners agreed to disband, depart in peace as they had come, and reconvene on 15 September 1557.[49] As a gesture of their mutual

44 *CSP Scot.*, I, 416, p.199.
45 *Ibid.*, I, 416, p.199.
46 LPL, Talbot MSS, 3195, f.44; *CSP Scot.*, I, 417, p.199.
47 PRO, SP51/1/26, 27.
48 LPL, Talbot MSS, 3195, f.36.
49 *CSP Scot.*, I, 419, pp. 200–1; LPL, Talbot MSS, 3195, f.46.

goodwill, it was further decided to issue a joint declaration of peace. On 17 July, 'standing together . . . at the highe crosse at Carlisle', the commissioners for both England and Scotland 'made open proclamation for peace, . . . and the like . . . sent to the wardens of both realms'.[50] As events would soon demonstrate, Mary of Guise had different ideas. She had no intention of enforcing the commissioners' instructions to the Wardens of the Marches to detain the principal 'owtrydars' of both realms in order to prevent future raids and incursions.

While the Scots were eager to declare publicly their commitment to the Anglo-Scottish peace and give the appearance that they 'covet peace [rather] then warr', their actions following the break-up of the Border Commission reveal their true feelings about England's declaration of war against France.[51] Almost immediately after its disbandment the Scots waged an 'unofficial' war against England. The English government had suspected that the Scots would engage in some sort of hostile activity, but they were unsure what form it would take – namely, '. . . if they denounce warr woll invade with an army or not, and that it may bee that they woll rather onely make incursions than otherwise'.[52] It did not take long for them to realise that the Scots' chosen means of expression, at least initially, was the launch of small-scale raids across the Border.

Conducted over a three-month period and overseen by Mary of Guise stationed at Dunbar, these guerrilla-like raids were led by such notables as d'Oisel, Maxwell, Huntly (lieutenant of the Borders) and other members of the Scottish nobility, and to devastating effect.[53] On 4 August Shrewsbury reported that 'The Scots nightly And dayly mayketh incursions And prepareth so to doo to dystroye the howses And cornes And thereby leave fortresses Towars and howses distytut. Ther haith ben great damaige done whereby the bordours is mych wasted'.[54] As Guise had intended, these raids were proving to be a 'grette annoyance' to the English.[55] But perhaps the most devastating of the raids in the summer of 1557 was the assault on Ford Castle. At five in the morning on 5 August, Lords James and Robert Stewart, Lord Home and a complement of Scottish soldiers invaded the East

50 *CSP Scot.*, I, 421, pp. 201–2.
51 LPL, Talbot MSS, 3195, fos. 34ᵛ; 40, 46, 49.
52 PRO, SP15/8/17.
53 LPL, Talbot MSS, 3195, fos. 42, 52, 103, 115; Lesley, *History*, p.260.
54 LPL, Talbot MSS, 3195, f.66. Reports that the Scots were making 'inrodes almost nyghtly and doth great Annoyaunce' were still being sent in September 1557. See, for example, *ibid*, 3195, f.177ᵛ.
55 *Ibid*, 3195, fos. 115, 253.

March. Armed with certain pieces of ordnance, they 'attempted to wynne the castell of forde, and . . . byrnt syndrie townes there aboute called the ten townes of glendale'. Cattle were seized and countless inhabitants either slain or taken hostage before the Scottish incursionary force retreated back into Scotland.[56]

While these raids were worries in themselves, the English government became seriously alarmed when reports that Mary of Guise was planning a full-scale military invasion of Northumberland began to come in. Throughout August and September details of an extensive military assault on Wark and Norham were received with increasing concern.[57] This was particularly true with respect to the news that the Queen Regent had assembled a great Scottish army to carry out the enterprise. In addition to the 3,000 hackbutters summoned from the burghs, Guise had also called a general muster of all men between the ages of 16 and 60 to assemble at Edinburgh provisioned with enough victuals to last 40 days.[58] The Scottish army was to be commanded by Châtelherault as Lieutenant-General, and supported by the 'holle nobylytie of Scotland', with Argyll, Cassillis, Morton and Huntly (who helped plan the siege) all playing prominent roles alongside d'Oisel and his contingent of French troops.[59] But the assembly of a Scottish army on the Anglo-Scottish Border was not the only cause for concern. Another factor that intensified the overall threat Scotland posed to England was the refortification of Eyemouth.

Mary of Guise ordered the reconstruction of Eyemouth, dismantled in accordance with the terms of the treaty of Norham, in direct response to England's declaration of war against France. Its strategic location as a defensive check to, and a potential launch pad for military campaigns against, England's principal Border stronghold at Berwick were no doubt major considerations in the Queen Regent's decision to resurrect Eyemouth. But of more immediate and practical value, especially in the light of the planned siege of Wark and Norham, was Eyemouth's capacity to serve as an arsenal of ordnance and munition. As Lord Herries noted in his *Historical Memoires*, '. . . it was thought necessar to build a fort at Aiimouth, which might both stop these incursions of the Engish and be a strength to keep cannon

---

56 LPL, Talbot MSS, 3195, fos. 72, 74, 115.

57 *Ibid*, 3195, fos. 98, 99, 150–1, 153, 162, 177, 179, 182, 189, 197, 200, 207, 214.

58 *Ibid*, 3195, fos. 98, 99, 153, 197.

59 *Ibid*, 3195, fos. 99, 197; Lesley, *History*, p.260. As recommended by Mary, Queen of Scots, Châtelherault was appointed the Lieutenant-General of Scotland upon resigning the regency in April 1554. He was discharged from this office on 25 October 1557. NLS, Adv.MSS, f.1; *RPC*, XIV, p.15.

and munition in that pairt of the cuntrie; for it was trublesome upon everie occasion to draw cannon and other necesars from Edinburgh'.[60] For defensive and offensive purposes, therefore, Eyemouth was deemed to be of paramount importance for Scotland's challenge to the Anglo-Imperial threat from England.

The actual refortification of Eyemouth was essentially a French endeavour. French soldiers under the supervision of d'Oisel, who were also garrisoned there, carried out most of the work. While the most intensive phase of its reconstruction and fortification occurred during the Anglo-Scottish truce in 1558,[61] work had nevertheless advanced enough in 1557 for Mary of Guise to declare in August that 'well uyset Aymowth shortly'.[62] English reports later confirmed that cannon, demi-cannon and other great pieces of ordnance intended for the assault against Wark and Norham were indeed being stored at Eyemouth.[63]

Yet, despite these extensive preparations and the steady stream of intelligence confirming that an invasion of England was imminent, no such event ever occurred, prompting Shrewsbury to complain that the Scots 'have dyvers tymes this yeare illudyd us with their apperences of settforwerds'.[64] By mid-October the military campaign was finally set in motion. The Scottish army advanced to the Border and assembled at Kelso, where they were joined by d'Oisel and the French troops and ordnance he brought with him from Eyemouth, in full readiness to cross the River Tweed and launch the assault against Wark.[65] Accompanied by Mary of Guise,

---

60 John Maxwell, lord Herries, *The Historical Memoires of the Reign of Mary Queen of Scots and a portion of the Reign of King James the Sixth* (Abbotsford Club, 1836), p.30. William Maitland of Lethington, conversely, regarded this decision in a far more cynical light: '. . . the Quein Regent be advyse of the Frenchemen and uthers of the Councill . . . did resolue to mak warre against Ingland and to induce or force the nobilitie and Cuntrie verye unwilling thai resolvit to mak ane fort neir to Heymouthe on the seysyde in the Mers and in 6 myles to Berwik vnder colour to be a fronteire to the cuntrie for safetie thairof in tyme of warre'. W.S. Fitch (ed.), *Maitland's Narrative of the Principal Acts of the Regency during the minority of Mary, Queen of Scotland* (Ipswich, 1842), p.9. See also Merriman, 'The Forts of Eyemouth', pp. 152–3.

61 *TA*, X, pp. 331, 334, 341, 344, 345, 353, 360, 368, 377, 387, 394, 401, 405, 409, 415, 418, 421–31; NAS, E34/21/5.

62 LPL, Talbot MSS, 3195, f.66ʳ. See also Astier's accounts for the refortification of Eyemouth (22 July – 18 December 1557) in NAS, E34/21/4.

63 LPL, Talbot MSS, 3195, f.99.

64 *Ibid*, 3195, fos. 105ᵛ, 153, 200, 214, 220, 228, 230.

65 *Ibid*, 3195, f.238; Knox, *History*, I, pp. 124–5 and *Works*, I, p.255.

who decided to oversee the military campaign from the safety of Home Castle just a few miles north of Kelso, the Franco-Scottish army heard rousing words of encouragement from their Queen Regent.[66] Words, however, were not enough to see the siege of Wark become a reality. On 18 October Châtelherault and other members of the Scottish nobility took the sudden and unilateral decision to disband the army and abort the siege of Wark even before it had begun.[67] The reason: to save the honour of Scotland. Foul weather conditions, being 'most contagious [for] the tyme of the yere', had weakened the resolve of the army and had resulted in many of the men 'Rynnyng away, dying and in mysery'.[68] This, in addition to the preparedness of the English to resist the Scots, rendered such an invasion unwise.[69]

The steady leak of information detailing Guise's planned assault of Wark and Norham had given the English ample time to set up their defences. The Scots had earlier misconstrued the absence of an English army on the Border as an encouraging sign of weakness.[70] They soon discovered that, in fact, a force of 4,000 men had arrived at Newcastle on 2 October 1557. This, in addition to the garrisons stationed at Wark, Norham and Berwick and the 600 horse and 400 foot which had also been levied for the occasion, meant that the English were not only well fortified, but amply prepared to meet any threat coming out of Scotland. The strength of England's Border defences was further enhanced by the presence of a sizeable naval force along the eastern seaboard, the mere sight of which was reported to have caused even more desertions from the Scottish army, as men returned home to protect their lands.[71] Even without an 'English army', England's Border defences were formidable – a fact that Shrewsbury had thought could be enough of a deterrent to avert a large-scale invasion at the hands of the Scots: 'it may now come to passe, that consyderynge the countenans of our force and prepar-

---

66 Knox, *History*, I, p.125 and *Works*, I, p.255; Pitscottie, *Historie*, II, pp. 119–20.

67 LPL, Tablot MSS, 3195, fos. 231, 248, 251–2, 253; Lesley, *History*, p.260; Knox, *History*, I, p.125 and *Works*, I, pp. 255–6; Pitscottie, *Historie*, II, pp. 119–20; *Diurnal of Occurrents*, p.267.

68 LPL, Talbot MSS, 3195, fos. 248, 253, 258.

69 *Ibid*, 3195, f.258.

70 Shrewsbury received the order from the English Council that 'Ye shall not nede to make any full assemblie of the armie oneless they sholde go abowte with theyr mayne power to invade the realme'. *Ibid*, 3195, fos. 153, 184.

71 Boscher, 'English provincial government', pp. 274–6; LPL, Talbot MSS, 3195, f.231.

acon, they may now chaunge ther purpose, to lye at the defence of ther owen contrey, then, otherwyse to invade till the light of the mone by wastyd'.[72]

But bad weather and the strength of England's defences may not have been the only reasons for the Scottish nobility's decision to abandon the siege of Wark. Events on the Continent may also have played a part. The summer of 1557 was not a particularly successful period in Henri's conflict with Philip. In August Emmanuel-Philibert, the exiled duke of Savoy, led a successful Spanish invasion of France's northern frontier that culminated in the fall and Imperial occupation of Saint-Quentin.[73] Montmorency's military expedition to relieve the town was, in short, disastrous on both a personal and national scale. Saint-Quentin remained in Imperial hands and, following a heavy loss of 3,000 French troops, an additional 7,000 were taken prisoner – Montmorency himself being captured on 10 August 1557.[74] Henri's losing battle against Philip and, in particular, the disaster at Saint-Quentin had a bad effect on Scottish morale and led some Scots to question their participation in France's war with England. As ever, English observers were keen to seize on this seemingly low ebb in Franco-Scottish relations and comment on the dissension that was apparently growing within the Scottish Court. On 18 September, Thomas Wharton reported:

> . . . the Scotts myche grudgeth against this warr ocasioned by the french And saith that there ar Sondrie noble men in Scotland who wold haue peace with this realme . . . they are Discontented with the greate vyctories the Kings Majesty [Philip] hath had over the frenche And that the Scotts do not trust the fayire promises of the french nor in their Assystaunce which [the] Scotts loked for.[75]

Discontent had also arisen, allegedly, over a disagreement as to the target of invasion. D'Oisel, it was reported, 'movet to Assaylle barwyk', but the Scots prevailed in their insistence that the targets remain Wark

---

72 LPL, Talbot MSS, 3195, f.228.
73 For more on the siege of Saint-Quentin, see Rodríguez-Salgado, *The Changing Face of Empire*, pp. 176–9; Potter, 'The Duc de Guise and the Fall of Calais', *EHR*, ccclxxxviii (1983), pp. 486–8; Baumgartner, *Henry II*, p.202; C.S.L. Davies, 'England and the French War, 1557–9', in J. Loach & R. Tittler (eds.), *The Mid-Tudor Polity, c.1540–1560* (London, 1980), pp. 165–6; Bouillé, *Histoire des Ducs de Guise*, I, pp. 397–401.
74 Davies, 'England and the French War', p.165.
75 LPL, Talbot MSS, 3195, fos. 177ʳ. See also his report of 23 September, *ibid*, 3195, f.189.

and Norham with devastation of the surrounding countryside.[76] Naturally, the English saw this as an ideal opportunity to exacerbate the situation and foster discord between the Scots and Mary of Guise. Shrewsbury, for one, suggested that 'such practyse myght have ben used and with money as at the least a dessention shold have bene sowne amongst them'.[77]

Some caution is necessary when considering these English observations. It is only natural to presume that the Scottish nobility would have some say in the logistics of a military exercise they were leading, and that in such discussions opposing or conflicting viewpoints should be expressed. Moreover, the fact that the Scottish army did advance to Kelso, ostensibly with every intention of carrying out the siege of Wark, suggests that some sort of consensus had been reached and that the final decision not to invade was, as Châtelherault implied, simply to avoid a humiliating defeat at the hands of the English. It should also be remembered that, at the outbreak of the Habsburg-Valois conflict in early 1557, the Scots had assured Mary of Guise that they would support Henri militarily in the event of an Anglo-French war, but only if they suffered an invasion at the hands of the English.[78] Their decision not to embark on a full-scale military campaign, complete with a 'national' army furnished with great pieces of ordnance, was consistent with their previous position. They were, however, more than willing to make small-scale incursions into England. Nevertheless, the fact that reports of internal dissension and the Scots decision to abandon the siege of Wark were contemporaneous with the fall of Saint-Quentin does suggest that Scottish support for France in the Habsburg-Valois conflict ultimately depended on whether Henri was winning or losing. The same cannot be said for their support of Mary of Guise. Contrary to the received view of contemporary and modern historians, such as Knox, Lesley, Pitscottie, Tytler, Marshall and Donaldson, the Scottish nobility's decision to abandon the siege of Wark did not mean they were abandoning either their Queen Regent or the war effort against England.[79]

Mary of Guise was, understandably, shocked and angered by the news that her magnates had unilaterally decided to act against her wishes. When Châtelherault informed Guise of what he and the others

76 LPL, Talbot MSS, 3195, f.177ʳ.
77 *Ibid*, 3195, f.189.
78 AÉ, *Mémoires et Documents*, Angleterre, XV, f.12ʳ.
79 Knox, *Works*, I, pp. 255–6 and *History*, I, p.125; Lesley, *History*, pp. 260–1; Pitscottie, *Historie*, II, pp. 119–20; Tytler, *History of Scotland*, IV, pp. 24–5; Marshall, *Mary of Guise*, pp. 214–5; Donaldson, *James V-James VII*, p.88.

had done, she 'raged and repreived them of theire promysses which was to Invade and anoy England. Theyre determynacione to departe and the consideracione they told hir and therupone arguments grew great betwene them wherwith she sorrowed and wepp openly'.[80] For his part, d'Oisel, 'in great hevynes and with high woords . . . wisshed hymself in Fraunce'.[81] Châtelherault, however, had not acted in accordance with the wishes of all the Scottish nobles. Huntly, for one, echoed Guise and d'Oisel's condemnation. According to English sources, the others were 'so offended with hym [Huntly] and said that he shuld have no rule of their doings and restrayned his Libertie for a day', and apparently 'axed playnely whatever he wolde be a Skottsman or a Frensheman'.[82] But the actions of some of the nobles had left Mary of Guise without an army and she had no choice but to discharge Châtelherault from his commission and order that the 'siege of the castell of Werk be left'.[83]

But a fact that most historians have ignored is that Scottish forces remained on the Border, and Scotland's 'unofficial' war against England continued after the Scottish army had disbanded.[84] Châtelherault proceeded to Jedburgh with an unidentified chosen few and placed garrisons along the Border, adopting what was primarily a defensive position against the English.[85] The Scottish nobility's abandonment of the siege of Wark, therefore, did not automatically mean that Guise's defensive policies would also be abandoned. Châtelher-

---

80 20 October 1557, LPL, Talbot MSS, 3195, f.253.
81 *Ibid*, 3195, f.253. In his commentary, Knox writes that the Scots' refusal to invade England 'putt ane effray in Monsieur Dosell his breathe, and kendilled such a fyre in the Quein Regentis stomak, as was nott weall slockened till hir braith failled'. Knox, *Works*, I, pp. 255–6 and *History*, I, p.125.
82 LPL, Talbot MSS, 3195, fos. 248, 253.
83 *RPC*, XIV, p.14; Lesley, *History*, p.261. D'Oisel was still determined to go ahead with the attack and, on 27 October, led his French troops across the Tweed with a few pieces of ordnance. Losing two men and eight horse by drowning in the process, all d'Oisel managed to achieve was a small and insignificant skirmish at Wark. According to English intelligence, d'Oisel felt so threatened upon returning to Scotland that he needed a bodyguard of 100 soldiers to ensure his personal safety. It was also alleged that d'Oisel was similarly concerned for Mary of Guise's safety, but there is no evidence to substantiate this claim. LPL, Talbot MSS, 3195, fos. 248, 253, 265; Boscher, 'English provincial government', p.275.
84 War was never formally declared between the 'auld enemies', and all Knox writes to indicate that the Scots still engaged in warlike activity against the English after the siege of Wark had been abandoned was, 'Butt yitt warre continewed'. Knox, *Works*, I, p.256 and *History*, I, p.125.
85 LPL, Talbot MSS, 3195, f.253.

ault had assured the Queen Regent in no uncertain terms that, despite their refusal to launch a full-scale attack against the English, they would 'devise [how] to furnyshe their fronters for this wynter'.[86] After this had been done, Châtelherault returned to the Borders to implement their resolutions, while others, such as Argyll and his 'company of Yrish men', returned to their own 'cuntries'.[87] But of even greater importance was the fact that Mary of Guise's offensive policies had not been entirely abandoned either. The Franco-Scottish force at Kelso and Eyemouth continued to conduct devastating guerrilla like raids into England.[88]

Both Northumberland and Shrewsbury were deeply concerned at the sustained threat to English national security. Northumberland sent urgent and repeated requests for reinforcements because the Scots had not only 'kept there own frontiers plenished to the uttermost but have destroyed and laid waste agreate parte of the borders of this realme.'[89] For Shrewsbury, the only solution to this Scottish problem was for the Scots '. . . to be scourged with armyes or with great garysons for frontier war or both'.[90] So, while the Scots were specifically unwilling to carry out the assault on Wark and Norham, they did not altogether withdraw their support for the Queen Regent's offensive policies. They continued to make incursions into England until an Anglo-Scottish truce was negotiated on 14 January 1558.[91]

The Scots' refusal to invade England on 18 October 1557 was not a demonstration against the Franco-Scottish dynastic alliance. If any-

---

86 LPL, Talbot MSS,, 3195, f.248.

87 *Ibid*, 3195, fos. 231, 253, 248; Lesley, *History*, pp. 260–1.

88 *Ibid*, p.261.

89 PRO, SP15/8/41.

90 *Ibid*, SP15/8/41, 52, 52i. For a discussion of England's Border defences at this time, see Boscher, 'English provincial government', pp. 276–7.

91 This was the first of many temporary peace agreements between the 'auld enemies', the negotiations for which cannot be dealt with effectively or comprehensively here. Suffice to say, the first truce was negotiated by Lord Home, the Earl of Northumberland and Sir Henry Percy on 14 January 1558 and was contracted to last for just 12 days. In February, the peace was extended to 15 March 1558 and, on 6 March, Bothwell and Northumberland contracted another truce to last two months. Fighting resumed in April and cut this last agreement short. See *CSP Scot.*, I, 422, 423, 426, 428, 429, 433, 434, pp. 202, 203–4, 204–5; *CSP Foreign, 1553–1558*, 665, pp. 335–6; *HMC Twelfth Report*, Appendix viii, pp. 183–4; Teulet, *Papiers*, I, pp. 285–91 and *Relations*, I, pp. 296–300, *TA*, X, pp. 331, 337, 420; *APC*, VI, p.275; and Boscher, 'English provincial government', pp. 296–301 for references concerning these truce negotiations and compacts.

thing, it served to highlight the importance and the need for the marriage of Mary, Queen of Scots to be concluded once and for all. Until the Franco-Scottish alliance was set on a more secure footing through dynastic union, the implementation of Franco-centric policies in Scotland would continue to be frustrated, while the political stability of both Mary of Guise and the Scottish political community would continue to be undermined and their working relationship counter-productive. Ironically, the disaster at Saint-Quentin sparked a chain of events in France that would bind the 'auld allies' closer and tighter than they had been in years. Montmorency's imprisonment marked the ascendancy of Les Guise at the French Court and, with it, a general desire to see the Valois-Stewart marriage formally concluded.

* * *

The Imperial occupation of France's northern frontier forced Henri to take prompt and drastic action. His immediate response was to recall the Duc de Guise from Italy and make him his Lieutenant General.[92] As such, the Duc was invested with extraordinary military and diplomatic powers, enjoying similar authority to the 'Constable of France', though without the title.[93] The Cardinal de Lorraine enjoyed similar powers in the realm of administration. The Guise brothers now reigned supreme at the French Court and exercised almost total control in all matters of state.[94] Their prestige at Court and, more importantly, their influence over Henri gave them the perfect platform from which to promote their dynastic ambitions and advance the Valois-Stewart marriage without fear of opposition or intrigue from Montmorency. But even in captivity, Montmorency still managed to pose a threat to Guise dynastic ambition. In December 1557 he had tried to throw a spanner in the works by suggesting that the Dauphin marry Philip's sister, and that Henri's daughter, Elisabeth, marry Philip's son, Carlos.[95] But by this time, Henri had already sent letters to the Three Estates acceding to their previous request that a delegation of commissioners be sent to France for the 'accompleishment' of the marriage of Mary, Queen of Scots to the Dauphin.[96]

While the influence of Les Guise cannot be dismissed as a factor

---

92 Michaud et Poujolat, *Mémoires-Journaux*, pp. 387–90.
93 *Ibid*, pp. 387–90; Bouillé, *Histoire des Ducs de Guise*, pp. 412–3; Baumgartner, *Henry II*, p.202.
94 Potter, 'The Duc de Guise', pp. 486–7.
95 Baumgartner, *Henry II*, p.207.
96 *APS*, II, p.504; AÉ, *Cor. Pol.*, Angleterre, XIII, f.178ᵛ and *Mémoires et Documents*, Angleterre, XV, f.12ᵛ; Teulet, *Papiers*, I, p.283 and *Relations*, I, p. 294.

behind Henri's decision to proceed with the marriage, events in Scotland arguably had a more immediate impact. The timing of his decision to send 'special lettres and writingis direct vnto the . . . thre estatis' on 29 October 1557 followed in the wake of the Scots' abandonment of the siege of Wark.[97] Significant as this was in its own right, the Scots' refusal to carry out the Queen Regent's orders against the English assumed even greater significance given that the English had assisted their Imperial allies in the capture of Saint-Quentin, Le Câtelet and Ham.[98] Control of Scottish foreign policy and, in particular, the obedience of the Scots in carrying out this policy were imperative, even more so now that a major assault on Calais was being planned for the winter of 1558.[99] If the Calais expedition was successful and France recaptured the last English-held territory on the Continent, Scotland would then become England's primary target against the French. In such an event, Scottish cooperation and their military assistance would be essential. As it happened, France's counter-attack on Calais was a resounding victory for France and for the commander of the campaign, the Duc de Guise. Launching his assault on 1 January 1558, Mary of Guise's brother easily took Rysbank and Newham Bridge before capturing Calais castle just one week after the campaign had begun. By the end of the month, he had also managed to take Guisnes and Ham, the two remaining fortresses in the Calais Pale.

Finally, one must not forget the role that Henri's imperial ambitions in the British Isles played in his decision to proceed with the Valois-Stewart marriage. Mary Tudor had still not produced an heir and, at forty-one, her chances of doing so were remote at best. Although the English Queen had reluctantly named her Protestant half-sister, Elizabeth, as her successor, there was the possibility that she could be kept off the throne on account of her illegitimacy. The next

97 *APS*, II, p.504.
98 Davies, 'England and the French War', pp. 165–6; Potter, 'The Duc de Guise', pp. 487–8; Rodrìguez-Salgado, *The Changing Face of Empire*, pp. 176–9. Although they missed the Duke of Savoy's initial assault on Saint-Quentin on 10 August, the Earl of Pembroke's 2000 English troops did participate in the battle that led to the fall of Saint-Quentin on 27 August. They remained in France to aid their Imperial allies in the subsequent capture and occupation of Le Câtelet and Ham, and stayed until 27 November 1557, when the Anglo-Imperial troops retreated from France's northern frontier.
99 See Potter, 'The Duc de Guise', pp. 481–512; Davies, 'England and the French War', pp. 168–78; and Bouillé, *Histoire des Ducs de Guise*, I, pp. 420–30, for detailed analyses and discussions of the siege and recapture of Calais.

legitimate and Catholic claimant to the English throne was Mary Stewart, whose marriage to the Dauphin would provide for the creation of a Franco-British Empire.

While these considerations may have prompted Henri to push for the marriage when he did, there was still the possibility that, given the events of the past few months, the Scots no longer wished to undergo dynastic union with France. Henri need not have worried, for the opposite was true. The marriage of Mary, Queen of Scots was still seen as the precondition of political stability. The Habsburg-Valois conflict and, in particular, the Anglo-French war served only to accentuate this need in the eyes of the Scots. On 14 December 1557, the Three Estates convened at Edinburgh to discuss the marriage question and issue a formal response to Henri's 'special lettres and writingis'.[100] It was determined that a delegation of eight commissioners would be sent to France to negotiate the terms of the marriage compact. Gilbert, earl of Cassillis, George, earl of Rothes, Lord James Stewart, James, lord Fleming, George, lord Seton and Provost of Edinburgh, John Erskine of Dun, Robert Reid, bishop of Orkney and James Beaton, archbishop of Glasgow, were all appointed to conduct the negotiations.[101] In her absence, Mary of Guise appointed her mother, Antoinette de Bourbon, to represent her in the negotiations.[102] The Three Estates then levied a tax of £15,000 to pay for the expedition.[103]

Armed with their instructions,[104] the negotiating commissioners set sail for France in early February 1558 and were escorted by a fleet of merchant and private vessels.[105] Upon arriving in France, they were 'honorable convoyit to Pareis, quhair thay war with gret honour and fawour receaved be the King of France and his nobilitie in the monethe of Merche'.[106] By 19 April 1558 an agreement had been

100 *APS*, II, pp. 501–2; Lesley, *History*, pp. 262–3.
101 *APS*, II, pp. 504–5, 506, 511, 514, 518; NLS, Adv.MSS, 54.1.2(i), f.1ʳ; NAS, GD/204/559.
102 NLS, Adv.MSS, 54.1.2(i), f.1ʳ.
103 *APS*, II, p.504; *RPC*, XIV, p.14; AÉ, *Cor. Pol.*, Angleterre, XIII, f.178ʳ and *Mémoires et Documents*, Angleterre, XV, fos. 12–3ʳ; Teulet, *Papiers*, I, pp. 282–3 and *Relations*, I, pp. 293–4.
104 See NLS, Adv.MSS, 54.1.2(i), fos. 1–5ʳ; *APS*, II, pp. 511–3, 504–6; and Prince Alexandre Labanoff, *Lettres, Instructions et Mémoires de Marie Stuart, Reine d'Écosse* (London, 1844), I, pp. 46–50, for the specific details of the Scots' commission.
105 *TA*, X, pp. 330, 332, 333. On 5 February 1558 Mary of Guise ordered 'all sindrie awnaris, skipparis and marinaris of schippis to be in reddines to depart witht the commissionaris the vj day of Februar instant, . . . and to pas fordwart witht thame unto the tyme the saidis commissionaris beis landit in France'. See also Lesley, *History*, pp. 262–3; *Papal Negotiations*, p.9.
106 Lesley, *History*, p.263.

reached and a treaty contracting the marriage of Mary, Queen of Scots and the Dauphin François was formally concluded.[107]

As with the treaties of Birgham, Greenwich and, to a lesser extent, Haddington, this treaty was fundamentally concerned with the protection of Scotland's cultural and institutional independence in a dynastic union. In the marriage, all 'heirs and successors sal observe and keip the fredomes Liberteis and priuilegeis of this realme and lawis of the samyn and In the samyn maner as hes bene keipit and obseruit in all kingis tymes of Scotland of before'.[108] The treaty also stipulated that if Mary should die without issue, the Scottish crown would revert, without impediment, to her nearest blood relative – namely, Châtelherault and his heirs and successors.[109] Châtelherault's rights to the Scottish succession were thus safeguarded in the dynastic union of the French and Scottish crowns.[110] A series of documents secretly signed by Mary, Queen of Scots on 4 April 1558, however, revealed the extent to which Henri was not prepared to relinquish his interests in Scotland in the event that his future daughter-in-law died without issue.[111]

Directly contravening the terms of the 'official' marriage treaty, these secret documents rejected the rights of the house of Hamilton to the Scottish succession in favour of the royal house of Valois. The first document was a letter of donation, whereby Mary willingly bequeathed the sovereignty of Scotland and all her claims to the English succession to the King of France and his successors.[112] It was decreed that, because of the special favour and affection Henri had bestowed on Scotland and its queen, Mary

> a donné et donné par ces présentes, par pure et libre
> donation, faicte pour cause de mort, au Roy de France qui

---

107 NLS, Adv.MSS, 54.1.2(i), fos. 1–5ʳ; *APS*, II, pp. 511–3. See also *ibid*, II, pp. 516–7; NAS, SP7/38, 39; and BL, Harley MSS, 1244.35, f.202, for the commission to investigate consanguinity (Mary and François were third cousins) and subsequent papal dispensation for the marriage.

108 *APS*, II, p.504.

109 *Ibid*, II, p.505; NAS, SP7/40.

110 The commissioners had been instructed to ensure that 'the richtuis blude of the croun of scotlande to succeid without any impediment Bot to be aydit fortifyit and supportit be the kingis maiestie and his successouris And all the auld Ligis in that cace to stand in effect as thai wer before the completing of the said mariage and obseruit betuix the twa realmis'. For his part, Châtelherault lodged a protest to ensure that his rights were safeguarded in the Franco-Scottish dynastic alliance. His rights and title were later confirmed by Mary and François in April 1558. *APS*, II, pp. 605, 517.

111 Labanoff, *Lettres*, I, pp. 50–6.

112 *Ibid*, I, pp. 50–2.

est ou sera, le royaulme d'Escosse selon qui se consiste et comporte, oultre tous et telz droictz que lui peuvent ou pourront, ores et pour l'advenir, compecter et appartenir au royaulme d'Angleterre, et aultres terres et seigneuryes, qui par ce tître lui sont escheuz ou pourrount escheoir et advenir; ensemble tous et chacuns les droictz, tant en pensions que aultrement, qui, à cause de ce, peuvent et pourront, ores et pour l'advenir, compecter à icelle Dame envers et contre toutes personnes, mesmes envers et à l'endroict du Roy de France et ses successeurs Roys, sur les terres de son royaulme, en quelque sorte que ce soit, dont les Roys ou Roynes d'Angleterre leur pourroient faire demande, débat ou querelle, desquelz icelle Dame, ou cas susdict, a fait à iceulx Roys de France don, quietance, cession et transport ces présentes.

[has given and gives by these letters, through a true and free settlement, established on account of death, the present or future King of France, the kingdom of Scotland as it consists and is compromised, with all and each right that can or could, now or in the future belong to it and to the kingdom of England, and also other lands and estates, which through this right fall or could fall to him; each and all the rights, whether pensions or otherwise, which for that reason can and could, now and in the future, belong to this Lady against everyone, even against the King of France and his heir Kings, on the lands of her kingdom, whatever the case, which the Kings or Queens of England could claim, contest and fight over with them, which this Lady, in these above cases, has given, confirmed, assigned and transferred these letters to these Kings of France].[113]

Mary's second letter of donation was also hedged in protectionist rhetoric, but this time the French King's voluntary 'protection, tuition and defence of the kingdom of Scotland' was revealed to have come at a price. In the event that Mary should die in the near future, it was decreed that the kingdom and the revenues of Scotland were to be retained by France until Henri was reimbursed for all the expenses he had incurred in Scotland's defence and Mary's education at the French Court.[114] Estimated to be in the region of one million *d'or*,

113 Labanoff, *Lettres*, I, p.51.
114 *Ibid*, I, pp. 52–4.

the sheer size of the Scots' debt to Henri was yet another guarantee that Scotland would remain in French possession for a very long time.

Henri now needed to find a way to protect his interests should the existence of these two documents be discovered by the Scots. So, on 4 April 1558, a letter of renunciation was issued in the name of Mary, Queen of Scots nullifying any future contract or agreement made by the Three Estates that contravened the terms of her two donations. The articles safeguarding Scotland's sovereignty and Châtelherault's claim to the Scottish succession in the 'official' treaty of 19 April 1558, therefore, would theoretically be null and void in the event of Mary's death by virtue of her letter of renunciation.[115] However valid this document would be in France, it would be illegal in Scotland – no precedent existed in Scots law that would enable Mary to make such an agreement. Nevertheless, this document does show how Henri was just as determined to protect the interests that Mary Stewart's dynasticism afforded him through marriage, as the Scots were to safeguard their cultural and institutional independence in a dynastic union with France.

Yet there were some terms of the 'official' marriage contract that were unaffected by the secret deal. It was agreed that, upon marriage, François would assume the title 'King of Scotland' and, until he succeeded his father, would be styled the 'King-Dauphin' and Mary the 'Queen-Dauphiness'.[116] Only when François acceded to the French throne would France and Scotland truly be united. In the meantime, the Franco-Scottish dynastic alliance would be celebrated and symbolised by the joining of the French and Scottish crowns on Mary and François' coat of arms (something which was later altered to include that of England following the death of Mary Tudor), and the naturalisation of both the Scots and the French in each other's kingdom.[117] Mary of Guise's position in Scotland was also safeguarded in the Franco-Scottish dynastic alliance. According to the Scottish Commissioners' instructions, it was agreed that a commission would be granted for Guise to retain the regency of Scotland for as long as Mary and François remained in France.[118] In accordance with the Scots' demand that the articles of the treaty of Haddington be confirmed and ratified by Mary and François, Henri's protectorate

115 Labanoff, *Lettres*, I, pp. 54–6.
116 The use of these styles was confirmed in an act of Parliament recognising the marriage of Mary to François (30 April 1558) and in a letter of congratulation (26 June 1558). *APS*, II, pp. 518, 519.
117 *Ibid*, II, pp. 518–9, 507, 513; Teulet, *Papiers*, I, pp. 303–6; Bonner, 'French Naturalization of the Scots', p.1115.
118 Guise's regency was confirmed by Mary and François on 29 April 1558. *APS*, II, pp. 519, 504; NAS, SP13/81.

of Scotland was similarly maintained.[119] Finally, provisions were made for the possibility the François predeceased Mary, and for the succession of any offspring this marriage might produce. In the first instance, Mary would have the option either to return to Scotland or stay in France, living off the income she received from her dowry (600,000 *livres* from lands assigned to her in Tours, Picardy, Champagne and Poitou, together with an annual pension of 30,000 *francs*).[120] If there existed an heir male, he would naturally inherit both the French and Scottish thrones, but if the marriage produced an heir female, she would only be able to lay claim to the Scottish succession as Salic law prohibited the succession of females to the French throne. These terms having been agreed, the marriage of Mary and François was then celebrated in a manner befitting a King and Queen at the Cathedral of Notre Dame in Paris on 24 April 1558.

As in Henri's triumphant entry into Rouen, the ceremony solemnising the marriage of Mary, Queen of Scots and the Dauphin François was a grand and lavish display celebrating the 'auld alliance'.[121] It was also a celebration of Les Guise, their recent accomplishments at Calais and the realisation of their dynastic ambitions. Accordingly, the Duc de Guise played a dominant role in the marriage ceremony. He led the massive procession to the Cathedral of Notre Dame which included musicians, a hundred gentlemen-in-waiting to the King, princes of the blood, abbots and bishops, among them the Cardinal de Lorraine and the Cardinal de Guise.[122] Next came the Dauphin, preceded by Antoine, King of Navarre, and escorted by his brothers, Charles, duc d'Orléans and Henri, duc d'Angoulême. Then came the bride. In a resplendent and, for the time, unconventional white gown, Mary was led by Henri and the Duc de Lorraine, and was followed by the French Queen, Catherine de Medici.[123] Crowds lined the streets and people strained to watch the ceremony through the windows of the cathedral, after which a festive string of banquets, balls and entertainment lasted for several days.[124] In

119 *APS*, II, pp. 504, 518–9; NAS, SP7/41.
120 *APS*, II, pp. 505, 517; Lesley, *History*, p.263.
121 Teulet, *Relations*, I, pp. 292–303 and *Relations*, I, pp. 302–11.
122 The fact that the Duc de Guise should lead the 'princes of the blood' is of great symbolic importance given that Les Guise were regarded as foreigners and, consequently, of lower status.
123 White was the traditional colour of mourning for royalty.
124 For more details of the wedding ceremony and celebrations in France, see W. Bentham (ed.), *Discours du Grand et Magnifique Triomphe Faict du Mariage de François et Marie Stuart* (Roxburghe Club, 1818); Lesley, *History*, pp. 264–5; Merriman, 'Mary, Queen of France', pp. 42–4; Fraser, *Mary, Queen of Scots*, pp. 98–102.

Scotland, news of their sovereign's marriage was also cause for celebration. Immediately following Mary and François' formal proclamation of marriage to the Estates on 26 June 1558, Mary of Guise ordered fires and processions throughout the entire kingdom in order to mark the 'completing and solemnizing of the mariage betuix our Soverane Ladie and the Dolphine of France'.[125]

For Les Guise, the marriage of their niece to the heir to the French throne consolidated their own power and position at the French Court, and marked the beginning of their ascendancy in France. But the dynastic ambitions of the House of Guise and the imperial ambitions of Henri were only partially realised with the marriage of Mary and François. Until the Dauphin had bestowed upon him the crown matrimonial, his kingship of Scotland was nominal – the sovereignty of Scotland and the rights to the English succession technically remained with his wife, Mary.

Having concluded their business at the French Court, the Scottish commissioners travelled to Dieppe in August 1558 to await their voyage home. There, a mysterious illness took the lives of four of the commissioners: Robert Reid, bishop of Orkney (6 September); George, earl of Rothes (9 November); Gilbert, earl of Cassillis (14 November); and James, lord Fleming (14 December at Paris). There was some suspicion that the illness was poison-induced and that Les Guise were behind it because the commissioners found out about the 'secret' marriage contract. This, however, has neither been proved nor disproved.[126] The four survivng commissioners returned to Scotland in November, and Mary of Guise wasted no time in summoning a Parliament to secure the Three Estates' ratification of the 'official' marriage contract, and, more importantly, to gain their consent for the crown matrimonial to be bestowed on the King-Dauphin.

The Parliament was held at Edinburgh on 29 November 1558 and was attended by 64 members of the Three Estates.[127] The only

---

125 NAS, SP13/82; NLS, MSS, 3137, fos. 13–4; *TA*, X, pp. 365, 366. Both
   Mary and François sent Mary of Guise personal letters announcing their
   marriage. NAS, SP13/79, 80.
126 If such a plot had been discovered, the question must then be asked why
   nothing was said by the remaining Commissioners to prevent the
   ratification of the 'official' marriage treaty, or mentioned in the
   Congregation's propaganda to substantiate their claims of French
   conquest. NAS, SP13/83–4; Labanoff, *Lettres*, I, pp. 57–60; *TA*, X, p.393;
   Knox, *History*, I, pp. 13 *n*.4, 130, 140–1; Lesely *History*, pp. 266–7; Fraser,
   Mary, Queen of Scots, pp. 111–2; Donaldson, *James V-James VII*, p.88.
127 *APS*, II, pp. 503–4. This was an average turn-out, although more people
   could have attended as sederunts were often incomplete.

member who was noticably absent was Châtelherault, who lodged a formal protest in defence of his rights and claim to the Scottish succession.[128] After conducting the usual business of discharging the negotiating commissioners from their commission, the Three Estates then ratified Mary and François' marriage contract. Mary of Guise's greatest accomplishment during this Parliament, though, was gaining the formal consent of the Three Estates for Mary, Queen of Scots to honour her husband with the crown of Scotland. In accordance with the wishes of their Queen, the crown matrimonial was granted to François:

> be way of gratificatioun during the mariage without ony maner of preiudice To hir hienes self the succesioun or hir body Or lauchfull successioun of hir blude quhatsumeuir And this crowne to be send with twa or thre of the lordis of hir Realme To the entent that the maist cristin king and king dolphine hir husband may vnderstand with quhat zele and affectioun hir subictis ar myndit To obswerue and recognosis hir said spous.[129]

With this, the Dauphin's kingship of Scotland was no longer nominal. He assumed all of Mary's rights and powers as sovereign and became King of Scots. To show further their support for and commitment to the Franco-Scottish dynastic alliance, the Three Estates then reciprocated Henri's earlier gesture and bestowed the same privileges and rights that the Scots enjoyed on all French subjects.[130] This Parliament was the culmination of Mary of Guise's political career in Scotland. Motivated by her own dynastic ambitions, and those of Les Guise in France, Mary of Guise had successfully provided for the union of the crowns and kingdoms of France and Scotland. In the wider context of European dynastic politics, however, the fulfilment of Guise's dynastic objectives assumed even greater significance because, in doing so, she had also laid the foundations for Henri's imperial scheme for a Franco-British empire.

The death of Mary Tudor on 17 November 1558 and the 'dubious' accession of Elizabeth, at least in Catholic eyes, brought Henri one step closer to realising his imperial ambitions within the British Isles. Mary Stewart had provided Henri, through marriage to his son, with the prospect of uniting Scotland, England and Ireland under one

128 *APS*, pp. 507–8.
129 *Ibid*, II, p.506. The outbreak of the Reformation Rebellion prevented the crown from being sent to France as Mary, Queen of Scots had wished.
130 *Ibid*, II, pp. 506–7; Teulet, *Papiers*, I, pp. 303–9 and *Relations*, I, pp. 312–7.

Catholic French crown. Upon Henri's death, these kingdoms would officially fall into the imperial dominion of France. Thus, upon hearing the news of Mary Tudor's death, the French King

> caused to make publict proclamatione in Paris, publishing the
> Quenis majestie of Scotlande to be Quene of Inglande,
> Scotlande and Irelande and caused hir and the dolphin hir
> husbande tak the armes of Inglande, and jone with the armes
> of Scotland and France, and make all thair seales conforme
> thairto, and mark thair silver plait, brodir thair tapestries,
> hingers and all uther thyngs with the same.[131]

As early as 16 January 1559, Mary and François had styled themselves 'Mary and François, King and Queen Dauphins of Scotland, England and Ireland', while Henri was actively trying to persuade the pope to declare Elizabeth Tudor illegitimate and recognise Mary Stewart's right to the English throne.[132]

On account of the international situation, however, Henri had to be careful not to push the claims of Mary and François to the English succession too vigorously as he was in the middle of negotiating a peace with Philip. Mary Tudor's death had undermined Philip's position regarding the relinquishment of Calais, but at the same time Henri did not want to push his claims to Calais too hard, lest Elizabeth become unreasonable over the terms for its reversion into French hands.[133] More importantly, though, the French King feared another Anglo-Imperial dynastic alliance. During the negotiations that culminated in the Peace of Câteau-Cambrésis on 2 April 1559, therefore, Henri pulled out all the stops to prevent Philip and Elizabeth marry-

131 Lesley, *History*, pp. 268–9.
132 *CSP Foreign, 1558–1559*, 235, 346, pp. 91, 145; *CSP Rome*, 4, pp. 1–2; *Papal Negotiations*, pp. 10–12. It is of interest to note that Elizabeth styled herself the sovereign of Scotland and France, so her anger at Mary and François was not without contradiction. See, for example, *CSP Foreign, 1558–1559*, 173, p.59. Mary, Queen of Scots' use of the styles and arms of England intensified after the death of Henri II in July 1559 and subsequent union of the French and Scottish crowns. This became a particular bone of contention for Elizabeth and her secretary, William Cecil, who saw this as a pretext for a French invasion of England. Mary and François' use of the arms of England was also a factor behind England's later decision to intervene financially and militarily on behalf of the Lords of the Congregation during the Reformation Rebellion in 1559–60. *Ibid*, 837, 840, 845, 868, pp. 311–2, 312–3, 314, 324–9; PRO, SP12/6, f.74ʳ; BL, Cotton MSS, Caligula B.x, fos. 17ᵛ-8ʳ; S. Alford, *The Early Elizabethan Polity: William Cecil and the British Succession Crisis, 1558–1569* (Cambridge, 1998), pp. 43–70.
133 Baumgartner, *Henry II*, p.224.

ing – a marriage that would inevitably be more fruitful than Philip's marriage to Elizabeth's aged and barren half-sister had been.[134] The actual terms of the treaty contracted between France, Spain and England reflect Henri's desire to safeguard his position and dynastic interests within the British Isles.[135] In lieu of the English Queen, Philip would instead marry Henri's daughter, Elisabeth, thereby keeping the Imperial threat out of the British Isles.[136] More importantly, it also provided for the possibility that Elizabeth could still be excommunicated by the pope, and enable Henri to put Mary and François on the prized throne of England.

With international peace and the dynastic and imperial interests of 'les Guises et Valois' safeguarded in Scotland and in England, the spring of 1559 seemed like the beginning of a 'golden age' for Henri and Mary of Guise. In reality, nothing could have been further from the truth. The reform movements in both Scotland and France soon began to translate into civil unrest, whilst Henri's untimely death in July 1559 instigated a series of events that would eventually see the collapse of Mary of Guise's régime in Scotland. But as we shall now see, the eventual outbreak of the so-called 'Reformation Rebellion' in May 1559 was not due to what Knox described as the 'altogether altered' mind of the Queen Regent towards her Protestant subjects upon fulfilling her dynastic objectives.[137] In fact, religion was a decidedly secondary concern for Mary of Guise until well after the marriage of her daughter and the bestowal of the crown matrimonial on the Dauphin. Seen in this light, the traditional view that Guise had to conciliate the reformers of her realm in order to achieve her dynastic objectives becomes highly questionable.

* * *

Throughout most of Mary of Guise's regency, religious issues had yielded to more pressing and immediate concerns such as the Franco-Scottish dynastic alliance, national security and the imposition of law and order.[138] However, Guise's preoccupation with these concerns

---

134 See *CSP Foreign, 1558–1559*, 321–2, 324–6, 335–7, 338–9, 340–1, 373, 390–4, 399, 405, 408, 419–20, 421–2, 439, 445–6, 447–8, 456, pp. 122–3, 137–44, 163–72, 175–9, 184, 186–8, 190, for references to the negotiations, in addition to Wernham, *Before the Armada*, pp. 244–6; Ruble, *Le Traité de Cateau Cambrésis* (Paris, 1889); Baumgartner, *Henry II*, pp. 221–5; Rodríguez-Salgado, *The Changing Face of Empire*, pp. 305–18.
135 *Foedera*, XV, pp. 505–12; *CSP Foreign, 1558–1559*, 475, 483, pp. 195, 196–8.
136 Baumgartner, *Henry II*, pp. 227–9; Rodríguez-Salgado, *The Changing Face of Empire*, pp. 319–23.
137 Knox, *Works*, I, p.315 and *History*, I, p.158.
138 *Papal Negotiations*, p.xiii.

did not mean that she was oblivious of the fact that the established Church was in need of internal reform or, for that matter, that there existed a small but powerful group of Protestants in her kingdom. In 1555 and 1556, for example, Pope Paul IV received numerous reports and petitions in the name of Mary, Queen of Scots,[139] detailing the degenerate and profligate state of the Scottish Church and requesting a visitation for the 'management and reform of our clergy'.[140] Church property had been alienated and neglected by prelates, parsons and holders of canonries and prebends, while ecclesiastical discipline had relaxed to such an extent that nuns wandered freely through the houses of the laity, admitted 'worthless and wicked men' to their monasteries and daily indulged in carnal lusts.[141] This was also evidenced by the fact that:

> divers abuses are introduced into the churches and very many crimes, iniquities, and scandalous enormities (some of them savouring of heresy) are committed by various persons of either sex, by ecclesiastics of various orders, both secular and regular, iniquities which give offence to the Divine Majesty, bring shame on the Christian religion, and cause loss of souls, and scandal to Christ's faithful.[142]

It is significant that this is the only reference to heresy in all the applications for a 'visitor' to Scotland. Even in Guise's letter to the Cardinal de Lorraine of 13 January 1557, in which she describes her problems in Scotland at great length, neither religion nor heresy is mentioned.[143] But it was at the instigation of the Queen Regent that Paul IV granted factory to Cardinal Anthony Trivulzio, legate *a latere* to the Apostolic See and to the Most Christian King of France, on 27 October 1557. Specifically, he was commissioned 'to visit, by means of some fit prelate, to be deputed by him, the churches, monasteries, and persons of either sex, ecclesiastical and secular, and regulars of every order in the realm of Scotland, and of the reforming and correcting of what he shall think deserving of reformation and correction'.[144] In 1556 Guise had already recommended the Scottish prelates who she

---

139 *Papal Negotiations*, pp. 4–9, 522–30, xviii-xx.
140 *Ibid*, p. 525.
141 *Ibid*, pp. 6–9, 528–9.
142 *Ibid*, p.7. Similar accusations had been made against the Church since the early 1400s, so the state of the Church had not really changed by the 1550s.
143 AÉ, *Mémoires et Documents*, Angleterre, XV, fos. 8–11; *Papal Negotiations*, pp. 423–30.
144 *Ibid*, pp. 8–9.

thought were the most capable and suitable candidates to hold the office of 'visitor'. The names of James Beaton, archbishop of Glasgow, Patrick Hepburn, bishop of Moray, Andrew Durie, bishop of Galloway, William Chisholm, bishop of Dunblane, and Robert Reid, bishop of Orkney, were all submitted for consideration.[145] It is not known, however, who was appointed, if anyone.

By 1557 the international situation was a more serious concern for the papacy than the internal reform of the Scottish Church. In December 1557 Trivulzio was sent on a special mission to France to pursue peace on the Continent. But Trivulzio also used his time in France to gather information on the 'state of Scottish affairs to which the queen's application to the Pope referred'.[146] In this, he was to be assisted not only by Henri and the Cardinal de Lorraine, but also by the delegation of Scottish commissioners negotiating Mary, Queen of Scots' marriage treaty. Expecting their arrival in two or three days' time, Henri informed Trivulzio that these 'Scotsmen of importance . . . would give full information as to the necessities of that kingdom'.[147] As proposed candidates to hold the office of visitor, Beaton and Reid could be expected to provide Trivulzio with pertinent and constructive information for the internal reform of the Scottish Church, but what the delegation's noted reformers, Cassillis, Erskine of Dun and Lord James, had to say on the matter is anyone's guess. Again, it is not known what information Trivulzio gathered from Henri or the Scots, if anything at all, but his appointment does reveal Mary of Guise's desire to see the internal reform of the Church.

She was similarly mindful that there existed a small but powerful group of Protestants in her kingdom that might oppose the Franco-Scottish dynastic alliance on religious grounds. To assure her Protestant subjects that her dynastic policies were not incompatible with the reformed faith, Guise adopted an accommodating position. Committed and noted reformers such as Glencairn, Argyll, Cassillis, Erskine of Dun and Lord James were shown no political bias in Guise's administration on account of their faith. Rather, they continued to play prominent roles in her government and, more importantly, were extensively involved in every stage of the process that culminated in Mary, Queen of Scots' marriage to the Dauphin. Reformers were recipients of French patronage alongside their Catholic peers and participated in Henri's triumphant entry into

145 *Papal Negotiations*, pp. 530, xx.
146 *Ibid*, p.9.
147 *Ibid*, pp. 9–10.

Rouen that celebrated, amongst other things, the Franco-Scottish dynastic alliance and projected Henri's imperial ambitions in the British Isles. Seven years later, Protestants elected to proceed with the Valois-Stewart marriage and were directly involved in the negotiations of the marriage treaty itself. Finally, in November 1558, having consented to grant the crown matrimonial to their new king, two of Scotland's most prominent reformers, Argyll and Lord James, were appointed to transport the crown itself to France.[148] By embracing a tolerant position with respect to religion and implementing a policy of inclusion rather than persecution, Guise sent a clear message to her Protestant subjects that they would not be marginalised, excluded or made to suffer personally or politically on account of their faith. This may also explain their support of her dynastic policies when most would see the union of the French and Scottish Catholic crowns as a direct threat to the reform movement in Scotland.[149]

Unlike Mary Tudor, Mary of Guise did not implement a policy of persecution. The controversial burning of Walter Miln in April 1558 was the work of Archbishop Hamilton.[150] John Knox, moreover, went unmolested during his preaching tour of Scotland in 1555–1556 and Guise did nothing to prevent him associating with Scots with Protestant sympathies such as Erskine of Dun, Argyll, Lord Lorne and Lord James.[151] Rather, she reinforced her assurances of inclusion and toleration with patronage. In November and December 1557 she entered into a bond a manrent with the Earl of Morton, while Donald Campbell, abbot of Coupar Angus, was nominated to the bishopric of

148 Knox, *Works*, I, p.294 and *History*, I, p.141; Lesley, *History*, p.268. Along with Glencairn, Argyll and Erskine of Dun, Lord James Stewart was one of those who invited Knox to return to Scotland on 10 March 1557. Knox, *Works*, I, pp. 267–8 and *History*, I, p.132.

149 Jenny Wormald has argued that leading Protestants such as Lord James and Erskine of Dun gave 'positive' support to the union with Catholic France because 'they saw it as a way to keep the Catholic-educated Mary out of Scotland, while maintaining their formal loyalty to her, [and] thereby maximizing the opportunity to advance the Protestant cause while minimizing the need to clash directly with their sovereign'. However, the relationship between Guise and her Protestant subjects appears to be far less cynical, and one based rather on a mutual understanding of religious toleration, than Wormald's argument allows. Wormald, *Mary, Queen of Scots*, pp.94–5 and *Court, Kirk, and Community*, p.114.

150 Dawson, 'The Scottish Reformation and the Theatre of Martyrdom', in D. Wood (ed.), *Martyrs and Martyrologies* (Oxford, 1993), pp. 259–70, especially pp. 269–70. Even Knox accepted Guise's protestations of innocence in this matter. Knox, *Works*, I, pp. 308–9, Appendix XIII, pp. 550–5, and *History*, I, pp. 153–4.

151 Donaldson, *James V-James VII*, pp. 85–6.

Brechin, a son of Glencairn received a pension of £900 from Kelso abbey, a nephew of Argyll was granted the temporalities from Brechin, and Adam Bothwell, son of the provost of Edinburgh, was nominated and provided with the bishopric of Orkney.[152]

So if Guise had adopted a tolerant position with respect to religion in a conscious effort to reassure her Protestant subjects that there would not be a backlash after the Valois-Stewart marriage, why did the Earls of Argyll, Glencairn and Morton, Lord Lorne and John Erskine of Dun sign the famous 'Common Band' of 3 December 1557? In this, they pledged to 'continually apply our hole power, substance, and our verray lyves to manteane, sett fordward and establish the most blessed word of God and his Congregatioun . . . and defend thame . . . at our haill poweris and waring of our lyves against Sathan, and all wicked power that does intend tyranny or truble'.[153] Was this a declaration against Mary of Guise and the Franco-Scottish dynastic alliance?

Unlike later proclamations, the 'First Band' of the Congregation was purely a religious manifesto. The subscribers, who subsequently became known as the Lords of the Congregation, were simply declaring their commitment to the reformed religion and its establishment in Scotland. Nothing contained within it suggests that the subscribers' motives were political. The purpose of the 'Common Band', therefore, was purely defensive. They knew Mary of Guise was a politique, who was ultimately concerned with her own dynastic interests and those of her daughter. As such, she was not above altering her religious policy if in the circumstances she deemed it necessary or advantageous to do so. In the event that Mary of Guise was not playing straight with them, this group of committed reformers took the precautionary step of setting up a private insurance policy against the *possibility* that once the marriage was accomplished, Guise would no longer need or, as would happen, could no longer afford to be so accommodating.[154] The fears of the Protestants, however, ensured that this became a self-fulfilling prophecy.

The year following the signing of the 'First Band' witnessed the systematic development of the Lords of the Congregation's religious policy, which they presented to the Queen Regent in their petitions of November 1558. Again, Guise showed her proclivity for accommoda-

---

152 Donaldson *James V-James VII*, p.86; Donaldson, *Reformed by Bishops*, pp. 1–52; Mahoney, 'The Scottish Hierarchy', p.53; Dowden, *Bishops*, pp. 190–1, 374, 267; *Papal Negotiations*, pp. 28, 30, 40, 55, 172; *Highland Papers*, IV, p.211; *ER*, XIX, p.451, *RSS*, IV, 1800, p.292 and V, 589, pp. 122–3.
153 Knox, *Works*, I, 273 and *History*, I, p.136.
154 Mason, *Kingship and the Commonweal*, p.150 *n*.40.

tion by promising to have them considered at a Provincial Council, which subsequently convened at Edinburgh on 1 March 1559.[155] Several statutes upholding the ancient faith and its authority as the established Church in Scotland were passed, and the Protestants' requests for such things as the legal assembly of Protestants in private or public, the reading of Scripture in the vernacular, the administration of the sacraments of baptism and communion in the vernacular (the latter in both kinds), and the reform of the Estate Ecclesiastical according to the above precepts, were rejected outright – not by Guise, but by the Provincial Council.[156] This casts doubt on the accuracy of Knox's assertion that:

> to gett the Matrimoniall Croune, the Quein Regent left no point of the compas unsailled Unto the Protestants she said, "I am nott unmyndfull how oft ye have suyted me for Reformatioun in religioun, and glaidly wald I consent thairunto; but ye see that the power and craft of the Bischop of Sanctandrois, togetther with the power of the Duck [Châtelherault], and of the Kirk-men, ever to be bent against me in all my proceadingis; So that I may do nothing, onless the full authoritie of this Realme be devolved to the King of France, which can nott be butt by donatioun of the Croune Matrimoniall; which thing yf ye will bring to passe, then devise ye what ye please in materis of religioun and thei shalbe granted".[157]

This version of events is, of course, coloured by Knox's personal bias as well as hindsight. It gives the impression that Guise needed to conciliate the Protestants by granting empty promises because their sheer political weight could have some bearing on the outcome of whether the crown matrimonial was granted to the Dauphin or not. Given the presumably small number of openly committed reformers at the time, this seems highly unlikely – especially as the decision was made in Parliament where consensus ruled. Of greater significance is Knox's inference that pro-reforming sympathies were synonymous with opposition to Franco-Scottish dynastic union. There is no evidence to suggest that such a correlation existed before the defence of Scotland's freedom and liberties became a central theme of the Lords of the Congregation's propaganda during the Reformation Rebellion.

155 Patrick, *Statutes*, liv, pp. 149–91.
156 *Ibid*, liv, pp. 156–62.
157 Knox, *Works*, pp. 293–4 and *History*, I, pp. 140–1.

The only formal protest lodged against the granting of the crown matrimonial to the Dauphin came from Châtelherault, who was noticeably absent from this session of Parliament and principally concerned with safeguarding his own dynastic ambitions and rights to the succession.[158]

If the Scots had any reservations about the effect Franco-Scottish dynastic union would have on their ancient laws or liberties, or their cultural or institutional independence, they could have refused to grant the crown matrimonial to the Dauphin. After all, they had already shown their ability to oppose Mary of Guise over the issue of taxation. The fact that the Three Estates did grant it, moreover, does not automatically mean that they did so because Mary of Guise made a secret deal with her Protestant subjects over matters of religion. Rather, their consent was more than likely owing to her dual policy of accommodation and inclusion, and the general assurances she gave to her Protestant subjects throughout her regency that her dynastic policies were not necessarily incompatible with the reform movement. Yet, despite these assurances, international and national events coinciding with the fulfilment of Guise's dynastic policies forced the Queen Regent to take a harder line in matters of religion. These same events also encouraged her Protestant subjects to take a far more assertive stance in their quest to advance and establish the reformed kirk in Scotland. The clash of interests resulted in civil war.

158 *APS*, II, pp. 507–8.

8

The Reformation Rebellion:
The Collapse of Mary of
Guise's Régime in Scotland?

O n 24 May 1559 a government force of 8,000 men assembled on the
outskirts of Perth to confront a riotous 'congregation' of Protestants who had embarked on a violent campaign of iconoclasm.[1] On the
face of it, Mary of Guise's decision to respond to this revolt militarily
seemed to confirm her 'altogether altered' mind towards the reform
movement since the fulfilment of her dynastic policies.[2] She had already
issued a religious proclamation on 23 March 1559 in support of the Third
Provincial Council upholding the authority and supremacy of the Scottish Church, and had made clear her determination to enforce this
proclamation by coming down hard on anyone who failed to observe the
order to return to the ancient faith by Easter (26 March).[3] Four Protestant
preachers were denounced as rebels when they failed to appear
before the Queen Regent at Stirling on 10 May to explain their non-
compliance.[4] Incensed by this turn of events and, in particular, by Mary of
Guise's *volte face,* John Knox preached a rancorous sermon 'vehemente
against idolatrie'.[5] The riot and iconoclasm that ensued officially marked
the beginning of the Reformation Rebellion in Scotland.[6]

Both contemporary and modern historians have used the timing of
this change of religious policy to suggest that Mary of Guise adopted a
conciliatory position towards her Protestant subjects with the sole

1 *CSP Foreign, 1558–1559*, 728, pp. 268–9; *CSP Scot.*, I, 457, p.213.
2 Knox, *Works*, I, p.315 and *History*, I, p.159.
3 Patrick, *Statutes*, pp. 149–91; D. Laing (ed.), 'Historie of the Estate of
   Scotland', *Wodrow Misc.*, I, p.56; W.L. Mathieson, *Politics and Religion: A
   Study in Scottish History from the Reformation to the Revolution* (Glasgow,
   1902), I, p.57; Lee, *James Stewart*, p.33.
4 Pitcairn, *Trials*, I.i, pp.406–7; *CSP Foreign, 1558–1559*, 710, pp. 263–4; *CSP
   Scot.*, I, 455, pp. 212–3; Knox, *Works*, I, pp. 315–9.
5 Knox, *Works*, I, p.321 and *History*, I, p.163.
6 Knox's accounts of the iconoclasm in Perth varied to suit his audience. A more
   realistic account can be found in his letters to Anna Locke in *CSP Foreign, 1558–
   1559*, 743, 877, pp. 278, 331–5, while a decidedly more favourable version of
   events is contained in his *Works*, I, pp. 319–23 and *History*, I, pp. 162–3.

purpose of achieving her dynastic objectives.[7] It is thus argued that, having secured the Three Estates' ratification of Mary, Queen of Scots' marriage contract and consent to grant the crown matrimonial to the Dauphin, Guise no longer required the political support of her Protestant subjects and promptly abandoned her policy of conciliation for one less accommodating. In reality, though, this alteration in policy was neither sudden nor extreme and did not represent the complete abandonment of Guise's accommodating position. Rather, a complex series of international and national events *coinciding* with the completion of her dynastic policies compelled her to take an increasingly hard line in matters of religion. As in so many other aspects of her regency, events in England dictated her actions at home, and the dynastic controversy that followed in the wake of Mary Tudor's death forced her to adopt a more assertive stance against the reform movement in Scotland. Mary of Guise's sudden preoccupation with religion in 1559, therefore, came not with the realisation of her dynastic ambitions, but directly as a result of the early Elizabethan succession crisis.

* * *

Following the death of Mary Tudor in November 1558 the question of religion in Scotland became a matter of crucial importance. Elizabeth Tudor's accession to the English throne physically prevented the immediate realisation of Henri's imperial vision of a Franco-British empire. Undeterred by this development, Henri immediately launched a campaign to advance Mary, Queen of Scots' claim to the English succession on the grounds that she was 'laitlie mareit to the dolphine his eldest sone, [and] was just heritour of the realme of Inglande, as nerrest and lauchfull to the croun thairof, being onelie dochtir to King James the Fyft of Scotlande, quhois moder Quene Margaret was eldest sister to Henry the viij'.[8] Henri's dynastic argument rested foursquare on religion. Because the Pope had not sanctioned Henry VIII's divorce from Catharine of Aragon, his subsequent marriage to Anne Boleyn was invalid and Elizabeth illegitimate in the eyes of the Catholic Church.

By contrast, there was no question of Mary Stewart's legitimacy in canon law, and Henri used this line of argument to try to persuade Pope Paul IV to 'declare Queen Elizabeth illegitimate, and, as it were, of incestuous birth and consequently incapable of succeeding to the throne'.[9] The credibility of his argument, however, would be seriously undermined if

---

7 Knox, *Works*, I, pp. 294, 312, and *History*, I, pp. 140–1, 156; Donaldson, *James V-James VII*, p.91; Lee, *James Stewart*, pp. 20, 32–3; Mathieson, *Politics and Religion*, I, pp. 42–4, 52, 56.
8 Lesley, *History*, pp. 268–9.
9 [December 1558], *CSP Rome*, 2, p.1.

the Queen of Scots' subjects were seen to favour Protestantism and, worse still, if the Scottish government was seen to accommodate them in their 'heretical' beliefs.[10] If Henri had any chance of receiving papal support for his daughter-in-law's claim and for realising his imperial ambitions within the British Isles, it was imperative that Scotland remain a kingdom favourable to Catholicism and a faithful adherent of the Holy See. Mary of Guise's religious proclamation of 23 March 1559 was a necessary and integral part of Henri's international campaign to strengthen Mary Stewart's Catholic claim to the English succession.[11]

10 After the outbreak of the Reformation Rebellion, Henri, Mary and François wrote to Pope Paul IV seeking financial assistance, papal intervention and, more importantly, to absolve themselves of any responsibility for their tolerance of heresy and growth of Protestantism in their respective kingdoms. In his letter of 29 June 1559, Henri went so far as to blame the Pope for the troubles in Scotland on account of the latter's failure to provide a remedy for the degenerate state of the Church. 'Having long foreseen the incredible disaster which has since befallen the realm of Scotland', he wrote, 'we have many and divers time heretofore written and made most instant request to your Holiness, that it might be your good pleasure to commit and delegate some good virtuous and notable personage among the prelates of that kingdom, such as our most dear and well-beloved good sister and cousin the queen dowager of this Scotland could well choose and select to introduce and establish some wholesome, holy and devout reform in the Church, correct, bridle and temper the corrupt customs, the depraved and dissolute lives of the said prelates and ecclesiastical ministers, who already begin to fall away very much and degenerate.' *Papal Negotiations*, pp. 17, xxviii-xxix, 13–20; NLS, Adv.MSS, 54.1.2(ii), fos. 6–7ʳ; Ribier, *Lettres et Mémoires*, II, p.808; P. Hume Brown, *John Knox* (London, 1895), II, Appendix B, pp. 300–2.

11 Henri's appeals to the Court of Rome were no doubt enhanced by his own commitment to extirpate heresy in France. While this was cited as a premise for the peace of Câteau-Cambrésis, Henri's declared intent to combat the Huguenot movement did not begin in earnest until the summer of 1559. In late May, Throckmorton reported that, 'The French King minds to make a journey to Poictou, Gascoigne, Guienne, and other places for the repressing of religion, and to use the extremist persecution he may against the Protestants in his countries and like in Scotland, and that with celerity'. It was only with the outbreak of the Reformation Rebellion in Scotland that Henri's declarations against heresy became more extreme. On 3 July Henri wrote to his ambassador in Rome that '. . . I'espere bien, puisque Dieu m'a donné la paix, d'employer le temps, et ce qu i'auray de force en main à faire punir, chastiser et extirper tous ceux qui se trouveront imitateurs de ces nouvelles Doctrines, sens y épargner personne, de quelque qualité or dignité qu'ils soient [I truly hope, as God has given me peace, to use the time and all the armed men I will have, to punish, chastise and extirpate all those who will be found following these new doctrines, sparing no one, whatever their nobility or office]'. Despite the projections of contemporary observers, such as Étiènne Pasquier, that as soon as the Valois-Habsburg peace was contracted, '. . . Monsieur le cont'd/

In the meantime, though, there was the danger that as long as Elizabeth sat on the throne, her religious sympathies would result in a Protestant religious settlement in England. The prospect of yet another Protestant English monarch posed a significantly greater threat to French interests in Scotland than the Anglo-Imperial dynastic and *Catholic* alliance had done during the reign of Mary Tudor. The stage would not only be set for renewed English intrigues in Scotland, but Elizabeth herself would become the focus of support for discontented Scottish reformers eager to revive the arguments in favour of Anglo-Scottish Protestant union and, more seriously, for any disaffected Scot in the realm.[12] The Elizabethan religious settlement, therefore, was eagerly anticipated by Catholics and Protestants alike: its outcome not only had the potential to change the political map of the British Isles, but of Europe as a whole.

Elizabeth assembled her first Parliament on 25 January 1559. The foremost topic of discussion was, unsurprisingly, the religious fate of England. All indications pointed to a return to Protestantism, but the final settlement was delayed until May 1559 because of the Lords' opposition to the proposed restoration of the Acts of Supremacy and Uniformity as they had been during the reigns of Henry VIII and

> *cont'd*   cardinal de Lorraine declara en plein Parlement, que l'opinion du Roy avoit esté de la faire a quelque prix et condition que ce fust pour de la en avant vacquer à son aise à l'extermination et banissment de l'heresie de Calvin [Monsieur the Cardinal of Lorraince will declare in the middle of the Parlement, that the King's decision had been to make [peace] whatever the cost and condition, to devote himself happily to the destruction and banishment of Calvin's heresy]' and, similarly, that 'Le Roy resolut, a quelque prix que ce fúst, de faire la paix en deliberation de s'armer contre les Heretiques de son Royaume [The King has decided, whatever the cost, to make peace with the intention of taking arms against the Heretics of his Kingdom]', Henri's threats of extremist persecution did not translate into effective action. *CSP Foreign, 1558–1559*, 732, 823, 833, pp. 272, 301, 308–11; Ribier, *Lettres et Mémoires*, II, p.806; É. Pasquier, *Les Oeuvres d'Estienne Pasquier, countenant ses recherches de la France* (Amsterdam, 1723), II, pp. 77, 450; Dickinson (ed.), 'Report by de la Brosse and d'Oysel on conditions in Scotland, 1559–60', *SHS Misc.*, IX, pp. 85–6.

> 12 In their letter to Pope Paul IV, Mary and François cited the Elizabethan religious settlement as one reason for the outbreak of the Reformation Rebellion in Scotland. They claimed they needed a papal subsidy for the 'soustenement et deffence de l'eglise Romaine contre les nouvelles sectes qui commancerent lors a seslever au dict Royaulme par le moyen de leurs voisins suivant l'eglise changee en Angleterre [support and defence of the Roman [Catholic] church against the new sects which began to emerge in the Kingdom through their neighbours following the reformed church in England]'. NLS, Adv.MSS, 54.1.2(ii), f.6ʳ; Brown, *John Knox*, II, p.301.

Edward VI.[13] The question throughout the spring of 1559, therefore, was not whether England would break with Rome, but the extent to which the Elizabethan Church would be a reformed church. All speculation ended when, on 8 May, the Elizabethan Acts of Uniformity and Supremacy received parliamentary sanction in both the Commons and the Lords.[14] With the restoration of the Edwardian *Book of Common Prayer and the Administration of Sacraments*, and 'to the Crown the ancient jurisdiction over the state ecclesiastical and spiritual', England once again became a Protestant kingdom and, in doing so, irrevocably changed the dynamics of Scottish politics.[15]

By May 1559 Scotland's Protestants had become decidedly more assertive in their demands for religious reform. Elizabeth's accession and religious settlement no doubt played a part in this new-found confidence, but so too did the return of John Knox to Scotland on 2 May 1559. On ending his exile on the Continent at the behest of Argyll, Lord Lorne, Glencairn, Morton and Erskine of Dun, Knox's return had an immediate impact on the progress of the reform movement in Scotland – even though he would have preferred to go to England.[16] Just four days after his return, the Lords of the Congregation sent a letter to Mary of Guise expressing their dissatisfaction at her sudden change of policy and, in particular, her religious proclamation of 23 March 1559:

> . . . now allace frustret of our howp to our greit hewines, we
> find the contrair, our lycht is changeit in myrknes, our
> myrth and joy in sorow and weping; ffor your letters
> proclamationis and the wordis dalie pronuncit of your awin
> mowthe, dois altogidder mak for the downputting of Godis
> gloir, his wird, and trew wirschiping, and to menten and to
> authoreis the idolatrie and abhominatioun of the Roman
> Antichrist.[17]

13 See, for example, Sir Simonds d'Ewes, *The Journals of all the Parliaments during the reign of Queen Elizabeth, Both of the House of Lords and House of Commons* (London, 1682), pp. 37–56; N.L. Jones, 'Elizabeth's First Year: The Conception and Birth of the Elizabethan Political World', in C. Haigh (ed.), *The Reign of Elizabeth I* (London, 1989), pp. 36–9, 43–8.

14 1559: 1 Eliz. I, c. 1 & 2, *Statutes of the Realm*, IV, pp. 350–5, 355–8.

15 1552: 5 & 6 Ed. VI, c.1 and 1559: 1 Eliz. I, c.1, *Statutes of the Realm*, IV, pp. 130–1, 350–5.

16 It was following his successful preaching tour in Scotland that Knox was invited to return in November 1558. Knox, *Works*, I, p. 274 and *History*, I, pp. 137, 161, 139 *n*.3.

17 'Appendix to the Dun Papers', *Spalding Misc.*, IV, p.88.

Of greater significance was the Congregation's latent threat that if Guise persisted in making 'ordinance aganis the word of God we of necessitie man disobey your ordinance'.[18] Whilst it is not known if Knox actually penned this letter himself, his influence on the Congregation's language and ideology is beyond question. Espousing Knox's covenanting ideology and theory of armed resistance, the Congregation's epistle clearly reflected their sense of duty as the elect bound in 'league and covenant' to the divine will. As such, they were obliged to disobey Guise as the constituted temporal authority if her laws contradicted those of God as revealed in Scripture.[19] Written just days before Paul Methven, John Christison, William Harlaw and John Willock were scheduled to appear before the Queen Regent at Stirling on 10 May, the Congregation's letter not only justified the Protestant preachers' act of defiance in failing to observe Guise's religious proclamation, but was also a poignant foreshadowing of things to come.

It was in support of the summoned preachers that a multitude of Protestants, including John Knox, assembled in Perth during the first week of May. According to Knox, this multitude, made up of men from 'the toune of Dundy, [and] the gentilmen of Anguss and Mearnis', was 'without armour, as peciable men, mynding onlie to geve confessioun with thare preachearis'.[20] Without armour they may have been, but they were armed with a ready supply of stones for use as projectiles, and they also had the element of surprise on their side. Their impromptu assembly in Perth had caught the Queen Regent unawares, and for Guise the Protestants' declared intention to accompany their preachers to Stirling made the assembly at Perth all the more alarming. In an attempt to defuse this dangerous situation, Guise asked Erskine of Dun 'to wret to those that war assembled at Sanct Johnestoun, to stay, and nott to come fordwarte'.[21] Knox claims that this staying order was taken to include the four summoned preachers who, consequently, remained in Perth. In the light of the Congregation's letter to the Queen Regent, though, the non-appearance of the preachers was taken as an open and deliberate act of defiance and prompted Guise, with justification, to give 'commandiment to putt thame to the horne, inhibiting all men under pane of thare rebellioun to assist, conforte, receave, or mayntenne thame in any sorte'.[22]

18 'Appendix to the Dun Papers', *Spalding Misc.*, IV, p.90.
19 Mason, 'Covenant and Commonweal', pp. 98–101.
20 Knox, *Works*, I, p.317 and *History*, I, p.160.
21 Knox, *Works*, I, p.318 and *History*, I, p.160.
22 Knox, *Works*, I, pp. 318–9 and *History*, I, pp. 160–1; Pitcairn, *Trials*, I.i, pp. 406–7; *CSP Foreign, 1558–1559*, 710, pp. 263–4; *CSP Scot.*, I, 455, pp. 212–3.

The Protestants had also assembled at Perth because of the 'Beggars Warning'.[23] Throughout January 1559 a summons appeared upon the gates and ports of friaries throughout Scotland. Written in the name of the 'Blynd, Cruked, Bedrelles, Wedowis, Ophelingis, and all uther Pure as may not worke', the 'Beggars Warning' sought to effect the 'Restitutioun of Wranges bypast, and Reformatioun in Tyme Cuming'. This was to be achieved by ordering friars to surrender their property so that the poor, 'the onelie lawfull proprietaris thairof may enter thairto, and efterward injoye thai commodities of the Kyrk, quhilke ye have heirunto wranguslie halden fra us'.[24] The day of eviction, or 'flitting Friday', fell on 12 May 1559 and coincided, unfortunately for Guise, with the scheduled appearance of the four preachers and their subsequent denunciation as rebels.[25] A mob of extremist Protestants none too pleased with the Queen Regent added a new element of danger to the threat that, if the friars did not meet their demands and surrender their properties, they would, 'at the said terme, [and] in haile number . . . enter and tak possessioun of our said patrimony, and eject yow utterlie furthe of the same'.[26] True to their word, the Protestants assembled at Perth ran 'without deliberatioun to the Gray and Blak Freris', after a riot suddenly broke out following John Knox's sermon 'vehement against idolatrie' on 11 May. In the iconoclasm that followed, these religious houses were attacked and utterly destroyed.[27] It is doubtful, though, whether John Knox and the Lords of the Congregation actually planned to start their rebellion for the reformation of religion at Perth in May 1559. The riot and outbreak of violence were unexpected, and once this chain of events had begun, they could not turn back. Instead, they had to impose some sort of control and give the impression that the riot was, in fact, all part of a grand plan. Similarly, the Queen Regent could not have expected, nor did she expect, that this assembly at Perth would quickly turn into an armed uprising. If she had, there would have been a military presence in Perth.

* * *

Upon hearing of the destruction in Perth, Mary of Guise immediately summoned the nobility and began making preparations to assert her

23 Knox, *Works*, I, pp. 320–1 *n*.1 and *History*, II, Appendix V, pp. 255–6.
24 Knox, *Works*, I, p.321 and *History*, II, p.256.
25 Knox, *Works*, I, pp. 320–1 and *History*, I, p.162; Donaldson, *James V-James VII*, p.92.
26 Knox, *Works*, I, p.321 and *History*, II, p.256.
27 Knox, *Works*, I, pp. 322–3 and *History*, I, pp. 162–3. According to one commentator, the Protestants also targeted the Charterhouse and 'pullit the hoill place downe, alsweill the Kirk thairof as uther housses, and all the coastlie bigginis quhilkis was maid be King James the First' in 1429. Lesley, *History*, p.272.

authority through a visible display of force.[28] Her decision to respond to the Congregation's revolt militarily was taken not because she was beginning to favour a policy of religious persecution, but because she believed that the aims of the Congregation had nothing to do with religion. For Guise, the Congregation's revolt in Perth was 'nothing bot a rebellioun' directed against the established authority.[29] The dictum *cuius regio, eius religio* was fast becoming a commonplace in Reformation Europe, and Guise, like Henri, believed that the religion of her subjects should be that of their sovereigns. Any challenge to the established Church was seen as a challenge to the temporal authority and, as such, political sedition. But as a *politique* whose dynastic interests took precedence over her own religious convictions, Guise had been willing to show a considerable degree of toleration towards the reform movement. But now, the relationship she had previously established with her Protestant subjects – namely, one of mutual accommodation – moved her to see the Congregation's revolt exclusively in political terms. Throughout their rebellion, she consistently maintained that the Congregation 'intended not religioun, bot the subversioun of authoritie'.[30]

28 Knox, *Works*, I, pp. 324–5 and *History*, I, p.163; *CSP Foreign, 1558–1559*, 728, 743, pp. 268–9, 278; *CSP Scot.*, I, 457, p.213.
29 Knox, *Works*, I, p.324 and *History*, I, p.163.
30 D. Calderwood, *The History of the Kirk of Scotland*, T. Thomson (ed.) (Wodrow Society, 1842–9), I, p.433. See similar comments that the Congregation 'pretended no religion, but a plain revolt from the Authority', in Knox, *Works*, I, pp. 324, 363–4, 397–9 and *History*, I, pp. 163, 193–4, 217–9. Only when seeking intervention from Pope Paul IV did Henri, Guise, Mary and François speak of the Congregation's rebellion in religious terms. The nobles and the third estate were described as 'seditious and scandalously insolent against religion', having 'certain apostate preachers of the learning or doctrine of Geneva to exhort, and induce the people to follow their damnable errors and heresies, whence the greater part of the said people is entirely infected and as it were lost. They constrain every one to follow their sect, wreck churches and monasteries, profane holy things, burn publicly the statues and pictures of the saints with their holy relics and bones. They have disinterred the bodies of the kings of Scotland, whom they have in like manner burnt and reduced to ashes; they have taken off and changed the habits of monks and nuns to make them become seculars and leave and abandon their orders and professions, boasting and bragging of attacking and bearing down the queen and all others who would oppose and refuse to join their new league, in such sort that cruel savages could not do worse'. With French military intervention, Henri hoped that the King and Queen Dauphin and the Queen Regent 'will overcome these heretics and schismatics, and force and power will be in their hands to chastise and punish their great temerity and arrogance, for the honour of the Creator, the exaltation of His Holy Name, and the increase of our holy faith and religion'. *Papal Negotiations*, pp. 17–8; NLS, Adv.MSS, 54.1.2(ii), fos. 6–7[r]; Ribier, *Lettres et Mémoires*, II, p.808; Brown, *John Knox*, II, pp. 300–2.

This questioning of motives ultimately gave the Queen Regent an edge over the Congregation in the war of words that continued between the two sides throughout 1559. This was especially true when the Congregation's actions began to substantiate her contentions. As Roger Mason points out, 'If credibility be ranked among the most treasured assets of any political movement, then it was the Congregation's singular misfortune that from the very outset their motives were questioned and their professed aims scoffed at and derided'.[31] Because Guise did not see the Congregation's revolt in religious terms, she did not employ a policy of persecution nor abandon her policy of accommodation towards the reformers. Instead, she continued to use notable Protestants such as John Erskine of Dun, Lord James Stewart and Archibald, 5th earl of Argyll, in the hope of suppressing the Congregation's revolt.

We have already seen how Mary of Guise tried to stay the multitude in Perth through the intervention of Erskine of Dun, whom Knox described as 'a zealous, prudent, and godly man most addict to please hir in all thingis not repugnant to God'.[32] During the initial stages of the rebellion, Guise also relied on the services of Lord James and Argyll to try to restore order through peaceful means. While Châtelherault and d'Oisel's troops were on standby in Auchterarder, Guise sent Argyll, Lord James and Lord Sempill (an ardent Catholic whom Knox described as 'a man sold under syne, enymye to God and to all godlynes'), to meet with representatives of the Congregation.[33] Their first task was to inquire into the nature of the Congregation's armed occupation of Perth. In the two weeks that had elapsed since the iconoclasm first began, the situation in Perth had taken a more serious turn with the arrival of Glencairn and a small contingent of lesser nobles in support of the Congregation.[34] The extent of Glencairn's reinforcements, however, was not substantial (numbering somewhere in the region of 2,500 men)[35] and should not be taken as a sign that Mary of Guise faced a groundswell of opposition from the nobility or the Protestant community at

31 Mason, 'Covenant and Commonweal', p.112.
32 Knox, Works, I, pp. 317–8 and History, I, p. 160.
33 Knox, Works, I, pp. 341, 339 and History, I, pp. 175, 173.
34 Glencairn was accompanied by the Lords Ochiltree and Boyd, Matthew Campbell of Loudon, John Wallace of Craigie, George Campbell of Cessnock, Hugh Wallace of Carnell, John Lockhart of Barr and James Chalmer of Gadgirth. Knox, Works, I, p.340 and History, I, p.175; CSP Foreign, 1558–1559, 822, 833, pp. 301, 308–11; CSP Scot., I, 464, p.215.
35 Knox, Works, I, p.341 and History, I, p.175; Sanderson, Ayrshire and the Reformation, pp. 98–9.

large.[36] Rather, support for the Congregation at this point was minimal and localised in nature. Glencairn was the only magnate of significance willing to risk his lands, liberty and life for the 'caus of religioun'.[37] Most of the gentry and leading reformers were still firmly in the Queen Regent's camp. As Sir James Croft observed, because 'a great number of those that rise with the Queen being of that religion that the other faction is, being also of kindred and alliance', it was his opinion that 'the matter will fall to some other appointment without battle'.[38]

Yet the reality of the situation was that Perth was a town being held against the Queen Regent, and the Congregation's assurances of 22 May 1559 did little to convince Guise that their rebellion was simply a revolt of conscience or that their promise of 'all humill obedience' was sincere.[39] Argyll, Lord James and Sempill's prime directive on 24 May was 'to inquire the caus of that convoctioun of liegis' in Perth and, more importantly, if the Congregation 'myndit nocht to hold that town against the authoritie, and against the Quene Regent'.[40] The response to this question did little to assure the Queen Regent. With Knox as their spokesperson, the Congregation reiterated their assurances of obedience, while simultaneously pledging to 'tak the sweard of just defence aganis all that should persew us for the mater of religioun'.[41] Upon

36 Upon hearing that Guise had summoned the nobility for the purpose of confronting them militarily, the Congregation hastily wrote a letter 'To the Nobilitie of Scotland', in which they earnestly required their 'moderatioun, and that ye stay your selfis, and the furye of utheris, from [the] persecuting of us'. Penned in the language of the covenant and espousing Knox's theory of armed resistance, the Congregation took great pains to stress the 'difference betuix the authoritie quhiche is Goddis ordinnance, and the personis of those whiche ar placit in the authoritie'. God's law was infallible, and if the nobility persecuted the Congregation for following God's will as revealed in Scripture, 'blynd zeale, nather yit the colour of authoritie' would excuse them in the eyes of God. Rather, it was the nobility's duty to 'defend innocentis, and to brydle the fury and raige of wicked men, wer it Princes or Emperouris'. And, as a foretaste of the patriotic stance they would later adopt, the Congregation played on the fact that, if the nobility carried out the will of the constituted temporal authority, namely, Mary of Guise, they would be doing so against their 'naturall cuntriemen'. Knox, *Works*, I, pp. 329–34 and *History*, I, pp. 167–71; Mason, *Knox: On Rebellion*, pp. 152–6.
37 As Knox himself admitted, support for the Congregation in Perth came only from the brethren of Fife, Angus [Dundee], Mearns, Cunningham and Kyle. Knox, *Works*, I, pp. 335–6, 327 and *History*, I, 171, 165.
38 *CSP Scot.*, I, 457, p.213; *CSP Foreign, 1558–1559*, 728, pp. 268–9.
39 Knox, *Works*, I, pp. 326–7 and *History*, I, pp. 164–5; Mason, *Knox: On Rebellion*, pp. 149–51.
40 Knox, *Works*, I, p.337 and *History*, I, p.173.
41 Knox, *Works*, I, pp. 339, 326 and *History*, I, pp. 173, 164; Mason, *Knox: On Rebellion*, pp. 149–50.

hearing Knox's reply, Guise immediately issued letters to her Lyon-King-at-Arms, Robert Forman, charging all men to avoid Perth on pain of treason.[42] No military force, however, was used to enforce this proclamation. Guise was still determined to reach some sort of agreement with the Congregation and restore the burgh to a state of obedience peacefully without using the sort of military force that might provoke accusations of heavy-handedness or repression.[43]

With the law and the majority of leading reformers still behind the Queen Regent, Knox knew that for the Congregation to succeed, more support was needed – particularly from high-ranking members of the nobility, such as Lord James and Argyll. The problem facing Knox was that these two nobles had bound themselves to the Regent, promising 'to laubour for concord, and to assist the Quene' against the Congregation if the latter refused to act reasonably and accept Guise's offer to negotiate a settlement.[44] Despite his attempts to goad Lord James and Argyll into breaking with the Regent by accusing them of 'infidelitie, in sa fer as thay had defrauded thair brethering of thair debtfull support and confort in thair gretest necessitie', honour prevented them from doing so.[45] Honour, however, worked both ways and Knox claims that Lord James and Argyll promised to side openly with the Congregation if, having concluded some sort of appointment with the Regent, 'the Quene did break in ony joit thairof'.[46] Whatever the premise, the negotiations that ensued culminated in the Perth Agreement of 29 May 1559. It was agreed that both armies would disband and leave Perth open to the Queen Regent; that none of the inhabitants would be molested on account of the late alteration in religion; that no Frenchmen would enter or be left to garrison the town when Guise retired; and finally, that all other controversies would be referred to the next Parliament.[47]

Guise's success in reducing Perth to obedience through diplomacy, however, was short-lived and ultimately lost her the crucial support of Argyll and Lord James. Upon entering Perth the next day, she immediately restored the Mass, replaced Lord Ruthven as Provost with a more faithful adherent to the crown, the Laird of Kinfauns, and

---

42 Knox, *Works*, I, p.340 and *History*, I, p.175.
43 In his *History*, Knox lets slip that an 'appointment' was what Guise 'required' at Perth – contradicting his inferences that the Regent's true intention was to persecute the Congregation and suppress them by force. Knox, *Works*, I, p.341 and *History*, I, p.175.
44 Knox, *Works*, I, p.343 and *History*, I, p.177.
45 Knox, *Works*, I, p.343 and *History*, I, p.177.
46 Knox, *Works*, I, p.343 and *History*, I, p.177.
47 *CSP Foreign, 1558–1559*, 784, p.289.

upon leaving the burgh, maintained a garrison of four Scottish companies there in French pay.[48] Guise's contravention of the Perth Agreement cost her dearly. The subsequent defection of Argyll and Lord James to assume the nominal leadership of the Congregation was a devastating blow to the Queen Regent and reinforced her view of the rebellion as one against the established authority. In other words, they had joined a rebellion against Mary of Guise's régime, not a movement that aimed to establish the reformed kirk in Scotland and leave the temporal authority unchanged.

Why Lord James and Argyll switched allegiance is slightly bemusing given that, just days before, Knox claims they were firmly on the side of Mary of Guise.[49] Knox has it that they remained loyal to the Queen Regent because she desired peace, but Guise had not resorted to violence at any time during the revolt or in her actual violation of the Perth Agreement.[50] Equally perplexing is the fact that the Perth riots had secured very little support for the Congregation – especially from the nobility. The 'Second Band' of the Congregation (31 May 1559) had only six subscribers, four of whom were new: Lord James, Matthew Campbell of Teringland, and the Lords Boyd and Ochiltree.[51] If the opposite had been true and the Congregation was seen as the stronger side, Lord James and Argyll's defection would be more understandable.

A slightly more sinister interpretation emerges, however, if Knox's version of events is accurate. Knowing that Guise was bent on peace and that Argyll and Lord James would break from the Regent if she violated any part of the agreement, it is possible that Knox entered into negotiations not with the intent of reaching a peaceful settlement, but rather to provide a pretext for Lord James and Argyll's defection. Although there is no evidence to substantiate such a theory,

---

48 Knox, *Works*, I, pp. 347–8 and *History*, I, pp. 179–80; Donaldson, *James V–James VII*, p.93; Lee, *James Stewart*, p.39.

49 Knox, *Works*, I, p.341 and *History*, I, pp. 175–6. In their negotiations with the Congregation, Knox writes that Argyll and Lord James 'had promesed to laubour for concord, and to assist the Quene, in case we refuised ressonable offerris, of conscience and honour, thay culd no na less than be faithfull in thair promeise maid'. But, as Maurice Lee points out, the terms of the Perth Agreement were far too favourable to the Congregation for Guise to abide by them permanently. Knox, *Works*, I, p.343 and *History*, I, p.177; Lee, *James Stewart*, p.36.

50 Knox, *Works*, I, pp. 337–8 and *History*, I, pp. 175–6; Lee, *James Stewart*, p.36.

51 Knox, *Works*, I, pp. 344–5 and *History*, I, pp. 178–9; *CSP Foreign, 1558–1559*, 799, p.296. Glencairn and Argyll were the only two subscribers to the 'First' and 'Second' Bands of the Congregation.

it is significant that it was only because of Lord James and Argyll's promise that Knox consented to negotiate with Guise in the first place.[52] Moreover, it was widely recognised that the terms of the Perth Agreement were decidedly favourable to the Congregation – too favourable for Guise to keep for any substantial length of time.[53] Knox was fully aware of this and preached a sermon on the day of the agreement, in which he predicted with a great deal of confidence that 'I am assured, that no pairt of this promeise maid shalbe longar keipit than the Quene and hir Frenchemen have the upper hand'.[54] While Maurice Lee and Jane Dawson contend that Lord James and Argyll sided with the Congregation because Guise, as her violation of the Perth Agreement clearly demonstrated, never had any intention of honouring her declarations of peace, it might also be said that Knox's pugnacity and determination to secure the support of Lord James and Argyll ensured that no settlement with the Queen Regent could be permanent – nor did he have any desire for it to be permanent.[55] With Guise's subsequent demands for their return dismissed,[56] Argyll and Lord James went on to become the *de facto* leaders of the Congregation until Châtelherault and his son, Arran, assumed nominal control in September 1559.[57]

* * *

As the Congregation's systematic campaign of iconoclasm continued throughout June and July 1559, news of the Queen Regent's troubles soon reached the shores of France and became a topic of concern at the French Court. On 7 June, Throckmorton informed Cecil that the Cardinal de Lorraine, the King and Queen Dauphin and the Duc de Guise . . . ' have had great consultation of Scotland, wherein, as yet, they have fallen to no determination. They are in doubt what to do and whom to send thither, being greatly perplexed with the news brought thence to the Court'.[58] Although military intervention was high on the list of considerations, Henri II and his ministers were

---

52 Knox, *Works*, I, p. 343 and *History*, I, p.177.
53 Lee, *James Stewart*, p.38.
54 Knox, *Works*, I, pp. 343–4 and *History*, I, p.178.
55 Lee, *James Stewart*, pp. 37, 39; Dawson, 'Protestantism and the Anglo-Scottish Alliance, 1558–60', in her forthcoming monograph on Archibald Campbell, 5th earl of Argyll. See also Argyll and Lord James' letter to the Queen Regent dated 15 June 1559, in Knox, *Works*, I, pp. 356–7 and *History*, I, pp. 187–8.
56 Knox, *Works*, I, p.347 and *History*, I, p.180.
57 Knox, *Works*, I, pp. 413–4 and *History*, I, pp. 229–30; *Sadler Papers*, I, pp. 455–7; Stevenson, *Documents*, pp. 73–5.
58 *CSP Foreign, 1558–1559*, 826, pp. 304–6.

reluctant to send reinforcements when it was really not clear what was going on in Scotland or, for that matter, what motives lay behind the Congregation's rebellion. So, amidst this uncertainty, they advised the Queen Regent 'to tolerate them [the Congregation] for a time till they may overcome these great matters here and so to take order accordingly'.[59] In the interim, Sir James Melville of Halhill was to be sent on a fact-finding mission to Scotland. His instructions clearly reveal Henri's private reservations about sending troops to Scotland, despite his public declarations and assurances to the contrary.

Melville had been assured that Henri 'myndit to wair and [to] hazard his crown, and all that he has, rather or your Quen want hir rycht, now seing that sche is maried vpon his son; and purposis to raise and send ane armye in Scotland for that effect'.[60] However, there were several factors preventing him from doing so. The most notable of these was 'that his Maieste hes hed wairres lang anough with his auld ennemys, and agreed with them for gud respectis, his is laith till enter again in a new vnnecessary wair with his auld frendis'.[61] Apart from the obvious financial and diplomatic considerations, Henri's reluctance to support Mary of Guise militarily was mainly due to the fact that he was unsure whether such intervention was justified. What, exactly, was the nature of the civil unrest in Scotland and why had it erupted? Was the Congregation's rebellion a revolt of conscience or was it politically motivated? Was Mary of Guise an innocent bystander or had she acted dishonourably towards her subjects, thereby inciting them to rebel? Many questions needed to be answered before Henri was prepared to translate his words into decisive action.

Melville's principal duty was to investigate the events surrounding Lord James' defection to the Congregation. As the bastard son of James V, Lord James' change of sides sparked fears, particularly in the Guise camp of the French Court, that he intended 'vnder pretext of this new religion, [to] vsurp the crown of Scotland, and pluk it clean away from the Quen'.[62] However, simultaneous reports that the Queen Regent had broken her word and violated the Perth Agreement added an altogether new dimension to the situation in Scotland.[63] Melville was thus commissioned to determine whether Lord James had designs on the crown or 'gene he be mouit to tak armes only of conscience, for deffence of his religion, him self and his

59 *CSP Foreign, 1558–1559*, 826, pp. 304–6.
60 Melville, *Memoirs*, p.79.
61 *Ibid*, p.79.
62 *Ibid*, pp. 78, 80.
63 *Ibid*, p.79.

dependers and associatis', what promises to Lord James and the Congregation had been broken, by whom and at whose instance.[64] Unlike Mary of Guise and d'Oisel, Henri was willing to concede that the Congregation's revolt might be religiously motivated.[65] If that was indeed the case, he was powerless to do anything about it, for 'Gif it be only religion that moues them, we mon commit Scottismens saules vnto God; for we haue anough ado to reull the consciences of our awen contre men'.[66] Rather, it was 'the obedience dew vnto ther lawfull Quen with ther bodyes' that the King desired, but again, Henri's hands were tied if Guise refused to keep her promises.[67] In short, the uncertainty surrounding what lay behind the Congregation's rebellion prevented Henri from intervening in support of Mary of Guise – especially in light of the reports that suggested she was not entirely blameless. Instead, Henri chose to place his faith in the Scots and the 'auld alliance', not wanting 'to geue haisty credence, that Scotland, wha haue keped salang frendschip with France, will now sa leichtly brek the auld band, nor abandon deute to ther lawfull prince'.[68]

This was a far cry from the offensive stance taken by the King in his supplication to Paul IV for a papal subsidy to finance his intended military campaign in Scotland.[69] Blaming the troubles on the internal degeneration of the Scottish Church and the heretical learning and doctrine of Geneva, Henri characterised the Congregation's rebellion in exclusively religious terms, making only a passing reference to the 'bragging of attacking and bearing down the queen and all others who

---

64 Melville, *Memoirs*, pp. 78, 80.
65 See d'Oisel's letter of 14 June 1559 to Gilles de Noailles, the new French ambassador resident in England, in which he writes that Argyll, Lord James and the Congregation 'disent que c'est pour la Religion Et de faict ilz ont des predicantz avec Eulx Gens de Mauvaise & dangereuse doctrine. Mais je cuyde qu'ilz ont autre desseing en l'esprit & n'y a autre apparence. Ilz disent bien qu'ilz veulent estre obeyssants a leurs Roy & Royne, mais il ne s'en void sortir effect du monde qui n'y soit du contraire, prenans Les armes tous les jours, pillant & destruissant les Abbayes ça et la [say that it is for Religion. In fact they have got preachers with them, men with an evil and dangerous doctrine. But I think they have got another purpose in mind, there is no other reason for it. They certainly say that they want to show obedience to their King and Queen, but one can only see people doing things to the contrary, taking up arms everyday, plundering and destroying abbeys here and there]'. AÉ, *Cor. Pol.*, Angleterre, XIII, f.257; Teulet, *Papiers*, I, pp. 310–11 and *Relations*, I, pp. 318–9.
66 Melville, *Memoirs*, p.80.
67 *Ibid*, p.80.
68 *Ibid*, p.79.
69 *Papal Negotiations*, pp. 13–20.

would oppose and refuse to join their new league'.[70] Henri conveyed none of the personal reservations he had as to the cause and nature of the rebellion or, significantly, what France's response should be. Rather, he had resolved

> to send immediately to Scotland a large and sufficient force or posse of French soldiers, both infantry and cavalry, with the hope of sending more after them very shortly, and of increasing and strengthening them with another large company or army, if need shall be; not intending to spare anything in sustaining and defending the cause of God, even though we have but just concluded a long war to enter on peace, after having borne and suffered an incredible expense as everyone knows. But our confidence is in God who is signally offended at this wretched pest of ruffians. He will so provide our most dear and well-beloved son and daughter, the king and queen dauphin, and the queen dowager their mother, with our aid and succour, will overcome these heretics and schismatics, and force and power will be in their hands to chastise and punish their great temerity and arrogance, for the honour of the Creator, the exaltation of His Holy Name, and the increase of our holy faith and religion.[71]

What Henri said to the pope was very different from practice. Henri had opted for a policy of temporisation – a policy that was also, but not exclusively, favoured by François II during his short reign.

Henri II died on 10 July 1559 from injuries sustained in a jousting tournament. François and Mary were now the King and Queen of France, and although François was old enough to rule at the age of 15, the kingdom was actually governed by Les Guise, whose power and position were now firmly entrenched at the French Court. The Duc de Guise replaced Montmorency as *grand maître* and Léonor d'Orléans, duc de Longueville, as the Grand Chamberlain. He now controlled François II's household and France's military affairs. The Cardinal de Lorraine, on the other hand, controlled the kingdom's administrative

---

70 *Papal Negotiations*, pp. 17–8.
71 *Ibid*, p.18. See also contemporary English reports detailing France's planned military intervention, which were more than likely deliberate leaks out of the French Court in order to frighten the Congregation into submission and to deter the English from joining the conflict. *CSP Foreign, 1558–1559*, 902, 928, 953, 962, pp. 346–8, 356, 365, 367–8; *CSP Scot.*, I, 486, p.223.

and financial affairs, and remained the most important ecclesiastic in the French Church.[72] Given their familial connection, Scotland naturally remained a high priority for Les Guise, but they were prevented from becoming too involved on account of certain domestic troubles that had been exacerbated by their own ascendancy.

As in the reign of Henri II, religion and finance continued to be major preoccupations, but as Stuart Carroll points out, the 'real problem was that Guise dominance at court and of patronage ensured that policy was perceived as the work of a single faction rather than the result of a consensus reached during the previous reign. The battle for supremacy at court destabilised France as excluded magnates sought a constituency among those opposed to the policies of Henri, among them protestants and unpaid soldiers'.[73] Whether they wanted to or not, the Duc de Guise and the Cardinal of Lorraine had no choice but to continue Henri's Scottish policy of temporisation rather than one of full-scale military intervention.

Shortly after François' accession, Béthencourt was sent to Scotland with new instructions for Mary of Guise. They echoed those of 7 June, and Guise was instructed to proceed 'leniently' against the Congregation.[74] Unlike the former missive, which advised Guise simply 'to tolerate them for a time', Béthencourt's commission included a specific plan of action for temporising with the Congregation. The most notable feature was an extensive letter-writing campaign aimed at leading members of the Congregation, who were promised absolution for past offences if they repented and returned to their due obedience to the crown.[75] Lord James was one such member of the Congregation who received letters from both the King and Queen of Scotland.[76] But fair

---

72 Carroll, *Noble Power during the French Wars of Religion*, pp. 92–4; Baumgartner, *Henry II*, pp. 252–5; Constant, *Les Guise*, pp. 37–40.

73 Carroll, *Noble Power during the French Wars of Religion*, p.93.

74 Béthencourt's instructions (16 July 1559) are printed in L. Paris, *Négotiations, Lettres et Pièces Diverses Relative au Relative au Règne au François II* (Paris, 1841), p.12. See also *Papal Negotiations*, pp. xxxiii-iv, and *CSP Foreign, 1558–1559*, 1094, pp. 428–9.

75 Béthencourt brought unaddressed letters from both Mary and François with him to Scotland; Guise was left to determine which members of the Congregation were to receive these letters and fill in the blanks accordingly. Paris, *Négotiations*, p.16; *Papal Negotiations*, pp. xxxiii-iv; *CSP Foreign, 1558–1559*, 1149, p.457.

76 AÉ, *Mémoires et Documents*, Angleterre, XV, fos. 27–8; *CSP Foreign, 1558–1559*, 1004, p.385; Knox, *Works*, I, pp. 384–6 and *History*, I, pp. 208–9; *Papal Negotiations*, p.432. Melville must have got to the bottom of Lord James' defection, at least to the French Court's satisfaction, as both Mary and François' letters charge the Prior with being the self-proclaimed head, principal beginner and nourisher of the tumults.

words and promises did not move him to repent. In his words, 'my conscience perswaidis me in thir proceidingis to have done na thing aganeis God, nor the debtfull obedience torwartis your Hienes and the Queneis Grace my Soverane'.[77] As in the 'rough wooing', it was hoped the distribution of patronage would secure support for the Queen Regent. Béthencourt brought with him 20,000 *livres* to induce members of the Congregation to abandon their cause, but it is not known how this money was dispensed or to whom.[78]

Mary of Guise, however, had already made efforts to appease her Protestant subjects before Béthencourt's arrival in August 1559. In accordance with her instructions of 7 June and despite their sustained campaign of iconoclasm, Guise was constrained to tolerate the Congregation, or at least give the appearance that she was doing so, by granting conciliatory promises. On 1 July 1559, for example, she issued a proclamation outlining the various concessions she had allegedly made to the Congregation over the recent controversy in religion.[79] Written in the name of Mary and François, this pronouncement claimed that the Queen Regent,

> perceaving the seditious tumult rased by ane parte of the our liegis, naming thame selffis THE CONGREGATIOUN, who, under pretense of religioun, have putt thame salffis in armes; and . . . for satisfeing of everie manis conscience, and pacifeing of the saidis trubles, had offerred unto thame to affix ane Parliament to be haldin in Januare nixt to cum, or sonnar, gyf that had pleased, for establissing of ane unversall ordour in matteris of religioun, be our advise and Estatis of our Realme; and in the meantyme, to suffer everie man to

77 Knox, *Works*, I, p.387 and *History*, I, p.209. For Lord James' reply dated 12 August 1559, see AÉ, *Mémoires et Documents*, Angleterre, XV, f.30; *Papal Negotiations*, pp. 433–4; *CSP Foreign, 1558–1559*, 1184, pp. 468–9 and Knox, *Works*, I, pp. 386–7 and *History*, I, p.210.

78 Paris, *Négotiations*, p.12; *CSP Foreign, 1558–1559*, 1149, p.457. Rumours of Henri's Scottish policy had reached England even before Béthencourt had arrived in France. On 8 July, Cecil informed Sir James Croft that 'the Protestants there [in Scotland] shall be essayed with all fair promises first, next with money, and last with arms'. In the end, Cecil was right – this was exactly how France's intervention in Scotland developed. Elizabeth responded accordingly by sending Sir Ralph Sadler north with £3,000 to counter the French offers. *CSP Foreign, 1558–1559*, 953, 1125, 1131, 1140, 1157, 1161, 1162, pp. 365, 450, 449, 453–4, 459–60, 460–1; *CSP Scot.*, I, 486, 520, 521, pp. 223, 241–2; AÉ, *Cor. Pol.*, Angleterre, XIII, fos. 319ᵛ-20ʳ; Teulet, *Papiers*, I, pp. 344–5 and *Relations*, I, pp. 348–9.

79 Knox, *Works*, I, pp. 363–5 and *History*, I, pp. 193–4; *CSP Foreign, 1558–1559*, 905, pp. 348–9.

leaf at libertie of conscience, without truble, unto the tyme
the said ordour war tackin be advise of our forsaid [Estates].
And at last, because it appeared mekle to stand upoun our
burght of Edinburght, what maner of religioun thai wald sett
up and use for the tyme; swa that na man mycht alledge that
he was forsed to do against his conscience: Quhilk offer the
Quenis Grace, was at all tymes, and yit is, ready to fulfill.[80]

This proclamation also served as an effective piece of propaganda in
which Guise was able to launch a scathing attack on the Congregation
by exposing the true aims of their rebellion. As they themselves had
declared 'by oppin dead [deed]', the Congregation's military occupation of Edinburgh on 29 June,[81] their suspected communication with
England and, most damning of all, their seizure of the kingdom's
coining irons at Holyrood on 21 July, were used by the Queen Regent
to show how it was not 'religioun . . . thai seak, bot onelie the
subversioun of our authoritie'.[82] In light of such blatant acts of
sedition, Mary and François charged all members of the Congregation
to withdraw from Edinburgh under pain of treason, and for 'all and
sindrie personis to leave thair cumpany, and adhear to our authoritie'.
Those who failed to observe this royal proclamation were warned that
they would be reputed and held as 'manifest traytouris to our
Crowne'.[83]

Clearly, the main function of this proclamation was to discredit the
Congregation by exposing the true aims of their rebellion as secular
rather than religious. Guise's position was further strengthened by the
concessions she had ostensibly granted to settle the religious controversy. While giving the impression that her conciliatory overtures
were genuine, in reality she had not conceded a thing. Guise's

---

80 Knox, *Works*, I, pp. 363–4 and *History*, I, p.193. Knox strenuously denies
   that Guise made an offer to settle their religious differences before the
   Congregation demanded it.
81 Following their voluntary withdrawal from Perth, and Guise's subsequent
   violation of the Perth Agreement, the Congregation mustered their
   forces at St Andrews. From there, they returned to Perth and re-took the
   burgh on 25 June 1559. The Congregation then made their way to
   Edinburgh by way of Stirling, which they entered on 29 June. Knox,
   Works, I, pp. 347–62 and *History*, I, pp. 180–92; *CSP Foreign, 1558–1559*,
   861, 862, 877, 878, pp. 319–20, 320–2, 331–5, 335–6; *CSP Scot.*, I, 469, 471,
   pp. 216–7; Donaldson, *James V–James VII*, pp. 93–4.
82 Knox, *Works*, I, p.364 and *History*, I, p.193.
83 Knox, *Works*, I, pp. 364–5 and *History*, I, pp. 193–4. The Congregation
   issued a formal response to this proclamation on 2 July 1559. Knox,
   Works, I, pp. 365–6 and *History*, I, pp. 194–5; *CSP Foreign, 1558–1559*, 925,
   p.355.

proclamation, therefore, enabled her to grant promises that she did not necessarily have to keep. This system of granting what were essentially 'empty promises' became the cornerstone of Guise's policy of toleration. Not only did they cast her in a favourable light, but they also bought time for reinforcements to arrive from France. It was in the hope that French military intervention would materialise that Guise re-entered negotiations with the Congregation later that month.

These negotiations culminated in what would prove to be the highly contentious Leith Agreement of 23/4 July 1559.[84] Central to the agreement was the offer previously made by Guise to have the religious controversy settled by the Three Estates in Parliament, which was scheduled to convene on 10 January 1560. This provision gave both the Regent and the Congregation just under six months to procure military support from France and England respectively. For their part, the Congregation agreed to withdraw from Edinburgh and relinquish the coining irons they had seized at Holyrood. They also promised to render their due obedience to their sovereigns and refrain from further outbreaks of iconoclasm and assaults on the clergy until the meeting of the said Parliament. For her part, Guise promised that the inhabitants of Edinburgh would be free to choose their own religion, having liberty of conscience, and that no interference or harm would befall members of the Congregation or their preachers.

Mary of Guise's attempts to stall the Congregation were effective. The Leith Agreement bought her the time she needed, and she emerged from the negotiations as the clear winner – something which the Congregation conceded in their band of 1 August 1559. Foreseeing 'the slycht of our adversaries, tending all maner of wayis to circumvene us' and, in particular, the 'desait' of the Queen Regent, they deemed it necessary to prohibit individual members of the Congregation from communicating or meeting with Guise 'without consent of the rest, and commone consultatioun thairupoun swa that nathing sall proceid heirin without commune consent of us all'.[85] This was the ultimate tribute to Mary of Guise's political

84 For details of the negotiations at Leith and the agreement itself, see Knox, *Works*, I, pp. 374–81 and *History*, I, pp. 202–6; *CSP Foreign, 1558–1559*, 1052, 1056, 1058, 1062, 1063/4, 1065, pp. 406–7, 408–9, 410, 411; *CSP Scot.*, I, 500, 503, 505, pp. 231–2, 233, 233–4; AÉ, *Cor. Pol.*, Angleterre, XIII, fos. 285, 303 and XIV, f.241; Teulet, *Papiers*, I, pp. 327–8, 329–32 and *Relations*, I, pp. 334–5, 335–7.

85 Knox, *Works*, I, p.382 and *History*, I, pp. 206–7; *CSP Foreign, 1558–1559*, 1108, p.435.

acumen, charm and charisma. By forbidding individual members to speak to the Queen Regent, the Congregation were inadvertently acknowledging the potential threat Guise posed to their cause by exposing the precarious loyalty of some members to the Congregation. Fears of Mary of Guise's powers of persuasion prompted the Congregation to take steps to discredit the Queen Regent and bring an end to the short-lived Leith Agreement.

The terms of the Leith Agreement initially came into dispute with the arrival of French reinforcements in August and September 1559. Unbeknownst to Mary of Guise, François II and Les Guise had decided to send military reinforcements as a token gesture of support in July.[86] Although it was widely believed that the situation in Scotland justified full-scale military intervention,[87] financial constraints and the delicate international situation, particularly with England, moved the young King of France to send only the bare minimum.[88] Temporising was still the preferred method at the French Court to combat the Congregation.[89] In August, Nicolas de Pellevé, bishop of Amiens, and Jacques de la Brosse were sent as envoys from the Courts of Rome and France respectively to try to effect a peaceful conclusion and bring the Regent all the comfort, counsel and aid that lay within their power.[90] In the meantime,

86 François to Noailles, 21 July 1559, AÉ, *Cor. Pol.*, Angleterre, XX, f.192. Béthencourt delivered this letter to Noailles on 30 July 1559 whilst en route to Scotland. Neither he nor François was aware that the Leith Agreement had been contracted when the decision to send troops had been made. *Brosse Missions*, pp. 164–5.
87 See, for example, AÉ, *Cor. Pol.*, Angleterre, XIII, f. 314ᵛ, XIV, f.239ʳ and XX, f.195; Teulet, *Papiers*, I, pp. 325–7, 340–3 and *Relations*, I, pp. 332–4, 345–8.
88 Neither François nor Les Guise wanted to rock the boat with Elizabeth. Noailles was instructed to give Elizabeth and her Council ample warning of the French King's intentions to dispel any suspicion that these troops were intended for an attack against England. AÉ, *Cor. Pol.*, Angleterre, XX, f.192; *CSP Foreign, 1558–1559*, 1118, 1143, 1151, 1187, 1190, 1255, 1270, pp. 444–5, 454–5, 458, 470–1, 476, 502, 507–8; *CSP Scot.*, I, 535, pp. 248–9.
89 AÉ, *Cor. Pol.*, Angleterre, XIII, fos. 316ʳ, 319ʳ; Teulet, *Papiers*, I, pp. 342–3 and *Relations*, I, pp. 347–8.
90 AÉ, *Mémoires et Documents*, Angleterre, XV, fos. 130ʳ-53ᵛ, and *Cor. Pol.*, Angleterre, XIII, fos. 319, 322ᵛ-3ʳ; NAS, SP13/85; NLS, MSS, 3137, fos. 16–8; Teulet, *Papiers*, I, pp. 348–9, 349–50 and *Relations*, I, pp.352–3, 353–4; Labanoff, *Lettres*, I, pp. 70–2; *CSP Foreign, 1558–1559*, 1187, 1190, 1274, pp. 470–1, 476, 508–9; Paris, *Négotiations*, p.15; Tytler, *History of Scotland*, IV, p.163. For details and analyses of de la Brosse's mission to Scotland in 1559–60, see *Brosse Missions*, pp. 175–271; Dickinson, 'Report by de la Brosse and d'Oisel', pp. 85–125; and J. de la Brosse, *Jacques de la Brosse 1485(?)-1562: Ses Missions en Écosse* (Paris, 1929), pp. 150–171.

d'Oisel was instructed to use the 'small forces' that de la Brosse and, later, Octavien Brosso brought with them, to dispel the Scottish insurgents and hinder their designs until François could deploy the greater reinforcements Guise was promised would come with her next supplication to the French Court.[91] No sooner had Brosso arrived with the 'first four ensigns which the King was pleased to send' than he was immediately despatched back to France to update François on the continuing troubles in Scotland and to urge him 'to have what remained of his assistance hastened'.[92] As the Congregation's rebellion developed and the situation in Scotland deteriorated, Guise became increasingly alarmed at the trickle of military aid coming out of France. Her urgent and desperate appeals for reinforcements to the King and her brothers seemed to fall on deaf ears.[93]

While the relatively small number of troops sent from France was far from adequate in the eyes of Mary of Guise and d'Oisel, the arrival of 1,000 men in August and another 800 in September was more than enough for the Congregation to accuse Guise of violating the Leith Agreement.[94] According to the Congregation, the entry of new French troops into the kingdom had been expressly forbidden in the truce which stipulated that 'with all diligent speed the Frenchmen here present shall be sent away, and none other shall come in this realm without the consent of the whole nobility [and Parliament]'.[95] Further condemnation followed when Guise decided to fortify and garrison Leith on 22 September 1559.[96] Again, the Congregation claimed that this contravened the article stipulating that Edinburgh was to be kept free of both Scottish and French garrisons.[97] While these articles were contained in the copies of the agreement sent to

---

91 AÉ, *Cor. Pol.*, Angleterre, XIII, fos. 316ʳ, 319ᵛ; Teulet, *Papiers*, I, pp. 343, 344 and *Relations*, I, pp. 347–8, 348–9; CSP *Foreign, 1558–1559*, 1151, p.458; Paris, *Négotiations*, p.12.

92 AÉ, *Cor. Pol.*, Angleterre, XIII, fos. 319ᵛ-20, 322ʳ and *Mémoires et Documents*, Angleterre, XV, f.39; Teulet, *Papiers*, I, p.344 and *Relations*, I, pp. 348–9; CSP *Foreign, 1558–1559*, 1355, p. 562.

93 See, for example, Guise's letters of 19 and 22 September 1559 in AÉ, *Mémoires et Documents*, Angleterre, XV, fos. 37ʳ-41ʳ.

94 Teulet, *Papiers*, I, pp. 342–3 and *Relations*, I, pp. 347–8; AÉ, *Cor. Pol.*, Angleterre, XIII, fos. 315ᵛ-6ʳ; CSP *Foreign, 1558–1559*, 1190, 1255, 1270, pp. 476, 502, 507–8; Donaldson, *James V-James VII*, p. 95; Mathieson, *Politics and Religion*, I, p.63.

95 CSP *Foreign, 1558–1559*, 1056, pp. 408–9.

96 AÉ, *Cor. Pol.*, Angleterre, XIII, fos. 322ᵛ-4ʳ and *Mémoires et Documents*, Angleterre, XV, f.39; Teulet, *Papiers*, I, pp. 349–50 and *Relations*, I, pp. 353–4.

97 CSP *Foreign, 1558–1559*, 1056, pp. 408–9; CSP *Scot.*, I, 505, pp. 233–4.

the English,[98] they were interestingly and conspicuously absent from Mary of Guise's.[99] The Congregation had altered the agreement in their favour. Like the Perth Agreement, the Congregation's alteration of the Leith Agreement was a desperate attempt to attract widespread support for their cause. Having informed Sir James Croft of the terms, William Kirkcaldy of Grange added this personal note:

> They [the Congregation] believe that never a word will be
> kept of these promises on the Queen's side, and therefore
> have taken bonds of my Lord Duke [Châtelherault], the Earl
> of Huntly and the rest of the nobility on her side for the
> performance thereof. With this condition, that if she break
> any point thereof, they will renounce her obedience and join
> themselves with the party of the writer.[100]

Given that some form of French intervention was inevitable, the invention of certain clauses that the Queen Regent was bound to break would attract more support nationally. More importantly, it would also strengthen the Congregation's appeals for English military aid and justify their rebellion on an international scale by showing how Guise had broken her word yet again.[101]

As Guise did not know that François had determined to send troops until Béthencourt arrived with the news in August 1559, after the conclusion of the truce, it was imperative for her to counter the Congregation's charges and implement some form of damage control. On 28 August, she issued a general proclamation defending and justifying the arrival of the first wave of French reinforcements.[102] Addressed to the Lords, Barons, Gentlemen and, as Knox terms them, the 'vulgar pepill' of the realm, this proclamation stressed that no violation of the Leith Agreement had occurred and that the current

98 See, for example, the report sent to Sir James Croft by William Kirkcaldy of Grange in *CSP Foreign, 1558–1559*, 1056, pp. 408–9, and *CSP Scot.*, I, 505, pp. 223–4. The same discrepancy also appeared in the two versions of the Congregation's proclamation of the appointment made on 25 July 1559. *CSP Foreign, 1558–1559*, 1062, 1063/4, p. 411; *CSP Scot.*, I, 503, p.233; Knox, *Works*, I, pp. 380–1 and *History*, I, pp. 205–6.
99 AÉ, *Cor. Pol.*, Angleterre, XIII, fos. 285, 303 and XIV, f.241; Teulet, *Papiers*, I, pp. 327–8 and *Relations*, I, pp. 334–5.
100 *CSP Foreign, 1558–1559*, 1056, pp. 408–9; *CSP Scot.*, I, 505, pp. 233–4.
101 Lee, *James Stewart*, p. 46; A. Lang, *Knox and the Reformation* (London, 1905), pp. 142–8.
102 Knox, *Works*, I, pp. 397–9 and *History*, I, pp. 217–9; Mason, 'Knox on Rebellion', pp. 157–9. The Queen Regent also embarked on an extensive letter-writing campaign, sending letters to 'everie Lord, Barroun, and Gentilman' justifying, as in her proclamation, her actions and those of the French. Knox, *Works*, I, pp. 395–7 and *History*, I, p.215.

controversy was the result of the Congregation's 'interprysing' against the 'authoratie, and tennour of the said Appointment'.[103] Accusing them specifically of inventing and 'blawin abrod dyvers rumouris and evill brutis', Guise asserted that there had been no stipulation in the compact that had 'communit or concludit to stope the sending in of Frensche men; as may cleirlie appeir be inspectioun of the said Appointmente', and denied unequivocally that the French were 'myndit to draw in greit forceis of men of weir furth of France, to suppress the libertie of this realme, oppres the inhabitantis thairof, and mak up straingaris with thair landis and goodis'.[104] Rather Guise, together with Mary and François, had nothing but a 'guid mynd' towards her Scottish subjects who, it was hoped, would not be led from their 'dew obedience', for there was held a 'moderlie luif towartis all' who showed themselves to be 'obedient subjectis'.[105] Condescending words like these, however, served only to reinforce the Congregation's growing contention that Scotland was not destined to be an equal partner in the Franco-Scottish dynastic union of the crowns and brought to the fore the implications of the Valois-Stewart marriage for Scotland's independence.

Although the deaths of Mary of Guise and François in 1560 prevent us from knowing what plans France actually had for Scotland, namely, whether it would be coalesced, conquered or follow the 'exampill of Brytanny', the Congregation nevertheless used the arrival of French troops, various other aspects of Guise's regency and the establishment of French power in Scotland as a whole, to infer that conquest was, indeed, the Queen Regent's true objective.[106] Their proclamation to

---

103 Knox, *Works*, I, p.397 and *History*, I, p.217; Mason, 'Knox on Rebellion', p.157.

104 Knox, *Works*, I, pp. 397–8 and *History*, I, p.217; Mason, 'Knox on Rebellion', p.157.

105 Knox, *Works*, I, pp. 398–9 and *History*, I, p.218; Mason, 'Knox on Rebellion', p.158.

106 As in Scotland, dynastic union was the pretext for Franco-Breton integration. As opposed to conquest, Anne of Brittany's successive marriages to Charles VIII and Louis XII of France resulted in the installation of a governor and the infiltration of Frenchmen into Breton institutions, such as the Court of Parliament and the Exchequer. Instead of imposing purely 'French' institutions, Brittany technically retained its cultural and institutional independence. Some Scots, such as the Earl of Argyll, feared that a similar fate was destined for Scotland in the Franco-Scottish dynastic union of the crowns. According to Archbishop Hamilton, Argyll was using France's military presence in Scotland and the occupation of certain of Scottish offices by Frenchmen to persuade the Scots that 'the France ar cumin in and sutin down in this realme to occupy it and to put furtht the inhabitantis tharoff, and siclik to occupy uther menis rowmes pece and pece, and to put avay the blud of the nobilitie'. *Scottish Correspondence*, cclxxxi, p.427 and *n*.1; McNeill, 'Discours', p.87.

the 'Nobilitie, Burghis, and Communitie of this Realme of Scot-land'[107] was not simply another public apology for their rebellion – it signalled the emergence of the Congregation as a patriotic party.[108] By playing on the xenophobia of the Scots and their fear of conquest by strangers, the Congregation became the self-proclaimed defenders of the true faith *and* the commonweal. Interestingly, it was not François II and Mary, Queen of Scots who were cited as the principal agents of France's alleged conquest of Scotland, but Mary of Guise, whose aim was to place the Scots 'under the perpetuall servitude of strangearis'.[109] She had revealed her true intentions by bringing in French troops with their 'wyffis and bairneis' to occupy the Scots 'houssis and possessiouns ancient rowmeis and heritageis'; by garri-soning Scottish strongholds with French soldiers in times of peace; by exorbitant taxation; and finally, by her debasement of the Scots coinage.[110] These were not displays of Guise's motherly care for Scotland's commonwealth, but acts of intended conquest and the suppression of the Scots' ancient laws and liberties.[111] The Congre-gation's rebellion was no longer a Protestant revolt against Catholi-cism. It was now a patriotic response to Guise dynasticism and the establishment of French power in Scotland.

The inherent problem with the Congregation's new platform, how-ever, was that the establishment of French power had not come about as a result of Guise's regency, but rather as a result of the treaty of Haddington and the Franco-Scottish protectoral alliance. But as we have seen, the establishment of French power, of which Guise's regency was but one feature, occurred with the consent and at the behest of the Scottish political community. In effect, the Congregation was now rebelling against something the Scots and many Protestants themselves had facilitated. More importantly, the Congregation was rebelling against the *possibility* and not the reality of conquest. Yet, despite these contradictions, the Congregation's association with patriotism was

---

107 Knox, *Works*, I, pp. 400–8 and *History*, I, pp. 219–28; Mason, 'Knox on Rebellion', pp. 159–65.
108 See Mason, 'Covenant and Commonweal', pp. 107–112, and Wormald, *Court, Kirk and Community*, pp. 118–9, for the ideology behind the Congregation's patriotism and their use of the concept and language of the commonweal.
109 Knox, *Works*, I, p.405 and *History*, I, p.223; Mason, 'Knox on Rebellion', p.162.
110 Knox, *Works*, I, pp. 407–8 and *History*, I, pp. 224–6; Mason, 'Knox on Rebellion', pp. 163–5.
111 Knox, *Works*, I, p.402 and *History*, I, p.221; Mason, 'Knox on Rebellion', p.160.

imperative if they were to have any chance of receiving the requested military aid from England and, in the short term, justifying their suspension of Mary of Guise from the regency. Contrary to the Congregation's assertions, Guise's decision to fortify Leith was not a motiveless act of aggression or evidence of her overall plan to conquer the realm.[112] Rather, it came as a direct response to the return of James, 3rd earl of Arran, to Scotland and Châtelherault's subsequent defection to the Congregation on 19 September 1559.[113] Mary of Guise was defending herself against an armed revolt, and the fact that she was being criticised for attempting to defend her position, as any regent or king would, is very unusual – especially when it was a rebellion that openly aimed to remove her from power.

The return of Châtelherault's son and heir to Scotland to assume nominal control of the Congregation with his father added a new, but not an entirely unexpected, dimension to the Congregation's rebellion. Guise knew something was afoot when she learned that the Congregation had summoned a convention to meet at Stirling on 10 May. Her immediate response was to write to Châtelherault and her nobility warning them that the Congregation was 'interprysing sum heycht purpoise aganis us, [and] our authoratie'.[114] She knew that Châtelherault's 'loyalty' was suspect at the best of times, and the very reason that his son and heir was in France to begin with was to act as surety for his support for the Franco-Scottish dynastic alliance. Arran's escape from France in June 1559, therefore, had serious implications – especially for the Congregation.[115] Châtelherault would not break with the Regent until he could be sure that his son had arrived safely in Scotland.[116] Until then, he could only promise the Congregation 'not to be [their] enemy'.[117] Arran's return was equally crucial in the

---

112 See, for example, the Congregation's letter to the Regent dated 19 September 1559. Hearing that Guise's 'army of Frensche men' were about to fortify Leith without the consent of the 'Nobilitie and Counsale of this realme', the Congregation claimed that this would not only be a breach of the Leith Agreement, but also 'verray prejudiciall to the commun-wealth, and playne contrair to our ancient lawis and libertieis'. Knox, *Works*, I, pp. 413–4; and *History*, I, pp. 229–30; *CSP Foreign, 1558–1559*, 1342, 1343, pp. 564–5.

113 Knox, *Works*, I, p.413 and *History*, I, p.229; AÉ, *Cor. Pol.*, Angleterre, XIII, fos. 322ᵛ-3ʳ; Teulet, *Papiers*, I, pp. 349–50 and *Relations*, I, pp. 353–4.

114 Knox, *Works*, I, p.395 and *History*, I, p.216.

115 *CSP Foreign, 1558–1559*, 848, 868, 888, pp. 316, 327, 340–1; *CSP Scot.*, I, 465, p.215.

116 *Ibid*, I, 466, 487, 525, pp. 216, 223, 242–3; *CSP Foreign, 1558–1559*, 888, 974, 1186, pp. 340–1, 372, 469–70.

117 *CSP Scot.*, I, 525, p.243.

Congregation's hope of gaining the formal support of Elizabeth I for their rebellion.

* * *

The Congregation's appeals for English military aid took on a fresh urgency with the arrival of French reinforcements in the summer of 1559. For William Cecil, Elizabeth's secretary, the deployment of these troops served only to substantiate his long-held contention that France was planning an invasion of England to advance the claim of Mary Stewart to the English succession. This, coupled with his notion of a united, Protestant British Isles, rendered Cecil more inclined than his mistress to support the Congregation.[118] To convince Elizabeth that intervention in Scotland was justified, Cecil not only stressed the immediate threat the establishment of French power in Scotland posed to Elizabeth's sovereignty and England's national security, but also used the 'sondry homagees done to this Crowne by the kinges of Scotland' to argue that 'england is of duty and in honour bound to preserve the realme of Scotland from such absolute Dominion of the french'.[119] On its own, Cecil's imperial and historical justification only managed to procure covert financial support for the Congregation's rebellion; full-scale military support would require the fulfilment of certain criteria on the part of the Congregation.[120] One such 'suggestion' was for the Congregation to emerge and establish themselves as a 'great council'. As the 'ancient blood of the realm', the Congregation would be the true and natural defenders of Scotland's ancient laws and liberties.[121] To legitimise this provisional government further, Cecil advised the Congregation to 'committ the Gouernance' of the realme to the 'nex heyres to the Croune the house of Hameltons'.[122] Only in this way could the

---

118 For more on Cecil's notion of an Anglo-British Protestant Empire and his dealings with the Congregation, see Alford, *The Early Elizabethan Polity*, pp. 43–70; Dawson, 'William Cecil and the British Dimension of early Elizabethan foreign policy', *History*, 74 (1989), pp. 205–7; W. MacCaffrey, 'Elizabethan Politics: The First Decade, 1558–68', *Past and Present*, 24 (1963), pp. 26–7.

119 BL Cotton MSS, Caligula B.x, f.86.

120 Contained within 'A memoriall of certain pointes meete for restoring the Realme of Scotland to the Anncient Weal', in BL, Lansdowne MSS, 4, fos. 26ʳ-7ʳ; *CSP Scot.*, I, 537, pp. 249–50; *CSP Foreign, 1558–1559*, 1297–99, pp. 518–9. See also *ibid*, 1300, pp. 519–23, BL, Cotton MSS, Caligula B.x, f.78, and especially Alford, *The Early Elizabethan Polity*, pp. 58–64, for a detailed discussion and analysis of this document.

121 BL, Lansdowne MSS, 4, fos. 26ᵛ-27ʳ; *CSP Foreign, 1558–1559*, 1297, p.518.

122 BL, Lansdowne MSS, 4, f.26ʳ.

Congregation effectively and legitimately oppose the Queen Regent and the 'Tyrannouse affection of fraunce'.[123] Châtelherault's position as second person in the realm provided the Congregation with a formidable defence against the potential usurpation of France and, more directly, against Mary of Guise and the Queen of Scots. If the French continued to act against the commonweal and threaten Scotland's ancient liberties and privileges, Châtelherault or his son could then be put forward as a suitable candidate for either the regency or the throne.[124] Arran's return, therefore, was not only crucial in gaining Châtelherault's support for the Congregation, but also for the realisation of Cecil's notion of an Anglo-British and Protestant Empire.[125]

With the help of the English,[126] Arran arrived safely in Scotland on 12 September 1559 in time to attend the Congregation's convention at Stirling.[127] Châtelherault had already written to Cecil on 9 August thanking him for the 'great kindness' he had shown in giving his son a 'veill' in order that he could return to Scotland undetected.[128] Cecil duly responded by advising the Duke 'not to neglect the present opportunity of doing good to his country', as there was nothing more he would like than 'to see this isle well united'.[129] Châtelherault was not about to pass up any opportunity that would enhance his position and the prestige of the House of Hamilton. After being reunited with his son, who had been in consultation with the principal lords of the Congregation since his arrival, Châtelherault and Arran officially became the nominal leaders of the Congregation on 19 September

123 BL, Lansdowne, MSS, 4, f.27^r.
124 *Ibid*, 4, f.27^r.
125 See, for example, Cecil's letter to Châtelherault on 24 August 1559 in *CSP Foreign, 1558–1559*, 1240, p.494. The Congregation also hoped to entice the English into supporting them by proposing Arran as a potential husband for Elizabeth. This proposal was not formally made, and rejected, until late 1560. *Ibid*, 743, 846, 878, pp. 278, 316, 335–6; *CSP Scot.*, I, 465, 466, 471, 926, 927, pp. 215–6, 216–7, 495–6; *APS*, II, pp. 605–6; Knox, *Works*, II, pp. 130–1, 137 and *History*, I, pp. 345–6, 350.
126 For correspondence concerning Arran and the details of his escape from France to Scotland, see *CSP Foreign, 1558–1559*, 998, 999, 1009, 1022, 1039, 1043, 1075, 1111, 1114, 1151, 1290, 1291, 1321, 1323, 1337, 1354, pp. 382–3, 383–4, 386–8, 391, 401, 402–3, 418, 436–7, 441, 451, 516, 542, 542–4, 551–2, 567; *CSP Scot.*, I, 538, 542, pp. 250, 251–2. See also Hannay, 'The Earl of Arran', pp. 264–6.
127 *CSP Scot.*, I, 538, p.250; *CSP Foreign, 1558–1559*, 1137, pp. 551–2.
128 *CSP Scot.*, I, 522, p.242; *CSP Foreign, 1558–1559*, 1176, p.465.
129 *Ibid*, 1240, p.494.

1559.[130] The full implications of Arran's return and Châtelherault's defection were realised on 21 October 1559 when the Congregation, as the 'borne Counsallouris' of the realm and the 'sworne protectouris and defendaris' of the commonweal, formally claimed the governance of Scotland and 'deposed' Mary of Guise as Regent in their 'Soverane Lord and Ladyeis name'.[131] Perceiving 'the interprysed destructioun of thair said commoun-weall, and overthrow of the libertie of thair native cuntree, be the meanes of the Quene Regent and certane strangearis', the Congregation regarded it as their 'dewtie' to suspend Guise's commission 'and all administratioun of the policy [her] Grace may pretend thairby'.[132]

For Mary of Guise, Châtelherault's defection and the Congregation's 'Act of Suspension' were the ultimate confirmation that they 'intended not religioun, bot the subversioun of authoritie'.[133] As such, she simply ignored their 'act', carried on in her capacity as Queen Regent and publicly accused Châtelherault and Arran of attempting to usurp 'the Croune and Authoritie of this Realme'.[134] For all her

130 Knox, *Works*, I, pp. 413–4 and *History*, I, pp. 229–30; *CSP Foreign, 1558–1559*, 1356, 1365, pp. 568, 571–2. On 19 September, the Congregation sent letters to the Queen Regent and John, 6th lord Erskine, subscribed by Châtelherault and Arran. *Ibid*, 1342–4, pp. 564–5; Knox, *Works*, I, pp. 413–7 and *History*, I, pp. 229–33. William Maitland of Lethington was then commissioned to begin formal negotiations with Elizabeth and her Council for English military support. *CSP Scot.*, I, 543, p.252.
131 Knox, *Works*, I, pp. 444–9 and *History*, I, pp. 249–55; Mason, 'Knox on Rebellion', pp. 171–4; BL, Cotton MSS, Caligula B.x, fos. 38, 42; NLS, Adv.MSS, 34.2.3, fos, 1–2.
132 Knox, *Works*, I, p.449 and *History*, I, p.255.
133 Calderwood, *The History of the Kirk of Scotland*, I, p.433.
134 Knox, *Works*, I, p. 439 and *History*, I, p. 248. The strength of Guise's position can be demonstrated by the fact that, in the words of Knox, 'because the rumour ceassed nott, that the Duke his Grace usurped the Authoritie, he was compelled, with the sound of trumpete, at the Mercat Croce of Edinburgh, to maik his purgatioun'. In this proclamation dated 19 October 1559, Châtelherault claimed he joined the Congregation because he was 'movit partlie by the violent persute of the religioun and trew professouris thairof, partlie by compassioun of the commoun-wealth and poore communitie of this realme, oppressed with strangearis'. Knox also admits that an extensive letter-writing campaign was undertaken by the Lords immediately following the Duke's defection, highlighting the danger 'giff the Frensche sould be sufferit to plant in this cuntrey at thair plesoure', their repeated pleas to Guise to 'send away to France hir Frensche men, quha war ane burding unproffitable and grevous to thair communwealth', and how the arrival of French troops with their wives and children was 'a declaratioun of ane plane conquiest'. On 6 October, for instance, Arran wrote to Sempill asking for his military support, not because of his 'conscience towartis the religioun', but 'for the commoun wealth and libertie of this youre native cuntray'. Knox, *Works*, I, pp. 438–40, 417–8 and *History*, I pp. 248–9, 232–3; *Scottish Correspondence*, cclxxxii, pp. 428–9.

confidence, Guise was not entirely flippant about the Congregation's 'Act of Suspension'; their rebellion had taken a very serious turn against which she had to defend her position and the authority of her daughter. Foreseeing what Châtelherault's defection would lead to, Guise proceeded in earnest with the fortification of Leith which was now viewed as a political and military necessity.[135] This was accompanied by renewed and urgent appeals to François for military and financial aid.[136] Detailing the nature of the Congregation's propaganda campaign following the Duke's defection, in which it was claimed that the French King wanted to 'overthrow all their laws and reduce them to utmost servitude', Guise begged her son-in-law to have pity on her and 'help us with more troops and money post-haste'.[137] Similar pleas came from Noailles in London with the emergence of the Congregation as a rival council to Guise's administration. On 30 September 1559, the French ambassador wrote to the Cardinal of Lorraine that the Congregation 'want to assume all authority and finally recognise no superior', which was made worse by the now certain likelihood that Elizabeth 'will be able to help them secretly with some incentives of money, arms and munitions to encourage them even more in the pursuit of their actions'.[138] 'Great help' was thus needed, which d'Oisel, the Queen Regent and 'all the French have yet not to suffer'.[139]

But neither these supplications, nor Guise's warning that Châtelherault and his accomplices would do all they could as soon as possible, translated into effective action on the part of France.[140] As a result, Guise was left to continue her war of words with the Congregation and to fortify Leith with what resources she had.[141] Needless to say, the Congregation's attempted deposition of Guise

135 AÉ, *Mémoires et Documents*, Angleterre, XV, fos. 37ʳ, 39ᵛ and *Cor. Pol.*, Angleterre, XIII, f.322ᵛ; Teulet, *Papiers*, I, pp. 349–50 and *Relations*, I, pp. 353–4.

136 AÉ, *Mémoires et Documents*, Angleterre, XV, fos. 37ʳ-8ᵛ; 39ᵛ-40ʳ. Similar appeals were contained in the Regent's letter to her brothers, *ibid*, XV, fos. 40r-1r. See also *CSP Foreign, 1558–1559*, 1346, pp. 565–6; *CSP Scot.*, I, 540, p.251.

137 AÉ, *Mémoires et Documents*, Angleterre, XV, f.40ʳ.

138 AÉ, *Cor. Pol.*, Angleterre, XIII, f.323r; Teulet, *Papiers*, I, p.354 and *Relations*, I, p. 358. A month later, Noailles wrote again to the Cardinal de Lorraine with certain proof that the Congregation's forces were being maintained with English money. AÉ, *Cor. Pol.*, Angleterre, XIII, f.335ʳ; Teulet, *Papiers*, I, pp. 360–1 and *Relations*, I, pp. 363–4.

139 Noialles to Constable Montmorency, 28 September 1559, AÉ, *Cor. Pol.*, Angleterre, XIII, f.322ᵛ.

140 AÉ, *Mémoires et Documents*, Angleterre, XV, f.40ʳ.

141 Knox, *Works*, I, pp. 417–21 and *History*, I, pp. 232–5.

sparked a flurry of new appeals to François for aid. He was told that 'a great number of men and vessels must be sent even though there were many more fortresses devoted to the Queen Regent than just Leith, like Dunbar, the island of Inchkeith and the very castle of Edinburgh'.[142] Even with this dramatic turn of events, military aid from France was still not forthcoming.

While Mary of Guise obviously felt the need to implement some precautionary defensive measures to counter the effects of the Congregation's patriotic campaign, their 'Act of Suspension' also served to strengthen her resolve to take the offensive in asserting her authority and that of Mary and François in Scotland. Not only was the Congregation's attempted deposition a blatant act of sedition, but the fact that it was done in the names of the very sovereigns who had granted the commission in the first place was also an act of hypocrisy.[143] Mary of Guise took her case, once again, to the public. Denouncing the Congregation's actions, which seemed 'to come from a Prince to his subjects, rather than from subjects to one that bears authority',[144] Guise declared that 'None can have the authority here except the Queen's daughter and her husband'. The Congregation's 'Act of Suspension' clearly indicated that they 'acknowledge[d] no other superiority'.[145] The Regent justified her position further by declaring that she would 'grant anything which may not resist the piety due to God, nor fight with their duty to their King and Queen', as she did 'not seek the overthrow of their laws and liberties, nor dream of conquering the kingdom by violence, for her daughter possesses it already'.[146] Finally, Guise defended her fortification of Leith by shifting the onus of blame onto the Congregation, for she 'had attempted nothing that way before' until they 'showed that they would shake off the lawful government, and made league and covenant with her ancient enemies [the English]'.[147]

Words were not the only way Guise chose to assert her authority. On 7 November, she re-entered Edinburgh and proceeded to have 'all things at her will'.[148] Her 'will' dictated that Mass be restored, St. Giles

---

142 AÉ, *Cor. Pol.*, Angleterre, XIII, fos. 338ᵛ-9ʳ. See also *ibid*, fos. 336ʳ-7ᵛ, 338ʳ-42ʳ; Teulet, *Papiers*, I, pp. 364–7, 367–76 and *Relations*, I, pp. 366–9, 369–78.

143 Knox, *Works*, I, pp. 448, 449 and *History*, I, pp. 254, 255; *APS*, II, p. 519; NAS, SP13/81.

144 *CSP Foreign, 1559–1560*, 107, p.45.

145 *Ibid*, 109, p.45.

146 *Ibid*, 109, p.46.

147 *Ibid*, 109, p.46.

148 *Ibid*, 234, p.100.

reconsecrated, and Leith continue to be fortified.[149] But it was the process of treason that was initiated against Châtelherault and Arran that reveals most about the French reaction to the Congregation's 'Act of Suspension' and who Mary, François, Les Guise and the Queen Regent ultimately held responsible.[150]

Throughout November, d'Oisel and Jacques de la Brosse began to assemble a case against the Congregation and their Hamilton figure-heads.[151] Instances of the Congregation's treasonable behaviour since the enlistment of Châtelherault and his son were cited in detail. This 'charge sheet' made specific reference to their convocation at Stirling on 19 September 1559, their taking up of arms and twenty-day siege of Edinburgh in October, their suspension of Mary of Guise from the regency (all the more treasonable since it was an office granted to her by Mary and François), their letters and proclamations written in the name of their sovereigns demanding that obedience be rendered instead to Châtelherault and Arran, and their seizure of coining irons and counterfeiting of coins.[152] The Congregation's illicit activities were then corroborated in depositions given by a wide range of witnesses, including the Archbishop of Glasgow, the Bishop of Dunblane, the Earl of Bothwell, and Sir Alexander Erskine, son of John, 5th Lord Erskine who, as custodian of Edinburgh Castle, had managed to stay neutral throughout the conflict.[153]

The evidence compiled by d'Oisel and de la Brosse was damning. Confirming the crown's suspicion that Châtelherault and Arran were guilty of treason, their report concluded that they had indeed committed

> crimes de leze maieste a lencontre de nous leurs princes souverains par les assemblees de gens en armes hostilitez et aultre actes de felonnye et Infidelite par eulx faictz Et quilz continuent encores chacun Jour pour de tout en tout

149 AÉ, *Cor. Pol.*, Angleterre, XIII, fos.336ᵛ-7ʳ; Teulet, *Papiers*, I, pp. 364–7 and *Relations*, I, pp. 366–9.
150 Mary and François' commission was dated 10 November 1559. AÉ, *Mémoires et Documents*, Angleterre, XV, f.130ʳ.
151 *Ibid*, XV, fos. 130ʳ-53ᵛ; Dickinson, 'Report by de la Brosse and d'Oisel', pp. 85–125.
152 AÉ, *Mémoires et Documents*, Angleterre, XV, fos. 131ʳ-39ᵛ; Dickinson, 'Report by de la Brosse and d'Oisel', pp. 90–8. Reference was also made to the iconoclasm and various skirmishes engaged in by the Congregation.
153 AÉ, *Mémoires et Documents*, Angleterre, XV, fos. 140ʳ-53ᵛ; Dickinson, 'Report by de la Brosse and d'Oisel', pp. 98–125.

opprimer audit royaulme notre auctorite et se lattribuer par
la force des armes contre tout droict divin et humain.

[crimes of lese-majesty against us their sovereigns with their
gatherings of armed men, hostilities and other acts of
treachery and disloyalty for which they were responsible and
which they still do everyday to suppress our authority entirely
in the kingdom and give it to themselves through armed
force against all divine and human right].[154]

On the strength of this evidence, Guise then commissioned James
Makgill of Nether Rankeillor and John Bellenden of Auchnoul,
Scotland's clerk register and justice register, to find historical and
legal precedents for the various acts of treason committed by the
Congregation as detailed in de la Brosse and d'Oisel's report. The
result was the *Discours Particulier d'Escosse*.[155]

While the *Discours* covered a wide range of topics, a dispropor-
tionate amount of the report was devoted to treason and the legal
process through which cases of lese-majesty were executed and
punished.[156] Specifically, the *Discours* outlined what acts constituted
treason and crimes of lese majesty as stipulated by the Three Estates in
Parliament. Not surprisingly, these included initiating, partaking or
assisting in a rebellion against the sovereign or his authority, taking up
arms or maintaining a stronghold against the crown, the counterfeiting of coin, and convoking an assembly of rebels.[157] Also contained
in their report were case studies of those against whom the process of
treason had been duly executed – the most notable of these were
James, 9th earl of Douglas (1455), Alexander Stewart, duke of Albany
(1483) and John MacDonald, lord of the Isles (1475).[158] Of particular
significance was the case of David Home of Wedderburn, who was
charged with treason for putting 'his people in order of battle against
James, earl of Arran, and for having invaded him'. The fact that Arran
'was then one of the regents of this kingdom' made Hume's invasion a
direct attack against 'the person of our sovereign'.[159] In an ironic twist

---

154 AÉ, *Mémoires et Documents*, Angleterre, XV, f.130ʳ.
155 Thomson (ed.), *Discovrs Particvlier D'Escosses escrit par commandement et
ordonnance de la Royne Dovariere et Regent, par Messires Iacques Makgill clerc
dv registere et Iean Bellenden clerk de la justice* (Bannatyne Club, 1824), pp.
3–32; NLS, Adv.MSS, 35.1.2; McNeill, 'Discours', pp. 86–131.
156 McNeill, 'Discours', pp. 117–31.
157 *Ibid*, pp. 123–5.
158 *Ibid*, pp. 127–31.
159 *Ibid*, p.129.

of fate, Châtelherault had become the perpetrator of a crime of which he had previously been a victim.

Together, the *Discours* and 'Information' provided the crown with a strong legal foundation on which to proceed against Châtelherault and Arran for treason and crimes of lese-majesty. But by the time Makgill and Bellenden had completed and submitted their report on 11 January 1560, circumstances had changed and the tide was beginning to turn decidedly against the Queen Regent. Any legal, ideological or constitutional strength she could derive from Châtelherault and Arran's nominal leadership of the Congregation and their 'Act of Suspension' was undermined by the military intervention of England on the side of the Congregation in February 1560. While this was unquestionably a factor contributing to the collapse of Mary of Guise's political régime in Scotland, France's failure to respond adequately to England's intervention would prove to be the most devastating.

* * *

England's military intervention in Scotland unofficially began in January 1560 when a naval fleet commanded by Admiral Winter 'accidentally' entered the Firth of Forth.[160] Officially, it was inaugurated on 27 February 1560 with the conclusion of the treaty of Berwick – an agreement written in the name of Mary, Queen of Scots, but contracted between James, Duke of Châtelherault, as second person in the realm, and Elizabeth I.[161] The pretext of the treaty, and England's military support of the Congregation on the whole, was the defence of Scotland's 'ancient right and liberty'.[162] In reality, the treaty facilitated the interference of a foreign monarch in what was essentially a domestic crisis. Hedged in the language of the commonweal, Elizabeth's intervention was justified by the fact that,

> the French intend to conquer the realm of Scotland, suppress the liberty thereof and unite it to France, and being required thereto by the said nobility in the name of the whole realm, shall accept this said realm, the apparent heir to the crown,

160 *Brosse Missions*, pp. 56–61; *CSP Foreign, 1559–1560*, 616, 636, 645, pp. 288–91, 311–2, 324.

161 *CSP Scot.*, I, 665, pp. 323–4; *CSP Foreign, 1559–1560*, 781, pp. 413–5; *Foedera*, XI, p.95 and X, p.47; BL, Cotton MSS, Caligula B.ix, f.34; Knox, *Works*, II, pp. 45–52, 53–6; *History*, I, pp. 302–7, 308–10. For a discussion of the negotiations and the treaty as it pertained to Cecil's 'British strategy' and notion of an Anglo-British Protestant Empire, see Alford, *The Early Elizabethan Polity*, pp. 64–79, and Dawson, 'William Cecil', pp. 207–10.

162 *CSP Foreign, 1559–1560*, 781, p.413.

the nobility and subjects thereof, for the protection of their old freedoms and liberties from conquest or oppression.[163]

In effect, the treaty of Berwick was a renunciation of the Franco-Scottish protectoral alliance that was established in the treaty of Haddington and the Congregation's formal appointment of Elizabeth as the new 'protector' of Scotland. It was also the culmination of the Congregation's patriotic platform. By accusing Mary of Guise of attempting to conquer the realm, and associating themselves with freedom, liberty and the defence of the commonweal, the Congregation, as Scotland's legitimate government, were able to secure the open and military support of England against the establishment of French power in Scotland.

The inherent contradiction in the Congregation's position, of course, was the simultaneous justification of their rebellion and alliance with England in terms of patriotism. In doing so, the Congregation revealed their true objective: the defence of their interests and position in Scotland as the natural-born councillors of the realm. Self-interest, and not altruism, was the prime motive behind the treaty of Berwick and the Congregation's appeal to patriotism as a whole. The treaty's additional stipulation that England and the Congregation 'shall never assent that the realm of Scotland shall be knit to the crown of France *otherwise than it is already*, only by marriage of the Queen to the French King', reinforced the Congregation's position.[164] As long as the Franco-Scottish dynastic union was nominal, the Scottish nobility's interests and traditional role in government were safeguarded. Anything beyond that, that is coalescence, integration or conquest, posed a direct threat to their traditional powers and was, therefore, unacceptable. But the fact that they accused Mary of Guise only of the *intent* to conquer the realm indicates how weak their justification really was. Ultimately, the treaty of Berwick was contracted against something that had not actually happened, and any sincerity that the Congregation hoped to convey in their professed recognition of François and Mary's authority was undermined by the simple fact that they had forged a military and protectoral alliance with England against the constituted authority of Scotland.

It therefore comes as no surprise that, as with the 'Act of Suspension', Mary of Guise refused to recognise the terms of the treaty of Berwick. On 27 March 1560, she reported to her brothers that she 'never saw anything so shameful as the Articles, as well for the honour of God as the

163 *CSP Foreign, 1559–1560*, 781, p.413.
164 *Ibid*, 781, p.413.

reputation of the King, and according to them there will rest no more but to render obedience to the Queen of England'.[165] Despite her indignation that the Congregation and Elizabeth should come to such an agreement in the first place, the arrival of English troops in March 1560 brought home the seriousness of the situation. Elizabeth had fulfilled her promise that she would 'send into Scotland sufficient aid of men to join with the Scots not only to expel the present power of French, but also to stop all greater forces to enter therein, and shall continue the same until they are "aluterly" expelled therefrom'.[166] But the Cardinal de Lorraine and the Duc de Guise would find themselves powerless to protect France's position in Scotland and help their sister in her most desperate time of need – a need that was made all the more urgent when news came that Mary of Guise was dying.

Help from France had been scheduled to come in the person of Mary of Guise's younger brother, René, Marquis d'Elboeuf, in December 1559. He was to arrive in Scotland with military reinforcements and a commission from François and Mary to replace Mary of Guise as Regent of Scotland.[167] Originally, René had been issued with a commission to serve as the King and Queen's lieutenant-general in Scotland 'during the absence of the Queen Dowager about to return to France for recovery of her health'.[168] Subsequent reports that the Queen Regent 'is nothing amended of hir diseas' and 'still languishes in great sickness from which her physicians have no hope of her recovery', dictated that a more permanent arrangement be made.[169] But when René's expedition was postponed indefinitely because of bad weather, all the Queen Regent's family could do was send encouraging messages and sit and wait for news of the progress of her health.[170] François, for one, sent a personal note to his mother-in-law saying that, when they were reunited, Guise would have 'no better "medicines" than her daughter and himself'.[171] Sadly, by January, the

---

165 *CSP Foreign, 1559–1560, 906, p. 480.*
166 *Ibid,* 781, p.413. England's military intervention in Scotland and the ensuing war between France and England in Scotland, which culminated in the siege of Leith, is a lengthy and complex topic in itself that cannot be fully explored here. See Brosse, *Jacques de la Brosse,* pp. 217–59 and 'The Journal of the siege of Leith, 1560' in *Brosse Missions,* pp. 51–179, for detailed accounts of the conflict, in addition to Marshall, *Mary of Guise,* pp. 242–53 and Tytler, *History of Scotland,* IV, pp. 114–23.
167 11 December 1559, BL, Cotton MSS, Caligula B.ix, fos. 46ʳ-7ᵛ.
168 *Cal. Scot.,* I, 590, p.271.
169 *Ibid,* I, 596(ii), 592, pp. 275, 272.
170 *Ibid,* I, 609 (i-vi), pp. 283–4.
171 23 December 1559, *ibid,* I, 609(ii), pp. 283–4.

growing civil unrest in France made it, once again, too dangerous for René to attempt the voyage.[172] The political and religious opposition to Les Guise in France had escalated and resulted in an attempt to abduct François at Amboise and remove the Duc de Guise and the Cardinal de Lorraine from power.[173] Although the 'Tumult of Amboise' on 15 March 1560 ultimately failed in its objective, it did prevent the Guise brothers 'from furnishing her with money as often as they would be glad to do. This they durst not adventure, nor the Marquis [d'Elboeuf] their brother, for the evident danger that might happen; but it cannot be long before they find some way open, when they will not lose one quarter of an hour'.[174] Fortunately for them, their sister's health improved enough for her to carry on in her capacity as Regent, and although the French troops in Scotland managed to withstand the English in their siege of Leith, the Guise brothers' failure to send additional reinforcements proved to be decisive in procuring widespread support for the Congregation. But if René had been successful in his mission, it is not only questionable whether these reinforcements would have been enough to defeat the English army, but also whether his assumption of the regency would have kept French interests alive in Scotland.

Realising that French reinforcements were not coming in aid of the Queen Regent, the Congregation were finally beginning to emerge as the winning side in the conflict. The number of subscribers to the Congregation's 'Third Band', drawn up at Leith on 27 April 1560, clearly shows that the tide had turned against Mary of Guise.[175] Approximately 140 Scots' signatures adorned the band and included such former stalwarts of the crown as Huntly.[176] Even more indicative is the fact that Catholics and Protestants alike had subscribed to a band that was not an exclusively political manifesto. After a long absence, the religious aims of the Congregation's rebellion reappeared alongside their now familiar political objective to defend

---

172 *CSP Foreign, 1559–1560*, 508, 575, 746, pp. 358–7, 460–1; *CSP Scot.*, I, p.135; AÉ, *Mémoires et Documents*, Angleterre, XV, fos. 56, 58, 65 and *Cor. Pol.*, XX, fos. 99, 100, 282, 291; Teulet, *Relations*, II, p.139; Brosse, *Jacques de la Brosse*, pp. 342, 344; Carroll, *Noble Power during the French Wars of Religion*, pp. 95–100.

173 The attempted coup was led by Louis I de Bourbon, Prince de Condé. It failed because the Cardinal had been forewarned of the conspiracy, and the rebels were massacred before they had a chance to attack. Bouillé, *Histoire des Ducs de Guise*, II, pp. 42–112; Constant, *Les Guise*, pp. 40–3.

174 *CSP Foreign, 1559–1560*, 879, pp. 460–1.

175 Knox, *Works*, II, pp. 61–4; *History*, I, pp. 314–5.

176 Donaldson, *All the Queen's Men*, pp. 33–4.

the commonweal against the oppression of the French. Unlike their religious bands of 1557 and 1559 which attracted minimal public support for the Congregation, the band of April 1560 reflects the Congregation's new-found strength and confidence. While this confidence may be attributed in part to England's formal entry into the conflict, the timing of the band clearly shows that it had more to do with France's failure to respond to this intervention – something which could only be determined in the months following the arrival of the English reinforcements.

For her part, Mary of Guise was still hoping that her brothers would 'find some way open' to send her aid, and, in an attempt to buy time, she re-entered negotiations with the Congregation.[177] Despite her obvious military disadvantage, the Queen Regent's stance was surprisingly adamantine in the series of talks that took place with the Congregation and their English representatives in the spring of 1560. She was particularly obstinate in her position when it came to the authority of Mary and François in Scotland. When presented with the demand that 'the whole number of French men at war at present in this realm be removed with speed so that we [the Scots] may live in peace without fear of disturbances from them', de la Brosse reports that Guise responded by saying that this article 'was quite beyond reason and could not be discussed'.[178] As she had told them the day before, the King and Queen would not receive orders from any prince in the world, much less from subjects, and that she, for her part, 'would in no wise consent thereto'.[179] Moreover, Elizabeth's intervention on behalf of the Congregation was regarded by Guise as an act of blatant interference in Scottish affairs that not only undermined her position and authority as Queen Regent, but also that of Mary and François. As a result, Guise was consistently unyielding in her demand that the Scots uphold and respect the authority of their own sovereigns and not the Queen of England.

Another point on which Mary of Guise was unyielding was her defence of the Franco-Scottish dynastic alliance. Just as the Congregation were persistent in their demands that the French leave Scotland,

177 In the spring of 1560 the French also sought to 'appease things in Scotland, and to find a means to win time' by sending two diplomatic envoys, the bishop of Valence and M. de Randan. The French position was weakened considerably, however, with the news that Mary of Guise had passed away on 11 June 1560. *CSP Foreign, 1559–1560*, 879, pp. 460–1.

178 *Ibid*, 879, pp. 460–1; *Brosse Missions*, p.101.

179 *Ibid*, p.103.

so too was Guise in her demand that the Congregation revoke their league with England. The refusal of both sides to renounce their respective allegiances resulted in stalemate and a temporary suspension of the negotiations.[180] On 12 May 1560, renewed attempts were made to reach a settlement and Lord James and William Maitland of Lethington presented Guise with a list of grievances about the establishment of French power in Scotland or, as they termed it, 'the stay the French had made'.[181] As we have seen in their propaganda as a whole, the establishment of French military power was a particularly sore point with the Congregation (or was it the English?). Reiterating their objections to Guise's importation of French troops in August and September 1559, the Congregation also took issue with the taxes raised for the French fortification of Inchkeith,[182] the French officers who had been appointed to the most important offices in the realm (a specific reference to the Vice-Chancellor, du Rubay) and Guise's desire to change their laws.[183] To each of these grievances, Mary of Guise responded by justifying and defending her position and that of the French in Scotland. She argued, quite correctly, that every one of these events had been agreed in Parliament and had the consent of the Scottish political community – with the exception of their last complaint which accused Guise of desiring to, but not actually succeeding in, changing their laws.[184]

Success ultimately came for the Congregation not as a result of their military might or ideological arguments, but with the death of Mary of Guise in the early hours of 11 June 1560.[185] After she fell seriously ill again on 1 June, the Queen Regent's health deteriorated rapidly and several of the leading members of the Congregation came to pay their last respects, including Châtelherault, Arran, Argyll, Huntly and

---

180 On 14 May, Maitland reported to Cecil that 'In the end they found that nothing could be agreed upon'. *CSP Foreign, 1559–1560*, 94, p.42. See *Brosse Missions*, pp. 151–7, for Guise's entire defence of the Franco-Scottish alliance and the establishment of French power in Scotland.

181 *Ibid*, p.151.

182 As we have already seen, the *Treasurer's Accounts* reveal that the fort at Langholm was the only stronghold whose modernisation was financed out of Crown revenues. Throughout 1558 Inchkeith was one of many strongholds, including Home Castle and Eyemouth, that was furnished with provisions for the war against England but paid for by the burghs of Leith and Edinburgh. If this is what the Congregation was referring to, why did it not mention these other strongplaces? *TA*, X, pp. 409, 421–45.

183 *Brosse Missions*, p.151.

184 *Ibid*, p.155.

185 *Ibid*, p.177.

Glencairn.[186] Although England's military intervention seriously weakened the foundations of her administration, the onus of failure for the collapse of her political régime ultimately lay with her allies in France. The failure of her brothers to meet the English challenge enabled the Congregation to emerge, and be seen, as the victors of the conflict. Yet, despite being seriously let down by Les Guise in France, the Queen Regent never gave up her fight to protect her own dynastic interests or those of her daughter. She not only maintained her ideological position against the Congregation to the very end, but also her hope that her appeals for French intervention would result in effective action.[187] Only in death did Mary of Guise abandon her fight to defend the Franco-Scottish dynastic alliance and the authority of Mary and François in Scotland, and only then can one say that her political régime truly collapsed. More significantly, her death also signalled the death of the French cause in Scotland. The loss of Mary of Guise as the acceptable face of French power witnessed the almost immediate removal of all French influence in Scotland. The death of François II in December 1560 merely confirmed it.

186 *Brosse Missions*, pp. 175–7; AÉ, *Mémoires et Documents*, Angleterre, XV, fos. 113–4; *CSP Foreign, 1559–60*, 276–89, pp. 116–21; Pitscottie, *Historie*, II, p.171; *Diurnal of Occurrents*, pp. 276–7; Lesley, *History*, pp. 439–41. Despite this ostensible display of respect, the Congregation snubbed Mary of Guise even after death. Following her autopsy, the Congregation refused her burial at Holyrood or to comply with the wishes Les Guise for her body to be shipped back to France. As a result, Mary of Guise's corpse remained in the Chapel of St. Margaret at Edinburgh Castle for several months. Negotiations did not begin for the Queen Regent's burial until August 1560. Only after François II passed away and Mary, Queen of Scots' had made the decision to return to Scotland, did she order that her mother's body be sent to France on 16 March 1561. Guise was finally laid to rest at the Convent of St. Peter at Rheims. A memorial service was then held in her honour at the Cathedral of Notre Dame, and was attended by her daughter and the entire French Court. *TA*, XI, p.24; *CSP Foreign, 1560–1561*, 218, p.133; Teulet, *Papiers*, I, pp. 615–6; *Diurnal of Occurrents*, p.64; Knox, *Works*, II, Appendix III, pp. 590–2; Tytler, *History of Scotland*, IV, p.398; Marshall, *Mary of Guise*, pp. 261–2.
187 AÉ, *Mémoires et Documents*, Angleterre, XV, fos. 86–105.

Conclusion

O n 6 July 1560 a treaty was contracted between England, Scotland and France that called for the withdrawal of all French troops from Scotland – the last vestiges of French power that remained after the death of Mary of Guise the previous month. In real terms, the treaty of Edinburgh marked the end of an alliance that had been unprecedented in its intimacy and transformed it into one of a purely nominal nature, whereby an absent queen ruled over a kingdom with a self-imposed system of government, and over subjects who had taken it upon themselves to define the duties of their sovereign. The 'divorce' was finalised when, six months later, François II's death severed the dynastic ties that had bound Scotland and France together since 1548, and that had slackened considerably since Mary of Guise's exit from the political arena. Mary of Guise not only proved to be the acceptable face of French power in Scotland, but was in many ways the linchpin of the Franco-Scottish alliance as a whole. Circumstances and the ever-changing international situation, however, dictated that she met with only limited success.

Mary of Guise was raised, and later operated, in a world where dynasticism took precedence over personal and religious convictions. The dynastic interests of Les Guise became inextricably associated with those of Mary Stewart when she became the Queen of Scots at six days old. But it was her Catholic claim to the English succession that made Mary Stewart a figure of extraordinary dynastic importance in sixteenth-century Europe – for it was possible that she alone could unite the kingdoms of Scotland, England and Ireland under one Catholic crown. As with any queenship, the question of marriage assumed great significance. For Mary Stewart, it was a question that dominated the politics of her minority, most notably because her marriage carried with it notions of British Imperialism for her future husband.

It was to protect and advance these dynastic and imperial interests that Mary of Guise formally entered into the factional high politics of Scotland during the 1540s in opposition to the Anglo-Scottish dynastic alliance contracted in the treaties of Greenwich. Guise's allegiances naturally lay with her native France and, aided by an unlikely bed-fellow in the person of Somerset, whose particularly aggressive Scot-tish policy produced tremendous support for the French cause, she played a key role in contracting a treaty of alliance with Henri II in July 1548. Mary of Guise's policies during the period 1548–1560, there-fore, were dictated by European dynastic politics and, more directly, by the Franco-Scottish protectoral and dynastic alliance established by the treaty of Haddington in 1548.

While Mary of Guise was instrumental in contracting the treaty of Haddington, her official political career in Scotland as Queen Regent was an inadvertent by-product of the treaty that facilitated the estab-lishment of French power in Scotland. Henri's protection of Scotland and its queen enabled him to establish a permanent foothold in the kingdom that served as the backdoor to England, and assume control over Scottish diplomacy and foreign policy. As the 'Protector' of Scotland, he was also able to determine when Mary, Queen of Scots reached her perfect age and who would govern her kingdom in her absence during her majority rule. Despite her role in forging this alliance, it should not be presumed that Mary of Guise had political designs in Scotland once the treaty of Haddington had been con-tracted and her daughter's future seemed secure. Her return to France in 1550, and even more surprising return to Scotland in 1551 to assume the regency in 1554, has conventionally been inter-preted to show that one of Guise's long-term objectives was to oust Châtelherault from power. But, as in the case of the Reformation Rebellion, this misconception is an example of the tendency of historians to read history backwards when assessing Mary of Guise's régime in order to provide convenient explanations for events that often defy such simplistic analyses. The decision behind Guise's return seems not to have been her own, but that of the Scots who had accompanied her to France and, latterly, that of Henri.

Mary of Guise's regency was dominated and, to a large extent, dictated by the international situation. The general aim of her policy was to restore stability to a realm that had endured a decade of plague, famine, war and the adverse affects of factionalism that accompanied any minority government. Like her late husband and his Stewart predecessors, she sought to achieve this by effecting a strong, yet personal monarchy and reasserting royal authority by advancing the interests of the crown at the expense of local jurisdictions. But it is her quest for law and order and the pursuit of royal justice that best characterise her domestic policy – particularly as these were seen as necessary prerequisites for facing the Anglo-Imperial threat from

England during the reign of Mary Tudor. But it was precisely because of this threat, and the Habsburg-Valois conflict on the Continent in general, that Guise's quest for law and order was undermined. Mary Tudor's accession and marriage to Philip of Spain meant that, through the forging of dynastic alliances, the Habsburg-Valois powers now met face to face on the Anglo-Scottish border, and Guise was forced to focus her attention on the more pressing and immediate concerns of defence and national security. The international situation also brought to the fore the importance of, and need for, Mary, Queen of Scots' marriage to the Dauphin. For many of Scotland's ruling élite, the Franco-Scottish protectoral alliance had run its course and now needed to be established on a more permanent footing that only dynastic union could bring about. Roughly translated, this meant that before they committed any more resources to finance Guise's defensive policies or to fight Henri's war on the Continent, they needed to know who their master was and where their allegiances formally lay. It was within this European context of the Habsburg-Valois conflict, therefore, that Mary of Guise fulfilled her dynastic objectives by securing not only the marriage of her daughter to the Dauphin, but also the consent of the Three Estates to grant the crown matrimonial to their new king.

Although Mary of Guise made a deliberate effort to reassure her Protestant subjects that the union of the French and Scottish Catholic crowns was not incompatible with the reform movement, she was not above abandoning her accommodating position if changes in the international or national scene made it advantageous to do so. Indeed, it was more than likely because she was recognised as a politique that a group of Scotland's leading Protestants signed a covenant pledging to 'manteane, sett fordward and establish the blessed word of God' on the eve of the Parliament that moved to advance the Valois-Stewart marriage.[1] The Lords of the Congregation were wise to take out such an insurance policy: changes in the international situation coinciding with the completion of her dynastic policies forced Guise to alter her religious policy and assume a less tolerant position towards the reform movement. The dubious legality of Elizabeth Tudor's accession saw the launch of a new campaign to advance the Catholic claims of Mary Stewart to the English throne by virtue of Elizabeth's illegitimacy in canon law. Once again, Guise's dynastic interests took precedence over religious considerations.

Conventional historiography has placed undue emphasis on the

1 Knox, *Works*, I, p.273 and *History*, I, p.136.

religious dimension of Mary of Guise's administration. Religion was a decidedly secondary concern for Guise throughout her regency. Dynasticism, not Catholicism, was the primary motive behind her policy in Scotland, and it is from a dynastic perspective that her régime must be examined. As a victim of circumstance, though, even Guise's dynastic policies met with limited success. While she showed herself to be an extremely shrewd and effective politician in fulfilling her dynastic objectives, the failure of her allies in France to respond accordingly to the changes in the international scene served to undermine all she had worked for during her political career in Scotland. In itself, the outbreak of the Congregation's rebellion did not pose a sufficient threat to her administration to cause its collapse. Guise's consistent belief that this was not a revolt of conscience, but a rebellion against duly constituted temporal authority, gained credence with every act of sedition the Congregation committed – none more so than their 'Act of Suspension'. Throughout 1559, Guise had the constitutional, legal, ideological and military edge over the Congregation. It was only when the rebellion adopted a British dimension with the formal intervention of England that the foundations of Guise's administration began to crumble.

As feared, Elizabeth's Protestant sympathies, and the religious settlement of May 1559, made her a source of support for Scotland's reformers and disaffected subjects in a way that her Catholic half-sister had never been, posing an arguably more dangerous threat than the Anglo-Imperial alliance had done during Mary Tudor's reign. Guise knew that with the military might of England behind the Congregation, ideological arguments would not be enough to maintain her position. The inability, or unwillingness, of her allies in France to respond adequately to this intervention was the most damaging blow to her régime. The onus of failure for the collapse of French power in Scotland and the Franco-Scottish alliance, therefore, lay with those who had wanted it the most – Les Guise. The fact that it did meet with limited success is solely down to Mary of Guise, whose death not only deprived the French cause of a respected and effective figurehead, but also what would prove to be the only acceptable face of French power in Scotland.

Much of the negative imagery surrounding Mary of Guise and her régime in Scotland derives from the propaganda of the Lords of the Congregation. Its emphasis on conquest and French domination at the hands of Mary of Guise was designed to play on Scottish xenophobia and identify the Congregation as a party of patriots. But the Reformation Rebellion is not a reliable or accurate context within which to assess Mary of Guise. Her régime must be examined within the wider context of European dynastic politics and, specifically, within the framework of the Franco-Scottish protectoral alliance of 1548–1560. If we change the perspective and read history forwards, Mary of Guise emerges as a pragmatic politique whose dynastic interests consistently took precedence over her religious convictions, while her assumption of the regency was the final part of a larger process establishing French power in Scotland that was intended to be consolidated by the marriage of Mary Stewart to François Valois. Despite the allegations of the Congregation to the contrary, the establishment of French power and the dynastic union of the French and Scottish crowns were both sanctioned and endorsed by the Scottish political élite. Moreover, Guise's domestic policy was the basic reassertion of traditional Stewart policies dating back to the reign of James I. Ironically, the Congregation's rebellion was not a revolt against French domination, but one against something that they themselves had established.

Appendix: Scots in France during Mary of Guise's Trip (1550–1551)

Unless otherwise cited, all biographical information has been taken from the *DNB*, *Scots Peerage* and Knox, *History* (index).

NAME	SCOTTISH & FRENCH PATRONAGE (1548–1551)	GENERAL COMMENTS	REFERENCES
Thomas Barclay, plus six servants*			*CSP Foreign, 1547–1553*, 311, p.81.
John Beaton of Creich*	100 *livres tournois* from Mary of Guise (1551).	Kinsman of Mary Beaton, one of the four 'Maries' who accompanied Mary, Queen of Scots to France in 1548; father-in-law to Walter Scott of Buccleuch and Branxholme, successor to his murdered namesake in 1552.	NLS, Adv.MSS. 29.2.5, f.151.
Sir Hugh Campbell of Loudon, heritable sheriff of Ayr, Agnes Drummond, his wife, and servants*	Gifts of non-entry of the lands of Cumnock, the five pound land of Raith and Leffnoll (1547–8); gift of escheat (1550).	After Arran's 'godly fit', supported the Angus/Lennox faction (1544); charged with treason and pardoned (1545); although a supporter of the English dynastic alliance, disapproved of Somerset's aggressive Scottish policy (1547); supporter of Guise administration; remonstrated with the Queen Regent after she issued a summons against the reformed preachers (May 1559); active member of the Congregation, but was later a supporter of the Marian party. [Did not accompany Mary of Guise personally to France; was still in Scotland in December 1550.]	*RSS*, III, 2533, 2757, 2840, pp. 406, 439, 450 and IV, 810, p.136; *CSP Foreign, 1547–1553*, 280, p.68.

* Not listed by Donaldson in Appendix C of *All the Queen's Men*

SCOTTISH & FRENCH PATRONAGE (1548–1551)

NAME	SCOTTISH & FRENCH PATRONAGE (1548–1551)	GENERAL COMMENTS	REFERENCES
Matthew Campbell of Loudon, his wife and servants*		Son and heir to Sir Hugh Campbell; although a reformer, he actively supported the Marian cause and fought at Langside, where he was taken prisoner (1568).	*CSP Foreign, 1547–1553*, 280, p.68.
Sir Robert Carnegy, 5th of Kinnaird*	Granted lands of Murdocairnie (1548); bond of manrent with Mary of Guise for an annual payment of £100 from the rents and duties of Orkney and Shetland (1550); received £500 Scots as expenses for his embassies to France and England (1551); gifts of escheat and non-entry (1551).	A lawyer by profession and loyal servant of the Crown during both Arran and Guise's administrations. Made a Senator of the College of Justice (1547); diplomatic envoy to negotiate the release of Huntly (1547–8); rewarded by Huntly with the possession of the Great Seal, a discharge and an assignation of the profits and duties of the Great Seal during the latter's trip to France (1548–51); Privy Councillor and Treasury Clerk (1548); member of the Queen's Household (1550); negotiating commissioner for the treaty of Norham (1551), member of several Border Commissions and ambassador to England (1557); appointed Collector General of Temporal Taxation during Guise's regency. Noted as a conservative, Carnegy reluctantly joined the Congregation during their Rebellion, but later supported the Marian party.	*RSS*, IV, 1284, 1285, 1420, pp. 204, 226; NAS, SP13/59; Fraser, *History of the Carnegies, Earls of Southesk and of their Kindred* (Edinburgh, 1867), I, pp. 25–40.
Alexander Cochrane	Granted a letter of protection and safeguard for his time in France (1550).	Travelled to France as part of Lord St. John's retinue.	*RSS*, IV, 882, pp. 147–8.

SCOTTISH & FRENCH PATRONAGE (1548–1551)

NAME	GENERAL COMMENTS	REFERENCES
Master Patrick Cockburn, parson/rector of Pitcox [Stenton]	Travelled to France as part of the Prior of St. Andrews' retinue.	*RSS*, IV, 879, p.146.
Robert Colville of Cleish	Natural son of Sir James Colville of Easter Wemyss; forfeited (1540) and restored (1543); after Arran's 'godly fit' supported the Angus/Lennox faction in favour of the English alliance and reformed faith (1544); one of the Fife lairds who conspired to murder Cardinal Beaton (1546); travelled to France as part of the Prior of St. Andrews' retinue and later became his Master of Household; sent by Archbishop Hamilton to warn Knox not to preach in St. Andrews (June 1559); eventually became an active promoter of the reform movement; killed at the siege of Leith (7 May 1560); his son, John, became a Presbyterian minister.	*RSS*, IV, 879, p.146.
Ninian Cranston*		*CSP Foreign, 1547–1553*, 281, p.68.

NAME	SCOTTISH & FRENCH PATRONAGE (1548–1551)	GENERAL COMMENTS	REFERENCES
Alexander Cunningham, 4th earl of Glencairn	Gift of non-entry of the lands and baronies of Kilmaurs, Finlaystone, Kilmarnock, Ranfurly-Cunningham, Glencairn, Stevenson, Hassendean and Hilton (1548); gift of escheat (1549); pension of 2,400 *francs* (1551).	Committed Protestant and principal promoter of the Reformation in Scotland. Entertained Knox during his preaching tour of 1555 and signed a letter inviting Knox to end his exile in Geneva (1557); subscriber to the 'First Band' of the Congregation (December 1557); remonstrated with the Queen Regent after she summoned the four Protestant preachers and supported the Congregation militarily against her with a force of 2,500 at Perth (May 1559); signed instructions to the negotiating commissioners for the treaty of Berwick, which he also ratified (1559–60); leading member of the Congregation.	*RSS*, III, 2944, pp. 466–7 and IV, 375, p.62; Knox, *Works*, I, p.241 and *History*, I, p.116; *Scottish Correspondence*, ccxxxvi, pp. 347–8.
Sir George Douglas of Pittendreich* (d.1552)	Gift of escheat (1548); nominated by Mary of Guise for a French title (1549); granted a remission (1550).	Younger brother of Archibald Douglas, 6th earl of Angus. Supporter of the Angus/Lennox faction and leader of the English party in Scotland during the 'rough wooing'; gave tactical advice to the English for their invasions into Scotland, but disapproved of Somerset's aggressive Scottish policy and did not actively fight against his fellow Scots; noted as a double dealer throughout the 1540s, but eventually became a loyal servant to Mary of Guise.	Knox, *Works*, I, p.241 and *History*, I, p.116; *RSS*, III, 2902, p.460 and IV, 907, p.151; NAS, E34/14/6; NLS, MSS.2991, f.67v; *Fourquevaux Mission*, p.18 *n.b*; *Scottish Correspondence*, ccxxxviii, pp. 349–51.

SCOTTISH & FRENCH PATRONAGE (1548–1551)

NAME	SCOTTISH & FRENCH PATRONAGE (1548–1551)	GENERAL COMMENTS	REFERENCES
Henry Douglas, younger of Drumgarland		Travelled to France as part of the Prior of St. Andrews' retinue; future member of the Lords of the Congregation.	*RSS*, IV, 879, p.146.
Sir James Douglas of Drumlanrig*	Gift of escheat (1551); granted a remission (1551).	Warden of the West Marches (1553); although a member of the Congregation, his pro-English activities had abated considerably by the time of the Reformation Rebellion.	*CSP Foreign, 1547–1553,* 283, p.69; *RSS,* IV, 1363, 1321, pp. 216, 210.
Master John Douglas, parson/ rector of Newlands		Travelled to France as part of the Prior of St. Andrews' retinue.	*RSS,* IV, 879, p.146.
Robert Drummond [of Carnock?]*	Gift of non-entry (1550).		*RSS,* IV, 719, pp. 122–3; *Scottish Correspondence,* ccxxxv, p.346.
Andrew Durie, bishop of Galloway and of the Chapel Royal at Stirling*		Brother to George Durie, Abbot of Dunfermline; Abbot of Melrose (1526); Lord of Session (1541); provided to Galloway (1541); supporter of the French cause and Mary of Guise; faithful adherent to the established Church, one of Guise's recommendations for papal visitor (1556); described by Knox as our 'ennemy of God'.	Knox, *Works,* I, pp. 242, 261–2 and *History,* I, pp. 116, 129; *HBC,* p.311.

SCOTTISH & FRENCH PATRONAGE (1548–1551)

NAME	SCOTTISH & FRENCH PATRONAGE (1548–1551)	GENERAL COMMENTS	REFERENCES
Sir Alexander Erskine of Gogar, second surviving son of John, 5th lord Erskine		Travelled to France as part of the Prior of St. Andrews' retinue; custodian of Stirling Castle and the young James VI (1572–8); Constable of Edinburgh Castle (1579); loyal servant to Mary, Queen of Scots and supporter of the Marian cause.	*RSS*, IV, 879, p.146; *CSP Foreign, 1547–1553*, 311, p.81.
John, 5th lord Erskine*		Guardian of James V and Mary, Queen of Scots, whom he accompanied to France in 1548; keeper of Edinburgh and Stirling Castles; neutral during the Reformation Rebellion (1559–60).	*CSP Foreign, 1547–1553*, 311, p.81.
Master Thomas Erskine*	Gifts of escheat and non-entry (1549); grant of crown lands (1550).	In France on diplomatic business on behalf of the Scottish government. [See *RSS*, IV, 690 for a list of his retinue.]	*CSP Foreign, 1547–1553*, 304, 309, 311, 356, pp. 78, 80–1, 118; *RSS*, IV, 654, 471, 506, 419, 690, pp. 112, 76, 83–4, 69, 118.

NAME	SCOTTISH & FRENCH PATRONAGE (1548–1551)	GENERAL COMMENTS	REFERENCES
James, 4th lord Fleming*	600 *écus* from Mary of Guise (1551).	Loyal servant to the Crown as Lord Chamberlain of Scotland and Warden of the East and Middle Marches (1553); negotiating commissioner and witness to Mary, Queen of Scots' marriage (1558); died in France on the return journey home (1558). His father, William, 3rd lord Fleming, was an 'assured Scot' and supporter of the Angus/Lennox faction (1544); abandoned the reformed cause and founded a collegiate church (1545); killed fighting the English at the battle of Pinkie (1547). His wife, Janet Fleming, accompanied Mary, Queen of Scots to France with their daughter, who was one of the four 'Maries' (1548), and was a mistress of Henri II, by whom she had a child.	Knox, *Works*, I, p.241 and *History*, I, p.116; NLS, Adv.MSS, 29.2.5, f.138.
John Forret		Catholic priest; close relation to Thomas Forret, vicar of Dollar who was burned for heresy at Edinburgh, 28 February 1539; travelled to France as part of the Prior of St. Andrews' retinue.	*RSS*, IV, 879, p.146.

NAME	SCOTTISH & FRENCH PATRONAGE (1548–1551)	GENERAL COMMENTS	REFERENCES
Alexander Gordon	Bond of manrent with Mary of Guise for an annual pension of £200 Scots (1548); obligation granted by Guise as compensation for his renunciation of the bishopric of Caithness, in which he was promised another benefice with an annual revenue of 500 merks Scots and a French pension of 400 *livres tournois* (1548); provided to the archbishopric of Glasgow (1549); received titular archbishopric of Athens, and Inchaffray *in commendam* as compensation for his loss of Glasgow (1551).	Brother to George, 4th earl of Huntly; postulate of Caithness (1544); provided to the Isles, with Iona *in commendam* (1553); bishop-elect of Galloway, never consecrated but acted as bishop from 1559; joined the Congregation and signed 'Third Band' at Leith (April 1560); signed ratification of treaty of Berwick (May 1560); attended Reformation Parliament and subscribed to *Book of Discipline* (1560–1); candidate for Superintendentship of Galloway (1566).	*CSP Foreign, 1547–1553*, 306, p.79; NAS, SP13/55; NLS, MSS.2991, f.68; *Fourquevaux Mission*, pp. 18–9; *Scottish Correspondence*, clxi-ii, clxxi, cxxvii, cxxxvii, cxxxix, pp. 227–9, 239–40, 323–4, 348–9, 352–4; Teulet, *Papiers*, I, pp. 662–3; *HBC*, pp. 311; 313; 315; *Blacarres Papers*, II, l and Appendix B, ii, pp. 68–9, 309–10; *RSS*, IV, 2253, 2298, 2536, 2961, pp. 375, 383, 425–6, 517; Hannay, 'Some Papal Bulls', pp. 32–5; Donaldson, *Reformed by Bishops*, pp. 1–18.

NAME	SCOTTISH & FRENCH PATRONAGE (1548–1551)	GENERAL COMMENTS	REFERENCES
George Gordon, 4th earl of Huntly, his wife and mother*	Gift of escheat and tack of the crown lands of Brae of Mar, Strathdee and Cromrar (1547). While imprisoned at Newcastle, Henri II promised to pay his ransom, invest him in the Order of St. Michael, award him an annual pension of £2,000, invest him in one of the earldoms of Orkney, Ross or Moray, and grant him provision for his kin and followers (1548); invested in the Order of St. Michael, which was confirmed during Mary of Guise's trip to France (1548 & 1550); granted the earldom of Moray (1549); granted a French pension of 6,000 *francs* (1549); received a charter for the hereditary bailiary of all the lands of the bishopric of Aberdeen (1549); granted 500 *écus* (1551).	Faithful adherent to the established Church, loyal supporter of the Franco-Scottish dynastic alliance and Mary of Guise's administration. Lord Chancellor (1543); disgraced for failing in his commission to impose order in the Highlands (1554); fined and imprisoned by the Queen Regent, losing his governorship of Orkney, his possession of the Great Seal and most of his powers as Chancellor to du Rubay, vice-Chancellor (1554); restored to favour (1555); helped plan the Scottish army's planned siege of Wark and disagreed with Châtelherault *et al*'s subsequent decision to abandon the expedition (1557); supported Guise throughout the Reformation Rebellion until April 1560, presumably when it became clear that France was not going to respond to England's military intervention; signed the 'Third Band' at Leith (April 1560) and the ratification of the treaty of Berwick (May 1560); wavering political loyalties during personal rule of Mary, Queen of Scots.	Knox, *History*, I, pp. 103, 116 and *Works*, I, pp. 217, 241; *RSS*, III, 2269, 2342, pp. 368, 379; *RMS*, IV, 299, 319, 366, 1904, 2006, pp. 71, 75, 84, 308, 328–9; NLS, MSS.2991, fos. 67^v-8^r and Adv.MSS, 29.2.5, f.140; *Fourquevaux Mission*, p.18 *n*.1 & b; NAS, SP13/58; BN, MSS.f.fr.18153, fos. 66–8.

NAME	SCOTTISH & FRENCH PATRONAGE (1548–1551)	GENERAL COMMENTS	REFERENCES
John Gordon, 10th earl of Sutherland*	Gift of escheat (1547); tack to crown lands in earldom of Moray and lordship of Abernethy (1548); bond of manrent with Mary of Guise in which he was granted tenancy in the earldom of Ross (1549).	Cousin of Huntly and faithful adherent to the French and Catholic cause; one of Guise's agents in the north commissioned to impose order in the Highlands (1554); future member of the Queen's Party and one of the few nobles who attended Mary, Queen of Scots' marriage to Bothwell (1567); died of poison (1567).	*RSS*, III, 2344, 2903, 2785, pp. 380, 460, 443–4; NAS, SP13/63; Fraser, *Sutherland Book*, III, p.107.
John Graham, 4th earl of Menteith*		Joined the Congregation in 1559 and remained a staunch supporter of the reform party. Defected to the Congregation in May 1559, ignoring a summons to return from Mary of Guise; signed the 'Third Band' at Leith (April 1560) and ratification of the treaty of Berwick (May 1560); subscribed to the *Book of Discipline* (1561); died (1565).	*Scots Peerage*, VI, p.160.
Archibald Hamilton of Letham	Granted a letter of protection during his time in France (1550).	Raised in the Protestant faith but converted to Catholicism after a public disputation with Knox; travelled to France in the company of Sir James Hamilton of Crawfordjohn; future member of the Congregation.	*RSS*, IV, 893, p.149.
Gavin Hamilton, commendator of Kilwinning Abbey*	9,600 *livres tournois* from Mary of Guise (1551).	Son of James Hamilton of Raploch; appointed dean of Glasgow in 1549, an office which he exchanged with Henry Sinclair for the commendatorship of Kilwinning (1550); Lord of Session (1555); cautious during the Reformation Rebellion, joining only in 1560.	NLS, Adv.MSS, 29.2.5, f.148.

NAME	SCOTTISH & FRENCH PATRONAGE (1548–1551)	GENERAL COMMENTS	REFERENCES
Master James Hamilton [later 3rd earl of Arran]*	Assigned a post in Guyenne worth 50,000 *francs* per year, and 50 lances once belonging to M. de St. Vallier by Henri II (1548); promised the daughter of the Duc de Montpensier in marriage (1548).	Committed reformer and son and heir to Châtelherault. Held as a pledge by Beaton in St. Andrews and as a hostage by the 'Castilians' (1546–7); sent to France as a pledge for his father's support of the proposed Franco-Scottish dynastic alliance (1548); escaped from France to become nominal leader of the Congregation with his father (1559); signed negotiating commissioners' instructions and ratification of the treaty of Berwick (1559–60); subscribed to the 'Third Band' at Leith (April 1560); proposed and rejected as husband to Elizabeth I (1560); signed *Book of Discipline* (1561); unsuccessfully sued for hand of Mary, Queen of Scots and went insane (1562); died (1609).	*TA*, IX, p.83; *CSP Scot*, 238, pp. 116–7; *CSP Spain*, X, pp. 303–4; *Balcarres Papers*, I, clix, xi, pp. 205–7 and II, cli, clxiii, clxviii, pp. 197–8, 245–8, 256–8; Hannay, 'The Earl of Arran', pp. 258–76; Durkan, 'James, Third Earl of Arran', pp. 154–66.
Sir James Hamilton of Crawfordjohn*	Granted a letter of protection for his time in France (1550).	After Arran's 'godly fit', supported the Angus/ Lennox faction in favour of an English dynastic alliance and reformed religion (1544); travelled to France in the company of Archibald Hamilton of Letham; future member of the Lords of the Congregation and King's Party.	*RSS*, IV, 893, p.149.

NAME	SCOTTISH & FRENCH PATRONAGE (1548–1551)	GENERAL COMMENTS	REFERENCES
James Hamilton, younger of Kincavill, plus one servant*		Future member of the Lords of the Congregation.	CSP Scot., I, 364, p.183.
Master David Henderson [Henrison], vicar of Rossie, chaplain of St. John of Bakie		Travelled to France as part of the Prior of St. Andrews' retinue.	RSS, IV, 839, 879, pp. 141, 146.
Alexander, 5th lord Home	Annual pension of 2,000 francs (1549); promised support from Henri II for maintaining Home Castle (May 1550); granted a charter of bailiary for Coldstream (1551).	Taken prisoner by the English at Pinkie (1547); Warden of the East March; supported Mary, Queen of Scots' marriage to Darnley, but after her marriage to Bothwell switched allegiances and supported Lord James; fought against Mary at Carberry and Langside (1568), but reverted to the Queen's Party (1569); forfeited (1573) and imprisoned (1573–5).	Scottish Correspondence, ccxxxv, p.346; NLS, MSS.2991, fos. 67^v–8^r; Fourquevaux Mission, p.18.

NAME	SCOTTISH & FRENCH PATRONAGE (1548–1551)	GENERAL COMMENTS	REFERENCES
William Keith, 4th earl Marischal*	Granted a remission (1548); nominated for a French title by Mary of Guise (1549); 6000 écus (1551); 500 écus [1551].	Accused of heresy (1543); favoured Tudor-Stewart marriage alliance (1543); present at George Wishart's sermon in Dundee (1544); supporter of the Lennox/Angus faction and associated with Glencairn against Arran (1544); consulted by Henry VIII for the murder of Cardinal Beaton, but refused to take part physically (1546); fought for Scotland at Pinkie, presumably disapproving of the aggressiveness of Somerset's Scottish policy (1547); appointed Commissioner for the Borders (1553); attended Knox's sermon in Edinburgh (1555); although he was sympathetic to the reformed doctrines, he remained neutral during the Reformation Rebellion, offering no practical support either to the Congregation or Mary of Guise, with whom he entered into Perth in 1559 and stayed with at Edinburgh Castle in 1560 until her death that June.	NLS, MSS. 2991, f.67^v and Adv.MSS, 29.2.5, fos. 140, 142; *Fourquevaux Mission*, p.18 *n.b*; *RSS*, IV, 7, p.2; Knox, *Works*, I, p.241 and *History*, I, p.116.
Gilbert Kennedy, 3rd earl of Cassillis*	Tack for lands of Turnberry (1548); nominated for a French title by Mary of Guise (1549); granted a remission (1550); invested in the Order of St. Michael (1550); 6,670 *livres* and 'six vingts dixsunt' *livres tournois* [1551].	Former pensioner of Henry VIII, 'assured Scot' and supporter of George Wishart; advised the English for an invasion of Scotland, but resisted Somerset at Pinkie (1547); appointed Lieutenant of the South (1548); Lord High Treasurer during Guise's regency (1554–58); negotiator and witness to Mary, Queen of Scots' marriage (1558); died in France en route to Scotland (1558).	Knox, *Works*, I, p.241 and *History*, I, p.116; *RSS*, III, 2579, pp. 412–3 and IV, 682, p.116; NLS, MSS.2991, f.67^v and Adv.MSS, 29.2.5, fos. 143, 146; *Fourquevaux Mission*, p.18 *n.b*.

NAME	SCOTTISH & FRENCH PATRONAGE (1548–1551) GENERAL COMMENTS	REFERENCES
Hugh Kennedy*		*CSP Foreign, 1547–1553*, 281, p.68.
William Lauder of Haltoun	Poet and playwright who probably took orders for the priesthood after completing his education at the University of St. Andrews; travelled to France as part of the Prior of St. Andrews' retinue; wrote a play for Mary of Guise's arrival in Edinburgh to assume the regency (1554); commissioned to write a play celebrating the marriage of Mary, Queen of Scots for which he was paid 10 *livres* (1558); joined the Lords of the Congregation (1560); appointed by Perth presbytery to minister at Forgandenny, Forteviot and Muckarsie (1563).	*RSS*, IV, 879, p.146.
Bartholomew Livingston	Travelled to France as part of the Prior of St. Andrews' retinue.	*RSS*, IV, 879, p.146.

NAME	SCOTTISH & FRENCH PATRONAGE (1548–1551)	GENERAL COMMENTS	REFERENCES
Robert, 6th lord Maxwell	Gift of non-entry (1549, 1550); granted a letter of protection, respect, safeguard and exemption for his time in France (1550); pension of 2,000 *francs* and made a gentleman of the French King's Bedchamber.	An 'assured Scot' who supported the Angus/Lennox faction in favour of the English dynastic alliance and reformed religion (1544); later switched allegiances and supported the French dynastic alliance, becoming a loyal agent of Mary of Guise and the French King [e.g. his mission to Scotland in February 1551 to join d'Oisel and Châtelherault on the Borders]; Warden of the West March for Scotland and an important figure in Anglo-Scottish Border affairs; died (1552).	Knox, *Works*, I, p.241 and *History*, I, p.116; *RSS*, IV, 880, p.147; *APC*, III, pp. 205–6; *CSP Foreign, 1547– 1553*, 291, 295, pp. 73, 75; *Scottish Correspon-dence*, ccxxxiv, ccxxxviii, pp. 334–5, 349–51.
Thomas Menzies of Pitfoddells*			*CSP Foreign, 1547– 1553*, 228, p.52.
Sir Angus Murray, chantor of Caithness	Granted a letter of protection and safeguard for his time in France (1550).	Travelled to France as part of Robert Stewart, bishop elect of Caithness' retinue.	*RSS*, IV, 883, p.148.
Sir William Murray of Tullibardine	Granted a letter of protection, safeguard and exemption for his time in France (1550).	After Arran's 'godly fit', supported the Angus/ Lennox faction in favour of the English dynastic alliance and reformed faith (1544); committed reformer and member of the Congregation; signed instructions to the negotiating commissioners for the treaty of Berwick (1560); comptroller (1565–56); future member of the King's Party.	*RSS*, IV, 887, p.148.

NAME	SCOTTISH & FRENCH PATRONAGE (1548–1551)	GENERAL COMMENTS	REFERENCES
James Ogilvy of Deskford and Findlater*	40 *écus* from Mary of Guise (1551).	Third son of George Gordon, earl of Huntly, who assumed the name Ogilvy; married a sister of Mary Livingston, one of the four 'Maries' and daughter to Lord Livingston, guardian of Mary, Queen of Scots; supporter of the Marian cause.	NLS, Adv.MSS, 29.2.5, f.150.
David Orme		Travelled to France as part of the Prior of St. Andrews' retinue.	*RSS*, IV, 879, p.146.
David Paniter, bishop of Ross	Gift of temporality of the abbey of Cambuskenneth (1549); gift of ward and non-entry (1551); gift of escheat (1551); given Abbey of l'Abyse in Poitou (1551).	Ambassador to France (1544–52); provided to the bishopric of Ross (1547); in France for Mary, Queen of Scots' marriage to the Dauphin (1558); died (1558).	*RSS*, IV, 136, 1049, 1139, pp. 21, 172, 184; NLS, Adv.MSS, 29.2.5, f.150; *Balcarres Papers*, II, ccxiii, pp. 245–8; *HBC*, p.319.
John Roull, prior of Pittenweem and Blantyre (plus his convent at Pittenweem)		Travelled to France as part of the Prior of St. Andrews' retinue.	*RSS*, IV, 879, p.146.

NAME	SCOTTISH & FRENCH PATRONAGE (1548–1551)	GENERAL COMMENTS	REFERENCES
Patrick, Master of Ruthven*	Granted a remission (1550); received 1,200 *livres tournois* from Mary of Guise on behalf of his father, William, 3rd lord Ruthven (1550), and 400 crowns for himself (1551).	Questionable loyalty in 1547 when it was thought he would surrender Perth to the English for a price; succeeded his father, William, lord Ruthven as heritable sheriff and provost of Perth (1552); refused to suppress the Congregation at Perth (May 1559); ignored a summons by the Queen Regent to support the Congregation militarily at Cupar (June 1559); negotiator for the Congregation with the Queen Regent; one of the commissioners who negotiated and signed the treaty of Berwick (1560); subscriber to the 'Third Band' at Leith (April 1560); played a leading role in the murder of Riccio (1566).	*RSS*, IV, 760, p.129; NLS, Adv.MSS, 29.2.5, f.134; *Scottish Correspondence*, ccxxxv, pp. 345–7.
Sir James Sandilands of Calder, lord St. John, preceptor of Torphichen, plus two or three pages.	Granted a letter of protection and safeguard for his time in France (1550).	Reformer and member of the Lords of the Congregation; presented the Congregation's petition to Mary of Guise (November 1558).	*RSS*, IV, p.882, pp. 147–8.
John Sempill of Fowlwod*		The Sempills were faithful adherents to the established Church and loyal supporters of Mary of Guise.	*RSS*, IV, 888, p.148; NLS, Adv.MSS, 29.2.5, f.134.

NAME	SCOTTISH & FRENCH PATRONAGE (1548–1551)	GENERAL COMMENTS	REFERENCES
Henry Sinclair, dean of Glasgow	Granted full license and free power and faculty to pass into France 'and ony uthir partis beyond sey to the sculis for doing of his uthiris lefull besynes and erandis' (1550).	Lord of Session (1537); Abbot of Kilwinning (1541); became Dean of Glasgow after exchanging Kilwinning with Gavin Hamilton (1550); did not return to Scotland from France until 1554; worked for the internal reform of abuses within the Church and was one of Guise's recommendations for papal visitor; negotiating commissioner for the treaty of Carlisle (1556) and Upsettlington (1559); succeeded Robert Reid as President of the College of Justice (1558); received gift of temporalities for the see of Ross upon the death of David Painter (1558) and provided to the bishopric in 1561; died at Paris (1565).	*CSP Foreign, 1547–1553,* 228, p.52; *RSS,* IV, 644–6, 820, pp. 109–110; 137–8.
James Somerville in Humbie, 6th lord Somerville	Gift of non-entry (1550).	Unlike his father, Hugh, 5th lord Somerville, who was an 'assured Scot' and pensioner of Henry VIII, James was a supporter of the Franco-Scottish alliance and Mary of Guise; helped to negotiate Châtelherault's resignation of the regency (1553–4); travelled to France as part of the Prior of St. Andrews' retinue (1550); negotiated with the Congregation on behalf of the Queen Regent (July 1559); defected to the Congregation in 1560, presumably when it was clear that France was not going to respond to England's intervention; signed 'Third Band' of the Congregation at Leith (April 1560) and the ratification of the treaty of Berwick (May 1560); voted against *Confession of Faith* in Parliament and refused to subscribe to the *Book of Discipline* (1560).	*RSS,* IV, 879, p.146.

NAME	SCOTTISH & FRENCH PATRONAGE (1548–1551)	GENERAL COMMENTS	REFERENCES
Master John Spottiswoode, rector/parson of Calder	Granted a letter of protection and safeguard for his time in France (1550).	Travelled to France as part of Lord St. John's retinue; zealous reformer and friend of Knox; accompanied Lord James Stewart to negotiate and witness Mary, Queen of Scots' marriage to the Dauphin (1558); played an active role in drawing up the *Book of Discipline* and *Confession of Faith* (1560); nominated and created Superintendent of Lothian (1560–1).	*RSS*, IV, 882, pp. 147–8.
Lord James Stewart, commendator of Kelso and Melrose*	3,000 *écus* from Mary of Guise (1551).	Natural son of James V with Elizabeth Shaw and half-brother to Mary, Queen of Scots.	Knox, *Works*, I, p.242 and *History*, I, p.116; NLS, Adv.MSS, 29.2.5, f.136.

NAME	SCOTTISH & FRENCH PATRONAGE (1548–1551)	GENERAL COMMENTS	REFERENCES
Lord James Stewart, Prior and Commendator of St. Andrews	Letters of legitimation (February 1551).	Natural son of James V with Margaret Erskine and half-brother to Mary, Queen of Scots; sympathetic to the reformed doctrines and rumoured to be an English agent (received 4 payments from the English Council, 1550–52); negotiated and witnessed Mary, Queen of Scots marriage to the Dauphin (1558); mediator between Mary of Guise and the Congregation at Perth (May 1559); defected to the Congregation with Argyll after Guise violated the Perth Agreement (June 1559); became *de facto* leader of the Congregation until the return of James, 3rd earl of Arran; created Earl of Moray (1562); opposed Mary, Queen of Scots' marriage to Darnley; forfeited (1565); became regent after Mary's abdication (1567); member of the King's Party; opposed Mary at Langside (1568); assassinated by the Hamiltons (1570).	Knox, *Works*, I, p.242 and *History*, I, p.116; *RSS*, IV, 879, 1064, pp. 146, 174; *RMS*, IV, 565, p.125; *APC*, III, pp. 103, 347 and IV pp. 103, 190.
Lord John Stewart, commendator of Coldingham*	Letters of legitimation (February 1551); nominated to the abbey of Flavigny (1551).	Natural son of James V with Elizabeth Carmichael and half-brother to Mary, Queen of Scots, whom he accompanied to France in 1548; commendator of Coldingham (1541); reported to be neutral by Maitland of Lethington in 1559; abetted Mary's celebration of Mass at Holyrood by protecting her priest (1561) and eventually married Bothwell's sister; died at Inverness (1563).	Knox, *Works*, I, p.242 and *History*, I, p.116; *Scottish Correspondence*, ccxxxiii, p.343; *RSS*, IV, 1064, p.174; *RMS*, IV, 565, p.125.

NAME	SCOTTISH & FRENCH PATRONAGE (1548–1551)	GENERAL COMMENTS	REFERENCES
Lord Robert Stewart, commendator of Holyrood*		Natural son of James V with Euphemia Elphinstone and half-brother to Mary, Queen of Scots, whom he accompanied to France in 1548; *in commendam* of Holyrood (1539); member of the Lords of the Congregation; married Jean Kennedy, eldest daughter to Gilbert, 3rd earl of Cassillis (1561); created 1st Earl of Orkney and Lord of Zetland (1581); died (1593).	Knox, *Works*, I, p.242 and *History*, I, p.116; *RSS*, IV
Robert Stewart, bishop [elect] of Caithness	Granted a letter of protection and safeguard for his time in France (1550); presentation of tenandry (1551).	Aristocratic bishop and brother to Matthew, 4th earl of Lennox; signed contract at Carlisle by which Lennox and Glencairn promised to aid Henry VIII in Scotland (1543); hostage in England during his brother's subsequent military expedition there, the failure of which resulted in Alexander Gordon replacing Stewart as postulate of Caithness by request of the Scottish government (1543–4); asked Mary of Guise if he could accompany her to France (1550); granted land and title to Earl of Sutherland (1553–60); organised reformed church in diocese of Caithness (*c.* 1560–1).	NAS, GD90/3/11; *Scottish Correspondence*, ccxxviii, p.338; *RSS*, IV, 883, 1372, pp. 148, 218; Donaldson, *Reformed by Bishops*, pp. 53–67.

NAME	SCOTTISH & FRENCH PATRONAGE (1548–1551)	GENERAL COMMENTS	REFERENCES
Dean John Winram, vicar of Dull & subprior of St. Andrews		Rumoured to be the author of Archbishop Hamilton's *Catechism* (1549); attended Provincial Councils of 1549, 1552 and 1559; initially sought to reform the Church from within, but joined the Lords of the Congregation when they emerged as the winning side; close associate of Lord James Stewart, Prior of St. Andrews; played a large part in drafting the *Confession of Faith*; Superintendent of Fife and Strathearn (1561–75).	*RSS*, IV, 879, p.146; Dunbar, 'John Winram c.1492–1582'.
Master Robert Winram of Ratho		Travelled to France as part of the Prior of St. Andrews' retinue.	*RSS*, IV, 879, p.146.

Bibliography

Manuscript Sources

ARCHIVES de MINISTÈRE des AFFAIRES ÉTRANGÈRES, PARIS.
Correspondence Politique, Angleterre, II, VIII-XXII.
Mémoires et Documents, Angleterre, XV.

BIBLIOTHÈQUE NATIONALE, PARIS.
Fonds français: 5467, 18153, 20457.

BRITISH LIBRARY, LONDON.
Cotton MSS. Caligula B.vii, B.viii, B.ix, B.x.; E.iv.
Harley MSS. 34, 36, 289, 290, 297, 353, 1244, 1582.
Lansdowne MSS. 4, 155, 159.

INNER TEMPLE, LONDON.
Petyt MSS. 538/47.

LAMBETH PALACE LIBRARY, LONDON.
Talbot MSS. 3194, 3195, 3196.

NATIONAL ARCHIVES OF SCOTLAND, EDINBURGH.
GD 90/3, 149/264, 150/3438, 204/559.
E33/4, 5.
E34/12, 14, 15, 17, 18, 20, 21, 25, 26, 27.
SP2/4.
SP7/34, 38–42.
SP6/49.
SP13/14, 55, 56, 58–61, 63, 65, 66, 68–73, 79–84.

NATIONAL LIBRARY of SCOTLAND, EDINBURGH.
MSS. 2991, 2992, 3112, 3137.
Advocate MSS. 1.2.2.
           19.1.25.
           29.2.1–3, 5.
           33.1.9.
           34.1.11.
           34.2.3, 17.
           35.1.2.
           54.1.2.
           54.1.5, 7.
Ch.2593.

PUBLIC RECORD OFFICE, LONDON.
MSS. 3/31/22, 23, 32, 33.
SP10/14, 15.
SP11/3.
SP12/6.
SP13/76.
SP15/7, 8.
SP31/3.
SP51/1, 8.

SPECIAL COLLECTIONS, UNIVERSITY LIBRARY, ST. ANDREWS.
msDA784.7
ms4347

Primary Printed Sources, Narrative Sources and Works of Reference

Accounts of the Masters of Works for Building and Repairing Royal Palaces and Castles, ed. H.M. Paton *et al*, 2 vols. (Edinburgh, 1957–82).

Acts of the Lords of Council in Public Affairs, 1501–1554: Selections from the Acta Dominorum Concilii introductory to the register of the Privy Council of Scotland, ed. R.K. Hannay (Edinburgh, 1932).

Acts of the Parliaments of Scotland, eds. T. Thomson and C. Innes, 12 vols. (Edinburgh, 1814–75).

Acts of the Privy Council of England, ed. J. R. Dasent *et al*, New Series, 46 vols. (London, 1890–1964).

Ambassades de Messieur de Noailles en Angleterre, ed. R.A. de Vertot, 2 vols. (Leiden, 1743).

'Appendix to the Dun Papers', *Spalding Miscellany*, IV (Spalding Club, Aberdeen, 1849).

Armstrong, R.B., *The History of Liddesdale, Eskdale, Ewesdale, Wauchopedale, and the Debateable Land* (Edinburgh, 1833).

Atlas of Scottish History to 1707, eds. P.G.B. McNeill and H.L. MacQueen (Edinburgh, 1996).

Bateson, M. (ed.), 'Aske's Examination', *English Historical Review*, v (1890).

Calderwood, D., *The History of the Kirk of Scotland*, ed. T. Thomson (Wodrow Society, Edinburgh, 1842–49).

Calendar of Documents relating to Scotland and Mary, Queen of Scots, ed. J Bain *et al*, 13 vols. (Edinburgh, 1881–1969).

Calendar of Letters and State Papers, relating to English Affairs of the reign of Elizabeth preserved in the Archives of Simancas, ed. M.A. Hume, 3 vols. (London, 1892–96).

Calendar of Letters, Despatches, and State Papers, relating to the negotiations between England and Spain, ed. J.M. Thomson *et al*, 13 vols. and 2 supplements (London, 1862–1954).

Calendar of State Papers, Domestic Series, of the reign of Edward VI, 1547–1553, ed. C.S. Knighton (revised edition, London, 1992).

Calendar of State Papers, Domestic Series, of the reign of Elizabeth, 1601–1603 and Addenda, 1547–65, ed. R.H. Brodie, 6 vols. (London, 1924–29).

Calendar of State Papers, Domestic Series, of the reign of Mary I, 1553–1558, ed. C.S. Knighton (revised edition, London, 1998).

Calendar of State Papers, Foreign Series, of the reign of Edward VI, 1547–1553, ed. W.B. Turnball (London, 1863).

Calendar of State Papers, Foreign Series, of the reign of Elizabeth, ed. J. Stevenson *et al*, 23 vols. (London, 1863–1950).

Calendar of State Papers, Foreign Series, of the reign of Mary, 1553–1558, ed. W.B. Turnball (London, 1861).

Calendar of State Papers, relating to English Affairs preserved principally at Rome in the Vatican Archives and Library, ed. J.M. Rigg (London, 1916).

Calendar of State Papers relating to Ireland, of the reigns of Henry VIII, Edward VI, Mary, and Elizabeth, 1509–1573, ed. H.C. Hamilton (London, 1860).

Calendar of State Papers relating to Scotland, 1547–1603, ed. M.J. Thorpe, 2 vols. (London, 1858).

Calendar of State Papers and Manuscripts, relating to English affairs, existing in the Archives and Collections of Venice, ed. R. Brown *et al*, 9 vols. (London, 1867–97).

Catalogue des actes de François II, ed. M.-T. de Martel, 2 vols. (Paris, 1991).

Catalogue des actes de Henri II, eds. M.-N. Baudoin-Matuszek *et al*, 2 vols. (Paris, 1979–86).

The Chronicle and Political Papers of King Edward VI, ed. W.K. Jordan (London, 1966).

The Chronicle of Queen Jane and two years of Queen Mary (Camden Society, 48, London, 1850).

The Complaynt of Scotlande vyth ane Exhortatione to the Thre Estaits to be vigilante in the Deffens of their Public veil (Paris, 1549?), ed. J.A.H. Murray (Early English Text Society, London, 1872–73).

Compota Thesaurariorum Regum Scotorum: Accounts of the Lord High Treasurer of Scotland, ed. T. Dickson *et al*, 13 vols. (Edinburgh, 1877–1978).

Correspondence Politique de Odet de Selve Ambassadeur de France en Angleterre (1546–1549), ed. G. Lefèvre-Pontalis (Paris, 1888).

Dickinson, G. (ed.), 'Instructions to the French Ambassador, 30 March 1550', *Scottish Historical Review*, xxvi (1947).

Dickinson, G. (ed.), *Mission of Beccarie de Pavie, Baron de Fourquevaux, en Ecosse, 1549. Documents originaux de fonds Fourquevaux* (Oxford, 1948).

Dickinson, G. (ed.), 'Report by de la Brosse and d'Oysel on conditions in Scotland, 1559–1560', *Scottish History Society Miscellany*, IX (Edinburgh, 1958).

Dickinson, G. (ed.), *Two missions of Jacques de la Brosse: An Account of the Affairs of Scotland in the year 1543 and the Journal of the Siege of Leith, 1560* (Scottish History Society, Edinburgh, 1942).

Dictionary of National Biography, ed. L. Stephen *et al*, 63 vols. and 6 supplements (London, 1885–1903).

Discours du Grand et Magnifique Triomphe Faict du Mariage de François et Marie Stuart, ed. W. Bentham (Roxburghe Club, Edinburgh, 1818).

Discovrs Particvlier d'Escosses escrit par commandement et ordonnance de la Royne Dovariere et Regent, par Messires Iacques Makgill clerc dv registere et Iean Bellenden clerc de la justice. XI Ianvier MDLIX., ed. T. Thomson (Bannatyne Club, Edinburgh, 1824).

A Diurnal of Remarkable Occurrents that have passed within the country of Scotland, since the death of James IV till the year 1575 (Bannatyne and Maitland Clubs, Edinburgh, 1833).

Dowden, J., *The Bishops of Scotland: being notes on the lives of all the bishops, under each of the sees, prior to the Reformation*, ed. J.M. Thomson (Glasgow, 1912).

Ellis, H. (ed.), *Original letters, illustrative of English history: including numerous royal letters from autographs in the British Museum*, 4 vols. (London, 1846).

An Epistle or exhortacion, to unitie & peace, sent from the Lorde Protector, & others the kynges moste honorable counsaill of England: To the Nobilitie, Gentlemen, and Commons, and al others the inhabitauntes of the Realme of Scotlande (London, 1548), reprinted in the *Complaynt*.

Ewes, Sir S. d', *The Journals of all the Parliaments during the reign of Queen Elizabeth, Both the House of Lords and House of Commons* (London, 1682).

Extracts from the Council Register of the Burgh of Aberdeen, 1398–1570, ed. J. Stuart, 2 vols. (Spalding Club, Aberdeen, 1844–48).

Extracts from the Records of the Burgh of Edinburgh, 1403–1589, ed. J.D. Marwick, 4 vols. (The Scottish Burgh Records Society, Edinburgh, 1871).

Foedera, conventiones, litterae, et cujuscunque generis acta publica inter reges Angliae et alios quosvis imperatores, reges, pontifices, principes, vel communitates, ed. T. Rymer, 20 vols. (London, 1704–35).

Foreign Correspondence with Marie de Lorraine Queen of Scotland, from the Originals in the Balcarres Papers, ed. M. Wood, 2 vols. (Scottish History Society, Edinburgh, 1923, 1925).

Fraser, J., *Chronicles of the Frasers: The Wardlaw Manuscript entitled 'Polichronicon seu Policratica Temporum', or, The True Genealogy of the Frasers, 916–1674* ed. W. MacKay (Scottish History Society, Edinburgh, 1905).

Fraser, W., *History of the Carnegies Earls of Southesk and of their Kindred*, 2 vols. (Edinburgh, 1867).

Fraser, W., *Memorials of the Family of Wemyss of Wemyss* (Edinburgh, 1888).

Fraser, W., *The Scotts of Buccleuch* (Edinburgh, 1878).

Fraser, W., *The Sutherland Book*, 3 vols. (Edinburgh, 1874).

Gail, J.B. (ed.), *Lettres inédits de Henri II, Diane de Poitiers, Marie Stuart, François, Roi Dauphin adressées au connétable Anne de Montmorency* (Paris, 1818).

Gregory, D., *The History of the Western Highlands and Isles of Scotland* (London, 1881).

Hall, E., *Chronicle*, ed. Sir H. Ellis (London, 1809).

The Hamilton Papers: Letters and Papers illustrating the political relations of England and Scotland in the XVIth century, ed. J. Bain, 2 vols. (Edinburgh, 1890–92). *Handbook of British Chronology*, ed. E.B. Froude *et al* (3rd edition, London, 1986). *Handbook of Dates*, ed. E. Cheney (London, 1991).

Haynes, S. (ed.), *A Collection of State Papers relating to affairs in the reigns of Henry VIII, Edward VI, Mary, and Elizabeth, from 1542 to 1570. Transcribed from original letters left by W. Cecill Lord Burghley, and now remaining at Hatfield House* (London, 1740).

Henrisoun, J., *An Exhortacion to the Scottes to conforme themselfes to the honorable, Expedient & godly Union betweene the two Realmes of Englande & Scotland* (London, 1547), reprinted in the *Complaynt.*

Herries, Maxwell, J., lord, *The Historical memoirs of the reign of Mary, Queen of Scots, and a portion of the reign of King James the Sixth*, ed. R. Pitcairn (Abbotsford Club, Edinburgh, 1836).

Highland Papers, ed. J.R.N. Macphail, 4 vols. (Scottish History Society, Edinburgh, 1914–34).

Histoire de la guerre d'Escosse: pendant les campagnes 1548 et 1549 par Jean de Beaugué, ed. J. Bain (Maitland Club, Glasgow, 1830).

The Historie of Scotland, wrytten first in Latin by the most reverend and worthy Jhone Leslie, Bishop of Rosse, and translated in Scottish by Father James Dalrymple 1596, eds. E.G. Cody and W. Murison, 2 vols. (Scottish Text Society, 1888–95).

History of the Church of Scotland by John Spottiswoode, eds. M. Russell and M. Napier, 3 vols. (Spottiswoode Society, Edinburgh, 1851).

History of the Kirk of Scotland by Mr. David Calderwood, eds. T. Thomson and D. Laing, 8 vols. (Woodrow Society, Edinburgh, 1842–49).

Holinshed, R., *The Chronicles of England, Scotland and Ireland*, ed. H. Ellis, 6 vols. (London, 1807–08).

Inventaire chronologique des documents relatifs à l'histoire d'Ecosse, ed. A. Teulet, 2 vols. (Abbotsford Club, Edinburgh, 1855).

John Knox: On Rebellion, ed. R.A. Mason (Cambridge, 1994).

John Knox's History of the Reformation in Scotland, ed. W.C. Dickinson, 2 vols. (Edinburgh, 1949).

Knox, J., *The First Blast of the Trumpet Against the Monstrous Regiment of Women*, in Laing (ed.), *Works of John Knox*, and Mason (ed.), *Knox: On Rebellion*.

Laing, D. (ed.), 'Historie of the Estate of Scotland', *Wodrow Miscellany*, I (Wodrow Society, Edinburgh, 1844).

Lesley, J., *The History of Scotland from the Death of King James I in the Year 1436 to the Year 1561* (Bannatyne Club, Edinburgh, 1830).

Letters and Papers, Foreign and Domestic, of the reign of Henry VIII, ed. J.S. Brewer *et al*, 21 vols. and 3 supplements (London, 1862–1932).

'Letters from Henry II King of France to His Cousin Mary Queen Dowager of Scotland', *Miscellany of the Maitland Club* (Maitland Club, Edinburgh, 1844).

The Letters of James V, ed. R.K. Hannay and D. Hay (Edinburgh, 1954).

Lettres et mémoires d'estat des roys, princes ambassadeurs et d'autres ministres sous les regnes de François Premier, Henri II et François II, par G. Ribier, ed. M. Belot, 2 vols. (Paris, 1666).

Lettres inédits de Marie Stuart, accompagnées de divers dépêches et instructions, 1558–1587, ed. Prince A. Labanoff (Paris, 1839).

Lettres, Instructions et Mémoires de Marie Stuart, Reine d'Écosse, ed. Prince A. Labanoff, 7 vols. (London, 1844).

'List of Abbreviated Titles of the Printed Sources of Scottish History to 1560', *Scottish Historical Review*, supplement (Edinburgh, October 1963).

Lodge, E. (ed.), *Illustrations of British history, biography and manners in the reigns of Henry VIII, Edward VI, Mary, Elizabeth, and James I exhibited in a series of original papers, selected from the manuscripts of the . . . families of Howard, Talbot, and Cecil* (London, 1791).

McFarlane, I.D. (ed.), *The Entry of Henri II into Paris, 16 June 1549* (Binghamton, New York, 1982).

Mackintosh, A.M., *The Mackintoshes and Clan Chattan* (Edinburgh, 1903).

McNeill, P.G.B. (ed.), 'Discours Particulier d'Escosse, 1559/60', *The Stair Society Miscellany*, II 35 (Stair Society, Edinburgh, 1984).

Maitland's Narrative of the Principal Acts of the Regency, during the minority; and other papers relating to the history of Mary, Queen of Scotland, ed. W.S. Fitch (Ipswich, 1842).

Marchand, C. (ed.), *Documents pour l'histoire du règne de Henri II* (Paris, 1902).

Melville of Halhill, Sir J., *Memoirs of his own life, 1549–1593*, ed. T. Thomson (Bannatyne Club, Edinburgh, 1827).

Mémoire justicatif du Droit qui appartient à M. le duc d'Hamilton de Porter le titre de duc de Chatelherault, ed. A Teulet (Paris, 1864).

Mémoires-Journaux de François de Lorraine, duc d'Aumale et de Guise, 1547 à 1563, eds. J.-P. Michaud et J.-J.-P. Poujoulat (Paris, 1854).

Nicolson, J. and Burn, R., *The History and Antiquities of the Counties of Westmorland and Cumberland* (London, 1777).

Nicolson, W., *Leges Marchiarum: Or, The Border-Laws* (London, 1714).

Papal Negotiations with Mary Queen of Scots during her reign in Scotland, 1561–1567, ed. J.H. Pollen (Scottish History Society, Edinburgh, 1901).

Papiers d'état relatif, pièces et documents inédits ou peu connus relatif à l'histoire de l'Ecosse au XVIème siècle, ed. A. Teulet, 2 vols. (Bannatyne Club, Edinburgh, 1852–60).

Paris, L., *Lettres et Pièces Diverses Relative au Règne de François II* (Paris, 1849).

Pasquier, É., *Les Oeuvres d'Estienne Pasquier, countenant ses recherches de la France* (Amsterdam, 1723).

Pitcairn, R. (ed.), *Criminal Trials in Scotland from 1488 to 1624*, 3 vols. (Edinburgh, 1833).

Pitscottie, R. Lindsay of, *The Historie and Cronicles of Scotland*, 3 vols. (Scottish Text Society, Edinburgh, 1899–1911).

Potter, D.L. (ed.), 'Documents concerning the negotiation of the Anglo-French treaty of March 1550', *Camden Miscellany*, xxviii/29 (1984).

Rait, R.S. (ed.), 'Muster-Roll of the French Garrison at Dunbar, 1553', *Miscellany of the Scottish History Society* II (Scottish History Society, Edinburgh, 1904).

The Register of the Privy Council of Scotland, 1545–1625, eds. J. Hill Burton and D. Masson, 14 vols. (Edinburgh, 1877–98).

Registrum Magni Sigilli Regum Scotorum: The Register of the Great Seal of Scotland, ed. J.M. Thomson *et al*, 11 vols. (Edinburgh, 1882–1914).

Registrum Secreti Sigilli Regum Scotorum: The Register of the Privy Seal of Scotland, ed. M. Livingstone *et al*, 8 vols. (Edinburgh, 1908–82).

Relations Politiques de la France et de l'Espagne au XVIe siècle, ed. A. Teulet, 5 vols. (Paris, 1862).

Reports of the Royal Commission on Historical Manuscripts (London, 1870–).

Rotuli Scaccarii Regum Scotorum: The Exchequer Rolls of Scotland, ed. J. Stewart *et al*, 23 vols. (Edinburgh, 1878–1908).

The Scots Peerage, ed. Sir J. Balfour Paul, 9 vols. (Edinburgh, 1904–14).

The Scottish Correspondence of Mary of Lorraine, ed. A.I. Cameron (Scottish History Society, Edinburgh, 1927).

A Source Book of Scottish History, ed. W.C. Dickinson *et al*, 3 vols. (Edinburgh, 1953–54).

State Papers, King Henry the Eighth, Correspondence Relative to Scotland and the Borders, 11 vols. (London, 1830–52).

The State Papers and Letters of Sir Ralph Sadler, ed. A. Clifford, 2 vols. (Edinburgh, 1809).

The Statutes of the Realm, ed. A. Luders *et al*, 11 vols. (London, 1810–28).

Statutes of the Scottish Church, ed. D. Patrick (Scottish History Society, Edinburgh, 1907).

Stevenson, J. (ed.), *Selections from unpublished manuscripts in the College of Arms and the British Museum, illustrating the reign of Mary Queen of Scotland, 1543–68* (Maitland Club, Edinburgh, 1837).

Thomson, T., *Memorial on Old Extent*, ed. J.D. Mackie (The Stair Society, Edinburgh, 1946).

'Treaty Between Argyll and O'Donnell', ed. J. Mackechnie, *Scottish Gaelic Studies*, vii (1953).

Tytler, P.F. (ed.), *England under the Reigns of Edward VI and Mary*, 2 vols. (London, 1839).

The Warrender Papers, ed. A.I. Cameron (Scottish History Society, Edinburgh, 1931).

The Works of John Knox, ed. D. Laing, 6 vols. (Edinburgh, 1846–64).

Secondary Sources

Alford, S., 'Knox, Cecil and the British Dimension of the Scottish Reformation', in Mason (ed.), *John Knox and the British Reformations*.

Alford, S., *The Early Elizabethan Polity: William Cecil and the British Succession Crisis, 1558–1569* (Cambridge, 1998).

Bardgett, F.D., *Scotland Reformed: the Reformation in Angus and the Mearns* (Edinburgh, 1989).

Baudouin-Matiszek, M.N., 'Henri II et les expéditions françaises en Ecosse', *Bibliothèque de l'Ecole des chartes*, cxlv (1987).

Baumgartner, F.J., *Henri II king of France, 1547–1560* (Durham and London, 1988).

Beer, B.L., *Northumberland: The Political Career of John Dudley, Earl of Warwick and Duke of Northumberland* (Kent, Ohio, 1973).

Bergin, J., 'The decline and fall of the House of Guise as an ecclesiastical dynasty', *Historical Journal*, 5 (1982).

Bonner, E., 'French Naturalization of the Scots in the Fifteenth and Sixteenth Centuries', *The Historical Journal*, xl/4 (1997).

Bonner, E., 'The French Reactions to the Rough Wooings of Mary Queen of Scots', *Journal of the Sydney Society for Scottish History*, 6 (1998).

Bonner, E., 'The Recovery of St. Andrews Castle in 1547: French Naval Policy and Diplomacy in the British Isles', *English Historical Review*, cxi (June 1996).

Bonner, E., 'Scotland's 'Auld Alliance' with France, 1295–1560', *Scottish Historical Review*, lxxxiv/273 (1999).

Bouillé, R. de. *Histoire des ducs de Guise*, 4 vols. (Paris, 1849–50).

Brady, C., 'Court, Castle and Country: the framework of government in Tudor Ireland', in Brady and Gillespie (eds.), *Natives and Newcomers.*

Brady, C., 'The Decline of the Irish Kingdom', in Greengrass (ed.), *Conquest and Coalescence.*

Brady, C. and Gillespie, R. (eds.), *Natives and Newcomers: Essays on the Making of Irish Colonial Society, 1534–1641* (Bungay, Suffolk, 1986).

Brosse, J. de la, *Jacques de la Brosse 1485(?)-1562: Ses Missions en Écosse* (Paris, 1929).

Brown, J.M., 'The exercise of power', in Brown (ed.), *Scottish Society.*

Brown, J.M. (ed.), *Scottish Society in the Fifteenth Century* (London, 1977).

Brown, K.M., *Bloodfeud in Scotland, 1573–1625. Violence, Justice and Politics in an Early Modern Society* (Edinburgh, 1986).

Brown, P.H., *John Knox*, 2 vols. (London, 1895).

Brown, M., *James I* (East Linton, 1994).

Bryce, W.M., 'Mary Stuart's Voyage to France in 1548', *English Historical Review*, xxii (1907).

Burns, J.H., 'John Knox and Revolution, 1558', *History Today*, viii (1958).

Burns, J.H., 'The Political Ideas of the Scottish Reformation', *Aberdeen University Review*, xxxvi (1956).

Burns, J.H., 'Reformation and Resistance: John Knox', *True Law of Kingship* (Oxford, 1996).

Bush, M.L., *The Government Policy of Protector Somerset* (London, 1975).

Cameron, J., *James V: The Personal Rule 1528–1542*, ed. N. Macdougall (East Linton, 1998).

Canny, N., 'Irish, Scottish and Welsh responses to centralisation, *c*.1530–*c*.1640: A comparative perspective', in Grant and Stringer (eds.), *Uniting the Kingdom?.*

Carroll, S., *Noble Power during the French Wars of Religion: The Guise Affinity and the Catholic Cause in Normandy* (Cambridge, 1998).

Cloulas, I., *Henri II* (Paris, 1985).

Colvin, H.M. (ed.), *History of the King's Works*, 6 vols. (London, 1963–76).

Constant, J.-M., *Les Guise* (Paris, 1984).

Cowan, I.B., *Regional Aspects of the Scottish Reformation* (Historical Association Pamphlet, 1978).

Cowan, I.B., *The Scottish Reformation* (London, 1982).

Davies, C.S.L., 'England and the French War, 1557–9', in Loach and Tittler (eds.), *The Mid-Tudor Polity.*

Dawson, J.E.A., 'Anglo-Scottish protestant culture and integration in sixteenth-century Britain', in Ellis and Barber (eds.), *Conquest and Union.*

Dawson, J.E.A., 'The Fifth Earl of Argyle, Gaelic Lordship and Political Power in Sixteenth-century Scotland', *Scottish Historical Review*, lxvii (1988).

Dawson, J.E.A., 'Resistance and revolution in sixteenth-century thought: the case of Christopher Goodman', in Van den Berg and Hoftijzer (eds.), *Church, Change and Revolution.*

Dawson, J.E.A., 'Revolutionary conclusions: the case of the Marian exiles', *History of Political Thought*, 11 (1990).

Dawson, J.E.A., 'The Scottish Reformation and the Theatre of Martyrdom', in D. Wood (ed.), *Martyrs and Martyrologies* (Oxford, 1993).

Dawson, J.E.A., 'Trumpeting Resistance: Christopher Goodman and John Knox', in Mason (ed.), *John Knox and the British Reformations*.

Dawson, J.E.A., 'The Two John Knoxes: England, Scotland and the 1558 Tracts', *Journal of Ecclesiastical History*, xlii (1991).

Dawson, J.E.A., 'Two kingdoms or three? Ireland in Anglo-Scottish relations in the middle of the sixteenth century', in Mason (ed.), *Scotland and England*.

Dawson, J.E.A., 'William Cecil and the British dimension of early Elizabethan foreign policy', *History*, 74 (1989).

Desplot, C., 'Louis XIII and the Union of Bearn to France', in Greengrass (ed.), *Conquest and Coalescence*.

Dickens, A.G., *The English Reformation* (New York, 1968 edn.).

Donaldson, G., *All the Queen's Men: Power and Politics in Mary Stewart's Scotland* (London, 1983).

Donaldson, G., *Reformed by Bishops: Galloway, Orkney and Caithness* (Edinburgh, 1987).

Donaldson, G., *Scotland: James V-James VII* (Edinburgh, 1994 edn.).

Donaldson, G. *The Scottish Reformation* (Cambridge, 1960).

Doran, S., *England and Europe, 1485–1603* (London, 1986).

Doran, S., *Monarchy and Matrimony: The Courtships of Elizabeth I* (London and New York, 1996).

Doran, S., 'Religion and Politics at the Court of Elizabeth I: the Habsburg Marriage Negotiations of 1559–1567', *English Historical Review*, 104 (1989).

Durkan, J., 'James, Third Earl of Arran: The Hidden Years', *Scottish Historical Review*, lxv (1986).

Dwyer J., Mason, R.A., and Murdoch, A. (eds.), *New Perspectives on the politics and culture of early modern Scotland* (Edinburgh, 1982).

Edington, C., *Court and Culture in Renaissance Scotland: Sir David Lindsay of the Mount (1486–1555)* (East Linton, 1994).

Edington, C., 'John Knox and the Castilians: A Crucible of Reforming Opinion?', in Mason (ed.), *John Knox and the British Reformations*.

Elliot, J.H., 'The Spanish Monarchy and the Kingdom of Portugal, 1580–1640', in Greengrass (ed.), *Conquest and Coalescence*.

Ellis, S.G. and Barber, S. (eds.), *Conquest and Union: Fashioning a British State, 1485–1725* (London, 1995).

Elton, G.R., 'Parliament', in Haigh (ed.), *The Reign of Elizabeth*.

Elton, G.R., *The Parliament of England, 1559–1581* (Cambridge, 1986).

Elton, G.R., *Studies in Tudor and Stuart Politics and Government*, 4 vols. (Cambridge, 1974–92).

Elton, G.R. (ed.), *The Tudor Constitution* (Cambridge, 1982).

Evenett, H.O., *The Cardinal of Lorraine and the Council of Trent: A Study in the Counter-Reformation* (Cambridge, 1930).

Finnie, E., 'The House of Hamilton: Patronage, Politics and the Church in the Reformation Period', *Innes Review*, xxxvi (1985).

Fleming, D.H., *Mary Queen of Scots* (2nd edition, London, 1898).

Forneron, H., *Les Ducs de Guises et Leur Epoque* (Paris, 1877).

Franklin, D., *The Scottish Regency of the Earl of Arran: A Study in the Failure of Anglo-Scottish Relations, Studies in British History*, Volume 35 (Lewiston, 1995).

Fraser, A., *Mary Queen of Scots* (London, 1971).

Goodare, J., 'Parliamentary Taxation in Scotland, 1560–1603', *Scottish Historical Review*, lxviii (1989).

Grant, A. and Stringer, K.J. (eds.), *Uniting the Kingdom? The Making of British History* (London and New York, 1995).

Gray, J.R., 'The Political Theory of John Knox', *Church History*, viii (1939).

Greaves, R.L., 'John Knox and the Covenant Tradition', *Journal of Ecclesiastical History*, xxiv (1973).

Greaves, R.L., *Theology and Revolution in the Scottish Reformation: Studies in the Thought of John Knox* (Grand Rapids, Michigan, 1980).

Greengrass, M. (ed.), *Conquest and Coalescence: The Shaping of the State in Early Modern Europe* (London, 1991).

Guerdan, R., *Marie Stuart: Reine de France et d'Écosse ou l'ambition trahie* (Paris, 1986).

Guy, J., *Tudor England* (Oxford, 1988).

Haigh, C., *Elizabeth I* (Harlow, 1988).

Haigh, C. (ed.), *The Reign of Elizabeth I* (London, 1984).

Hannay, R.K., 'Some Papal Bulls among the Hamilton Papers', *Scottish Historical Review*, xxii (1924).

Hannay, R.K., 'The Earl of Arran and Queen Mary', *Scottish Historical Review*, xviii (1921).

Harbison, E.H., *Rival Ambassadors at the Court of Queen Mary* (Princeton, 1940).

Head, D.M., 'Henry VIII's Scottish Policy: a Reassessment', *Innes Review*, lxi (1982).

Hoak, D., 'Rehabilitating the Duke of Northumberland: Politics and Political Control, 1549–1553', in Loach and Tittler (eds.), *The Mid-Tudor Polity*.

Hoak, D. (ed.), *Tudor Political Culture* (Cambridge, 1995).

Jones, N.L., 'Elizabeth's First Year: the Conception and Birth of the Elizabethan Political World', in Haigh (ed.), *The Reign of Elizabeth I.*

Jones, N.L., *Faith by Statute: Parliament and the Settlement of Relgion, 1559* (London, 1982).

Jordan, C., 'Woman's Rule in Sixteenth-Century British Political Thought', *Renaissance Quarterly*, xl (1987).

Knecht, R.J., *Francis I* (Cambridge, 1982).

Knecht, R.J., *French Renaissance Monarchy: Francis I and Henry II* (London, 1984).

Lee, M., *James Stewart, Earl of Moray* (New York, 1953).

Lee, M., 'Sir Richard Maitland of Lethington: A Christian Laird in the Age of Reformation', in Rabb and Seigel (eds.), *Action and Conviction.*

Levack, B.P., *The formation of the British state: England, Scotland and the union of 1603–1707* (Oxford, 1987).

Levine, M., *The Early Elizabethan Succession Question, 1558–1568* (Stanford, 1966).

Levine, M., *Tudor Dynastic Problems, 1460–1571* (London, 1973).

Loach, J. and Tittler, R. (eds.), *The Mid-Tudor Polity, c.1540–1560* (London, 1980).

Loades, D.M., *John Dudley, Duke of Northumberland: 1504–1553* (Oxford, 1996).

Loades, D.M., *The Reign of Mary Tudor: Politics, government and religion in England, 1553–58* (2nd edition, London 1991).

Loades, D.M. *Two Tudor Conspiracies* (Cambridge, 1965).

Lynch, M., 'Calvinism in Scotland, 1559–1638', in M. Prestwich (ed.), *International Calvinism, 1541–1715* (Oxford, 1985).

Lynch, M. (ed.), *The Early Modern Town in Scotland* (London, 1987).

Lynch, M., *Edinburgh and the Reformation* (Edinburgh, 1981).

Lynch, M. (ed.), *Mary Stewart: Queen in Three Kingdoms* (Oxford, 1988).

Lynch, M., *Scotland: A New History* (2nd edition, London, 1992).

MacCaffrey, W.T., 'Elizabethan Politics: the First Decade, 1558–1568', *Past and Present*, 24 (1963).

Macdougall, N. (ed.), *Church, Politics and Society: Scotland, 1408–1929* (Edinburgh, 1983).

Macdougall, N., *James III: A Political Study* (Edinburgh, 1982)

Macdougall, N., *James IV* (East Linton, 1989).

McDonald, R.A., *The Kingdom of the Isles, c.1100–c.1136* (East Linton, 1997).

McGowan, M.B., 'Forms and themes in Henri II's entry in Rouen', *Renaissance Drama*, i (1968).

Mackenzie, W.M., 'The Debatable Land', *Scottish Historical Review*, xxx (1951).

McKerlie, E.M.H., *Mary of Guise-Lorraine Queen of Scotland* (London, 1931).

McRoberts, D. (ed.), *Essays on the Scottish Reformation, 1513–1625* (Glasgow, 1962).

Mahoney, M., 'The Scottish Hierarchy, 1513–1565', in D. McRoberts (ed.), *Essays on the Scottish Reformation*.

Malament, B.C. (ed.), *After the Reformation: essays in honour of J.H. Hexter, William Bouwsma et al* (Manchester, 1980).

Marshall, R.K., *Mary of Guise* (London, 1977).

Mason, R.A., 'Covenant and Commonweal: the Language of Politics in Reformation Scotland', in Macdougall (ed.), *Church, Politics and Society*.

Mason, R.A., 'Imagining Scotland: Scottish Political Thought and the Problem of Britain, 1560–1650', in Mason (ed.), *Scots and Britons*.

Mason, R.A. (ed.), *John Knox and the British Reformations* (Aldershot, 1998).

Mason, R.A., 'Kingship, nobility and Anglo-Scottish union: John Mair's *History of Greater Britain* (1521)', *Innes Review*, 41 (1990).

Mason, R.A., *Kingship and the Commonweal: Political Thought in Renaissance and Reformation Scotland* (Edinburgh, 1998).

Mason, R.A., 'Knox on Rebellion', in Mason (ed.), *Kingship and the Commonweal*.

Mason, R.A., 'Knox, Resistance and the Moral Imperative', *History of Political Thought*, I (1980).

Mason, R.A., 'Knox, Resistance and the Royal Supremacy', in Mason (ed.), *John Knox and the British Reformations*.

Mason, R.A., 'Scotching the Brut: Politics, History and National Myth in sixteenth-century Britain', in Mason (ed.), *Scotland and England*.

Mason, R.A. (ed.), *Scotland and England, 1286–1815* (Edinburgh, 1987).

Mason, R.A. (ed.), *Scots and Britons. Scottish Political Thought and the Union of 1603* (Cambridge, 1994).

Mason, R.A., 'The Scottish Reformation and the origins of Anglo-British imperialism', in Mason (ed.), *Scots and Britons*.

Mathieson, W.L., *Politics and Religion: A Study in Scottish History from the Reformation to the Revolution*, 2 vols. (Glasgow, 1902).

Meikle, M.M., 'The Invisible Divide: The Greater Lairds and the Nobility of Jacobean Scotland', *Scottish Historical Review*, lxxi (1992).

Merriman, M.H., 'The assured Scots: Scottish Collaborators with England during the 'Rough Wooing'', *Scottish Historical Review*, xlvii (1968).

Merriman, M.H., 'The Forts of Eyemouth: Anvils of British Union?', *Scottish Historical Review*, lxvii (1988).

Merriman, M.H., 'James Henrisoun and 'Great Britain': British Union and the Scottish Commonweal', in Mason (ed.), *Scotland and England*.

Merriman, M.H., 'Mary, Queen of France', in Lynch (ed.), *Mary Stewart*.

Merriman, M.H., *The Rough Wooings: Mary Queen of Scots, 1542–1551* (East Linton, 2000).

Merriman, M.H., 'Stewarts and Tudors in the mid-sixteenth century', in Grant and Stringer (eds.), *Uniting the Kingdom?*.

Merriman, M.H., 'War and Propaganda during the "Rough Wooing"', *Scottish Tradition*, ix/x (1979–80).

Mitchison, R., *A History of Scotland* (2nd edition, London, 1982).

Neale, J.E., *Queen Elizabeth I* (London, 1988 edn.).

Palmer, W., *The Problem of Ireland in Tudor Foreign Policy, 1485–1603* (Woodbridge, Suffolk, 1994).

Pariset, J.-D., 'France et les princes allemands', *Francia*, 10 (1980).

Pariset, J.-D., *Relations entre la France et l'Allemagne au milieu du seizième siècle* (Strasbourg, 1983).

Paul, J.B., 'Edinburgh in 1544 and Hertford's Invasion', *Scottish Historical Review*, viii (1911).

Pimodan, G. de, *La Mère des Guises: Antoinette de Bourbon, 1494–1583* (Paris, 1925).

Pollard, A.F., *England Under the Protector Somerset* (New York, 1966).

Potter, D.L., 'The Duc de Guise and the Fall of Calais', *English Historical Review*, ccclxxxviii (1983).

Potter, D.L., 'French Intrigue in Ireland during the Reign of Henri II, 1547–1559', *International History Review*, v (1983).

Potter, D.L., 'The Treaty of Boulogne and European Diplomacy, 1549–50', *Bulletin of the Institute of Historical Research*, lv (1982).

Rabb, T.K. and Seigel, J.E. (eds.), *Action and Conviction in Early Modern Europe* (Princeton, 1969).

Rae, T.I., *The Administration of the Scottish Frontier, 1513–1603* (Edinburgh, 1966).

Read, C., *Mr. Secretary Cecil and Queen Elizabeth* (London, 1955).

Reid, N., 'Margaret 'Maid of Norway' and Scottish Queenship', *Reading Medieval Studies*, iii, (1982).

Rodríguez-Salgado, M.J., *The Changing Face of Empire: Charles V, Philip II and Habsburg Authority, 1551–1559* (Cambridge, 1988).

Romier, L., 'La mort de Henri II', *Revue de seizième siècle*, I (1913).

Rooseboom, M.P., *The Scottish Staple in the Netherlands* (The Hague, 1910).

Rowen, H.H., *The King's State: Proprietary Dynasticism in Early Modern France* (New Brunswick, 1985).

Roy, I. (ed.), *The Habsburg-Valois Wars and the French Wars of Religion; Blaise de Monluc [translated from the French by Charles Cotton]* (Harlow, 1971).

Ruble, A. de., *La première jeunesse de Marie Stuart* (Paris, 1891).

Ruble, A. de., *La Traité de Cateau Cambrésis* (Paris, 1889).

Salmon, J.H.M., *Society in Crisis, France in the Sixteenth Century* (New York, 1975).

Sanderson, M.H.B., *Ayrshire and the Reformation: People and Change, 1490–1600* (East Linton, 1997).

Scaligni, P.L., 'The sceptre and the distaff: the question of female sovereignty, 1516–1607', *The Historian*, xli (1978).

Scarisbrick, J.J., *Henry VIII* (Berkeley, 1970 edn.).

Shepard, A., *Gender and Authority in Sixteenth-Century England* (Keele, 1994).

Skinner, Q., 'The Origins of the Calvinist Theory of Revolution', in Malament (ed.), *After the Reformation*.

Tanner, R.J., *The Late Medieval Scottish Parliament: Politics and the Three Estates, 1424–1488* (East Linton, 2001).

Tough, D.L.W., *The Last Years of a Frontier: A History of the Borders during the Reign of Elizabeth* (Oxford, 1928).

Tytler, P.F., *History of Scotland*, 7 vols. (3rd edition, Edinburgh, 1845).

Van den Berg, J. and Hoftijzer, P.G. (eds.), *Church, Change and Revolution. Transactions of the fourth Anglo-Dutch Church History Colloquium* (Publications of the Sir Thomas Browne Institute, new series; Leiden, 1991).

Verschuur, M., 'Merchants and craftsmen in 16th-century Perth', in Lynch (ed.), *The Early Modern Town*.

Watson, F.J., *Under the Hammer: Edward I and Scotland, 1286–1306* (East Linton, 1998).

Wernham, R.B., *Before the Armada: The Growth of English Foreign Policy, 1485–1588* (London, 1966).

Williams, H.N., *The Brood of False Lorraine: The House of Guise* (London, 1914).

Williams, H.N., *Henri II: His Court and Times* (London, 1910).

Williamson, A.H., 'Scotland, Antichrist and the Invention of Great Britain', in Dwyer, Mason and Murdoch (eds.), *New Perspectives.*

Williamson, A.H., 'Scots, Indians and the Empire: the Scottish Politics of Civilization, 1519–1609', *Past and Present,* 150 (1996).

Wintroub, M., 'Civilizing the Savage and Making a King: The Royal Entry Festival of Henri II (Rouen, 1550)', *Sixteenth Century Journal,* xxix/2 (1998).

Wormald, J., 'Bloodfeud, Kindred and Government in Early Modern Scotland', *Past and Present,* 87 (1980).

Wormald, J., *Court, Kirk and Community: Scotland, 1470–1625* (London, 1981).

Wormald, J., 'Godly Reformer, Godless Monarch: John Knox and Mary Queen of Scots', in Mason (ed.), *John Knox and the British Reformations.*

Wormald, J., *Lords and Men in Scotland: Bonds of Manrent, 1442–1603* (Edinburgh, 1985).

Wormald, J., *Mary Queen of Scots: A Study in Failure* (London, 1988).

Wormald, J., ''Princes' in the Scottish Reformation', in Macdougall (ed.), *Church, Politics and Society.*

Zweig, S. *The Queen of Scots,* translated by C. & E. Paul (London, 1935).

Unpublished Works

Alford, S., 'William Cecil and the British succession crisis of the 1560s' (unpublished PhD thesis, University of St. Andrews, 1996).

Baker, J., 'The House of Guise and the church, c.1550–1558' (unpublished D.Phil thesis, University of Oxford, 1995).

Boscher, P.G., 'Politics, Administration and Diplomacy: The Anglo-Scottish Border, 1550–1560' (unpublished PhD thesis, University of Durham, 1985).

Dunbar, L.J., 'John Winram c.1492–1582: A Study of his life and his role in the pre- and post-Reformation Scottish Church', (unpublished PhD thesis, University of Edinburgh, 1998).

Meikle, M.M., 'Lairds and Gentlemen: A Study of the Landed Families of the Eastern Anglo-Scottish Border c.1540–1603' (2 vols., unpublished PhD thesis, University of Edinburgh, 1989).

Merriman, M.H., 'The Struggle for the Marriage of Mary Queen of Scots: English and French Intervention in Scotland, 1543–1550' (unpublished PhD Thesis, University of London, 1974).

Index

H
Habsburgs *see* Charles V; Mary of
     Hungary; Philip of Spain
Habsburg-Valois conflict 6, 33, 34,
     44, 90, 96, 99, 103, 105, 110,
     119–22, 128, 143, 155, 167–8
     & *n.*, 173, 175, 177, 184,
     185, 190, 247
Haddington 154, 165 *n.*
  abbey of 25
  fortification at 21, 27, 28
  Parliament at (1548) 19, 25
Haddington, treaty of (1548) 4, 16
     & *n.*, 19, 25, 26, 27, 28, 30,
     33, 61, 68, 78 *n.*, 142 & *n.*,
     191, 193, 229, 239, 246
Ham 189 & *n.*
HAMILTON, house of 41–2, 79
  and the Scottish succession 17,
     23
Hamilton, Elizabeth 17
Hamilton, Gavin, commendator of
     Kilwinning 82, 259
Hamilton, James, 1st earl of 17
Hamilton, James, 2nd earl of Arran
     and duc de Châtelherault
  and Beaton 157, 158
  and Cecil 231, 232 & *n.*
  and Charles V 41
  and the Congregation 8, 217,
     230, 232–3 & *n.*, 234, 238
  dynasticism 17, 23, 24, 191, 204,
     232
    and the Scottish succession 17,
     23, 191 & *n.*, 193, 196, 204,
     231
    second person of the realm 17,
     94, 232, 238
  and the Franco-Scottish alliance
     191, 230, 233 *n.*
    support for 25, 64, 72, 78, 85,
     158
    negotiations for 24–5
    terms of 24, 25 & *n.*, 230
    and the treaty of Haddington
     25
  and Henri II 23–5, 34, 37, 41–2,
     91, 92 & *n.*, 93, 127–8
    patronage from 5, 24, 25, 41,
     72, 77, 78 & *n.*, 93–4
  legitimacy 17
  and Lennox 101, 102

  as Lieutenant-General 93, 181 &
     n., 183, 185–7
  and Mary of Guise 22, 24, 61–2,
     64, 91, 92 *n.*, 93, 94, 101–2,
     158, 162–3, 185–7, 227, 230
     & *n.*, 233 *n.*, 237–8, 243
  and d'Oisel 24, 82, 84, 92 *n.*, 94,
     186, 213
  as Regent 25 & *n.*, 37, 38, 44–6,
     48 *n.*, 49, 52, 54 & *n.*, 57, 76
     n., 74 *n.*, 79–81, 82, 85 & *n.*,
     87, 91–2, 94, 123, 151 *n.*,
     157
    council 124–5 & *n.*
    ecclesiastical nominations
     79 & *n.*
    financial policy 25, 124, 133–4
     & *n.*, 136, 139
    Highland policy 157–62, 163–4
    intrigues 93, 101–2
    law & order 146 & *n.*
    political skills as 88, 127–8,
     136, 157
    resignation of 5, 86–7, 91–2 &
     n., 93–4, 100, 181 *n.*
      terms of 94 & *n.*, 133
  religion 17–8, 203, 233 *n.*134
Hamilton, James, 3rd earl of Arran
  and the Congregation 8, 130,
     217, 230–31, 232–3 & *n.*,
     236, 238
  in France 25, 78, 230, 260
    escape from 230, 232 & *n.*
  and marriage, question of 23,
     24, 25
    Elizabeth I 232 *n.*
    Mary Queen of Scots 23–4
    Mlle de Montpensier 25 & *n.*
  and Mary of Guise 243
Hamilton, James, dean of Brechin
     79
Hamilton, Jean, 134 *n.*
Hamilton, John, archbishop of St
     Andrews 17, 41–2, 79–81,
     201, 203, 228 *n.*
  Catechism 271
Hamilton of Crawfordjohn, Sir
     James 260
Hamilton of Kincavill, James,
     younger 261
Hamilton of Letham, Archibald 259
Harbottle 151